plant sciences

plant sciences

VOLUME 4
Ra–Ye
Cumulative Index

Richard Robinson, Editor in Chief

Macmillan Reference USA
an imprint of the Gale Group
rk • Detroit • San Francisco • London • Boston • Woodbridge, CT

Macmillan Reference USA
1633 Broadway
New York, NY 10019

Gale Group
27500 Drake Rd.
Farmington Hills, MI 48331-3535

Printed in Canada
1 2 3 4 5 6 7 8 9 10

Library of Congress Cataloging-in-Publication Data
Plant sciences / Richard Robinson, editor in chief.
   p.   cm.
Includes bibliographical references (p.).
ISBN 0-02-865434–X (hardcover : set) — ISBN 0-02–865430-7 (vol. 1) —
ISBN 0-02-865431-5 (vol. 2) — ISBN 0-02-865432-3 (vol. 3) —
ISBN 0-02-865433-1 (vol. 4)
   1. Botany—Juvenile literature. 2. Plants—Juvenile literature. [1.
     Botany—Encyclopedias.] I. Robinson, Richard, 1956-
QK49.P52 2000
580—dc21
00—046064

Preface

Someone once said that if you want to find an alien life form, just go into your backyard and grab the first green thing you see. Although plants evolved on Earth along with the rest of us, they really are about as different and strange and wonderful a group of creatures as one is likely to find anywhere in the universe.

The World of Plants

Consider for a minute just how different plants are. They have no mouths, no eyes or ears, no brain, no muscles. They stand still for their entire lives, planted in the soil like enormous drinking straws wicking gallon after gallon of water from the earth to the atmosphere. Plants live on little more than water, air, and sunshine and have mastered the trick of transmuting these simple things into almost everything they (and we) need. In this encyclopedia, readers will find out how plants accomplish this photosynthetic alchemy and learn about the extraordinary variety of form and function within the plant kingdom. In addition, readers will be able to trace their 450-million-year history and diversification, from the very first primitive land plants to the more than 250,000 species living today.

✳Explore further in Photosynthesis, Light Reactions and Evolution of Plants

All animals ultimately depend on photosynthesis for their food, and humans are no exception. Over the past ten thousand years, we have cultivated such an intimate relationship with a few species of grains that it is hardly an exaggeration to say, in the words of one scientist, that "humans domesticated wheat, and vice versa." With the help of agriculture, humans were transformed from a nomadic, hunting and gathering species numbering in the low millions, into the most dominant species on the planet, with a population that currently exceeds six billion. Agriculture has shaped human culture profoundly, and together the two have reshaped the planet. In this encyclopedia, readers can explore the history of agriculture, learn how it is practiced today, both conventionally and organically, and what the impact of it and other human activities has been on the land, the atmosphere, and the other creatures who share the planet with us.

✳Explore further in Agriculture, Modern and Human Impacts

Throughout history—even before the development of the modern scientific method—humans experimented with plants, finding the ones that provided the best meal, the strongest fiber, or the sweetest wine. Naming a thing is such a basic and powerful way of knowing it that all cultures have created some type of taxonomy for the plants they use. The scientific understanding of plants through experimentation, and the development of ra-

tional classification schemes based on evolution, has a rich history that is explored in detail in this encyclopedia. There are biographies of more than two dozen botanists who shaped our modern understanding, and essays on the history of physiology, ecology, taxonomy, and evolution. Across the spectrum of the botanical sciences, progress has accelerated in the last two decades, and a range of entries describe the still-changing understanding of evolutionary relationships, genetic control, and biodiversity.

With the development of our modern scientific society, a wide range of new careers has opened up for people interested in plant sciences, many of which are described in this encyclopedia. Most of these jobs require a college degree, and the better-paying ones often require advanced training. While all are centered around plants, they draw on skills that range from envisioning a landscape in one's imagination (landscape architect) to solving differential equations (an ecological modeler) to budgeting and personnel management (curator of a botanical garden).

*Explore further in Ecology, History of; Biodiversity; and Phylogeny

*Explore further in Curator of a Botanical Garden and Landscape Architect

Organization of the Material

Each of the 280 entries in *Plant Sciences* has been newly commissioned for this work. Our contributors are drawn from academic and research institutions, industry, and nonprofit organizations throughout North America. In many cases, the authors literally "wrote the book" on their subject, and all have brought their expertise to bear in writing authoritative, up-to-date entries that are nonetheless accessible to high school students. Almost every entry is illustrated and there are numerous photos, tables, boxes, and sidebars to enhance understanding. Unfamiliar terms are highlighted and defined in the margin. Most entries are followed by a list of related articles and a short reading list for readers seeking more information. Front and back matter include a geologic timescale, a topic outline that groups entries thematically, and a glossary. Each volume has its own index, and volume 4 contains a cumulative index covering the entire encyclopedia.

Acknowledgments and Thanks

I wish to thank the many people at Macmillan Reference USA and the Gale Group for their leadership in bringing this work to fruition, and their assiduous attention to the many details that make such a work possible. In particular, thanks to Hélène Potter, Brian Kinsey, Betz Des Chenes, and Diane Sawinski. The editorial board members—Robert Evans, Wendy Mechaber, and Robert Wallace—were outstanding, providing invaluable expertise and extraordinary hard work. Wendy is also my wife, and I wish to thank her for her support and encouragement throughout this project. My own love of plants began with three outstanding biology teachers, Marjorie Holland, James Howell, and Walt Tulecke, and I am in their debt. My many students at the Commonwealth School in Boston were also great teachers— their enthusiastic questions over the years deepened my own understanding and appreciation of the mysteries of the plant world. I hope that a new generation of students can discover some of the excitement and mystery of this world in *Plant Sciences*.

Richard Robinson
Editor in Chief

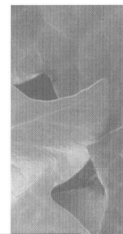

Geologic Timescale

ERA	PERIOD		EPOCH	STARTED (millions of years ago)
Cenozoic: 66.4 millions of years ago–present time	**Quaternary**		Holocene	0.01
			Pleistocene	1.6
	Tertiary	**Neogene**	Pliocene	5.3
			Miocene	23.7
		Paleogene	Oligocene	36.6
			Eocene	57.8
			Paleocene	66.4
Mesozoic: 245–66.4 millions of years ago	**Cretaceous**		Late	97.5
			Early	144
	Jurassic		Late	163
			Middle	187
			Early	208
	Triassic		Late	230
			Middle	240
			Early	245
Paleozoic: 570–245 millions of years ago	**Permian**		Late	258
			Early	286
	Carboniferous	**Pennsylvanian**	Late	320
		Mississippian	Early	360
	Devonian		Late	374
			Middle	387
			Early	408
	Silurian		Late	421
			Early	438
	Ordovician		Late	458
			Middle	478
			Early	505
	Cambrian		Late	523
			Middle	540
			Early	570
Precambrian time: 4500–570 millions of years ago				4500

Contributors

Miguel Altieri
University of California, Berkeley

Sherwin Toshio Amimoto
Redondo Beach, CA

Edward F. Anderson
Desert Botanical Garden, Phoenix, AZ

Gregory J. Anderson
University of Connecticut

Mary Anne Andrei
Minneapolis, MN

Wendy L. Applequist
Iowa State University

Rebecca Baker
Cotati, CA

Peter S. Bakwin
National Oceanic and Atmospheric Administration

Jo Ann Banks
Purdue University

Theodore M. Barkley
Botanical Research Institute of Texas

Ronald D. Barnett
University of Florida

Patricia A. Batchelor
Milwaukee Public Museum

Hank W. Bass
Florida State University

Yves Basset
Smithsonian Tropical Research Institute

Stuart F. Baum
University of California, Davis

Gabriel Bernardello
University of Connecticut

Paul E. Berry
University of Wisconsin-Madison

Paul C. Bethke
University of California, Berkeley

J. Derek Bewley
University of Guelph

Christopher J. Biermann
Philomath, OR

Franco Biondi
University of Nevada

Richard E. Bir
North Carolina State University

Jane H. Bock
University of Colorado

Hans Bohnert
Nara Institute of Science and Technology

Brian M. Boom
New York Botanical Garden

David E. Boufford
Harvard University Herbaria

John L. Bowman
University of California, Davis

James R. Boyle
Oregon State University

James M. Bradeen
University of Wisconsin-Madison

Irwin M. Brodo
Canadian Museum of Nature

Robert C. Brown
Iowa State University

Leo P. Bruederle
University of Colorado, Denver

Robert Buchsbaum
Massachusetts Audubon Society

Stephen C. Bunting
University of Idaho

John M. Burke
Indiana University

Charles A. Butterworth
Iowa State University

Christian E. Butzke
University of California, Davis

Kenneth M. Cameron
New York Botanical Garden

Deborah K. Canington
University of California, Davis

Vernon B. Cardwell
American Society of Agronomy

Don Cawthon
Texas A & M University

Russell L. Chapman
Louisiana State University

Arthur H. Chappelka
Auburn University

Lynn G. Clark
Iowa State University

W. Dean Cocking
James Madison University

James T. Colbert
Iowa State University

Daniel J. Cosgrove
Pennsylvania State University

Barbara Crandall-Stotler
Southern Illinois University

Donald L. Crawford
University of Idaho

Thomas B. Croat
Missouri Botanical Garden

Lawrence J. Crockett
Pace University

Sunburst Shell Crockett
Society of American Foresters

Richard Cronn
Iowa State University

Anne Fernald Cross
Oklahoma State University

Rodney Croteau
Washington State University

Judith G. Croxdale
University of Wisconsin

Peter J. Davies
Cornell University

Jerrold I. Davis
Cornell University

Elizabeth L. Davison
University of Arizona

Ira W. Deep
Ohio State University

Nancy G. Dengler
University of Toronto

Steven L. Dickie
Iowa State University

David L. Dilcher
University of Florida

Rebecca W. Doerge
Purdue University

Susan A. Dunford
University of Cincinnati

Frank A. Einhellig
Southwest Missouri State University

George S. Ellmore
Tufts University

Roland Ennos
University of Manchester

Emanuel Epstein
University of California, Davis

M. Susan Erich
University of Maine

Robert C. Evans
Rutgers University

Donald R. Farrar
Iowa State University

Charles B. Fenster
Botanisk Institutt

Manfred A. Fischer
University of Vienna, Austria

Theodore H. Fleming
Tuscon, AZ

Dennis Francis
Cardiff University

Arthur W. Galston
Yale University

Grace Gershuny
St. Johnsbury, VT

Peter Gerstenberger
National Arborist Association, Inc.

Stephen R. Gliessman
University of California, Santa Cruz

J. Peter Gogarten
University of Connecticut

Govindjee
University of Illinois, Urbana-Champaign

Linda E. Graham
University of Wisconsin, Madison

Peter H. Graham
University of Minnesota

Michael A. Grusak
U.S. Department of Agriculture, Children's Nutrition Research Center

Gerald F. Guala
Fairchild Tropical Garden, Miami

Robert Gutman
Athens, GA

Charles J. Gwo
University of New Mexico

Ardell D. Halvorson
U.S. Department of Agriculture, Agricultural Research Service

Earl G. Hammond
Iowa State University

Jeffrey B. Harborne
University of Reading

Elizabeth M. Harris
Ohio State University Herbarium

Frederick V. Hebard
American Chestnut Foundation

Steven R. Hill
Center for Biodiversity

J. Kenneth Hoober
Arizona State University

Roger F. Horton
University of Guelph

D. Michael Jackson
U.S. Department of Agriculture, Agricultural Research Service

William P. Jacobs
Princeton, NJ

David M. Jarzen
University of Florida

Roger V. Jean
University of Quebec

Philip D. Jenkins
University of Arizona

Russell L. Jones
University of California, Berkeley

Lee B. Kass
Cornell University

George B. Kauffman
California State University, Fresno

Jon E. Keeley
National Park Service

Dean G. Kelch
University of California, Berkeley

Nancy M. Kerk
Yale University

Alan K. Knapp
Kansas State University

Erich Kombrink
Max-Planck-Institut für Züchtungsforschung

Ross E. Koning
Eastern Connecticut State University

Thomas G. Lammers
University of Wisconsin, Oshkosh

Mark A. Largent
University of Minnesota

Donald W. Larson
Columbus, OH

Matthew Lavin
Montana State University

Roger H. Lawson
Columbia, MD

Michael Lee
Iowa State University

Michael J. Lewis
University of California, Davis

Walter H. Lewis
Washington University

Douglas T. Linde
Delaware Valley College

Bradford Carlton Lister
Rensselaer Polytechnic Institute

Margaret D. Lowman
Marie Selby Botanical Gardens, Sarasota, FL

Peter J. Lumsden
University of Central Lancashire

Lynn Margulis
University of Massachusetts, Amherst

Wendy Mechaber
University of Arizona

Alan W. Meerow
U.S. Department of Agriculture, Agricultural Research Service

T. Lawrence Mellichamp
University of North Carolina, Charlotte

Scott Merkle
University of Georgia

Jan E. Mikesell
Gettysburg College

Orson K. Miller Jr.
Virginia Polytechnic Institute

Thomas Minney
The New Forests Project

Thomas S. Moore
Louisiana State University

David R. Morgan
Western Washington University

Gisèle Muller-Parker
Western Washington University

Suzanne C. Nelson
Native Seeds/SEARCH

Robert Newgarden
Brooklyn Botanic Gardens

Daniel L. Nickrent
Southern Illinois University

John S. Niederhauser
Tucson, AZ

David O. Norris
University of Colorado

Lorraine Olendzenski
University of Connecticut

Micheal D. K. Owen
Iowa State University

James C. Parks
Millersville University

Wayne Parrott
University of Georgia

Andrew H. Paterson
University of Georgia

Jessica P. Penney
Allston, MA

Terry L. Peppard
Warren, NJ

John H. Perkins
The Evergreen State College

Kim Moreau Peterson
University of Alaska, Anchorage

Peter A. Peterson
Iowa State University

Richard B. Peterson
Connecticut Agricultural Experiment Station

D. Mason Pharr
North Carolina State University

Bobby J. Phipps
Delta Research Center

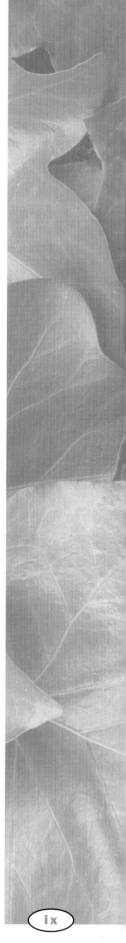

Janet M. Pine
Iowa State University

Ghillean T. Prance
The Old Vicarage, Dorset, UK

Robert A. Price
University of Georgia

Richard B. Primack
Boston University

V. Raghavan
Ohio State University

James A. Rasmussen
Southern Arkansas University

Linda A. Raubeson
Central Washington University

A. S. N. Reddy
Colorado State University

Robert A. Rice
Smithsonian Migratory Bird Center

Loren H. Rieseberg
Indiana University

Richard Robinson
Tuscon, AZ

Curt R. Rom
University of Arkansas

Thomas L. Rost
University of California, Davis

Sabine J. Rundle
Western Carolina University

Scott D. Russell
University of Oklahoma

J. Neil Rutger
*U.S. Department of Agriculture,
Dale Bumpers National Rice
Research Center*

Fred D. Sack
Ohio State University

Dorion Sagan
Amherst, MA

Ann K. Sakai
University of California-Irvine

Frank B. Salisbury
Utah State University

Mark A. Schneegurt
Witchita State University

Randy Scholl
Ohio State University

Jack C. Schultz
Pennsylvania State University

Hanna Rose Shell
New Haven, CT

Timothy W. Short
*Queens College of the City
University of New York*

Philipp W. Simon
University of Wisconsin-Madison

Garry A. Smith
Canon City, CO

James F. Smith
Boise State University

Vassiliki Betty Smocovitis
University of Florida

Doug Soltis
Washington State University

Pam Soltis
Washington State University

Paul C. Spector
*The Holden Arboretum, Kirtland,
OH*

David M. Spooner
University of Wisconsin

Helen A. Stafford
Reed College

Craig Steely
Elm Research Institute

Taylor A. Steeves
University of Saskatchewan

Hans K. Stenoien
Botanisk Institutt

Peter F. Stevens
University of Missouri, St. Louis

Ian M. Sussex
Yale University

Charlotte A. Tancin
Carnegie Mellon University

Edith L. Taylor
University of Kansas

Thomas N. Taylor
University of Kansas

W. Carl Taylor
Milwaukee Public Museum

Mark Tebbitt
Brooklyn Botanical Gardens

Barbara M. Thiers
New York Botanical Garden

Sean C. Thomas
University of Toronto

Sue A. Thompson
Pittsburgh, PA

Barbara N. Timmermann
University of Arizona

Ward M. Tingey
Cornell University

Alyson K. Tobin
University of St. Andrews

Dwight T. Tomes
Johnston, IA

Nancy J. Turner
University of Victoria

Sarah E. Turner
University of Victoria

Miguel L. Vasquez
Northern Arizona University

Robert S. Wallace
Iowa State University

Debra A. Waters
Louisiana State University

Elizabeth Fortson Wells
George Washington University

Molly M. Welsh
*U.S. Department of Agriculture,
Agricultural Research Service*

James J. White
Carnegie Mellon University

Michael A. White
University of Montana

John Whitmarsh
*University of Illinois, Urbana-
Champaign*

Garrison Wilkes
University of Massachusetts, Boston

John D. Williamson
North Carolina State University

Thomas Wirth
*Thomas Wirth Associates, Inc.,
Sherborn, MA*

Jianguo Wu
Arizona State University

Table of Contents

VOLUME 1:

PREFACE v
GEOLOGIC TIMESCALE vii
LIST OF CONTRIBUTORS viii

A

Acid Rain 1
Agricultural Ecosystems 3
Agriculture, History of 5
Agriculture, Modern 10
Agriculture, Organic 12
Agronomist 16
Alcoholic Beverage Industry 18
Alcoholic Beverages 22
Algae 26
Alkaloids 32
Allelopathy 35
Alliaceae 35
Anatomy of Plants 36
Angiosperms 43
Anthocyanins 48
Aquatic Ecosystems 49
Aquatic Plants 52
Arborist 54
Archaea 56
Asteraceae 57
Atmosphere and Plants 59

B

Bamboo 62
Bark 64
Bessey, Charles 65
Biodiversity 66
Biogeochemical Cycles 73
Biogeography 75
Biomass Fuels 79

Biome 80
Bioremediation 84
Bonsai 86
Borlaug, Norman E. 88
Botanical and Scientific Illustrator 89
Botanical Gardens and Arboreta 91
Botany 93
Breeder 93
Breeding 95
Breeding Systems 99
Britton, Nathaniel 102
Brongniart, Adolphe 103
Bryophytes 104
Burbank, Luther 109

C

Cacao 111
Cacti 113
Calvin, Melvin 116
Candolle, Augustin de 117
Cannabis 119
Carbohydrates 120
Carbon Cycle 122
Carnivorous Plants 126
Carotenoids 129
Carver, George Washington 131
Cell Cycle 132
Cells 135
Cells, Specialized Types 140
Cellulose 144
Cell Walls 145
Chaparral 147
Chestnut Blight 151
Chlorophyll 151
Chloroplasts 153

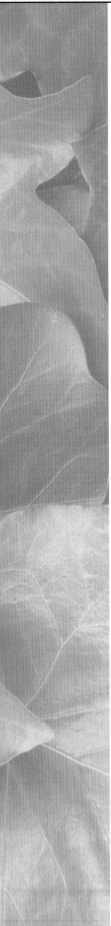

Chromosomes 157
Clements, Frederic 160
Clines and Ecotypes 161

VOLUME 2:

Coastal Ecosystems 1
Coca 4
Coevolution 6
Coffee 10
College Professor 14
Compost 15
Coniferous Forests 17
Conifers 21
Cordus, Valerius 24
Cork 25
Corn 28
Cotton 31
Creighton, Harriet 33
Cultivar 34
Curator of a Botanical Garden 35
Curator of an Herbarium 36
Cyanobacteria 38

D

Darwin, Charles 40
Deciduous Forests 46
Deciduous Plants 51
Decomposers 53
Defenses, Chemical 54
Defenses, Physical 60
Deforestation 63
Dendrochronology 65
de Saussure, Nicolas-Théodore 68
Desertification 70
Deserts 73
Dicots 78
Differentiation and Development 80
Dioscorea 83
Dutch Elm Disease 83

E

Ecology 84
Ecology, Energy Flow 90
Ecology, Fire 92
Ecology, History of 96
Economic Importance of Plants 99
Ecosystems 102
Embryogenesis 104

Endangered Species 106
Endosymbiosis 111
Epiphytes 113
Ethnobotany 115
Eubacteria 119
Evolution of Plants 121
Evolution of Plants, History of 127

F

Fabaceae 130
Family 132
Ferns 133
Fertilizer 135
Fiber and Fiber Products 137
Flavonoids 140
Flavor and Fragrance Chemist 141
Flora 142
Flowers 144
Food Scientist 149
Forensic Botany 150
Forester 152
Forestry 153
Fruits 156
Fruits, Seedless 160
Fungi 162

G

Gametophyte 165
Genetic Engineer 166
Genetic Engineering 168
Genetic Mechanisms and Development . 173
Germination 174
Germination and Growth 176
Ginkgo 179
Global Warming 181
Grains 184
Grasses 185
Grasslands 189
Gray, Asa 194
Green Revolution 196
Gymnosperms 197

VOLUME 3:

H

Hales, Stephen 1
Halophytes 2
Herbals and Herbalists 3
Herbaria 5

Herbicides 9
Herbs and Spices 11
Hooker, Joseph Dalton 12
Hormonal Control and Development . . . 13
Hormones 17
Horticulture 21
Horticulturist 23
Human Impacts 25
Humboldt, Alexander von 30
Hybrids and Hybridization 32
Hydroponics 35

I

Identification of Plants 36
Inflorescence 37
Ingenhousz, Jan 39
Interactions, Plant-Fungal 40
Interactions, Plant-Insect 41
Interactions, Plant-Plant 43
Interactions, Plant-Vertebrate 45
Invasive Species 47

K

Kudzu 50

L

Landscape Architect 52
Leaves 53
Lichens 58
Linnaeus, Carolus 61
Lipids 65

M

McClintock, Barbara 66
Medicinal Plants 69
Mendel, Gregor 73
Meristems 76
Molecular Plant Genetics 80
Monocots 86
Mycorrhizae 88

N

Native Food Crops 91
Nitrogen Fixation 91
Nutrients 95

O

Odum, Eugene 99
Oils, Plant-Derived 100

Opium Poppy 102
Orchidaceae 103
Ornamental Plants 105

P

Palms 106
Palynology 107
Paper 109
Parasitic Plants 110
Pathogens 113
Pathologist 120
Peat Bogs 121
Pharmaceutical Scientist 123
Photoperiodism 125
Photosynthesis, Carbon Fixation and . . . 128
Photosynthesis, Light Reactions and . . . 133
Phyllotaxis 140
Phylogeny 143
Physiologist 146
Physiology 148
Physiology, History of 153
Phytochrome 155
Pigments 156
Plant Community Processes 157
Plant Prospecting 164
Plants 165
Plastids 166
Poison Ivy 169
Poisonous Plants 170
Pollination Biology 175
Polyploidy 180
Potato 184
Potato Blight 185
Propagation 186
Psychoactive Plants 192

Q

Quantitative Trait Loci 195

VOLUME 4:

R

Rain Forest Canopy 1
Rain Forests 4
Record-Holding Plants 13
Reproduction, Alternation of
    Generations and 16
Reproduction, Asexual 18
Reproduction, Fertilization and 20

Reproduction, Sexual 21

Rhythms in Plant Life 24

Rice 26

Roots 29

Rosaceae 35

S

Sachs, Julius von 36

Savanna 38

Seed Dispersal 41

Seedless Vascular Plants 45

Seed Preservation 48

Seeds 50

Senescence 56

Sequoia 57

Shape and Form of Plants 58

Soil, Chemistry of 62

Soil, Physical Characteristics of 65

Solanaceae 68

Soybean 69

Speciation 71

Species 75

Sporophyte 76

Stems 78

Succulents 80

Sugar 81

Symbiosis 84

Systematics, Molecular 87

Systematics, Plant 90

T

Taxonomic Keys 96

Taxonomist 96

Taxonomy 98

Taxonomy, History of 103

Tea 105

Terpenes 108

Tissue Culture 109

Tissues 110

Tobacco 115

Torrey, John 116

Transgenic Plants 117

Translocation 118

Tree Architecture 123

Trees 126

Trichomes 129

Tropisms and Nastic Movements 130

Tundra 138

Turf Management 140

V

Vacuoles 142

van Helmont, Jan 143

van Niel, C. B. 145

Variety 146

Vascular Tissues 146

Vavilov, N. I. 152

Vegetables 155

W

Warming, Johannes 156

Water Movement 158

Weeds 165

Wetlands 166

Wheat 169

Wood Anatomy 171

Wood Products 174

PHOTO AND ILLUSTRATION CREDITS 181

GLOSSARY 183

TOPIC OUTLINE 199

CUMULATIVE INDEX 209

plant sciences

Rain Forest Canopy

The rain forest canopy consists of the treetop region or, more precisely, of the aggregate of every tree crown in the rain forest, including foliage, twigs, fine branches, and **epiphytes**. The upper canopy represents the interface between the uppermost layer of leaves and the atmosphere, and, for practical purposes, many researchers consider this layer to be only a few meters deep. Most of the biological activity in and **biodiversity** within tropical rain forests appears to be concentrated in the upper canopy.

Many **abiotic** and **biotic** characteristics of the canopy are different from the understory beneath. Its higher illumination levels promote more rapid rates of photosynthesis, which, in turn, promote higher vegetal production, and consequently sustain a more abundant and diverse **community** of animals than in the understory. In a much publicized article in 1983, Terry Erwin termed the canopy of tropical forests "the last biotic frontier," referring to the vast, but poorly studied, richness of organisms, particularly arthropods, resident in the canopy.

Many regional and global ecological processes depend crucially on the integrity of the rain forest canopy, which possesses features unique to this environment. Hence, canopy science represents a young, but blossoming, discipline in the field of natural sciences.

Significance of the Rain Forest Canopy in Ecological Processes

Canopies of all types, including boreal and tropical forests, play a crucial role in the maintenance of ecological processes, although thus far, the attention of researchers has tended to concentrate on those in the tropics, rather than those in temperate climates.

The forest canopy is the principal site for the interchange of heat, oxygen, water vapor, and carbon dioxide. It has been estimated that most photosynthetic activities in the **biosphere** occur in the canopy. Forest canopies account for almost half of the carbon stored in terrestrial vegetation and fix more carbon per year than any other habitat. **Ecophysiological** studies are therefore crucial to predict the impact of increasing atmospheric concentrations of carbon dioxide in global warming. Thus,

epiphytes plants that grow on other plants

biodiversity degree of variety of life

abiotic nonliving

biotic involving or related to life

community a group of organisms of different species living in a region

biosphere the region of the Earth in which life exists

ecophysiological related to how an organism's physiology affects its function in an ecosystem

A man climbing into a
rain forest canopy in
Braulio Carrillo National
Park in Costa Rica.

ecosystem an ecological community together
with its environment

forest canopies both control regional climate and play an important role
in regulating global climate.

Rain forest canopies sustain countless species of animals and plants, and
the majority of them are undiscovered and potentially unexploited resources.
This important reservoir of genetic diversity ensures that vital ecological
processes are performed by a variety of species, rather than a few, thus maintaining the integrity of the forest **ecosystem** in case of light disturbance. Adequate pollination and seed dispersal by a variety of organisms ensure the regeneration of the forest, whereas herbivory hastens the return of nutrients to
ground level and their recycling; all three processes are prevalent in the canopy.

Unique Features of the Rain Forest Canopy

The uppermost canopy leaves are typically thicker, more upright, and have higher specific leaf mass and higher photosynthetic rates than understory leaves. In closed tropical forests, the upper canopy is more akin to chaparral shrub vegetation than to rain forest understory vegetation. Leaf area density and the abundance of young leaves, flowers, and seeds are also higher in the canopy than in the understory. Microclimatic conditions differ markedly between the canopy and the understory; illumination, air temperature, wind, fluctuation of relative humidity, and water condensation at night are appreciably higher in the former.

Further, the array of tree crowns in the canopy are rather heterogeneous, including different species, size, **phenologies** (e.g., flowering and leaf flushing), and age state. Thus, forest canopies are best considered as spatially complex, three-dimensional structures that are temporally dynamic. Such systems are particularly conductive to the **stratification**, niche differentiation, and habitat selection of canopy organisms.

Indeed, the rain forest canopy may represent one of the most biodiverse **biotas**, perhaps containing between 50 and 80 percent of terrestrial species, depending on estimates. Besides the support trees, not only are many epiphytic plants (such as lianas, ferns, and orchids), arboreal mammals and reptiles, birds, and bats encountered, but unrivaled numbers of species of insects, spiders, mites, and other arthropods are also present. Ants represent the most regularly abundant animal group in the canopy, both in terms of numbers and **biomass**, whereas the most species-rich groups appear to be rove beetles (Staphylinidae) and weevils (Curculionidae). Typically, arthropod abundance and diversity are between two and four times higher in the canopy than in the understory.

Many of these organisms show distinct physical or behavioral adaptations to arboreal life. These include the canopy root system of several tree species that tap into the **humus** accumulated within epiphytes; the **coalescing roots** of strangling figs; the prehensile tails and gliding membranes of various arboreal mammals; the foraging behavior of particular bird species visiting epiphytes to search for various food resources; or the many peculiar life cycles and specializations (e.g., symbiotic associations) of a multitude of arthropod species. In particular, it is probable that herbivorous insects in the canopy are more host-specific to their host plants than their counterparts in the understory. Interactions between canopy organisms are often complex, due to heterogeneous **substrates** and patchy food resources, often resulting in intriguing **mutualisms**, such as ant gardens, in which ants harvest leaves to feed to cultures of fungi maintained by the colony. However, very little is known of most canopy organisms and their interactions with the canopy environment.

Canopy Access

The means for gaining access to the canopy, a major impediment to canopy science, was developed in the tropics. A pioneering attempt to study the canopy in situ by means of ladders and pulley systems was utilized during Oxford University's expedition of 1929 in Guyana, led by Major R. W. G. Hingston. The few studies performed before the late 1970s used fixed

phenology seasonal or other time-related aspects of an organism's life

stratification layering, or separation in space

biota the sum total of living organisms in a region of a given size

biomass the total dry weight of an organism or group of organisms

humus the organic material in soil, formed from decaying organisms

coalescing roots roots that grow together

substrate the physical structure to which an organism attaches

mutualism a symbiosis between two organisms in which both benefit

systems such as various towers, platforms, walkways, and ladders. In 1978, Donald Perry reported the inexpensive adaptation of a single-rope technique (used by cave explorers to ascend vertical shafts) to the safe climbing of tall forest trees. This led to an expansion of canopy studies, augmented in the following decade with newer methods permitting access to the upper canopy, including the canopy raft (and accompanying sledge) and canopy cranes. In addition, **entomologists** collect large quantities of canopy arthropods by insecticide knockdown or by hoisting various designs of traps into the canopy. Landscape ecologists also study the canopy with satellite remote sensing. By December 1999, the canopy raft had completed four successful missions, and four canopy cranes were in continuous use in the tropics. The scientific exploration and study of one of the most significant, exciting, and endangered habitats on Earth has only just begun. SEE ALSO PLANT PROSPECTING; RAIN FORESTS.

Yves Basset

entomologist a scientist who studies insects

Bibliography

Erwin, Terry L. "Tropical Forest Canopies: The Last Biotic Frontier."*Bulletin of the Entomological Society of America* 29 (1983): 14–19.

Hallé, Francis. *The Canopy Raft.* 1999. [Online] Available at http://www.radeau-des-cimes.com/.

Lowman, Margaret D. *Life in the Treetops. Adventures of a Woman in Field Biology.* New Haven, CT: Yale University Press, 1999.

———, and Nalini M. Nadkarni, eds. *Forest Canopies.* San Diego, CA: Academic Press, 1995.

Mitchell, Andrew W. *The Enchanted Canopy: Secrets from the Rainforest Roof.* London: Collins, 1986.

Moffett, Mark W. *The High Frontier: Exploring the Tropical Rainforest Canopy.* Cambridge, MA: Harvard University Press, 1993.

Mulkey, Stephen S. *The Panama Canopy Crane at the Smithsonian Tropical Research Institute.* 1997. [Online] Available at http://atb.botany.ufl.edu/crane/crane.html.

Nadkarni, Nalini M. *The International Canopy Network.* 1999. [Online] Available at http://192.211.16.13/individuals/nadkarnn/info.htm.

Perry, Donald R. "A Method of Access into Crowns of Emergent and Canopy Trees."*Biotropica* 10 (1978): 155–57.

Rain Forests

Since rainfall controls tropical vegetation in the tropics, rain forest types may be classified with reference to local climate. These include lowland, **montane**, subtropical, and temperate rain forests. Their common features are at least 1,500 millimeters (approximately 33 inches) of annual rainfall and evergreen vegetation with lianas and **epiphytes**. Most widespread are lowland tropical rain forests, accounting for less than one-third of the tropical land surface, growing in areas receiving between 2,000 to 5,000 millimeters of annual rainfall, with relatively high and constant air temperature (annual mean ± 25°C) never below freezing point. They persist in Central America, the Amazon Basin, the Congo Basin, Southeast Asia, New Guinea, and northern Australia. Their canopy is often 25 to 45 meters or higher.

In the monsoonal tropics, characterized by similar total annual rainfall, but unevenly distributed between dry and wet seasons, a related type of low-

montane growing in a mountainous region

epiphytes plants that grow on other plants

land forest is found, which becomes partly leafless during the driest months. These tropical evergreen seasonal forests occur in Central America, the northern coast of South America, Africa, India, Southeast Asia, and in some of the Pacific Islands.

Montane tropical rain forests grow in the same regions that lowland forests do, but at higher altitudes, often above 1,000 meters. Local climate is cooler (15 to 25°C), with high annual rainfall (2,000 to 4,000 millimeters or more). The canopy is often 15 to 35 meters in lower montane forest, while above 2,000 meters, in upper montane forests, it is only 10 meters or less. Fog is frequent, and in moss forests relative humidity varies little from saturation point.

Subtropical rain forests are found in the southeastern United States, southwestern South America, southern China, Japan, eastern Australia, and New Zealand, often within cooler climates (15 to 20°C) and lower rainfall (1,500 to 2,000 millimeters). The canopy generally ranges between 35 and 40 meters. Temperate rain forests occur mostly along the Pacific Coast of North America (where the canopy may be 60 meters or higher), Tasmania, and New Zealand. Although temperatures often fall below freezing point, annual rainfall remains high. In addition, wetland forests include mangrove forests, occurring in saline coastal waters, and various peat and freshwater swamp forests. The rest of this overview concentrates on tropical lowland rain forests.

Lush tropical rain forest vegetation on Atiu Island in the Cook Islands.

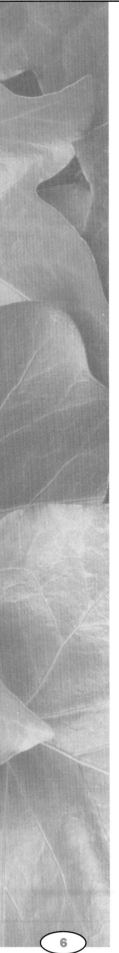

Rain Forest Structure

Rain forest structure is highly complex and determined by competition for light among plant species. Isolated trees, emerging above the canopy, are often present and can be 70 to 80 meters in height. Different tree species grow following various architectural models related to bud location and branching patterns and may or may not form distinct forest layers. Lianas rooted in the ground and epiphytes (e.g., ferns, orchids, and bromeliads) growing on support branches are common in the canopy. Leaves are often medium to large in size, lustrous, and tough. Their shape is often simple, ending with a "drip tip" to shed rainfall. Compound leaves are thought to represent an adaptation to rapid upward growth or seasonal drought and occur more commonly among plants growing in light gaps, in early successional vegetation, or in tropical evergreen seasonal forests. Very little of the light falling on the canopy reaches the ground (0.5 to 2 percent of the illumination available in the canopy), so that the herb layer is much reduced but also includes some **saprophytes** and root-parasites. Although larger herbs from *Zingiberales* and *Arales* may occasionally form denser understory, in mature rain forests it is usually not difficult to penetrate.

saprophytes plants that feed on decaying parts of other plants

This structural complexity is complicated by the temporal dynamics of the rain forest. Often, leaf fall occurs during the driest months and leaf flushing (budding and growth) during the wettest. Furthermore, rain forest trees show a variety of leafing **phenologies**, from continuous leafing, intermittent flushing to deciduous habits. Within the same species or individual crown, flushing may be synchronous or not. Patterns of flowering and fruiting are equally complex, with sometimes mass flowering or fruiting. Understory leaves are often long-lived, more than five years, and covered with mats of epiphytes (such as mosses, lichens, and algae).

phenology seasonal or other time-related aspects of an organism's life

Plant Diversity in Rain Forests

Several theories account for the higher plant and animal diversity in tropical forests compared to temperate forests. First, a greater stability may have existed in the tropics, in comparison with temperate lands, where **biotas** have been depleted by recent glaciations. During the Pleistocene epoch, ten thousand years ago, climatic changes transformed many rain forests into drier savanna. Some rain forests persisted as refugia (isolated refuges), later rejoining together as the climate became more favorable, increasing species richness within. Second, tropical **ecosystems** may provide more ecological niches than temperate ones, thereby supporting more species. Third, **predation** and competition in the tropics may promote higher speciation rates. Last, high species richness in the tropics may result from solar energy controlling **biodiversity** in near-saturated humid conditions.

biota the sum total of living organisms in a region of a given size

ecosystem an ecological community together with its environment

predation the act of preying upon; consuming for food

biodiversity degree of variety of life

genera plural of genus

The great majority of plants in rain forests consist of dicotyledonous trees. For example, the **genera** *Ficus* (Moraceae) and *Piper* (Piperaceae) are diverse throughout the tropics, whereas *Eperua* (Caesalpiniaceae) and *Shorea* (Dipterocarpaceae) are species-rich in Neotropical and Asian forests, respectively. Some families that are herbaceous in temperate areas develop as woody trees in rain forests (e.g., Verbenaceae, Urticaceae, and Polygalaceae). Monocotyledons are less common but include palm trees, various herbs, orchids, and grasses. Abundant woody climbers (often dicotyledons) are characteristic of rain forest vegetation. Their broad stems may cover several kilo-

Epiphytes cover trees in an Ecuadoran rain forest.

meters of canopy. Herbaceous or shrubby epiphytes, semiparasitic mistletoes, and strangling figs (*Ficus*) are also species-rich.

Although tropical rain forests cover less than 6 percent of land masses, they may sustain half or more of Earth's biodiversity. For example, the Malay Peninsula contains about 7,900 plant species compared to Britain's 1,430. Further, a typical hectare of rain forest may include 150 to 200 species of trees with a diameter greater than 10 centimeters, with records of 300 species per hectare in Peruvian Amazonia. In contrast, a hectare of temperate deciduous forest might contain only one-tenth as many species. Still, many rain forest tree species are rare, with average densities of 0.3 to 0.6 trees per species and per hectare. This results in a large average distance between trees of the same species that may affect pollinating and foraging animals, as well as the plants themselves. Indeed, pests or diseases are rarely a problem in mixed rain forests, while uniform vegetation in the same area, such as plantations, is often heavily defoliated.

Contrasting strongly with mixed rain forests, monodominant rain forests are dominated by a single canopy species, such as *Mora* (Caesalpiniaceae) in the Neotropical region, *Gilbertiodendron* (Caesalpiniaceae) in Africa, and *Dryobalanops* (Dipterocarpacea) or *Nothofagus* (Fagaceae) in Australasia. These are competitively superior, shade-tolerant, slow-growing, long-lived species with large and poorly dispersed seeds.

Animal Diversity in Rain Forests

Rain forests sustain more faunal diversity than any other habitat on Earth. In particular, the Amazonian forests of Peru and Ecuador are the most diverse for mammals, birds, reptiles, amphibians, and butterflies. Arthropods are particularly diverse in rain forests since they exploit every niche from the soil to the canopy. For example, one large tree in Peru yielded 43 species of ants, equivalent to their entire British fauna, and 134 species of leaf beetles (Chrysomelidae) were collected from ten tree species in New Guinea in comparison with a total fauna of 255 British species.

herbivore an organism that feeds on plant parts

entomologist a scientist who studies insects

euglossine bees a group of bees that pollinate orchids and other rainforest plants

diurnal daily, or by day

population a group of organisms of a single species that exist in the same region and interbreed

The most abundant vertebrates in rain forests are frugivores, feeding on fruits and seeds. Among invertebrates (aside from earthworms in soil and epiphytes), the dominant groups rely on a variety of food ressources. These include ants (Formicidae: predators, **herbivores**, or fungal-feeders), rove beetles (Staphylinidae: predators, scavengers, or fungal-feeders) or weevils (Curculionidae: leaf-chewers, wood-, seed-, or flower-eaters). Other important invertebrate groups in rain forests include parasitoid wasps, moths, leaf beetles, and spiders. However, most of these species are little known and many are yet to be described.

In 1982, **entomologist** Terry Erwin suggested that there may be as many as 30 million species of arthropods, instead of the previously estimated 1.5 million, although this has not been substantiated. Erwin's estimates attracted considerable attention to the vast, but endangered, reservoir of genetic diversity represented by rain forest arthropods. In 1988, Erwin stated "no matter what the number we are talking about, whether 1 million or 20 million [arthropod species], it is massive destruction of the biological richness of Earth."

Rain Forest Dynamics: Regeneration

Rain forest regeneration and continuity is assured through the important processes of pollination and seed dispersal, which occur primarily through the movements of rain forest animals. Their loss in severely disturbed rain forests drastically affects regeneration capacity. Wind pollination, common in temperate regions, is rarer due to the absence of wind currents; 90 percent of rain forest plants may be insect-pollinated, with nectar the reward for pollinators. They may be strong fliers that forage over long distances, such as birds, bats, hawk moths, and large **euglossine bees**, which may fly up to 23 kilometers. Other short-range pollinators may include stingless, carpenter, and bumblebees, wasps, butterflies, thrips, beetles, midges, and flies. Depending on the timing of flower opening, pollinators may be either **diurnal** or nocturnal.

Another important aspect of pollination is fidelity to particular plant species, which ensures cross-pollination. Some pollinators are generalists (e.g., stingless bees) but restrict their visits to particular plant species. However, many rain forest plants have developed intricate relationships with their pollinators. For example, the petal tube of many flowers corresponds exactly in length and curvature to either the beaks of hummingbirds or to the tongue of certain hawk moths. Further, pollinator activities are attuned to different flowering phenologies, the most specialized of these involving figs (*Ficus*) and fig wasps (Agaonidae), the former totally dependent on the latter for pollination. Usually, one particular species of fig is pollinated only by its own species of wasp.

Some rain forest plants may be dispersed by wind or gravity. However, many of them rely on animals such as ants, fish, reptiles, birds, bats, primates, deer, pigs, civets, rodents, and elephants to disperse seeds. This ensures pollination and cross-fertilization of distant tree **populations** to produce more vigorous and successful offspring and that seedlings have enough space and light to grow and develop. Fruits represent fleshy rewards for animals; swallowed with their seeds, the latter emerge intact in feces and ready to germinate. Animals often specialize in particular seeds or similar seed

Leaf-cutter ants carry their quarry in a Peruvian rain forest.

types, with larger animals often dispersing the seeds at great distance from the parent tree.

Figs are a year-round resource for rain forest frugivores and are particularly important when other fruits become scare. Fig trees are referred to as a keystone species, those that have a crucial importance in the maintenance of the rain forest ecosystem.

Insects (e.g., Bruchidae and Curculionidae), parrots, or squirrels may overcome the chemical defenses of seeds, feeding on them without dispersal. Many insects and fungi also attack the leaves and stems of seedlings. Patterns of herbivore attack below the parent trees may depend on seedling density and decrease with increasing distance from the parent. This may result from specific insect herbivores colonizing seedlings from parent trees, promoting botanical diversity by prohibiting the establishment of young trees near conspecific parents. However, this is not universal, and this model requires validation and refinement.

Rain Forest Dynamics: Succession

Natural disturbance induces a succession of vegetation. After clearance, rain forest succession may start with almost bare soil, proceed with a different kind of vegetation (called secondary forest or growth), and end with the restoration of the original, climax, vegetation. For example, the fall of a large crown of 20 meters in diameter may produce a forest gap of 400 m^2. Some plants will be damaged from the tree fall, but others will have improved growth opportunities, due to increased access to light. Forest gaps are common and promote local plant and animal diversity.

Secondary rain forests contain smaller trees, with many small climbers and young saplings in an understory that is often difficult to penetrate. The floral composition of these forests is different from primary rain forests. Although a few secondary species may live in natural gaps created by treefalls in primary forests, they are more abundant in secondary forests. These are dominated by a few plant species and are less species rich than primary

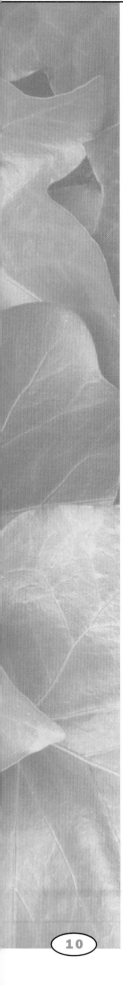

forests. Secondary genera include *Cecropia* (Cecropiaceae) in the Neotropical region, *Musanga* (Moraceae) in Africa, and *Macaranga* (Euphorbiaceae) in Asia. Typically, these "pioneer species" (as opposed to the shade-tolerant species of primary rain forests) produce large quantities of small seeds carried by wind or small animals. In contrast, shade-tolerant species often bear large seeds in fleshy fruits that are dispersed by large animals. Pioneers germinate and grow rapidly (often several meters in two to three years), producing thin, short-lived, and large leaves on weak stems that break easily. Secondary vegetation is not long-lived, since species needing much sunlight to germinate and grow eventually die in the shade of their parents. These stands of pioneers are unable to regenerate under new ecological conditions, giving way to slower-growing, stronger trees that regenerate primary forest, a process that takes place over many centuries.

Herbivory and Decomposition in Rain Forests

Both herbivory and decomposition hasten the return and recycling of nutrients in the ground and promote regeneration of the forest. Most rain forest plants contain more chemical defenses than temperate plants. This may be a response to year-round high herbivore pressure, particularly from insects that represent the bulk of leaf-eating, sap-sucking, flower- and seed-eating fauna. Chemical defenses are often by-products of plant metabolism and are termed secondary metabolites, including lectins, resins, **alkaloids**, protease inhibitors, **cyanogenic** glycosides, or rare amino acids. Each plant species may contain fifty or more in its leaves, bark, or seeds. Many may be pharmacologically active, with subtle differences often due to the high genetic variation of rain forest plants. Since 99 percent of rain forest plants have not been yet chemically screened, biological prospecting for secondary metabolites was undervalued until recently—with an even greater percentage of arthropods untreated.

Herbivorous insects have developed assorted strategies to counter the plants' chemical defenses and concentrate their damage on young leaves. They may produce **enzymes** capable of breaking down secondary metabolites, thus becoming restricted to feeding on one or a few related plant species sharing similar chemical properties. About 9 percent of leaf area is usually lost to herbivores in tropical rain forests, a figure often considerably lower in forests growing on nutrient-poor soils. Since they invest most of their energy in growth and less in chemical defenses, herbivory on pioneer trees tends to be greater than those that are shade tolerant.

Decomposition of organic matter, performed by fungi, bacteria, and invertebrates, particularly earthworms, is rapid in rain forests. Termites are the primary decomposers of wood, often transporting rotting wood to great depths in their underground galleries. In terms of dominance, termites are ranked second to ants with up to 870 colonies per hectare, including underground and arboreal nests.

Nutrient Cycling in Rain Forests and the Consequences of Deforestation

Although most tropical rain forests grow on nutrient-poor soils, their primary production is the highest of any natural system, ranging from 300 to 900 tons of **biomass** per hectare. This is due to the efficient cycling of

alkaloids bitter secondary plant compounds, often used for defense

cyanogenic giving rise to cyanide

enzyme a protein that controls a reaction in a cell

biomass the total dry weight of an organism or group of organisms

nutrients through a virtually leak-proof system, since up to 90 percent of nutrients may be stored at anytime in the vegetation.

The main source of nutrients is rainfall, which represents as much as 3 kilograms of phosphorus, 2 kilograms of iron, and 10 kilograms of nitrogen per hectare per year. The forest filters out nutrients from the water as it passes through. Epiphytes growing on leaf surfaces often fix nitrogen. At ground level, tree roots, which may extend near the soil surface 100 meters away from the tree trunks, may be three times as dense as in temperate forests and are very efficient at absorbing nutrients from the soil, whether from rainfall or from decaying organic matter. Symbiotic associations between roots and fungus or bacteria (termed mycorrhizae) are particularly efficient in recovering minerals, particularly phosphorus, from leaf litter.

Since most nutrients are held in the vegetation aboveground, clearing and burning of rain forests concentrates nutrients in the ground. Some nitrogen and sulfur are lost during burning, but large quantities of other nutrients are deposited in ash. Leaching, due to heavy rainfall, washes these nutrients far beyond the shorter roots of new grasses or shrubs. This severely disrupts the nutrient cycle, leaving barren tracts that remain unproductive or that require the ecologically unsound overapplication of fertilizers. Moreover, the clearing and removal of logs by heavy machinery result in soil **compaction**, water runoff, and, eventually, soil erosion. When a large area of forest is cleared, the soil becomes drier and warmer, and most of the mycorrhizae die out. Aided by nutrients, mycorrhizae, and seeds from nearby intact rain forest patches, regrowth occurs in small areas of clearance, but this is impossible for large clearings, where herbaceous vegetation **colonizes** infertile soils.

compaction compacting of soil, leading to loss of air spaces

colonize to inhabit a new area

Indigenous People and Rain Forests

The indigenous dwellers of rain forests are dependent on them and, similarly, are endangered by habitat fragmentation and destruction. This includes several groups in Malaysia (the Orang Asli), Sarawak (the Penan), Sabah, New Guinea, the Philippines, the African Pygmy groups in Cameroon, Gabon, and Congo; and many Amerindian groups, such as the Yanomami of Brazil or Jívaro of Ecuador.

The encyclopedic knowledge of the natural world of many indigenous groups is well known and discussed by many rain forest ecologists. For example, Papua New Guineans know hundreds of plant and animal species living in their forests, and they have developed detailed **nomenclatural** systems in their local languages. This knowledge is not restricted to medicinal plants but also extends to the smallest of creatures. Indigenous knowledge is an inspiration for scientific research and an opportunity for inclusion of local assistants within research projects. Such knowledge also requires reward through the sharing of profits that may result from economically important discoveries.

nomenclatural related to naming or naming conventions

Environmental Threats to Rain Forests

The major threats to rain forests are, in order of decreasing importance:

1. cattle ranching and farming, leading to habitat fragmentation and destruction

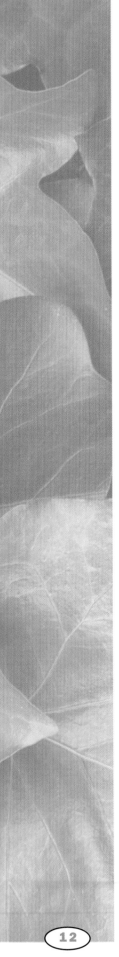

2. clear-cutting for timber and pulp, with similar outcomes

3. plantation **cultivation**, creating large areas of secondary regrowth

4. selective logging of particular tree species, leading to an irregularly structured patchwork of primary and secondary forests

5. shifting cultivation (slash-and-burn), creating small patches of secondary growth

6. natural disasters, including localized landslides and fires, leading to secondary regrowth and natural succession.

The ever-increasing and often irreversible human damage to rain forests shows no sign of slowing down. Although much controversy exists regarding rates of its loss (perhaps 50 hectares per minute) and biodiversity, it is probable that, in a few decades, large tracts of rain forests will remain only in the Guianas, upper Amazon, Congo Basin, and New Guinea. Tragically, a substantial part of Earth's biodiversity and genetic resources will be lost forever, with the potential for concomitantly disastrous effects on local and global climates. Belief that recent advances in biotechnology will remedy this situation is erroneous. The best way to slow down these alarming rates of loss is through education, conservation, and rehabilitation of the organismic components of ecology, botany, zoology, and taxonomy. SEE ALSO BIODIVERSITY; DEFENSES, CHEMICAL; DEFORESTATION; ENDANGERED SPECIES; PLANT PROSPECTING; POLLINATION; RAIN FOREST CANOPY; SEED DISPERSAL.

Yves Basset

Bibliography

Barry, Glen R. *Gaia's Forest & Conservation Archives and Portal.* 1999. [Online] Available at http://forests.org/.

Carrere, Ricardo. *World Rainforest Movement.* 1999. [Online] Available at http://www.wrm.org.uy/.

Diamond, Jared M. "This-Fellow Frog, Name Belong-him Dawko." *Natural History* 98 (1989): 16, 18–20, 23.

Erwin, Terry L. "Tropical Forests: Their Richness in Coleoptera and Other Arthropod Species." *The Coleopterists Bulletin* 36 (1982): 74–75.

———."The Tropical Forest Canopy: The Heart of Biotic Diversity." In *Biodiversity*, ed. Edward O. Wilson. Washington, DC: National Academy Press, 1988.

Gentry, Alwyn H. *Four Neotropical Forests.* New Haven, CT: Yale University Press, 1990.

———. "Tropical Forest Biodiversity: Distributional Patterns and Their Conservational Significance."*Oikos* 63 (1992): 19–28.

Hallé, Francis, Roelof, A. A. Oldeman, and Peter B. Tomlinson. *Tropical Trees and Forests: An Architectural Analysis.* Berlin: Springer, 1978.

Hubbell, Stephen P., and Robin B. Foster. "Commonness and Rarity in a Neotropical Forest: Implications for Tropical Tree Conservation." In *Conservation Biology, The Science of Scarcity and Diversity*, ed. Michael E. Soulé. Sunderland, MA: Sinauer Associates, 1986.

Hyatt, Paul. Rainforest Action Network. [Online] Available at http://www.ran.org/ran/intro.html.

Janzen, Daniel H. "Herbivores and the Number of Tree Species in Tropical Forests." *American Naturalist* 104 (1970): 501–528.

———. *Ecology of Plants in the Tropics.* London: Edward Arnold, 1975.

Leigh, Egbert G. Jr., A. S. Rand, and Donald M. Windsor, eds. *The Ecology of a Tropical Forest*, 2nd ed. Washington, DC: Smithsonian Tropical Research Institute, 1996.

Lieth, Helmut, and M. J. A. Werger. *Tropical Rain Forest Ecosystems. Bigeographical and Ecological Studies.* Amsterdam: Elsevier, 1989.

Longman, K. A., and J. Kenik. *Tropical Forest and Its Environment.* London: Longman, 1974.

Maas, Jelle. European Tropical Forest Research Network (ETFRN). [Online] Available at http://www.etfrn.org/etfrn/.

Mabberley, D. J. *Tropical Rain Forest Ecology.* Glasgow and London: Blackie, 1983.

McDade, Lucida A., Henry A. Hespenheide, and Gary S. Hartshorn, eds. *La Selva, Ecology and Natural History of a Neotropical Rain Forest.* Chicago: University of Chicago Press, 1993.

Prance, Ghillean T., ed. *Biological Diversification in the Tropics.* New York: Columbia University Press, 1982.

———, and Thomas E. Lovejoy. *Key Environments: Amazonia.* Oxford: Pergamon Press, 1985.

Price, Peter W., Thomas M. Lewinsohn, G. Wilson Fernandes, and Woodruff W. Benson, eds. *Plant-Animal Interactions: Evolutionary Ecology in Tropical and Temperate Regions.* New York: John Wiley & Sons, 1991.

Richards, Paul W. *The Tropical Rain Forest*, 2nd ed. Cambridge: Cambridge University Press, 1996.

Sutton, Stephen L., T. C. Whitmore, and A. C. Chadwick. *Tropical Rain Forest: Ecology and Management.* Oxford: Blackwell, 1983.

Tomlinson, Peter B., and M. H. Zimmerman. *Tropical Trees as Living Systems.* Cambridge: Cambridge University Press, 1978.

Whitmore, T. C. *Tropical Rain Forests of the Far East*, 2nd ed. Oxford: Clarendon Press, 1984.

Record-Holding Plants

Of all the kingdoms of living organisms, the plant kingdom exhibits the greatest extremes of size and scale of individuals. From gigantic, massive organisms to extremely small ones, the plant species truly demonstrate the immense range of growth forms and size differences. Some record-holding plants are listed in this article; however, additional research may disclose new records of interest to botanists.

Largest Plant. An individual plant of giant sequoia (*Sequoiadendron giganteum*) in Sequoia National Park, California, named the "General Sherman Tree" is considered to be the largest living plant, as well as the largest living thing on Earth. It is a cone-bearing **gymnosperm** with a height of 84 meters (275 feet) and a measured trunk girth of 31.3 meters (102.6 feet). This plant has enough wood in its trunk to supply the lumber to build about forty small houses.

gymnosperm a major group of plants that includes the conifers

Largest Leaves. Two related plants compete for the title of the largest-leaved plant: the raffia palm (*Raphia farinifera*) of the Mascarene Islands and the bamboo palm (*Raphia taedigera*) of the Amazon basin in South America both have leaves of similar, gigantic size. The blades of their leaves have been measured to be 20 meters (65.2 feet) and their **petioles** measured approximately 4 meters (13 feet). Their total leaf length (24 meters; 78 feet) is equivalent to the height of a seven-story building.

petiole the stalk of a leaf, by which it attaches to the stem

Longest Total Root Length. A plant of the grass known as rye (*Secale cereale*), which has an extensive fibrous root system, was shown to have a total root length of 623 kilometers (387 miles).

A specimen of *Puya raymondii,* which holds the record for the world's largest inflorescence, grows at the foot of mountains in Peru's Huascaran National Park.

inflorescence an arrangement of flowers on a stalk

panicle type of inflorescence (flower cluster) that is loosely packed and irregularly branched

Deepest Roots. A species of fig (*Ficus,* family Moraceae) from the Transvaal of South Africa was determined to have roots reaching at least 122 meters (400 feet).

Largest Inflorescence. The **inflorescence** of *Puya raimondii,* a rosette-leaved member of the pineapple family (Bromeliaceae), is produced after 80 to 150 years of nonreproductive growth. It develops a **panicle** of over 10 meters (35 feet) in height, and produces up to eight thousand white flowers. After flowering and producing thousands of fruit on its gigantic inflorescence, the plant dies.

Largest Flower. A vining tropical plant from the jungles of Southeast Asia, *Rafflesia arnoldii*, known as the corpse lily, has individual flowers that weigh up to 15 kilograms (33 pounds) and diameters reaching 1 meter (39 inches) across. The flowers are pollinated by flies and beetles.

Smallest Plant. The world's smallest flowering plant is a member of the duckweed family (Lemnaceae), *Wolffia angusta*, which is found in Australia. This extremely diminutive aquatic plant measures only 0.61 millimeters (0.024 inches) long and 0.33 millimeters (0.013 inches) wide, and consists of one or two leaves and a very tiny root. The plant floats on the surface of fresh water lakes and ponds and rivers. It flowers annually and produces a very tiny fruit.

Oldest Living Plant. A single individual plant, the creosote bush, in Southern California (*Larrea tridentata* of the sunflower family [Asteraceae]), is estimated to be 11,700 years old.

Oldest Recorded Tree. A coast redwood (*Sequoia sempervirens*), the Eon Tree of Humboldt County, California, fell in December 1977, and was estimated to be more than 6,200 years old. The oldest living tree is a bristle-cone pine, *Pinus longaeva*, found in the White Mountains of California. It has been documented to be at least 4,700 years old (measured in 1974).

Largest Tree (Biomass). A giant sequoia (*Sequoiadendron giganteum*), named the General Sherman Tree, is found in Sequoia National Park, California, and is considered the largest living thing in the world. It is also the largest plant.

Tallest Tree (Height). A plant in the myrtle family (Myrtaceae), *Eucalyptus regnans*, from Watts River, Victoria, Australia, was recorded in 1872 to have measured 132.6 meters (435 feet) tall. The tallest presently living tree is the National Geographic Society tree, a coast redwood (*Sequoia sempervirens*) found in Redwood National Park, California, determined to be 111.4 meters (365.5 feet) in height.

Greatest Tree Girth. One individual tree of the European chestnut (*Castanea sativa*) discovered on the island of Sicily was measured in 1780 and found to be 58 meters (190 feet) in circumference. Since that time, the tree's growth has caused it to divide, and it is now separated into three distinct parts.

Tallest Grass. A bamboo species, *Bambusa arundinacea*, from India was measured with a height of 37 meters (121.5 feet) in 1904.

Largest Cactus. The saguaro (*Carnegiea gigantea*) of the Sonoran Desert in Mexico and Arizona is considered the world's largest (tallest) cactus; one individual plant from southern Arizona was measured at nearly 17.8 meters (58 feet) in height. Another species of related columnar cactus, *Pachycereus weberi*, from the state of Oaxaca, Mexico, is likely the largest cactus by weight. While not as tall as the saguaro, it has many more branches and trunk diameters of more than 2 meters, and its mass can only be estimated to be in the range of 3,600 kilograms (4 tons) or more.

Largest Seed. Seeds of the giant fan palm (*Lodoicea maldivica*) called the double coconut weigh approximately 22 kilograms (44 pounds) and are more than 41 centimeters (16 inches) in their longest dimension. Giant fan palms are found on the Seychelles Islands of the Indian Ocean.

Smallest Seed. The nearly microscopic seeds of epiphytic orchids are dispersed by wind currents (similar to pollen), carrying the seeds from the ripe, opened orchid fruits (capsules) and allowing them to land on suitable locations in trees to establish new plants far from the original mother plant.

Fastest-Growing Plant. Various species of bamboo, members of the grass family (Poaceae), have been recorded as having grown up to 1 meter (3 feet) per day. A record on the island of Scilly, England, from 1978 documented that an individual *Hesperoyucca whipplei* (family Agavaceae) grew 4 meters (12 feet) in 14 days, or about 25 centimeters (10 inches) per day.

Slowest-Growing Tree. Of naturally occurring plants, a cycad (a gymnosperm) *Dioon edule*, has been reported as having the slowest growth rate: 0.76 millimeters (0.03 inches) per year. A plant with an age of 120 years measured only 10 centimeters (4 inches) tall. SEE ALSO DENDROCHRONOLOGY; SEQUOIA; TREES.

Robert S. Wallace

Bibliography

Mauseth, J. D. *Botany: An Introduction to Plant Biology.* Boston: Jones and Bartlett Publishers, 1998.

Quinn, J. R. *Nature's World Records.* New York: Walker Publishing Co., 1977.

Raven, Peter. H., Ray F. Evert, and Susan E. Eichhorn. *Biology of Plants*, 6th ed. New York: W. H. Freeman and Co., 1999.

Young, M. C., ed. *The Guinness Book of World Records.* Enfield, England: Guinness Publishing Ltd., 1997.

Reproduction, Alternation of Generations and

haploid having one set of chromosomes, versus having two (diploid)

zygote the egg immediately after it has been fertilized; the one-cell stage of a new individual

diploid having two of each type of chromosome; twice the haploid number

During sexual reproduction two gametes, each of which is **haploid**, unite to form a single-celled **zygote**, which is **diploid**. As a consequence of the chromosome doubling that occurs during fertilization, at some point in the organism's reproductive cycle meiosis, or reductive cell division, must also occur to restore the haploid condition. In many organisms, including most animals, the zygote develops into a multicellular individual, and meiosis occurs during gamete production. In such organisms, gametes are the only haploid cells in the life cycle. In many algae and fungi, in contrast, the diploid zygote undergoes meiosis immediately to form haploid cells, called spores. Spores subsequently grow into multicellular haploid individuals. In both of these life cycles there is only one multicellular phase. In some algae and in all plants, however, there are actually two multicellular phases, one haploid and one diploid, which alternate with each other in the life cycle. This type of reproductive cycle is referred to as alternation of generations.

In organisms with alternation of generations, the diploid generation, or sporophyte, is formed by mitotic divisions of the diploid zygote, just as in animals. When mature, the sporophyte produces asexual reproductive organs called sporangia. Meiosis within the sporangia produces the one-celled, haploid spores that are released when the sporangia open. Each spore then gives rise to a multicellular haploid individual, or gametophyte. The gametophyte produces the sexual reproductive organs, or gametangia, in which

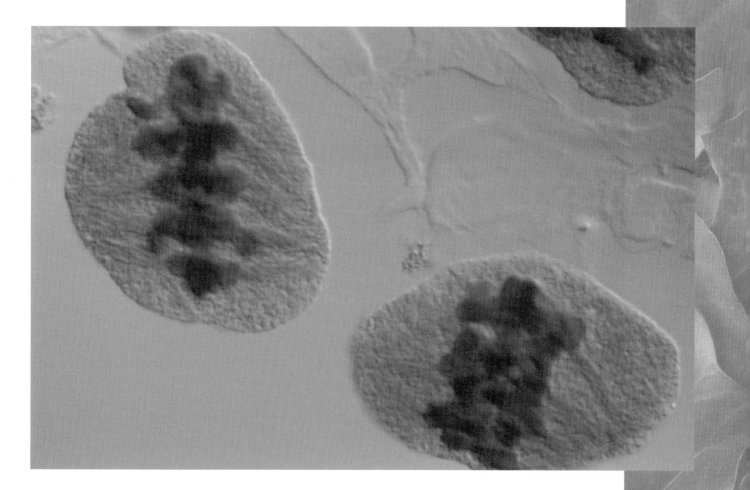

haploid gametes are formed by **mitosis**. Gametes then fuse to form the zygote, completing the cycle.

Occasionally, sporophyte and gametophyte generations look identical, as in many red and some green and brown algae, in which case alternation of generations is described as isomorphic. In other algae and all plants, the two generations are structurally different, and alternation of generations is said to be heteromorphic.

It is notable that isomorphic alternation of generations occurs only in certain algae and aquatic molds, while heteromorphic alternation of generations is the rule in land plants. In bryophytes the gametophyte is the ecologically persistent, independent generation, and the sporophyte is ephemeral and dependent upon the gametophyte for its nutrition. In all other plants the sporophyte dominates the life cycle. The fern gametophyte, for example, is a small thalloid plant, which is soon destroyed by the growth of the large, leafy sporophyte. In **gymnosperms** and **angiosperms**, the gametophyte is reduced to but a few cells of the pollen grain (the male gametophyte) and the embryo sac (the female gametophyte).

Two theories have been proposed to explain how alternation of generations evolved. Both theories hypothesize that the haploid generation is ancestral and that the diploid generation developed as a consequence of mitosis replacing immediate meiosis in the unicellular zygote. One theory proposes that originally the developmental potential of the diploid zygote

A micrograph of the first metaphase of meiosis in cells of a member of the lily family.

mitosis the part of the cell cycle in which chromosomes are separated to give each daughter cell an identical chromosome set

gymnosperm a major group of plants that includes the conifers

angiosperm a flowering plant

was identical to that of the haploid spores, resulting in isomorphic sporophytes and gametophytes. Sporophytes became structurally different from gametophytes as a result of spores and zygotes being exposed to different environmental pressures. In land plants, for example, spores are released as unicells into the environment, while zygotes begin their development within the confines of the female gametangium. As a consequence, gametophytes, which develop from spores, and sporophytes, which develop from zygotes, are structurally very different.

The second theory proposes that the sporophyte generation evolved gradually by stepwise delays in zygotic meiosis, accompanied by the elaboration of vegetative diploid cells. The first sporophytes were little more than single sporangia, probably embedded in the much larger gametophytes. As evolution progressed, sporophytes became larger and larger, and gametophytes became more and more reduced. Even today, there is no consensus as to which theory best explains the diversity seen in modern organisms. SEE ALSO ALGAE; ANGIOSPERMS; BRYOPHYTES; FERNS; GAMETOPHYTE; GYMNOSPERMS; REPRODUCTION, FERTILIZATION AND; REPRODUCTION, SEXUAL; SPOROPHYTE.

Barbara Crandall-Stotler

Bibliography

Graham, Linda. "The Origin of the Life Cycle of Land Plants." *American Scientist* 73 (1985): 178–86.

Reproduction, Asexual

Although sexual reproduction is more frequent, asexual reproduction also commonly occurs in the plant kingdom. The technical term for asexual reproduction in plants is *apomixis*, derived from *apo* meaning "without," and *mixis* meaning "mingling." Apomixis thus refers to the fact that asexual reproduction lacks the mixing of genes that occurs in sexual reproduction. In apomixis, a new individual is produced by a single parent without pollination or mixing genetic material. A familiar example of apomixis is the production of new plants by the growth of horizontal stems (runners) in strawberries (genus *Fragaria*). Other familiar plants with asexual reproduction include blackberries (genus *Rubus*) and dandelions (genus *Taraxacum*), both of which produce asexually formed seeds. Apomixis is of great interest to plant breeders, because it allows the production of exact genetic duplicates of plants with favorable characteristics.

Asexual reproduction in plants is divided into two general types: vegetative reproduction and agamospermy. Vegetative reproduction refers to the formation of new plants by the growth of specialized structures that can survive after physical separation from the parent. Examples include growth by above- or below-ground stems (called stolons and rhizomes), and layering, in which the stem of a woody plant forms roots upon contact with the soil. Fragments of some plants can also grow to form new individuals. Poplar trees (genus *Populus*), for example, often shed branches that become rooted and produce new trees below the parent. Poplar trees can be easily **propagated** by simply cutting off branches and planting them directly in the ground.

propagate to create more of through sexual or asexual reproduction

The feathery parachutes of dandelion seeds (*Taraxacum officinale*) are the result of agamospermy.

Asexual reproduction by seed, called agamospermy, occurs when a single parent plant forms seeds without pollination. Agamospermy thus differs from self-pollination, in which pollen produced by a plant fertilizes its own ovules. Asexually produced seeds also differ in their development from typical, sexually produced seeds. In some plants, maternal **diploid** cells (which, in a normal seed, do not contribute to the new embryo) divide via **mitosis** and overgrow the developing ovule. The seed produced is thus genetically identical to the parent plant. A number of tropical fruit trees, such as mangos (*Mangifera* spp.), can reproduce in this manner.

Asexual reproduction is thought to be an important adaptation for plants that **colonize** open areas and harsh environments and, as such, is perhaps most common in plant species in arctic and alpine environments. The advantage may be that an asexually reproducing individual reaching a new area can always reproduce, even if no other plants of that species are present. Asexual reproduction also means that a plant's offspring will share 100 percent of its genes, while sexually produced offspring share only 50 percent of their genes with each parent. Evolutionary theorists have argued that, all other things being equal, this should act to favor asexual reproduction, since a parent thereby guarantees that all of its genes are represented in the next generation.

The main disadvantage of asexual reproduction is lack of genetic variation. For example, a disease or pest that has a large effect on one individual may be able to quickly infect all other individuals that share the same exact genetic makeup. In the long run, asexual reproduction may often be an evolutionary dead-end because plants that only reproduce asexually cannot recombine genes to produce new genetic variants. SEE ALSO PROPAGATION; REPRODUCTION, SEXUAL; STEMS; TISSUE CULTURE.

Sean C. Thomas

diploid having two of each type of chromosome; twice the haploid number

mitosis the part of the cell cycle in which chromosomes are separated to give each daughter cell an identical chromosome set

colonize to inhabit a new area

Bibliography

Raven, Peter. H., Ray F. Evert, and Susan E. Eichhorn. *Biology of Plants*, 6th ed. New York: W. H. Freeman and Co., 1999.

Richards, A. J. *Plant Breeding Systems*, 2nd ed. London: Chapman & Hall, 1997.

Reproduction, Fertilization and

diploid having two of each type of chromosome; twice the haploid number

sporophyte the diploid, spore-producing individual in the plant life cycle

haploid having one set of chromosomes, versus having two (diploid)

gametophyte the haploid organism in the life cycle

meiosis division of chromosomes in which the resulting cells have half the original number of chromosomes

flagella threadlike extension of the cell membrane, used for movement

zygote the egg immediately after it has been fertilized; the one-cell stage of a new individual

nonmotile not moving

Gametes in plants—unlike those of animals—are not produced directly by meiotic division of a **diploid** organism, but by an entirely different haploid plant, in a process known as alternation of generations. In this process, embryos grow into **sporophytes**, and sporophytes release **haploid** spores. Spores grow into **gametophytes**, and gametophytes release gametes. Gametes fuse to form embryos.

In mosses and liverworts, the embryo produces a small, but visible, sporophyte in which thousands of spores are produced through **meiosis**. The sporophyte that we see—the capsule and stalk of the moss—remains dependent on the dominant gametophyte (which is the vegetative moss plant).

In ferns and so-called fern allies, the embryo produces a large sporophyte as the dominant generation (which is recognized as the vegetative plant). Keen observation is needed to see the free-living fern gametophytes, as they rarely reach 1/4 inch, but this is where sexual reproduction occurs in these plants.

In mosses, liverworts, and ferns, the sperm cells have **flagella** and can swim. Sperm cells are released under moist conditions. Often the sperm are helped by being splashed out of the sperm-producing organ to within swimming distance of the eggs. Just one egg cell is found in each archegonium, which is the female protective organ on the gametophyte. A chemical signal or erotactin may be produced that attracts the sperm cells. When the egg cell is fertilized, it forms the **zygote**, which divides to form the embryo.

In seed plants, the gamete-producing organs are highly protected and dependent on the sporophyte. Sperm cells form inside male gametophytes, known as pollen. The egg cells form inside female gametophytes, which in turn are located inside ovules. Each pollen grain forms only two sperm cells. The more primitive seed plants—*Ginkgo* and the cycads—have large sperm cells with hundreds or thousands of flagella. Most seed plants, however, have sperm that lack flagella and are **nonmotile**. Once pollination occurs, the

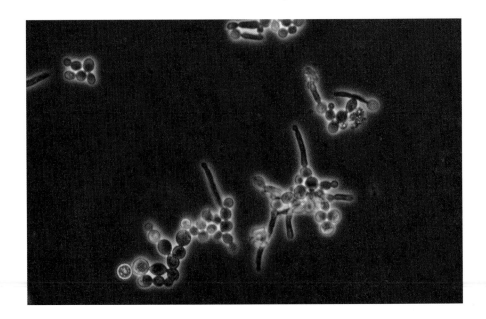

Magnification of pollen reveals the growth of sperm-conveying tubes from the microspores.

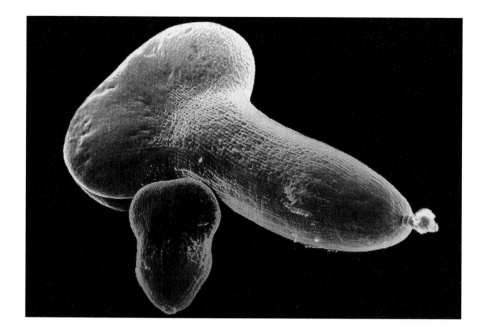

False color scanning electron micrograph of two young turnip (*Brassica campestris*) embryos seven days (small) and twelve days (large) after fertilization. Each has a well-developed root (brown) and a shoot embedded between two embryonic leaves, or cotyledons (green). The structure at the tip of the larger embryo's root is the remnant of the suspensor, which delivers food for the developing embryo from the mother plant.

pollen germinates and forms a tube. Nonmotile sperm cells depend on pollen tube growth for their transportation. Guided by chemical signals, the pollen tube grows over and through protective layers and deposits the sperm cells precisely next to the egg cell.

The egg cell is located within the ovule. In **gymnosperms** (e.g., conifers), the ovule contains a large female gametophyte with multiple archegonia and eggs. In **angiosperms** (flowering plants), the female gametophyte—reduced to one egg and six other cells—is known as an embryo sac. One of the two cells (called synergids) located next to the egg receives the successful pollen tube. Sperm cells are discharged from the pollen tube near the egg cell, and soon fuse with the egg cell to form the embryo. In angiosperms, a second sperm fuses with the central cell to form a nutritive **endosperm** during double fertilization. Fusion of sperm cells with each egg cell and central cell is required to produce the nutrition-rich endosperm needed for development of the embryo in flowering plants.

During fertilization in plants, male and female gametes: 1) contact one another; 2) adhere; 3) fuse their cells; and 4) fuse their nuclei. Fertilization triggers later embryo development. SEE ALSO BRYOPHYTES; FERNS; FLOWERS; FRUITS; POLLINATION BIOLOGY; REPRODUCTION, ALTERNATION OF GENERATIONS AND; REPRODUCTION, ASEXUAL; REPRODUCTION, SEXUAL; SEEDS.

Scott D. Russell

gymnosperm a major group of plants that includes the conifers

angiosperm a flowering plant

endosperm the nutritive tissue in a seed, formed by fertilization of a diploid egg tissue by a sperm from pollen

Bibliography

Cresti, M., S. Blackmore, and J. L. Van Went. *Atlas of Sexual Reproduction in Flowering Plants.* New York: Springer-Verlag, 1992.

Reproduction, Sexual

Sexual reproduction is a fundamental process in plants that involves the production of egg and sperm followed by their fusion to form a **zygote**, which then divides and eventually develops into a new plant. Sexual reproduction

zygote the egg immediately after it has been fertilized; the one-cell stage of a new individual

Seed spores along the ribs of a fern leaf.

in flowering plants involves four sequential processes: sporogenesis, gametogenesis, pollination, and fertilization, all of which occur within the reproductive organs (the anthers and ovules) of the flower. Anthers are the site of (male) pollen formation, and ovules are the site of (female) egg formation.

Sporogenesis and Gametogenesis

Sporogenesis, or spore formation, begins with the differentiation of specialized spore mother cells within the anthers and ovules. The spore mother cells are unique because they undergo **meiosis**, a division that reduces the chromosome number by one-half, or from **diploid** to **haploid**. The haploid spores produced by meiosis in the anthers are called microspores (small spores), while those in the ovules are called megaspores (big spores).

During male gametogenesis, each microspore divides twice to produce a pollen grain, or mature male **gametophyte**, that consists of only three cells: two sperm cells and one vegetative cell. Female gametogenesis is slightly more complex. Of the four haploid megaspores formed following meiosis of the female spore mother cells, one typically divides four times to produce an eight-nucleate, seven-celled embryo sac, or mature female gametophyte. One of these cells becomes the egg.

Fertilization

Following gametogenesis, the sperm within the pollen grain must somehow reach the egg, which is buried within the ovary of the flower, before fertilization can occur. Flowering plants have evolved numerous adaptations that aid in the transfer of pollen to the tip of the **pistil**, or stigma. This process is referred to as pollination, and can be mediated by wind, insects, bats, or rodents. Once the pollen reaches the stigma, which is often sticky or hairy to trap the pollen grain, the pollen grain swells and germinates. It then sends a tip-growing tube through the style of the pistil to the egg. The vegetative cell of the pollen aids in tube growth. Once the tip of the pollen tube reaches the egg, it discharges the two sperm cells. One sperm cell fuses with the egg to form the diploid zygote, while the other sperm cell fuses

meiosis division of chromosomes in which the resulting cells have half the original number of chromosomes

diploid having two of each type of chromosome; twice the haploid number

haploid having one set of chromosomes, versus having two (diploid)

gametophyte the haploid organism in the life cycle

pistil the female reproductive organ

with two nuclei that reside very close to the egg cell within the embryo sac. The triploid cell that results from this second fertilization event divides to form triploid **endosperm**, which is starchy material stored in the seed and provides nutrition for the developing embryo. Coconut milk and cornstarch are familiar examples of endosperm.

Although not all plants produce flowers or seeds, all land plants do form gametophytes of various shapes and sizes. In many lower plants, such as mosses and ferns, the haploid spores are shed from their parent and can remain **dormant** for many years. Once in a favorable environment, the spores germinate and divide to form a multicellular gametophyte that develops independently of the parent plant. Each gametophyte produces **motile** sperm and **nonmotile** egg cells. Until it develops a root system, the young embryo remains attached to and dependent upon the gametophyte. Because the gametophytes of these plants lack water-conducting tissues and require water for the sperm to swim to the egg, they can only be found in places that are damp for at least part of the year. While the fern gametophyte is small (0.25 inches), the moss gametophyte is the lush green carpet we think of as the moss plant.

Evolution of Sexual Reproduction

Most flowering plants produce "perfect" or hermaphroditic flowers with both male and female parts and can readily self-fertilize. One consequence of self-fertilization is inbreeding, which can have negative effects on offspring because they have a high probability of being homozygous for lethal recessive mutations. To avoid self-fertilization, flowering plants have evolved a number of adaptations or modifications to promote out-crossing, or mating between two individuals. Among these are genetic incompatibility, temporal (time-related) separation of pollen and egg maturation, as well as physical separation of the sexes into different flowers or individuals. Monoecious ("one house") plants, such as maize (corn), produce unisexual male flowers or female flowers, but both types are present on the same plant. Dioecious ("two house") plants, such as holly, produce unisexual male or female flowers on different plants. In some dioecious species, the sex of the individual is determined by sex chromosomes, while in other species, the sex of the flower is determined normally, and can be manipulated by applying plant growth hormones. Monoecious and dioecious species are thought to have evolved from species that produced perfect flowers.

Scientists have only recently begun to study and identify the genes that are involved in the evolution of reproductive structures in plants by studying the evolution of maize. The domestication of modern maize (*Zea mays* spp. *mays*) from its wild **progenitor** species, teosinte (*Zea mays* ssp. *parviglumis*) began approximately ten thousand years ago. During this period, agriculturists selected for traits, such as the monoecious condition, that affect the reproductive structures of this plant. What is known at this point is that the large differences one observes between maize and teosinte are attributed to differences in a very small number of genetic **loci**. Once all of these loci have been cloned, scientists will be able to understand at the molecular level how reproductive characteristics evolve.

endosperm the nutritive tissue in a seed, formed by fertilization of a diploid egg tissue by a sperm from pollen

dormant inactive, not growing

motile capable of movement

nonmotile not moving

progenitor parent or ancestor

loci (singular: locus) sites or locations

Advantages and Disadvantages of Sexual Reproduction

propagate to create more of through sexual or asexual reproduction

Many plants **propagate** themselves readily by asexual reproduction. Cattails (*Typha latifolia*), for example, vegetatively multiply by underground stems to form large stands of genetically identical individuals. Why do such plants expend great amounts of energy to produce the floral structures necessary for sexual reproduction when they can successfully reproduce without sexual reproduction? Scientists believe that sexual reproduction is widespread among living organisms because the advantages it provides to the species outweigh the disadvantages. The key to understanding these advantages has to do with the genetic processes that occur during meiosis and fertilization. During meiosis, homologous pairs of chromosomes (each chromosome of a pair previously contributed by each parent) pair with each other and recombine, or exchange genetic material. The resulting haploid cell or gamete contains only one of each chromosome pair, yet each chromosome has a mixture of genetic material from both parents. This mixing of genetic information during sexual reproduction results in offspring that are genetically and **morphologically** different (compare the appearance of genetically identical twins to nonidentical siblings). These differences allow natural selection and adaption to changing conditions. Sexual reproduction thus serves two purposes: in many cases, it is necessary to propagate the species and in all cases is needed to maintain genetic diversity within a species. The long-term consequence of a species that lacks genetic diversity between its members is extinction. SEE ALSO BREEDING SYSTEMS; CORN; FLOWERS; POLLINATION; REPRODUCTION, ALTERNATION OF GENERATIONS AND; REPRODUCTION, FERTILIZATION AND; REPRODUCTION, SEXUAL; SEEDS.

morphologically related to shape or form

Jo Ann Banks

Bibliography

Banks, J. "Gemetophyte Development in Ferns."*Annual Review of Plant Physiology and Plant Molecular Biology* 50 (1999): 163–86.

Doebley, J., and A. Stec. "Inheritance of the Morphological Differences Between Maize and Teosinte: Comparison of Results for Two F2 Populations." *Genetics* 134 (1993): 559–70.

Rhythms in Plant Life

The natural environment is always changing, sometimes predictably, but more often not. Unlike animals, plants cannot move away or seek shelter from unfavorable conditions, so it is crucial that they are able to adapt quickly to such changes. Unpredictable changes include daily temperature, rainfall, and amount of light, and plants have developed a range of responses to deal with these changes. However, some aspects of the environment change regularly, such as the seasons; the monthly waxing and waning of the moon; the cycle of the tides coming in and out; and, of course, the daily changing of light and dark. It is therefore not surprising that, like most other living organisms, plants have evolved so that their behavior or development changes in synchrony with these predictable changes in the environment.

Types of Rhythms

A rhythm is a process that changes regularly and continuously. It can best be represented as a wave, as with light or radio waves, or on a graph where response is plotted against time. The distance between successive peaks or troughs of the wave is then referred to as the period of the rhythm. Rhythms in plants have a range of periods. For example, the circular growth of some stems has a period of less than one hour, but the flowering in some bamboos has a period of seven years. The most widespread rhythms are those with a period of about twenty-four hours, referred to as circadian rhythms (from the Latin *circa*, meaning "about," and *diem*, meaning "day"). Some examples of processes that show circadian rhythms are photosynthesis, stomatal movements, root pressure, nitrogen fixation, bioluminescence, cell division, leaf movements, flower opening, and fragrance emissions. Circadian rhythms, which match the daily twenty-four-hour cycle of day and night, have almost certainly been selected for during evolution, and it is thought that they are the visible expression of a biological clock in plants.

Characteristics of Circadian Rhythms

Perhaps the first observation of a circadian rhythm associated with a plant was made by Androsthenes, scribe to Alexander the Great, who noticed that the leaves of certain trees were elevated by day and drooped at night. More recently, an eighteenth century French astronomer, Jean de Mairan, observed that the leaves of certain "sensitive" plants, probably mimosa, continued to open and close even during long periods of darkness. In the first half of the twentieth century the German plant physiologist Erwin Bünning made detailed observations of the movement of bean leaves. He confirmed that the leaves continued to move up and down in constant darkness, and established that the period was 25.4 hours.

Bünning's work also established the most important property of these rhythms, which is that they are truly internal and thus generated by the plant. The rhythm continues running under constant environmental conditions (called a free running rhythm), which indicates that it is driven from within and not by a rhythm of the environment. Another important property is that the phase of the rhythm can be changed by light. This means that every day, at the onset of daylight (dawn) the rhythm is reset so as to coincide with the daily light-dark cycle in the environment. This phenomenon is known as entrainment and is crucial to the functioning of the biological clock.

Nature of Biological Clocks

The biological clock allows an organism to match its internal system with the time of day, so that in some sense it could be said to "know" what the time is. Inside every cell are processes that change rhythmically and that drive the observed rhythms. The actual mechanism of the clockwork is not known, although recent research in organisms such as fruit flies and fungi suggests that a cycle of gene transcription and protein synthesis is an important part. Another part of the clock is one or more photoreceptors through which light entrains or sets the clock to match up with the daily light cycle. Having many internal processes matched with the daily light

A boojum tree in Mexico during the dry season. The plant adapts to seasonal changes in precipitation by restricting the growth of its foliage in the dry season.

A boojum tree in Mexico during the moist season. The plant adapts to seasonal changes in precipitation by maintaining foliage in the moist season.

cyanobacteria photosynthetic prokaryotic bacteria formerly known as blue-green algae

population a group of organisms of a single species that exist in the same region and interbreed

cultivation growth of crop plants, or turning the soil for this purpose

cycle allows the plant to anticipate changes that occur during the day, such as switching on genes associated with photosynthesis before the onset of daylight. It also allows them to carry out incompatible processes at different times, such as nitrogen fixation and photosynthesis in unicellular **cyanobacteria**.

Having a biological clock that is reset by light and dark means that plants can measure the length of day and/or night. This also allows them to tell what season it is by whether days are getting longer or shorter. Many developmental responses are triggered by changes in the length of day, a type of behavior termed photoperiodism. While some changes occur in response to shortening of the daylength, others occur as days get longer. These two types of photoperiodic response were first recorded for the induction of flowering and led to the classification of plants as short-day plants or long-day plants. Those plants that do not respond to daylength are called day-neutral plants.

There are several advantages to having developmental responses controlled by daylength. For flowering, it means that members of a **population** will flower at the same time, which increases the chances of outbreeding and thus genetic recombination. If a pollinating insect's behavior is also photoperiodically controlled, this further improves the chance of successful pollination. Another example of the survival value of seasonal timing of flowering is that woodland plants can flower and set seed before the dense leaf canopy is formed. Other changes that occur in response to daylength include the formation of storage organs such as bulbs or tubers, the onset of dormancy, and the development of cold hardiness in trees. These changes help plants survive through the winter and are triggered by the shortening daylength during autumn. SEE ALSO PHOTOPERIODISM; SENESCENCE; TROPISMS AND NASTIC MOVEMENTS.

Peter J. Lumsden

Bibliography

Johnson, Carl H. "The Elusive Mechanism of the Circadian Clock." *American Scientist* 74 (1986): 29–36.

Sweeney, Beatrice. *Rhythmic Phenomena in Plants*. Academic Press, 1987.

Thomas, Brian, and Daphne Vince-Prue. *Photoperiodism in Plants*. Academic Press, 1996.

Rice

Rice (*Oryza sativa*) is a staple food for nearly half of the world's population. Rice is a member of the grass family, which also includes wheat, corn, sorghum, barley, oats, and rye. Unlike other grains, rice is well adapted to aquatic environments. Rice originated in Southeast Asia, where archeological evidence—including carbon-dated grain imprints in pottery shards—indicates that it was under **cultivation** at least six thousand years ago. Cultivated rice consists of two subspecies, *O. sativa* subsp. *indica*, which is grown in the tropics and subtropics, and *O. sativa* subsp. *japonica*, which is grown in temperate regions.

Although rice is grown in 115 countries, over 90 percent of the crop is in Asia. In 1999 world rice area was 153 million hectares (Mha), and total

Terraced rice paddies in Ubud, Bali.

production was 589 million metric tons (Mmt). India had the largest area, 43.0 million hectares, and China was second with 31.7 million hectares. However, yields in China averaged 6.33 metric tons per hectare (mt/ha) compared to 2.97 metric tons per hectare in India, so China had the largest total production. Other leading rice countries in 1999 were: Indonesia, 11.5 million hectares; Bangladesh, 10.5 million hectares; Thailand, 10.3 million hectares; Myanmar, 5.6 million hectares; Brazil, 3.7 million hectares; the Philippines, 3.9 million hectares; and Pakistan, 2.4 million hectares. The United States was far down the list at 1.4 million hectares, but with yields of 6.65 metric tons per hectare was well ahead of the world average yield of 3.84 metric tons per hectare.

Except for a small amount for seed, all rice is used for human consumption. Most rice is consumed in the country where it is grown, with about 5 percent going into international trade. In the late 1990s, five countries dominated export markets, in the following descending order: Thailand, Vietnam, the United States, India, and Pakistan. About 40 percent of the U.S. crop is exported, with leading destinations being Latin America, Europe, Africa, and the Middle East.

Cultivation Techniques

Rice is grown under conditions ranging from full flood to rainfed upland conditions. Highest yields are obtained under flood, so the half of the world's rice area that is flooded produces 75 percent of the total crop. U.S. production is all flooded. Although rice is primarily a tropical or subtropical crop, it is grown from 53°N to 40°S. Interestingly, highest yields are obtained in high-latitude temperate areas such as Australia, Egypt, Korea, Italy, Spain, Uruguay, and the United States. High yields in the temperate areas occur because of longer day length, fewer storms, and relative freedom from the traditional diseases and insect pests of the tropics.

In the tropics and subtropics, rice is transplanted into flooded fields, following two or three weeks of initial growth in seedbeds. Most transplanting is by hand, but machine transplanting is becoming popular as labor costs increase. In temperate regions rice is direct seeded, either with grain drills into soil or water seeded by airplane into flooded fields. In all cultivation systems, highest yields are obtained by keeping the floodwater on for as much of the season as possible. Fertilizers are applied before and during the growing season, and weeds are controlled by handweeding and herbicides. About two or three weeks before harvest, fields are drained. In the tropics and subtropics, harvest is by hand while in temperate regions grain combines are used. All harvesting techniques involve threshing the grains from the **panicles** at the top of the plant. Man-hours per hectare for producing rice are as high as 300 in hand-transplanting cultivation, but are as little as 20 in mechanized cultivation in the United States. Total length of the growing season is 100 to 130 days. In the tropics two or even three rice crops may be produced per year, but in temperate areas only one crop is grown per year.

Harvest and Milling

At harvest, rice grain is called paddy or rough rice. In preparation for consumption, the hulls are removed by dehulling machines. Hulls, which are 18 percent by weight of paddy, have high silica content and are of little value except for onsite fuel or mixing into compost materials. Hull removal produces brown rice, which then is milled to remove the grain's outer layers, called bran, 10 percent by weight of paddy, and white rice, 72 percent by weight of paddy. Edible oil, about 2 percent by weight of paddy, is extracted from the bran and the remainder of the bran goes into pet food. Virtually all human consumption is as milled white rice, except for a small amount as brown rice in health food markets. In much of the world the milled rice goes into food use. In the United States, 81 percent of the domestic use of rice is for food, 15 percent for brewing, and the remaining 4 percent for seeding the next crop.

panicle the grain-bearing head of the plant

Worldwide, per-capita consumption of milled rice is 84 kilograms per year. Per-capita consumption is declining in developing nations as they become more affluent. In the United States, per-capita consumption is now 12 kilograms, which represents a doubling since the early 1980s. The increase in the United States is due to growth in ethnic groups who prefer rice, to recognition that rice is a healthful food, and to rice industry promotion efforts.

Rice and the Green Revolution

The Green Revolution began in the 1960s, when tall, **lodging**-susceptible rice and wheat varieties were converted to semidwarf varieties. The semidwarfs stand up better, produce more panicles per unit area, are more responsive to fertilization, and yield more. For example, in the pre-Green Revolution era of the early 1960s, world average rice yields were about 2 metric tons per hectare, compared to the 1999 average of 3.8 metric tons per hectare. The combination of high yielding semidwarfs plus more intensive cultural practices has driven the increase.

lodging falling over while still growing

Wild Rice

In North America the term *wild rice* refers to an unrelated aquatic crop, *Zizania palustris*, which is grown in cooler areas such as Manitoba, Canada, and Minnesota. Small portions of *Z. palustris* grain are blended into gourmet preparations of regular rice. In Asia the term wild rice refers to the twenty related species of *Oryza*, which also are called weedy rice. One of these related species, *Oryza glaberrima*, is cultivated in Africa, but is being rapidly replaced by the higher-yielding *O. sativa*. The wild or weedy species of *Oryza* serve as sources of resistance to diseases and insects of cultivated rice. SEE ALSO AGRICULTURE, HISTORY OF; AGRICULTURE, MODERN; BORLAUG, NORMAN; ECONOMIC IMPORTANCE OF PLANTS; GRAINS; GRASSES; GREEN REVOLUTION.

J. Neil Rutger

Bibliography

Food and Agricultural Organization Statistical Databases. 1999. [Online] Available at http://apps.fao.org.

Riceweb. 1999. [Online] Available at http://www.riceweb.org.

Rutger, J. Neil, and D. Marlon Brandon. "California Rice Culture." *Scientific American* 244 2 (1981): 42–51.

Teubner, Christian, Eckart Witzigmann, and Tony Khoo. *The Rice Bible*. New York: Penguin Putnam, Inc., 1999.

Roots

Plants have three organs: roots, stems, and leaves. Growth, flowering, food production, and storage all depend on the activities of these three organs. The combination of stems and leaves makes up the shoot system that is usually visible because it grows above the ground and gives rise to flowers, fruits, and seeds. Roots, on the other hand, are often underground, but the root system can be every bit as massive as the aboveground shoot system. An active root system makes it possible for the plant to carry out growth, photosynthesis and other chemical reactions, branching, flowering, fruiting, and seed production.

Roots are so critical to plant survival that a sprouting seedling devotes its first days to root growth before allowing leaves to pop out of the seed. During this time of early germination, the root anchors the plant in the soil and begins to deliver a reliable water supply to the growing seedling. In dry climates, the time taken by roots to find reliable water can take years. The two-year-old sprouts of some California oaks can have a three-foot long root, while their shoots are restricted to only two leaves. In the Namib Desert of Southwest Africa, *Welwitschia* plants spend their entire one-hundred-year life growing underground roots, leaving only two leaves on the plant even after a century of growth. These examples illustrate the priority placed on root growth over shoot growth in specialized (dry) environments. In moister climates, roots will still be the first organs to emerge from seeds, but leaves will follow them within about ten days.

The primary root, or radicle, is the first root to emerge from the seed. From there, the plant can develop a taproot system or a fibrous root system. In dicotyledons, including most trees (except palms), the radicle grows into a strong taproot that sends small branch roots out to the side. In monocotyledons, especially grasses and palms, the radicle stops growing early on and many roots emerge from the seed, each forming similar-sized branch roots that combine into a fibrous root system. Long taproots allow plants to reach deep reliable water supplies, while fibrous roots absorb surface water before it evaporates. Fibrous roots also stabilize soil, reducing erosion.

Root Functions

Most root functions take place in the youngest part of roots, usually 10 centimeters from the growing root tip. Four activities are accomplished in that area:

Roots Stabilize the Plant. Roots anchor plants in soil by pressing between soil particles. Loose or wet sand or mud makes it much harder for roots to

Roots of an elephant ficus tree spread out on the surface from the base of its trunk.

secure mechanical anchorage. Trees topple when high winds sweep sandy areas, wetlands, or rainsoaked slopes. In free-floating aquatic plants, such as duckweed and water hyacinth, roots stabilize the plant by dangling into the water, acting as a keel to keep the leaves upright and preventing plants from toppling over. When roots are experimentally removed from water hyacinth, the plants tip over and die.

Roots Absorb Water and Minerals. Roots absorb water and minerals and transport them to the shoot. In a root system, each root elongates from its tip, entering new soil that can be exploited as an undepleted source of minerals and water. Delicate single-celled root hairs grow from the epidermis and greatly increase the root surface area devoted to absorption. Conditions that harm root hairs in the soil will **impede** nutrient uptake and harm the entire plant as leaves turn yellow and plant growth slows. Soil **compaction** and salt accumulation are two environmental factors that harm plants by killing root hairs. In 1999, decline in fruit quality from date orchards in Southern California was slowed by reducing tractor traffic near the trees. This decreased the likelihood of crushing root hairs on the shallow fibrous root systems of date palms.

There are more than fifteen elements needed by plants to grow. Of these, roots absorb nitrogen (N), phosphorus (P), and potassium (K) in the largest amounts. The soil minerals most commonly available for root uptake are those that are stuck onto tiny colloid particles in the soil. Colloids are abundant in clay and in broken-down compost. They enhance soil fertility by anchoring minerals in the soil and preventing them from being washed (leached) down and away from plant roots. Colloids are negatively charged particles, allowing minerals with positive charges (potassium, calcium, iron, etc.) to stick to them. Roots can free these stuck minerals by releasing protons (H^+) from inside the root and exchanging them for positively charged minerals on the colloid surface in a process called cation exchange. The cation exchange capacity of a soil is a strong indicator of soil fertility, the ability of a soil to provide roots with essential minerals over long periods of time. Acid rain (high in H^+) in Europe and Northeastern North America (Canada and the United States) decreases soil fertility by displacing minerals from soil colloids, thereby lowering the soil's exchange capacity.

Roots Attract Microbes. The roots of many species attract beneficial soil microbes by secreting a paste (mucigel) rich in sugar. The sugars support large populations of soil bacteria and fungi that help roots absorb minerals, especially nitrogen and phosphorus. The bacteria involved are nitrogen fixing bacteria. The fungi are mycorrhizae, long threadlike fungi that attach to plant roots and form a bridge connecting roots to minerals that would have been out of reach of the shorter root hairs. Almost all major agricultural crops have fungi or bacteria associated with their roots. Plants invest up to 10 percent of all food made by leaves to the paste they secrete out of roots. In some cases, the mucigel can feed more than just microbes. In lava tubes such as the Kaumana caves of Hawaii, entire populations of insects live in total darkness, fed only by mucigel from roots pushing through the cave ceiling.

Roots Store Food. Since roots are underground and away from light, making their own food by photosynthesis is impossible. Instead, sugar made by

impede slow down or inhibit

compaction compacting of soil, leading to loss of air spaces

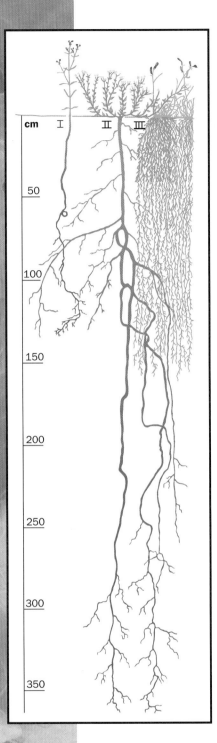

Comparisons of roots: tap (I and II) and fibrous (III). Redrawn from Kutschera, 1960.

commodities goods that are traded, especially agricultural goods

leaves is transported to roots for storage as starch. The stored food can power root growth, or it can enlarge roots in some cases, turning them into economically important **commodities** such as cassava (*Manihot*) from West Africa and the Caribbean, sweet potato (*Ipomoea*), and ginseng (*Panax*) from China and North Carolina.

Root Anatomy

Four features help distinguish roots from shoots. In roots: 1) a protective cap covers the growing tip, 2) single-celled root hairs are present, 3) branching starts deep within the root, and 4) xylem and phloem alternate around the vascular cylinder.

The root cap protects the tender growing tip against **abrasion** by soil particles. By secreting mucilage, the cap may help lubricate passage of the growing root through the soil. The cap helps attract nitrogen fixing bacteria and mycorrhizal fungi by secreting sugars that feed them. Finally, the root cap detects gravity and directs most roots to grow downward in a process called gravitropism. Corn roots with caps removed by microsurgery grow in random directions until the cap regenerates, after which time they return to growing downward.

When viewed from the outside in, root cross sections show six tissues. The epidermis is the interface between the soil environment and the living root. There is no water-repellent **cuticle** over the epidermis of roots growing in moist media such as soil or water. Everything absorbed by the root must pass through the epidermis including water, minerals, and pollutants such as heavy metals and pesticides. The surface area devoted to uptake of water and minerals is greatly increased by single-celled root hairs extending from thousands of epidermal cells. Root hairs are especially important for water uptake from soil. Aquatic plants with ample supplies of water, such as *Elodea* and water chestnut (*Trapa*), produce no root hairs.

The root cortex contains food-storage cells usually filled with starch. The cortex is especially large in storage roots such as those of cassava, sweet potato, and tropical yam (*Dioscorea*). The cortex spans from the epidermis to the endodermis, which is the innermost layer of cortex. The endodermis helps regulate which **compounds** spread throughout the plant. Cell walls of mature endodermal cells contain a ribbon of wax called the Casparian band, which prevents water from passing from the cortex into the root vein through the cell walls. Instead, water (and the compounds dissolved in it) must pass through the cytoplasm of endodermal cells before it can spread throughout the plant. This allows the plasma membrane of endodermal cells to regulate which compounds pass deeper into the root. Calcium absorption is regulated this way, as is the uptake of pollutants, including soil-borne lead, which are known to accumulate at the endodermis and to pass no farther.

The root vein, or vascular cylinder, is at the center of the root. In dicotyledons, xylem with two to six armlike lobes in a starlike configuration is at the core of the root. In monocotyledons, there can be twenty or more xylem arms in a circle around a central pith. Patches of phloem are tucked between each of the xylem arms. Water and minerals absorbed by the root move upward through the root xylem to the above-ground shoot system. At

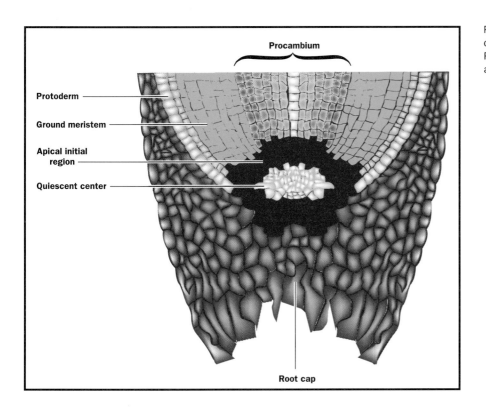

Protoderm

Ground meristem

Apical initial
region

Quiescent center

Procambium

Root cap

Parts of root cap and
quiescent center.
Redrawn from Moore et
al., 1998, Figure 15.6.

the same time, in the phloem, the solution of sugars and other carbon compounds made by leaves moves down into the roots.

The pericycle occupies the space between the outmost reaches of xylem arms and the endodermis. It ranges from one to six cell layers wide. Branch roots develop from the pericycle. By combining mechanical force with parent cell breakdown, the young branch root pushes through the endodermis, cortex, and epidermis of the parent root before reaching the soil. Developing from the pericycle allows branch roots to connect to xylem of the parent root at the earliest stages of their development. Root branching increases in response to pockets of enhanced resources in soil, leading to root proliferation around fertilizer pellets, dissolving rock, decaying animals, buried reptile eggs, or water drops.

Root Growth

Roots grow 1 to 6 centimeters each day by cell division and cell elongation near their tip. Growth depends on oxygen and temperature. Air space takes up 30 to 50 percent of productive soil volume, and depletion of that space by soil compaction or by flooding will reduce or stop root growth. The growing root tip is organized into three distinct zones, with an inactive zone sandwiched between two actively dividing meristems. The cap meristem is a layer of rapidly dividing cells between the root cap and the root body. It maintains the root cap, whose tip cells are **abraded** by soil particles. Behind the cap meristem is a lens- or bowl-shaped group of cells that seldom, if ever, divide. This is called the quiescent center, and its roles are to produce growth regulators (including cytokinin) that regulate root growth, to provide a reserve of cells that can replace injured cells of the cap and body meristems, and to physically regulate the size of those meristems.

abrasion wearing away through contact

cuticle the waxy outer coating of a leaf or other structure, providing protection against predators, infection, and water loss

compound a substance formed from two or more elements

abrade wear away through contact

Behind the quiescent center is the body meristem responsible for creating all root tissues except the cap.

Modified Roots and Their Economic Importance

In warm climates where freezing is not a problem, roots can grow above ground where they assume diverse functions. Above-ground roots are well developed in orchids, fig trees, and mangroves growing throughout the tropics and subtropics.

epiphytes plants that grow on other plants

The orchid family includes climbing orchids and **epiphytes** that live on tree branches, close to sunlight but away from soil. Roots of the vanilla orchid emerge from the stem and support this climbing vine by twining around sticks and branches of trees. Roots of epiphytic orchids are out in the open where they have access to sunlight and rainwater, but not to soil. Long-term studies at Hummingbird Cay Tropical Field Station in the Bahamas show these orchids grow very slowly but live for decades. Their aerial roots have a spongy multilayered epidermis called velamen that enables roots to store water from rain and bark runoff. To the inside of the velamen the cortex is modified for photosynthesis, performing a function usually restricted to leaves. Photosynthesis by the elaborate green roots of epiphytic orchids in the tropics and Japan compensates for the reduced leaves in these plants.

Ficus trees such as figs and banyans use buttress roots and stilt roots to support large canopies atop shallow tropical soil. Buttress roots resemble rocket fins at the bottom of large tree trunks. They develop from the fusion of the upper side of a horizontal root with the vertical tree trunk in response to tension as the tree leans away from the developing buttress. Trees growing on hillsides show larger buttresses on the uphill side of the trunk than on the downhill side. Buttresses are prominent on Brazilian rubber tree (*Hevea*), and kapok (*Ceiba*). Stilt roots develop from horizontal branches and grow down to the soil where they thicken and become long-lived supports for the tree canopy.

ecosystem an ecological community together with its environment

Mangroves are trees living in tropical coastal areas. Their roots are of enormous value in stabilizing tropical coast lines against typhoons, hurricanes, and wave action, and they give refuge to young stages of commercially important fish. The global value of such **ecosystem** services provided by mangroves was estimated in 1997 to exceed $600 billion. To help restore damaged environments, mangroves are being replanted in Vietnam, the Philippines, and Mexico. Mangrove roots allow these coastal trees to grow in shifting sand and oxygen-poor soil. The stilt roots of red mangrove (*Rhizophora*) spread down into sand from dozens of canopy branches, thereby stabilizing the tree. Pores, called lenticels, on the root surface allow oxygen to enter the aerial part of the root and diffuse down to submerged tissues in oxygen-depleted soil. Massive intertwined root systems of red mangrove forests prevent hurricanes from removing acres of land from south Florida and the Caribbean. The root system of black mangrove (*Avicennia*) has at least three root types. Underground cable roots radiate horizontally from the central tree trunk and stabilize the tree. They produce upward-growing roots (pneumatophores) that grow out of the soil and act as snorkels to bring oxygen into belowground roots. Feeder roots branch from the base of each pneumatophore where their large surface area absorbs minerals from the soil. SEE ALSO ANATOMY OF PLANTS; COMPOST; EPIPHYTES; NITROGEN FIX-

ATION; NUTRIENTS; ORCHIDACEAE; TISSUES; TROPISM; VASCULAR TISSUES; WATER MOVEMENT.

George S. Ellmore

Bibliography

Kutschera, L. *Wurzelatals.* Frankfurt: DLG-Verlag, 1960.

McCully, Margaret E. "Roots in Soil: Unearthing the Complexities of Roots and Their Rhizospheres."*Annual Review of Plant Physiology and Plant Molecular Biology* 50 (1999): 695–71.

Moore, Randy, W. Dennis Clark, and Darrell S. Vodopich. *Botany,* 2nd ed. New York: McGraw-Hill, 1998.

Pimm, Stuart L. "The Value of Everything." *Nature* 387 (1997): 231–32.

Russell, R. Scott. *Plant Root Systems: Their Function and Interaction with the Soil.* London: McGraw-Hill, 1977.

Stegmann, Edwin W., Richard B. Primack, and George. S. Ellmore. "Absorption of Nutrient Exudates from Terrapin Eggs by Roots of *Ammophila breviligulata* (Gramineae)." *Canadian Journal of Botany* 66 (1988): 714–18.

Waisel, Yoav, and Eshel Amram, eds. *Plant Roots: The Hidden Half,* 2nd ed. New York: Dekker, Marcel, Inc., 1996.

Weaver-Missick, Tara. "Dates Go Under Cover."*Agricultural Research* 48 (2000): 15.

Rosaceae

The family Rosaceae consists of about one hundred **genera** and three thousand species. It is distributed throughout the world, being especially common in North America, Europe, and Asia. Many members of the family are woody shrubs or trees. Others are perennial herbs: the stems die back at the end of each season and the root lives on to produce new stems in following seasons. The flowers of Rosaceae are distinctive because of the presence of a hypanthium, a cup-shaped structure forming the base of the flower. The **sepals**, petals, and stamens are attached to the edge of the hypanthium, while the **pistil** or pistils (which develop into the fruit or fruits) sit in the bottom of it.

One of the most conspicuous characteristics of Rosaceae is the variety of fruits produced by its species. Many Rosaceae have **achenes** and follicles, both of which are nonfleshy. Achenes contain one seed and have a hard fruit wall that does not split open at maturity, whereas follicles contain more than one seed and split open at maturity. Most fleshy fruits of Rosaceae are either drupes or pomes. A drupe (or stone fruit) contains one seed; the inner part of the fruit wall (the pit) is hard, and the outer fruit wall is usually fleshy. Peaches, plums, and cherries are examples of fleshy drupes, while almonds are nonfleshy. The fruits of raspberries and blackberries are clusters of many very small drupes. Pomes such as apples and pears are unusual fruits because the fleshy part does not develop from the pistil but from the hypanthium. The mature pistil containing the seeds is enclosed by the fleshy hypanthium. The fleshy part of the strawberry fruit is also not made from the pistil but from the base of the flower, which has expanded and become fleshy (accessory tissue). The fruits are achenes that are attached to the outside of the fleshy structure.

Rosaceae is very important economically. Many members of the family are important as ornamentals because of their foliage or flowers. Others are important components of diets in countries throughout the world because of

genera plural of genus; a taxonomic level above species

sepals the outermost whorl of flower parts; usually green and leaf-like, they protect the inner parts of the flower

pistil the female reproductive organ

achene a small, dry, thinwalled type of fruit

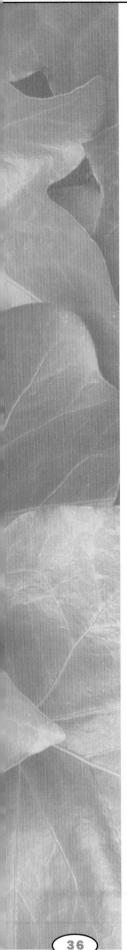

ECONOMICALLY IMPORTANT ROSACEAE SPECIES

Scientific Name	Common Name	Uses
Ornamental shrubs and trees		
Chaenomeles species	Flowering quince	Flower ornamental
Cotoneaster species	Cotoneaster	Foliage and flower ornamental
Crataegus species	Hawthorn	Foliage and fruit ornamental, hedgerows
Eriobotrya japonica	Loquat	Foliage ornamental
Kerria japonica	Kerria	Flower ornamental
Malus species	Crabapple	Flower ornamental
Prunus species	Flowering cherry	Flower ornamental
Pyracantha species	Firethorn	Foliage ornamental
Rosa species	Rose	Flower ornamental
Spiraea species	Bridal wreath	Foliage and flower ornamental
Ornamental herbs		
Alchemilla species	Lady's mantle	Foliage ornamental
Filipendula species	Meadowsweet	Foliage and flower ornamental
Geum species	Avens	Foliage and flower ornamental
Potentilla species	Cinquefoil	Foliage and flower ornamental
Food and wood plants		
Cydonia oblonga	Quince	Fruit
Fragaria species	Strawberry	Fruit
Malus domesticus	Apple	Fruit, wood
Mespilus germanica	Medlar	Fruit
Prunus species	Cherry	Fruit
Prunus species	Plum	Fruit
Prunus amygdalus	Almond	Fruit
Prunus armeniaca	Apricot	Fruit
Prunus persica	Peach	Fruit
Prunus serotina	Wild black cherry	Wood
Pyrus communis	Pear	Fruit, wood
Rubus species	Blackberry, raspberry	Fruit

the fiber, phytochemicals, and vitamins they contain. Much of the fresh fruit eaten by people in temperate regions (apples, pears, strawberries, and cherries, for example) are members of family Rosaceae. Some members of Rosaceae are large enough to be sources of wood. The wood of wild black cherry (*Prunus serotina;* the largest species of Rosaceae) is a desirable furniture wood, and the wood of pear is used to make musical instruments such as recorders. SEE ALSO ECONOMIC IMPORTANCE OF PLANTS; FRUITS; HORTICULTURE.

David R. Morgan

Bibliography

Bailey, L. H. *Manual of Cultivated Plants.* New York: Macmillan, 1951.

Heywood, V. H., ed. *Flowering Plants of the World.* New York: Oxford University Press, 1993.

Simpson, B. B., and M. C. Ogorzaly. *Economic Botany: Plants in Our World*, 2nd ed. New York: McGraw-Hill, 1995.

Sachs, Julius von

German botanist
1832–1897

Julius von Sachs was born October 2, 1832, in what is now Poland. Although his family was very poor, his brilliance and constant hard work helped him become in his day the foremost authority on the new science of plant

physiology. He was made a member of many scientific societies and academies, and was awarded a grant of nobility that allowed him to use "von" before his name. Sachs published several books that became the definitive plant physiology references for many years. His *Lehrbuch der Botanik* (*Textbook of Botany*) went through many editions and is still read today.

Sachs's main scientific contributions to plant science came with his early research in the mid-1800s. He enjoyed lab research more than attending lectures in school and he worked with incredible energy and determination. Throughout his career, Sachs strove to find general principles and large concepts involved in botany, rather than focus on smaller, more specific questions. He used microscopic and chemical techniques to study three main areas of plant physiology: carbon use in plants, the mineral requirements of plants, and the effect of temperature on plants. This work laid the foundation for the study of plant physiology among his successors.

In examining the fate of carbon in plants, Sachs used an iodine test to show that carbon was first accumulated as starch in the leaves of plants. He also demonstrated that this accumulation occurred in the **chloroplasts** and that chlorophyll, light, and carbon dioxide were necessary for carbon fixation. Sachs also observed the way in which the carbon in starch was converted into different compounds in the plant, such as oils, sugars, and proteins. He was one of the first researchers to believe that **enzymes** did essential work in these metabolic conversions.

Sachs developed a method to culture plants in water instead of soil, which allowed him to experiment with the nutrient content of the water he gave the plants. He used this technique to demonstrate that plants can grow with just water, the right nutrients, and sunlight. Many other scientists believed at first that he must have faked his results—they were certain that soil was necessary for plant growth. Later, of course, Sachs's pioneering research led to the development of **hydroponics** and the agricultural fertilizer industry.

Sachs's examination of the effects of temperature on plants showed that plants have minimum, maximum, and optimum temperatures at which they grow. These ideas became important later in the study of ecology.

As one of the founders of the modern study of plant physiology, Sachs developed new techniques and scientific instruments, and he helped make plant physiology into a scientific discipline with its own methods and laws. His great authority occasionally led him to be unfair in disagreeing with other scientists (including Charles Darwin) and just his disapproval of an idea could delay research into it. Despite this, Sachs made very important advances in the plant sciences and he was very well respected when he died in Germany on May 29, 1897. SEE ALSO DARWIN, CHARLES; HYDROPONICS; PHOTOSYNTHESIS, CARBON FIXATION AND; PHYSIOLOGIST; PHYSIOLOGY; PHYSIOLOGY, HISTORY OF.

Jessica P. Penney

physiology the biochemical processes carried out by an organism

chloroplast the photosynthetic organelle of plants and algae

enzyme a protein that controls a reaction in a cell

hydroponic growing without soil, in a watery medium

Bibliography

Morton, A.G. *History of Botanical Science.* London: Academic Press, 1981.

Sachs, Julius von. *History of Botany.* Translated by Henry E. F. Garnsey. New York: Russel and Russel, 1890.

Savanna

ecosystem an ecological community together with its environment

Grass-dominated **ecosystems** that contain a significant number of widely spaced trees are termed savannas. Trees may make up as little as 5 percent or as much as 30 percent of the cover of all plants in savannas, but grasses and grasslike plants form a continuous ground cover. Originally, savanna was a term used to describe primarily tropical and subtropical grasslands, which usually have more woody plants than temperate grasslands. These tropical and subtropical savannas occupy large land areas. Almost 65 percent of Africa is covered by savanna, much of the northern region of Australia has savanna vegetation and South America has extensive savannas. Worldwide, estimated land cover by savanna is nearly 20 percent.

Savannas may be a product of climatic factors, they may result from unique soil types, or they may be narrow to broad transitional zones between forests and grasslands. Fire and periods of water limitation are present in all savannas whether they occur in the tropics or in temperate zones.

Tropical and Subtropical Savannas

The extensive savannas of Africa, South America (locally known as cerrado) and Australia are primarily a result of either the climate or unique soil characteristics. Climatically derived savannas are warm all year but have distinct wet and dry (winter) seasons with annual rainfall varying widely from 30 to more than 100 centimeters of rainfall. What is critical about these climates is that during the dry season, rainfall amounts are very low. It is during these dry periods that the grasses are **dormant** and the trees experience water stress. Fires are also common at this time because the fine, dry fuel (dead foliage) that the grasses produce is very flammable. This allows fires, started by lightning or humans, to start easily and spread quickly. This combination of water stress and fire keeps the tree density low and distinguishes savanna from the adjacent forest.

dormant inactive, not growing

Other savannas occur in areas where there are unique soil conditions. Although most tropical and subtropical savanna soils are poor in nutrients, some also have a hard crust or barrier at some depth in the soil. This crust separates the shallow soil layer that the grasses rely on for water, and which dries during periods of low rainfall, from the deeper soil layers that may retain moisture all year. Trees in these savannas are located where cracks in the crust occur. In these places the roots of trees can access this deep soil water. Such savannas are referred to as edaphic (related to the soil) savannas.

Savannas as Transitional Zones

Savannas in both tropical and temperate zones may occur along the edge of forests where the dominant vegetation shifts from trees to grasses. This tension zone (also called an ecotone) between forest and grassland may be relatively narrow or 50 to more than 100 kilometers wide. These savannas usually occur where annual rainfall is not quite high enough to support a closed forest and where fire is common. In North America, the aspen parkland of Canada is an example of a temperate savanna and in the United States there are the oak savannas that extend from Minnesota to Texas. His-

A baobab tree on the African savanna.

torically, the region occupied by oak savanna moved eastward in periods of aridity and with frequent fire. In contrast, with fire suppression these savannas may be converted to closed canopy forest. Much of the original extent of North American savanna was found on deep fertile soils, but greater than 99 percent has been lost because the land was so valuable for row crop agriculture.

Savannas and Biodiversity

Savannas contain a mixture of forest and grassland species, as well as some species unique to this ecosystem type. Because of this they are important zones of high **biodiversity** for both plants and animals. In North America, oak trees embedded in tallgrass prairie vegetation are joined by species specifically adapted to partial shade and frequent fire. In Africa and Australia, thorny acacia, eucalyptus, and baobab trees are scattered among the grasses. Savanna grasses are well adapted to fire because their buds are protected below ground. Like the grasses, some mature savanna tree species are resistant to fire, particularly compared to other forest species. Many savanna trees (such as the oaks) have thick insulating bark that protects the

biodiversity degree of variety of life

Zebras on the savanna in Masai Mara, Kenya.

herbivore an organism that feeds on plant parts

population a group of organisms of a single species that exist in the same region and inter-breed

biomass the total dry weight of an organism or group of organisms

inner growing layers of the tree from fire. Others, such as the baobab tree in Africa, can store tremendous amounts of water in their bark and trunk, protecting them from both fire and drought. Other savanna trees are capable of resprouting vigorously after fire. Despite these adaptations, frequent fire decreases the density of trees in most savannas, with tree seedlings especially susceptible to fire.

Savannas support a diverse array of **herbivores**, especially so in the African savannas. Grassland grazers such as zebras and wildebeest are found with herbivores that feed on trees, such as giraffes and elephants. Elephants have been termed a keystone species of African savannas for the role they play in determining the density of trees. When elephant **populations** are low, acacia trees and shrubs may become so dense that the grasses are shaded out and grassland species disappear. Conversely, if elephant populations are too high, the trees may disappear along with those species that depend on woody plants for food and shelter. Another group of organisms that is particularly notable in tropical savannas for their diversity and numbers, if not their individual size, are the termites. Conspicuous above-ground termite mounds are present in Australian and African savannas, but most termites live underground without building mounds. Termites fill a very important role as one of the major decomposers in savannas. As much as 90 percent of the grass **biomass** that is decomposed in some savannas can be attributed to termites. Thus, these organisms are valuable for making nutrients available to plants.

Savanna Management and Conservation

Most of the larger savannas in tropical and subtropical regions are grazed by livestock. Fire is used as a management tool to keep the density of trees low and stimulate the productivity of the grasses. Savannas can produce abundant plant biomass for grazers in regions with high rainfall, but savannas in the driest regions and with the most nutrient-poor soils can support only a modest number of livestock. In Africa, human-induced shifts in the populations of large native herbivores (elephants) have altered the density of trees in some savannas, and conservation programs for these species must also take into account their effect on other species as well as the savanna vegetation.

Interest in conserving and restoring savanna ecosystems is also great in North America, where the greatest proportion of the original savanna ecosystems has been lost. Controlled fire and even mechanical removal of woody species is typically used in areas where dense shrubs and tree seedlings have displaced the grasses. SEE ALSO BIOME; FABACEAE; GRASSES; GRASSLANDS.

Alan K. Knapp

Bibliography

Archibold, O. W. *Ecology of World Vegetation*. New York: Chapman & Hall, 1995.

Barbour, Michael G., Jack H. Burk, Wanna D. Pitts, Frank S. Gilliam, and Mark W. Schwartz. *Terrestrial Plant Ecology*. Menlo Park, CA: Addison Wesley Longman, Inc., 1998.

Cole, M. M. *The Savannas: Biogeography and Geobotany*. New York: Academic Press, 1986.

Daubenmire, Rexford. *Plant Geography*. New York: Academic Press, 1978.

Seed Dispersal

Seed dispersal refers to the processes by which mature seeds disperse from the parent plant. Dispersal decreases competition with the parent and increases the likelihood of finding a suitable environment for growth. Sexual reproduction generally results in the production of fruits whose sole purpose is to enable the species to disperse and multiply. The part of the plant that acts in the dispersal is the diaspore (a term incorporating both fruit and seed). Although diaspore dispersal is the obvious end of reproduction, some plants rarely flower or set fruit and instead have evolved a very efficient system of vegetative reproduction by means of sucker shoots. Vegetative reproduction is very common in herbaceous plants that may spread by **stolons**, **bulbils**, or stem suckering. Still, most plants that reproduce vegetatively also reproduce sexually since this enables them to remain genetically variable and more adaptable to changes in the environment.

stolons underground stems that may form new individuals by sprouting

bulbil a small above-ground bulb

Wind Dispersal

The simplest form of seed dispersal is by wind and, not surprisingly, wind-dispersed fruits in temperate areas usually develop in breezy spring months. The same species that are wind-pollinated in temperate areas often bear wind-dispersed seed such as maple (*Acer* in Aceraceae), willow and poplar (*Salix* and *Populus* in Salicaceae), and ash (*Fraxinus* in Oleaceae).

A pisonia plant's seed clings to the feathers of a black noddy on Heron Island, Australia.

samara a winged seed

morphological related to shape

Typically the wind-dispersed seeds are developed quickly and dispersed in the same season. Wind-dispersed tree species are numerous in the warm, moist forests of the tropics—especially for tall trees in areas where there is a slight to prominent dry season. The height of the tree is important to enable the diaspore to catch the wind currents. The shape of wind-dispersed diaspores is often critical to their dispersal as well. Maple seeds have a **samara** and set up a whirling pattern as they fall, which may assist them in implantation. Poplar and willow seed are borne in a loose, cottony mass, which is extremely buoyant even in weak air currents. Although different **morphological** structures have evolved to disperse tree seed, the most common form of seed dispersal is wind-dispersed.

Typically, wind-dispersed species in tropical areas with seasonally dry periods lose their fruits late in the dry season or in the early rainy season that follows. This ensures adequate moisture for germinating seeds and adequate establishment before the next dry season. Wind-dispersed seeds have the distinct disadvantage of being at the peril of the elements. Most do not get carried very far away from the mother plant, and the population of insects that feed on the particular plant increases greatly at the time of flowering and can often destroy much of the crop. Some tropical species successfully avoid this by fruiting irregularly or even by what is known as mass fruiting, in which hundreds of individuals somehow manage to flower all at one time, literally swamping the predator population with more food than it can eat and thus preventing the insects from eating all the fruit.

The manner in which wind-dispersed diaspores are released is often critical to their dispersal. Because wet seeds do not float well on the air, most do not disperse except when the capsule is dry. Seeds are often contained within the capsule walls, and the valves of the capsule open increasingly further with only the uppermost seeds being capable of being blown free.

The same capsules may release seeds not from wind alone, but in part by mechanical motions and the inertia built up by movements of animals passing through a population. Each time a plant is bumped more seeds are cast away from it. This is a short distance but common type of seed dispersal in many prairie and forest edge plant populations.

Animal Dispersal

Animal-dispersed fruits are more common than wind-dispersed fruits and occur in species with a wider variety of life forms, including herbs, many vines, a modest number of tropical lianas, and shrubs as well as some trees. The morphology of animal-dispersed fruits varies depending on the organism doing the dispersal. The animals vary from those as small as ants to as large as horses or elephants.

Both birds and mammals are very effective dispersers. Birds are particularly effective dispersers since they can move the diaspore the farthest and the fastest. Diaspores dispersed by birds are usually colorful and lack any obvious scent (birds have keen vision but a poor sense of smell). Often the fruits feature contrasting colors so they are more easily seen. Frequently the outer covering of such fruit might be green or brown, but when the fruit opens the inner surface is bright red with a black seed. Often birds eat only the sweet portion of the diaspore and spit out the seed. If eaten, most seeds pass rather quickly through the bird's system and are ejected. Many times tiny colorful berries, such as those of *Anthurium* (Araceae), are initially quite sweet but quickly turn bitter after being eaten to encourage rejection. *Anthurium* also produces seeds with a sticky **appendage** that causes the seeds to stick to the bird's bill.

appendages parts that are attached to a central stalk or axis

Mammal dispersers are common in both temperate and tropical areas. Mammal-dispersed diaspores are usually not particularly colorful but may be tasty and even have a distinct aroma when mature. (Mammals have only average sight compared to birds but typically have a good sense of smell.) Squirrels and rodents in temperate regions gather and hoard oak and hickory fruits while tropical agoutis "scatter hoard" fruits by burying them seemingly at random on the forest floor. Those fruits that are not found later in the late rainy season—when fruit is rare—are already planted and ready to grow. Monkeys in the tropics have a diverse diet with a broad array of fruits that are dispersed by them. They are amazingly adept at dispersal, but seemingly wasteful since they gather many fruits, eat part of them, and then discard the remainder along with the seeds. Some less common animal dispersers are horses, which are known to eat and disperse the seeds of calabash (*Cresentia cujete* in Bignoniaceae) in Central America.

In the case of epizoochorous fruits, animals are responsible for dispersing fruits without actually consuming them. These are diaspores that attach themselves to fur or clothing. Among the most effective types are beggar's ticks (*Bidens* in Asteraceae), tick-trefoil (*Desmodium* in Fabaceae), and Queen Anne's lace (*Daucus carota* in Apiaceae). These fruits are difficult to avoid and are difficult to remove, so they are usually picked off and discarded far from where they were first encountered.

Mechanical Dispersal

Mechanically dispersed seeds are common in both temperate and tropical areas. Many **legumes** (Fabaceae) have fruits that dry under torsion, and are suddenly released when the two halves of the fruits fall apart. In this instant the two halves of the valve twist **laterally** and sometimes also longitudinally, which causes the dry seeds along their length to be thrown for considerable distances. One of the most remarkable mechanically dispersed seeds is that of *Hura crepitans* (Euphorbiaceae), which is made up of a series of pie-shaped segments that burst open with such force that it sounds like a rifle shot. Its small flat seeds are carried for great distances.

Water Dispersal

Water dispersal is quite effective in estuarian populations of plants. The nature of water-dispersed fruits is important since a seed that lacks buoyancy would sink to the bottom near the mother plant and have to compete with it. A diaspore that was too buoyant would perhaps never sink at all and thus might never be implanted. *Urospatha*, a tropical aroid, has fruits with seeds that are embedded in a thick, buoyant, gelatinous mass, which allows them to float for a period and then sink into the water. The seeds of some tropical trees that occur along water courses are known to be consumed by fish. It is not yet known, however, whether the movement of the fish are important to the dispersal of the seeds.

Seed germination and the establishment of the young plant is, of course, the only true sign of reproductive success. Dispersal without establishment is to no avail. In every case the rate of germination is critical. Many diaspores do not fall into the proper situation for germination. Often large numbers of seeds are killed by a wide variety of beetles or weevils that specialize on seeds. Different species have developed various methods of survival. Some, such as orchids, produce thousands of minute seeds per capsule, giving some a good chance of success. Other species use the opposite strategy of producing large and heavy fruits with a lot of stored food material to ensure survival after germination. Some species, such as the seeds of the *Beilschmiedia* in the Lauraceae, have an increased chance of survival by having the seeds begin the germination process while still on the trees, where they are less susceptible to attacks. The red mangrove *Rhizophora mangle* (Rhizophoraceae) goes even further by actually establishing a young plant on the tree that has a pointed base that actually implants in the soil when it falls. SEE ALSO Germination; Interactions, Plant-Vertebrate; Seeds.

Thomas B. Croat

Bibliography

Van der Pijl, L. *Principles of Dispersal in Higher Plants.* New York: Springer-Verlag, 1969.

legumes beans and other members of the Fabaceae family

lateral to the side of

Seedless Vascular Plants

The Lycophyta, Equisetophyta, and Psilophyta are collectively referred to as the fern allies because, like the ferns (Pterophyta), they reproduce by single-celled spores released from sporangia (spore sacs). They do not produce flowers or seeds and both ferns and fern allies contain well-developed conducting tissues to transport fluids within the plant. Fern allies, however, differ greatly in appearance from ferns because they generally bear small, simple leaves with an unbranched vein, whereas almost all ferns have larger, often lacy cut leaves called fronds that contain branching veins. The fern allies include some of the earliest known land plants, many of which are long extinct. Today, there are probably fewer species of fern allies than there were many millions of years ago.

The life cycles of the fern allies and ferns are similar. Alternating generations of sporophytes (**diploid** plants producing spores) live independently of gametophytes (**haploid** plants producing eggs and sperm). The **sporophyte** is the dominant of the two generations; it has two sets of chromosomes per cell and is larger and more conspicuous. Through meiosis in the sporangia (spore sacs), the number of chromosomes in some cells is reduced by half; these cells develop into spores. If a spore lands on a suitable site it will germinate to form a gametophyte, usually less than 1 centimeter across. The resulting gametophyte, with a single set of chromosomes per cell, produces an egg in each archegonium (vase-shaped structure) and sperm in each spherical antheridium. Sperm are released from antheridia and, in a drop of water, they swim to an egg and unite with it to create another sporophyte with two sets of chromosomes.

diploid having two sets of chromosomes, versus having one (haploid)

haploid having one set of chromosomes, versus having two (diploid)

sporophyte the diploid, spore-producing individual in the plant life cycle

Lycophyta

In the Carboniferous period (over three hundred million years ago), Lycophyta included large trees that are now extinct, but which have left remains preserved as coal. This division of fern allies is represented today by three distantly related families of small herbaceous plants called club mosses, spikemosses, and quillworts. The club mosses are homosporous (producing spores of one size) while spikemosses and quillworts are heterosporous (producing spores of two sizes). These plants generally grow to less than 20 centimeters high, rarely up to 1 meter. They have branched or unbranched stems that are erect, creeping, or hanging, and covered with simple, one-veined leaves. Their roots branch with equal forks. Sporangia are borne singly in the upper angle formed between leaf and stem. Leaves associated with sporangia are clustered in zones along the stem or packed into terminal cones. Heterosporous lycophytes are distinctive for the small flap of tissue on the upper surface of each leaf called a ligule.

Club Mosses (Lycopodiaceae). There are about 375 species of club mosses distributed worldwide, especially in mountainous tropical habitats. These large mosslike plants, whether terrestrial or epiphytic, have branching stems that are densely covered with small, narrow leaves. Unlike spikemosses and quillworts, club mosses are homosporous and have kidney-shaped sporangia that open like clams. The sporangia may be clustered in zones or packed in terminal cones. The small, disc- or carrot-shaped gametophytes associate with fungi for assistance with the uptake of nutrients. Princess pine (*lycopodium* sp) is a common lycopod in eastern forests.

Spikemosses (Selaginellaceae). Most of the approximately 750 species of spikemosses occur in tropical and subtropical regions where they occupy a variety of habitats ranging from rain forests to deserts. These mosslike terrestrial plants typically are less than 2 centimeters high. Like the club mosses, they have branching stems densely covered with small, narrow leaves. The sporangia of most species are packed in four-sided, terminal cones. They are heterosporous, usually producing four megaspores in each megasporangium and hundreds of microspores in each microsporangium. Upon germination, the tiny megagametophytes produce eggs and the minute microgametophytes release numerous sperm when the spore wall opens.

globose rounded and swollen; globe-shaped

Quillworts (Isoetaceae). There are probably over two hundred species of quillworts distributed worldwide in a range of habitats including lakes, streams, roadside ditches, and soil pockets on exposed rocks. The slender leaves of these terrestrial or aquatic plants can grow up to 50 centimeters long, and some can grow up to 1 meter. The short and squat to **globose** stems are covered with long, thin leaves, giving the plants the appearance of a tuft of grass. The sporangia are embedded in a basal cavity of the leaf. They are heterosporous, usually producing tens to hundreds of megaspores in each megasporangium and thousands of microspores in each microsporangium. Upon germination, the tiny megagametophytes produce eggs and the minute microgametophytes release four sperm when the spore wall opens.

Equisetophyta (Horsetails and Scouring Rushes)

These plants are distinctive for their tubular, grooved, and jointed stems. Although more diverse in the fossil record, today they are represented by only fifteen species, which are distributed nearly worldwide in moist to wet, often-disturbed habitats including shores, roadsides, marshes, and woodlands. Silica in the stems makes them useful for scouring and sanding— hence, one of their common names is "scouring rushes." These plants are usually less than 1 meter tall, but on occasion can grow to several meters. Their stems range from horizontal to erect and can be branched or unbranched. They bear **whorls** of leaves fused along their edges to form a slightly expanded sheath at each joint. In cross section, stems are seen to have a large central canal and smaller canals under the grooves and ridges. The sporangia hang from six-sided, umbrellalike sporangiophores, which are packed into terminal cones. The plants are homosporous and the spores are notable for the tiny, straplike **elaters** that coil and uncoil to aid in their dispersal. The small, lobed, cushionlike gametophytes initially produce either eggs or sperm. Gametophytes of some species, initially producing archegiona, later develop antheridia.

whorls rings

elater an elongated, thickened filament

Psilophyta (Fork Ferns)

The Psilophyta have long been thought to be among the most primitive of all living vascular plants because of their similarity in form to some of the oldest land plant fossils. Recent studies, however, indicate that they may be more closely related to the ferns than to the fern allies. There are about seventeen species, growing mainly in the tropics and subtropics. Most grow as **epiphytes** on tree fern trunks. They are called fork ferns (or whisk ferns) because the leaves associated with the sporangia (sporophylls) are forked, whereas their other leaves are simple or absent. Fork ferns grow less

epiphytes plants that grow on other plants

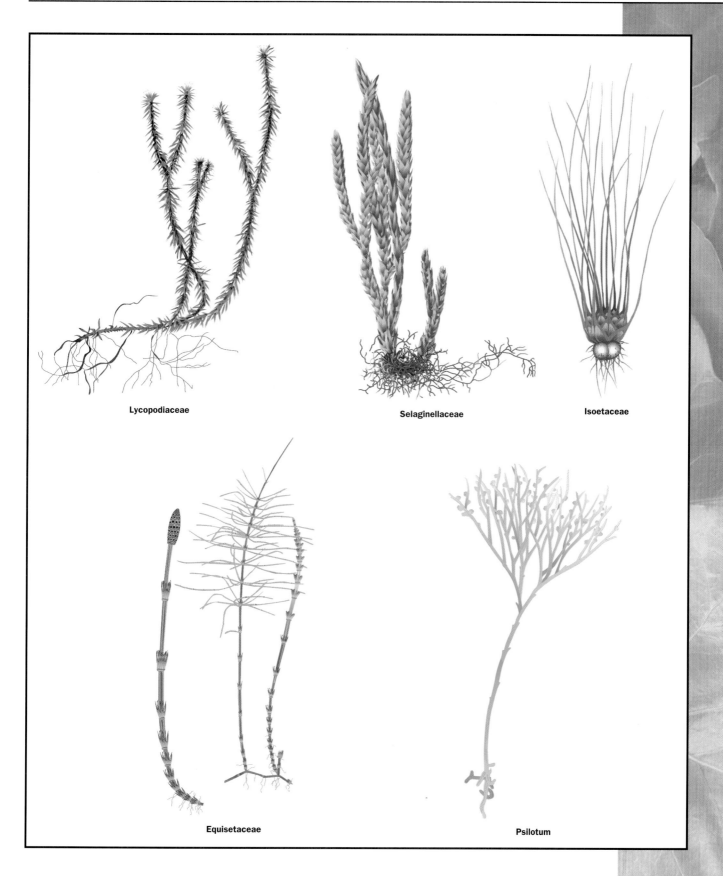

Lycopodiaceae

Selaginellaceae

Isoetaceae

Equisetaceae

Psilotum

Various types of seedless
vascular plants.

than 0.5 meters high and are without roots. They have horizontal, erect, or hanging stems that may be branched or unbranched. Their leaves are scale-like and with or without a vein. They are homosporous, bearing two- or three-lobed, fused sporangia on or above the sporophylls. The spores produce small subterranean gametophytes that associate with fungi for assistance with the uptake of nutrients. Gametophytes look similar to the underground branches of the sporophyte. SEE ALSO BRYOPHYTES; EPIPHYTES; EVOLUTION OF PLANTS; FERNS; VASCULAR TISSUES.

W. Carl Taylor and Patricia A. Batchelor

Bibliography

Gifford, Ernest M., and Adriance S. Foster. *Morphology and Evolution of Vascular Plants*, 3rd ed. New York: W. H. Freeman and Company, 1989.

Judd, Walter S., Christopher S. Campbell, Elizabeth A. Kellogg, and Peter F. Stevens. *Plant Systematics: A Phylogenetic Approach*. Sunderland, MA: Sinauer Associates, Inc., 1999.

Raven, Peter. H., Ray F. Evert, and Susan E. Eichhorn. *Biology of Plants*, 6th ed. New York: W. H. Freeman and Co., 1999.

Walters, Dirk R., and David J. Keil. *Vascular Plant Taxonomy*, 4th ed. Dubuque, IA: Kendall/Hunt Publishing Company, 1996.

Seed Preservation

Conservation of crop genetic resources is important to the long-term health of the world's food production systems. Genetic diversity provides the raw materials for selecting and improving plant traits such as resistance to pests, diseases, and environmental stresses. Genetic engineering has greatly increased our ability to manipulate genes for the benefit of agriculture, including transferring genes between unlike species. However, until individual genes that code for a specific trait or set of traits can be designed and developed in the lab, researchers and plant breeders must rely on existing genes. Thus, saving and preserving seeds, and their genes, is critical to future food security and stability.

Providing access to a reservoir of plant genetic resources has been the goal of ex situ (outside of the place of origin or natural occurrence) conservation at both the national and international levels. Ex situ strategies include the storage of plant genetic resources in seed banks, clonal repositories, and living collections. An extensive system for the ex situ conservation of plant genetic resources has been developed in the United States under the auspices of the Agricultural Research Service (ARS), the main research agency of the USDA (United States Department of Agriculture). The National Plant Germplasm System (NPGS), established to preserve and promote the use of plant genetic diversity, is a collaborative effort between state, federal, and private entities to acquire and manage plant genetic resources, including wild and weedy crop relatives, **landraces**, obsolete cultivars, and elite lines or **populations** of agricultural, horticultural, industrial, and medicinal crops. Though the NPGS focuses on building a strong, competitive U.S. agricultural industry, all **germplasm** held in the NPGS collections is made available to researchers around the world upon request.

Germplasm from all over the world is preserved in the NPGS system. Because many of the commercial crops produced in the United States are

landrace a variety of a cultivated plant, occurring in a particular region

population a group of organisms of a single species that exist in the same region and interbreed

germplasm hereditary material, especially stored seed or other embryonic forms

Scientists at the Vavilov Plant Industry Institute in St. Petersburg, Russia, work with the seeds of such plants as drought-resistant wheat, barley, and corn. The institute is the storehouse of seeds gathered by geneticist N. I. Vavilov, who roamed Africa, Asia, and Latin America in the early twentieth century to establish one of the world's largest collections of genetic plant stock.

Structure of several species of seeds. Strictly, lettuce and wheat are not seeds, but fruits.

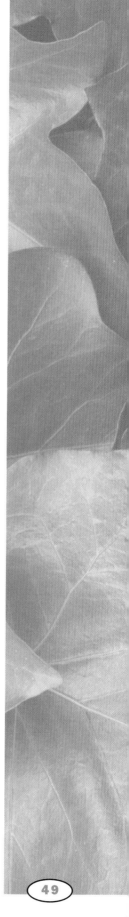

from nonnative sources, American agricultural productivity has depended on plant introductions from other countries, particularly from the tropics and subtropics. There are over four hundred thousand **accessions** from more than ten thousand species in the U.S. germplasm reserves. Responsibility for maintaining and distributing this large collection is divided between different NPGS sites, such as the eight National Germplasm Repositories, four Regional Plant Introduction Stations, the National Seed Storage Laboratory (NSSL), and other NPGS sites. Each site is charged with maintaining different species.

accession an individual sample of seed

The NSSL preserves the base collection of the NPGS and conducts research to develop new technologies for preserving seed and other types of plant germplasm. Seeds are stored either in conventional storage at -18°C or in cryogenic storage (liquid nitrogen) at -196°C. The National Germplasm Repositories are responsible for acquiring, preserving, increasing, evaluating, documenting, and distributing plant genetic resources of specific genera. United States germplasm collections of maize (corn), pumpkins, sunflowers, melons, cucumbers, and carrots are maintained at the North Central Regional Plant Introduction Station located in Ames, Iowa. The Western Regional Plant Introduction Station in Pullman, Washington, maintains lettuce, beet, bean, chickpea, forage and turf grass, and pea germplasm. Collections of pears, strawberries, blueberries, raspberries, and others are maintained at the National Clonal Germplasm Repository in Corvallis, Oregon, as living plants or, in the case of wild species, as seeds. Fruit and nut tree germplasm is maintained at the National Clonal Germplasm Repository in Davis, California.

Long-term storage of seed samples carries with it some inherent problems. The primary objective of seed banks is to maintain the genetic diversity and integrity of germplasm. Maintaining seeds in frozen storage requires adequate temperature and humidity controls. Even under ideal conditions, however, seeds eventually begin to lose viability—the ability to germinate.

genotype the genetic makeup of an organism

Thus, periodically, new seed needs to be produced in order to replace aging seed samples. This process is referred to as regeneration. The loss of unique **genotypes** within a collection—whether from natural causes, small sample sizes, or random drift—nonetheless would constitute a change in the presence or frequency of genes within a germplasm collection.

During regeneration, plants are exposed to the risks inherent with agriculture—insects, diseases, drought, hail, temperature extremes, and wind, depending on whether they are grown under field or greenhouse conditions. When susceptible genotypes succumb to insect or disease pressures, the genetic variability and integrity of the collection may be compromised unless the genes lost are present in surviving genotypes. Thus, the need to regenerate a collection must be weighed against the need to minimize risks associated with regeneration. Additionally, genetic contamination through cross pollination or accidental mixing during post-harvest processes such as cleaning can also result in a loss of integrity.

Many small, independent organizations are also involved in seed saving. Together, they have created what is known as the heirloom seed movement. These organizations, groups, and individuals have helped bring about global awareness of genetic erosion—a reduction in the number of varieties, and, hence, genetic diversity—in commercially available vegetable and crop seed. Of the approximately five thousand heirloom varieties of vegetables available in the 1984 seed catalogs, 88 percent were no longer available by 1998. On average, there is a 6 percent loss in available varieties every year. Comparison of a USDA inventory of varieties available at the beginning of the twentieth century with a list of holdings in the NSSL at the end of the twentieth century revealed that only 3 percent of this germplasm survived in American germplasm reserves.

More than twenty-five small seed companies in the United States focus their efforts on slowing or preventing the loss of open-pollinated, heirloom seeds. Founded in 1975, Seed Savers Exchange collects, maintains, and distributes precious heirloom seeds through a network of eight thousand members. The vast collection of rare, heirloom seeds includes over eighteen thousand varieties of tomatoes, beans, peppers, squash, peas, lettuce, corn, melons, garlic, and watermelons from countries around the world. SEE ALSO BIODIVERSITY; CULTIVAR; NATIVE CROPS; SEEDS; VAVILOV, N. I.

Suzanne C. Nelson

Bibliography

USDA-ARS/National Seed Storage Laboratory Preservation Page. 1997. [Online] Available at http://checkers.nssl.colostate.edu/preserve/prestour.htm.

USDA-ARS/North Central Regional Plant Introduction Station Page. 1999. [Online] Available at http://www.ars-grin.gov/ars/MidWest/Ames/.

Whealy, Kent. *Garden Seed Inventory*, 5th ed. Seed Savers Publications, 1985.

angiosperm a flowering plant

gymnosperm a major group of plants that includes the conifers

Seeds

The seed is the dispersal stage of the life cycle of **angiosperms** and **gymnosperms**. It contains the embryo, the next generation of plant in miniature. Many seeds are dry when shed from their parent plant and are thus adapted to withstand harsh environments until conditions suitable for germination are achieved.

The evolution of plants to produce seeds is poorly understood because the fossil evidence is incomplete. The advantage of reproducing through seeds is apparent, however: The embryo is encased in a protective coat and is provided with a source of nutrients until, as a young seedling following germination, it becomes established as an independent photosynthetic (**autotrophic**) entity.

Seeds account for 70 percent of food consumed by humans, and are also the major feeds for domestic animals. Their importance cannot be overstated. World seed production is dominated by the cereals, and even the production of wheat, maize, or rice alone by far exceeds that of all the other crops. As a concentrated source of carbohydrate, cereals provide for the human diet, livestock feed, and industrial raw materials. They are also an important source of protein, oil, vitamins, and fiber. Grain **legumes**, particularly soybeans and groundnuts (peanuts) are an important source of proteins and vegetable oils, which are used in margarine and cooking fats, and have applications in paints, varnishes, and plastics, as well as the manufacture of soaps and detergents. An understanding of seeds is therefore an essential prelude to human attempts to improve their quality and yield, whether it be by conventional breeding techniques or the novel approach of genetic engineering.

Seed Structure

A seed is a combination of maternal tissues, embryo tissues, and (in angiosperms) **endosperm** tissue. Seeds of different species are variable in size and internal structure at the time they are shed from their parent plant. They may be barely visible to the naked eye (for example, orchids), weigh a few micrograms to milligrams (for example, poppy, tobacco, and many annual weeds), weigh up to several hundred milligrams to grams (for example, soybean, maize, pea, and bean) or even several kilograms (coconut and *Lodoicea maldivica*).

Non-Maternal Tissues

The seed develops from the ovule after the egg cell within has been fertilized by a male gamete from a germinated pollen grain. The resulting **diploid zygote** cell then undergoes extensive mitotic divisions to form the embryo. In angiosperms, the process of double-fertilization occurs when a second male gamete from the pollen tube fuses with two female nuclei in the ovule, yielding a triploid nucleus containing one set of paternal genes and two maternal sets. This also undergoes extensive mitotic divisions to produce the endosperm, usually a storage tissue that may (cereals, castor bean) or may not (peas, beans) persist in the mature seed, or it may be reduced to a thin layer of cells (lettuce, tomato, soybean).

Maternal Tissues

The seed coat (testa) develops from the outer layers of the ovule, the integuments, and is a diploid maternal tissue. In many angiosperm species the ovary wall surrounding the ovule also divides and develops at the same time as the seed to form an enclosing fruit. While many species form a fleshy fruit, in others the fruit tissues (pericarp) develop as only a few layers of cells,

autotroph "self-feeder"; any organism that uses sunlight or chemical energy

legumes beans and other members of the Fabaceae family

endosperm the nutritive tissue in a seed, formed by fertilization of a diploid egg tissue by a sperm from pollen

diploid having two of each type of chromosome; twice the haploid number

zygote the egg immediately after it has been fertilized; the one-cell stage of a new individual

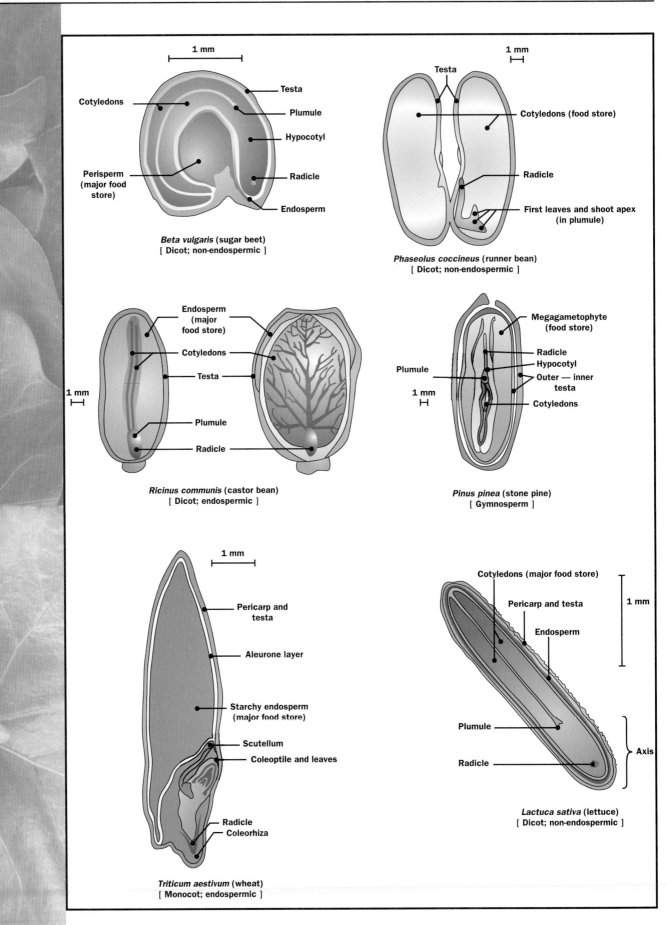

1 mm

Cotyledons — Testa
— Plumule
— Hypocotyl
Perisperm (major food store) — Radicle
— Endosperm

Beta vulgaris (sugar beet)
[Dicot; non-endospermic]

1 mm

Testa
— Cotyledons (food store)
— Radicle
— First leaves and shoot apex (in plumule)

Phaseolus coccineus (runner bean)
[Dicot; non-endospermic]

1 mm

Endosperm (major food store)
Cotyledons
Testa
Plumule
Radicle

Ricinus communis (castor bean)
[Dicot; endospermic]

1 mm

Megagametophyte (food store)
Radicle
Hypocotyl
Outer — inner testa
Cotyledons
Plumule

Pinus pinea (stone pine)
[Gymnosperm]

1 mm

Pericarp and testa
Aleurone layer
Starchy endosperm (major food store)
Scutellum
Coleoptile and leaves
Radicle
Coleorhiza

Triticum aestivum (wheat)
[Monocot; endospermic]

Cotyledons (major food store)
Pericarp and testa
1 mm
Endosperm
Plumule
Radicle
Axis

Lactuca sativa (lettuce)
[Dicot; non-endospermic]

Structure of several species of seeds. Strictly, lettuce and wheat are not seeds, but fruits.

become dry, and adhere to the outside of an equally thin or thinner seed coat. Strictly, by botanical definition, such dispersal structures are fruits (for example, cereal grains, lettuce, sunflower, oak). Nonetheless, for convenience, and because they contain the embryo, they are usually called seeds.

In some angiosperm seeds, following the completion of fertilization, another part of the ovule, the nucellar tissue, may divide mitotically and grow to produce a nutritive perisperm (sugar beet, coffee). In gymnosperm (conifer) seeds, the tissue surrounding the mature embryo is the megagametophyte, a **haploid** maternal tissue into which the fertilized zygote grows during seed development; it is still substantially present in the mature seed as a source of stored reserves.

The Embryo

The embryo is made up of an axis bearing one or more cotyledons. The axial region contains a hypocotyl to which the cotyledons are attached, a radicle that will become the primary root following germination, and the plumule, the shoot axis bearing the first true leaves. These parts are usually easy to discern in dicot angiosperm seeds and in those of the polycotyledonous (many cotyledons) gymnosperms. But in seeds of monocot plants, particularly the cereal grains, the single cotyledon is much reduced and modified to form the scutellum, an absorptive structure that lies against the endosperm and absorbs material from it. The basal sheath of the cotyledon is elongated to form a **coleoptile**, which covers the first leaves.

The shapes of the embryos and their position within the seed are variable between species. In those dicot species that have a substantial endosperm (endospermic seeds) the embryo occupies proportionately less of the seed than when the endosperm is rudimentary or absent (compare castor bean with lettuce or runner bean). In contrast, the cotyledons of nonendospermic seeds are much bulkier and are the storage tissues, and in peas and beans account for over 90 percent of the mass of the seed.

Several variations on this general theme occur. In the Brazil nut the cotyledons are much reduced and the bulk of the seed is occupied by a storage hypocotyl. Because the Brazil nut is primarily a single hypocotyl, it does not split in two like most other nuts made from two enlarged cotyledons. Cotyledons are absent from the seeds of many parasitic species. In orchids, seeds are shed when the embryos are extremely small and contain only a few cells, and completion of development occurs afterward.

Non-Embryonic Storage Tissues

In most species, the maternally derived perisperm fails to develop and is quickly absorbed by the developing embryo. Where it does persist, it is a major storage tissue, sometimes in conjunction with an endosperm, or the cotyledons (for example, sugar beet).

As noted, seeds are categorized as endospermic or nonendospermic in relation to the presence or absence of a well-formed endosperm within the mature seed. The relatively massive endosperm is the major source of stored seed reserves in species such as the cereals, castor bean, date palm, and endospermic legumes (carob, fenugreek). In the cereal grains and seeds of some endospermic legumes (for example, fenugreek) the storage cells of the endo-

haploid having one set of chromosomes, versus having two (diploid)

coleoptile the growing tip of a monocot seedling

sperm are nonliving at maturity, and the cytoplasmic contents have been replaced entirely by the stored reserves (starch and protein in cereals; hemicellulose cell walls in fenugreek). But on the outside of the endosperm there remains a living tissue of one to a few cell layers in thickness, the aleurone layer, whose role is to synthesize and secrete **enzymes** to mobilize those reserves following germination.

The Seed Coat (Testa)

The anatomy of the seed coat is highly variable, and differences among species have been used for taxonomic purposes. The coat is of considerable importance to the seed because it is a protective barrier between the embryo and the outside environment (in some species the fruit coat may augment or be a substitute for this role). Protection by the seed coat is aided by the presence of an inner and outer **cuticle**, impregnated with fats and waxes, and **lignified** cell walls. Phenolics or crystals (of calcium oxalate, for example) may be deposited in the coat to discourage **predation** by insects. Mucilage-containing cells may be present that burst on contact with water, retaining and absorbing moisture as a supply to the germinating embryo. Rarely, hairs or wings develop on the seed coat to aid dispersal (willow, lily); more frequently the dispersal structures are a modification of the surrounding fruit coat.

Quiescence and Dormancy

The completion of seed development and the acquisition of the mature structure is marked in many species by a loss of water, so that the mature seed can be dispersed in the dry state. The water content of a dry seed is usually 5 to 15 percent, versus 70 percent or more for the plant as a whole. When dry, a seed can withstand extremes of temperature that would rapidly result in death in the hydrated state. Not surprisingly, then, dry seeds are more or less in a state of suspended animation, with little or no metabolic activity. As such, they are said to be quiescent. When introduced to water again, under favorable conditions such seeds will rapidly resume metabolism and complete germination.

The phenomenon of seed quiescence is very different from that of dormancy. The latter is when seeds in a hydrated state fail to complete germination even when conditions are favorable; that is, temperature, water and oxygen supply are not limiting. **Dormant** seeds are metabolically active, in fact as active as their nondormant counterparts, but there exists within the seed a block (or blocks) that must be removed before germination can be completed. To be released from dormancy, a seed must experience a particular stimulus, or undergo certain metabolic changes. The cause of dormancy is not clearly understood, but at least one factor is the growth regulator hormone abscisic acid (ABA), which is imported from the parent plant into the seed during its development.

Many seeds lose dormancy (while remaining quiescent) while still in the mature dry state, in a process called after-ripening, which may extend over several weeks to many years. Dormancy of hydrated seeds in the soil may be broken by one or more environmental cues, whose effectiveness depends on the species. These cues include: 1) light, usually for a short duration, with sunlight being the most effective; 2) low temperature, around 1 to 5°C for several to many weeks; 3) fluctuating temperatures, usually day-night

enzyme a protein that controls a reaction in a cell

cuticle the waxy outer coating of a leaf or other structure, providing protection against predators, infection, and water loss

lignified composed of lignin, a tough and resistant plant compound

predation the act of preying upon; consuming for food

dormant inactive, not growing

CONDITIONS THAT TERMINATE SEED DORMANCY

Species	Common Name	Light	Chilling	Alternating Temperatures	After-ripening
Acer pseudoplatanus	Great maple		+		+
Avena fatua	Wild oat		+		+
Betula pubescens	Birch	+	+		+
Hordeum species	Barley		+		+
Lactuca sativa	Lettuce	+	+		+
Nicotiana tabacum	Tobacco	+		+	
Pinus sylvestris	Scot's pine	+	+		
Prunus domestica	Plum		+		+
Triticum aestivum	Wheat		+		+

fluctuations of 5 to 10°C; and 4) chemicals, of which nitrate is the most important in the soil.

Dormancy is a mechanism to ensure the optimum distribution of seed germination in time and space. For example, seeds that require weeks of cold temperatures to break their dormancy cannot complete germination immediately after being shed from their parent plant in early fall, but will do so only following the cold winter months. This ensures that they are not in the delicate seedling stage at the onset of winter, which would be detrimental to their survival. Dormancy of light-requiring seeds will be removed only when seeds are at the soil surface, a mechanism that prevents germination at too great a depth. This is crucial for small seeds whose stored reserves are insufficient to support growth through the soil to carry the seedling leaves into the light to begin photosynthesis. Seeds on the forest floor receive light that is poor in the red wavelengths, since this is absorbed by the leaves of the overarching canopy. Thus, seeds in this environment must wait for the appearance of gaps in the canopy (tree fall or logging) before their dormancy can be broken, and they can then emerge in situations where there is reduced competition for resources from established plants. Phytochrome is the light-perception system in dormant seeds and is activated by wavelengths rich in red.

While the significance of dormancy can best be understood in an ecological context, it is important in agriculture too. Prolonged dormancy in crop species is undesirable since germination could be spread out over several years, resulting in unpredictable and low annual yields. On the other hand, lack of at least a temporary dormancy can be harmful also because, for example, mature seeds of barley or wheat could germinate on the ear if wetted by rain before harvest, resulting in crop spoilage. SEE ALSO EMBRYOGENESIS; FLOWERS; FRUITS; FRUITS, SEEDLESS; GERMINATION; GERMINATION AND GROWTH; GRAINS; PHYTOCHROME; POLLINATION; REPRODUCTION, FERTILIZATION AND; REPRODUCTION, SEXUAL; SEED DISPERSAL; SEED PRESERVATION.

J. Derek Bewley

Bibliography

Bewley, J. Derek, and Michael Black. *Seeds: Physiology of Development and Germination*, 2nd ed. New York: Plenum, 1994.

Bradbeer, J. W. *Seed Dormancy and Germination.* Glasgow and London: Blackie, 1988.

Chrispeels, Maarten J., and David E. Sadava. *Plants, Genes and Agriculture.* Boston and London: Jones and Bartlett, 1994.

Senescence

Senescence refers to all of the many changes that inevitably lead to the death of part or all of a plant. Two related terms, *aging* and *longevity*, are also often used when senescence and eventual death are being discussed. Aging means all of the changes that occur over time, whether or not these changes lead to death, and longevity refers to how long a seed, or plant, or part of a plant, survives.

Senescence occurs in all plants and at all stages of the life cycle. Even in a young bean seedling, senescence processes have begun. The cotyledonary leaves, which were present in the dry seed, will rapidly give up their nutritive reserves to the growing plant, undergo senescence, and fall off.

tracheid a type of xylem cell for water transport

transpiration movement of water from soil to atmosphere through a plant

At the same time, root hairs and root cap cells are dying and being continuously replaced as the root grows. Elsewhere in the plant, cells are dividing, expanding, and differentiating. In the final stages of formation of vessels and **tracheids**, the living cell contents will undergo senescence and be removed. The remaining hollow tubes, consisting of just the cell walls, become the water-conducting pipes of the xylem tissues used in **transpiration**. Thus both whole-organ senescence (for example, a leaf, petal, or fruit) as well as specific-cell senescence, occur as a normal part of plant development.

pigments colored molecules

One of the visible symptoms of leaf senescence is the loss of the green chlorophyll **pigments** allowing the yellow carotenoid pigments to show through. In some maples (*Acer* spp.) in North America, red pigments, the anthocyanins, are made at this time. The senescence of leaves is triggered by environmental shifts (i.e., temperature and the relative lengths of night and day) and is also dramatically altered by applications of plant hormones. Cytokinins, auxins, and gibberellins can often delay senescence, while abscisic acid, ethylene, and jasmonates will accelerate these processes in some species. Some plants (for example, annuals like wheat, or perennial, deciduous maple trees that drop their leaves) have highly synchronous leaf senescence. In contrast, the bristlecone pine (*Pinus aristata*) may keep individual needles for up to thirty years. Among other plant structures, petals often undergo rapid senescence after the flower has been pollinated, and the final part of the ripening and softening processes in fruits is also a form of senescence. The manipulation of these processes—from the vase-life of cut flowers to the shelf-life of tomatoes—will remain an important economic target.

Underlying many, and perhaps all, of these diverse, visible patterns of senescence is an ordered sequence of gene expression, called programmed cell death, which is triggered either by environmental shifts or by internal mechanisms in the plant. By mutating, eliminating, or altering the expression of these genes, the pattern of senescence can be changed. A full understanding of these genetic processes, and their linkage to the environmental, hormonal, and time-dependent expressions of senescence in specific cells, tissues, and organs, will provide a new view of death in the plant kingdom. SEE ALSO DECIDUOUS PLANTS; GENETIC MECHANISMS AND DEVELOPMENT; HORMONAL CONTROL AND DEVELOPMENT; HORMONES.

Roger F. Horton

Bibliography

Buckner, Brent, Diane Janick-Buckner, John Gray, and Guri S. Johal. "Cell Death Mechanisms in Maize." *Trends in Plant Science* 3 (1992): 218–23.

Nooden, Larry D., and A. Carl Leopold, eds. *Senescence and Aging in Plants.* London: Academic Press, 1988.

Thimann, Kenneth Vivian, ed. *Senescence in Plants.* Boca Baton, FL: CRC Press, 1980

Sequoia

Sequoia is a genus of conifer containing one species, *Sequoia sempervirens*, the coast redwood. It is named for a Georgian Indian chieftain who invented the Cherokee alphabet. Traditionally included in the Taxodiaceae, current workers combine this family with the cypress family, Cupressaceae. One of the world's tallest tree species, sequoias can exceed 115 meters (360 feet) in height. The trunk, covered in red, shredding bark, is about 3 to 5 meters (10 to 16 feet) in diameter, but may reach 10 meters (33 feet). The branches bear both triangular and needlelike leaves. Male (pollen-producing) and female (seed-bearing) cones are borne on the same tree, but on different branches. *Sequoiadendron giganteum*, the giant redwood, formerly included in *Sequoia*, was placed in its own genus in 1939.

Coast redwoods form coniferous forests in western North America, from coastal central California to southernmost Oregon. Here they receive fog that provides moisture and cool conditions during the dry summer months. Coast redwoods are relics, plants that had wider distribution in the milder, moister climate of the past. Adult trees can live 2,200 years, and their thick bark resists most fires, which clear the undergrowth and create the open conditions needed for seedling establishment.

Redwood lumber is greatly desired, as it is rot resistant and straight grained. Therefore, redwood trees have been logged heavily during the last 150 years. Trees readily resprout from roots and stumps, so forests grow back quickly. Nevertheless, concern for the disappearance of virgin groves

A man stands besides a fallen redwood tree in California's Prairie Creek Redwoods State Park.

prompted the creation of Muir Woods National Monument in 1908. Less than five percent of the ancient redwood forests are intact, and most of those survive only through the protection of parks and National Forests. SEE ALSO CONIFEROUS FORESTS; CONIFERS; GYMNOSPERMS; RECORD-HOLDING PLANTS; TREES.

Dean G. Kelch

Bibliography

Lanner, Ronald M. *Conifers of California.* Los Olivos, CA: Cachuma Press, 1999.

Shape and Form of Plants

Plants exhibit an enormous range of shape and form. Common shapes include the conical form of conifers, the vase shape of many shrubs, the linearity of scrambling vines, and the clumped form of a daylily. Ferns have a range of forms nearly as great as flowering plants, while mosses usually take the form of miniature herbs. These plant forms result from enhanced growth in one region occurring at the expense of growth in another area. Shape results from differential growth, localized cell division, and cell expansion.

apical meristem region of dividing cells at the tips of growing plants

New plant cells come from single embryonic cells or groups of embryonic cells called meristems. Two groups of embryonic cells are responsible for the origin of all new shoot parts in seed plants: the shoot **apical meristems** and the lateral meristems. Shoot apical meristems, also called primary meristems or growing points, are found at the tips of all stems. Cells from these meristems grow primarily by elongation. The meristems may be active simultaneously, with the apical meristems of branches increasing branch length while the apical meristem of the main stem increasing plant height.

The lateral meristems, which are also called secondary meristems, produce the secondary growth or the widening of plant stems. The two lateral meristems (the vascular cambium and the cork cambium) increase the diameter of the stem. The vascular cambium is a continuous circle of cells in

Branching in Japanese maples produces trees with a broad crown but a less regular form.

the stem interior and when active produces the woody portions of the stem. The cork cambium, also a continuous circle of cells, lies near the stem surface and when active produces the outer bark region. The activity of the lateral meristems is responsible for the increasing girth of plants as they age. Lateral meristems are active in plant regions where primary growth has ceased. Although increases in stem girth are associated with perennial plants, lateral meristems are also active in some annual plants (e.g., soybean) and increase their girth during the season.

Contribution of the Stem

Stems contribute to overall form in five major ways: growth direction, diameter, length between leaves, branches, and branch location.

Growth Direction. Stems are upright in most plants (such as corn or oak), growing away from gravity, but may be prostrate, as in creeping plants (e.g., creeping devil cactus), which grow at right angles to or without respect to gravity. Creeping stems of pot-grown plants may grow beyond the pot edge, down the side of the pot, and across the table the pot is on. This type of stem growth is contact dependent. The stems are not weak, but often quite stout. Stems of other shoots are lax (e.g., ivy), unable to support themselves, and their direction of growth is related to the availability of a host plant or a **substrate** to provide support.

substrate the physical structure to which an organism attaches

The number, location, and growth angle of the branches regulate tree form. Stems growing in different orientations are frequently found on the same plant. Christmas trees (fir or spruce, usually) have a main stem, which grows upright, and many side stems (branches) that grow at a regular angle to the stem. Many branches grow out at the same location and their orientation with respect to the stem yields a highly symmetrical, regular tree. On the other hand, branching in oaks and maples produces trees with a broad crown but a less regular form. Herbaceous plants exhibit the same features, although they are not as obvious as in conifers or large trees. The branches in these examples duplicate the architecture of the main stem, sometimes with great precision, to provide additional surface area for continued vegetative growth. Profuse branching in one plant shades out neighbor plants and limits their ability to compete for sunlight.

Branches may also be specialized for propagation and for reproduction rather than photosynthetic activity. Herbaceous plants such as strawberries have a main stem with only a few branches. Each branch extends far from the parent plant but finally touches the ground to establish a new plant. The new plant becomes independent of the parent and the linking stem can be severed with no harm to the new plant. These branches are called runners or stolons. Runners do not change the form of the parent plant, but instead duplicate the entire plant at a nearby location. The length of the runner prevents both plants from competing for the same resources, and the strategy is an effective means of vegetative propagation.

Reproduction often triggers change in plant form, commonly by enormous extension of the main axis, which might be topped by a single flower (e.g., iris, amaryllis, spring bulbs). Flowering in other species results in the outgrowth of branches from the main axis; reproductive branches may perfectly replicate or produce a slight modification of the pattern of flowers on the main stem.

Stem Diameter. Stem diameter may be the same along its entire length, either narrow (many annuals) or broad (palms). Other plants have conical stems (the main stem of a woody perennial), which result from secondary growth occurring at the base of the stem, while primary growth occurs at the top of the stem. With each new season of growth the stem base broadens. Lastly, stems may have an obconate form (upside-down cone), broader at the top than the base. Such a stem is inherently unstable and two conditions are common. In corn, the stem has roots that grow out from lower leaf positions. These stem-borne roots act as guide wires to stabilize the plant. In other species, secondary growth from an active vascular cambium stabilizes the plant and masks the obconate form.

Length Between Leaves. The stem length between adjacent leaves, leaf pairs, or **whorls** of leaves varies. When it is very short, a rosette plant is produced (e.g., strawberry, lettuce, ferns) that hugs the ground with a tight cluster of leaves. Tree ferns and palms have aerial rosettes, a series of closely spaced leaves produced each growing season. The stem is exposed as the old leaves die and fall, leaving a clump of green leaves at the top of the stem. Neither of these plants grows quickly, so tall tree ferns and palms are often more than one hundred years old. At the other extreme is papyrus, which bears a single **internode** topped by a cluster of leaves and associated floral branches. Sweet woodruff, a common garden plant, has stems with what appear to be whorls of leaves clustered at a single point on the stem followed by a substantial internode. When studied carefully, the whorl is a spiral of leaves with very short internodes, but a long internode separates each pseudowhorl of leaves. This is an obvious example of how differential growth yields variation in plant form.

Plants often have internodes of different length along the stem. A common pattern is short internodes at the base followed by long internodes and topped by short internodes. The diameter of these internodes changes as well, with short basal internodes having a greater diameter than the short internodes at the top. Again, differential growth regulates plant form. There may be a structural advantage to this organization: the short broad internodes at the bottom supporting a tall stem with short terminal internodes in the reproductive region. This organization would be advantageous in flower display to pollinators and in pollen dissemination by the wind.

Vines display an entirely different growth that is linked to their life strategy. In these plants, the internodes are long, even near the shoot tip, and leaf growth is limited. However, once the vine has made contact with a support, then leaf growth occurs. Vines put their energy into extending the stem into the light and attaching themselves to the substrate, and then the leaves expand.

Branches and Branch Location. A branch develops from a bud located where the leaf joins the stem (the **axil**). Each bud has growth potential, but some buds never grow out and sometimes only buds in particular locations extend. Differential growth of the shoot apical meristems regulates overall plant form. If the buds do not develop, the stem remains unbranched. In some instances, the terminal apical meristem prevents the outgrowth of lateral buds, but the buds grow out if the meristem is removed or damaged. Gardeners often remove the main shoot apical meristem so new buds will grow out and ultimately produce more flowers. On some plant species (such

whorls rings

internode the distance on the stem between leaves

axil the angle or crotch where a leaf stalk meets the stem

as chrysanthemum), meristem removal takes place several times during the season to create a bushy plant covered with flowers.

In other species, only buds located at the base of the stem extend as branches, which results in a shrub that with each succeeding season grows more dense. In yet other plants, like the conifers, buds at a particular location (produced near the beginning or end of a growing season) will expand to give the plant a tiered appearance. Thus, the lower tiers have longer branches than those near the top because they have grown for more seasons. This gives the Christmas tree its conical shape.

Some trees take on a candelabra appearance (e.g., buckthorn, lilac) because the apical meristem on the main axis dies at the end of the year and two or more branches grow out in its place. In the following year, the apical meristem of each branch dies and two new branches grow out in place of the old one. The death and replacement strategy creates plants with highly regular forms. The same strategy is found in *Philodendron* and *Anthurium*, common houseplants, and many orchids, although it is less obvious in these species because only a single replacement branch grows out and subsequent plant growth obscures the branching pattern. The horsechestnut (*Aesculus*) also has single replacement branches.

Contribution of the Leaf

Leaves contribute to overall plant form through their size, shape, and arrangement around the stem. Leaves consist of two or three parts. Corn and leek leaves have two parts, a basal ensheathing portion and a long blade region. Geranium and oak leaves have three parts, a base region, a stalk called the petiole, and a terminal blade. The blade may be simple, an entire unit, or dissected, divided into several units called leaflets. The leaflets occur in two arrangements. When leaflets lie on opposite sides of a central axis and are terminated by a leaflet, the arrangement is featherlike or pinnate. When all leaflets are attached to the end of the petiole, the arrangement is fanlike or palmate (like the digits of a hand). Sometimes leaflets are attached around the entire circumference of the petiole, as in lupines, or the petiole is attached to the middle of the leaf blade, as in nasturtium.

Leaves are frequently similar in shape but differ in size. For example, leaves of banana and scallion or green onions are united by shape, as are those of feather palms and many common ferns. Leaves on a single plant may also differ in shape; sometimes shape change is dramatic and other times quite subtle. These changes may be related to the life history of the plant or result from a change in the direction of growth.

Leaves are present either in spirals (one leaf at each stem position) or in whorls (two or more leaves at each stem position). The most obvious spiral leaf arrangement is shown by *Costus*, a member of the ginger family, in which single leaves are arranged in an ascending spiral around the stem. Corn, which has leaves present in two vertical rows along the stem, also has a spiral arrangement. One can demonstrate a plant's spiral nature by winding a string from one leaf position to the next higher leaf position. In a few plants, a spiral of leaves will have little space between each leaf, making them appear whorled, and a large gap before the next spiral of leaves. These are

Pseudo-whorled leaf arrangements are found in select species of sweet woodruff, this common garden plant.

pseudo-whorled arrangements and found in select species of *Impatiens* and *Peperomia* and in a common garden plant, sweet woodruff.

The simplest form of whorled leaf arrangement is that of two leaves at a common stem position, seen in sunflowers, plants with opposite leaf arrangements. In members of the mint family, which includes garden mints and the common houseplant coleus, leaves originate in pairs, but each successive pair is offset 90 degrees from the previous pair. There are also plants with whorls of three leaves, such as oleander, where the succeeding set of leaves is offset from the preceding set. Looking down the length of the stem, there are six leaf positions, but only three positions are filled by each individual whorl. SEE ALSO ANATOMY OF PLANTS; MERISTEMS; PHYLLOTAXIS; TREE ARCHITECTURE.

Judith Croxdale

Bibliography

Esau, K. *Anatomy of Seed Plants*, 2nd ed. New York: John Wiley & Sons, 1977.

Fahn, A. *Plant Anatomy*, 4th ed. New York: Pergamon Press, 1990.

Gifford, E. M., and A. S. Foster. *Morphology and Evolution of Vascular Plants*, 3rd ed. New York: W. H. Freeman, 1988.

Raven, Peter. H., Ray F. Evert, and Susan E. Eichhorn. *Biology of Plants*, 6th ed. New York: W. H. Freeman and Co., 1999.

Soil, Chemistry of

The chemistry and fertility of soils have been of concern to humans since ancient times. One of the earliest books to correctly identify the soil as the source of plant mineral nutrients is *Organic Chemistry in its Application to Agriculture and Physiology*, authored by the German chemist Justus von Liebig (1803–1873) and published in 1840. Liebig's book was based, in part, on research conducted and reported in the 1820s and 1830s by German agronomist Carl Sprengel (1787–1859). Although this field still includes study of plant nutrients, modern research is also focused on the reactions and chemistry of pollutants such as mercury, arsenic, and organic pesticides in soils.

The sundew (*Drosera petiolaris*), found in Papua New Guinea and Indonesia, utilizes the sticky, shiny droplets on the end of its stem to trap small insects, which it digests to supplement the lack of nitrogen and phosphate in the soil.

Soil Components

The mineral fraction of soils is derived from rocks and minerals and composed largely of oxygen, silicon, and aluminum. After these elements, the most abundant in soil are iron, carbon, calcium, potassium, sodium, and magnesium. The organic fraction of soils is usually about 1 to 5 percent by weight; it forms during microbial decomposition of dead plant and animal material. Carbon, oxygen, and hydrogen are the major constituents of soil organic matter, which also contains nitrogen, phosphorus, and sulfur. Although plants do not directly absorb organic forms of nutrients, microbial processes can transform the nitrogen, phosphorus, and sulfur in soil organic matter into plant-available (inorganic) forms.

The chemical structure of clay minerals gives them charge; most have a net negative charge or a very low net charge close to zero. Negatively charged soils retain positively charged ions called cations (e.g., Mg^{2+}, Ca^{2+}). The total amount of negative charge in a soil is called cation exchange capacity (CEC). Some plant nutrients, such as calcium, magnesium, and potassium, are cations, and, therefore, soils with higher CEC values are able to retain more plant nutrients than those with lower CEC values. Organic matter has a higher CEC value than clay minerals and increases a soil's fertility.

Essential Elements for Plant Growth

An element is considered essential for plant growth when plants are unable to complete their life cycles without it. Sixteen to eighteen elements are recognized as essential including carbon, hydrogen, oxygen, nitrogen, phosphorus, potassium, sulfur, calcium, magnesium, iron, manganese, copper, zinc, boron, molybdenum, chlorine, and, for some plants, cobalt and nickel. Plant carbon comes from carbon dioxide in the atmosphere, and plant hydrogen and oxygen from water in soil. The other elements come primarily from the inorganic and organic fractions of soil. Macronutrients (nitrogen, phosphorus, potassium, sulfur, calcium, and magnesium) are needed by plants in relatively large quantities. Micronutrients, also called trace elements, are those elements usually contained in concentrations less than 100 milligrams/kilogram plant tissue (iron, manganese, copper, zinc, boron, molybdenum, chlorine, cobalt, and nickel).

Importance of Soil pH

Soil **pH** is an important property that influences many chemical and biological processes occurring in soils. Acidification of soils is a natural geologic process. Rainwater contains carbonic acid produced when atmospheric carbon dioxide dissolves in the rain. In addition, plants may acidify the soil around their roots by releasing hydrogen ions. Human processes, such as combustion of fossil fuels, may add acidity to the atmosphere; this acidity eventually reaches soils via precipitation (acid rain) and deposition of dry particles. Although many soils have a large capacity to neutralize incoming acidity without changes in their pH values, over geologic time soil pH values decrease.

Soils in arid environments tend to have pH values above 7. The presence of soluble carbonates in these alkaline soils maintains high pH values. Soils containing high amounts of sodium carbonate can have pH values in the range of 8.5 to 10. These soils are called sodic and generally present severe limitations to plant growth. Alkaline and sodic soils may become neutral over time if exposed to enough precipitation to remove all the carbonates by dissolution and leaching. Neutral soils, which contain no carbonate minerals, tend to have pH values between 6.6 and 7.3 and are generally suitable for the growth of a wide range of plant species. Acid soils, which have pH values of 6.5 and below, tend to be found in regions with abundant rainfall and moderate to high temperatures.

One of the most important consequences of soil acidity is the dissolution of aluminum (Al^{3+}), which is toxic to plants, from soil minerals. Aluminum in soil solution interferes with both cell division and cell elongation and produces short, stubby root systems. Because of its strong positive charge, aluminum is strongly held on negative exchange sites, partially displacing calcium, potassium, and magnesium and reducing their availability. It may be difficult for plants to take up sufficient phosphorus when growing in acid soils because of chemical reactions between aluminum and phosphorus. Many micronutrients become more soluble at lower pH values, including manganese. Manganese is abundant enough to be toxic to plants in some low-pH soils. Lime (ground calcium and magnesium carbonate) is often added to acid soils to correct these problems and improve the soil environment for plant growth.

Effects of Excess Nutrients on Ecosystems

The nutrients most commonly limiting for plant growth in both terrestrial and aquatic systems are nitrogen and phosphorus. Both are often added as fertilizer to agricultural **ecosystems**. Nitrogen is generally readily soluble and leaches from soils to surface and ground waters. Phosphorus is strongly absorbed in most soils and typically reaches surface waters attached to particles eroded from agricultural fields. Both nutrients may promote excess algal growth in lakes and the ocean. When large quantities of algae grow, die, and are decomposed in the water, dissolved oxygen is depleted and aquatic organisms may die. Scientists have known since the 1960s

PH LEVELS

pH is a measure of acidity (determined by hydrogen ions [H^+]) or alkalinity (determined by hydroxyl ions [OH^-]). In a pure water solution the concentration of hydrogen ions equals the concentration of hydroxyl ions at a value of 10^{-7} M (moles per liter). Such a solution of equal amounts of hydrogen and hydroxyl ions is said to be neutral and have a pH of 7. Acid solutions contain a higher concentration of hydrogen ions than of hydroxyl ions. Solution acidity is usually reported as the negative logarithm of the hydrogen ion concentration. So a solution with a hydrogen ion concentration of 10^{-4} moles per liter has a pH value of 4. In an aqueous solution, pH values less than 7 indicate an acid solution while pH values greater than 7 indicate an alkaline solution. In soils pH values generally range between about 4 and 10.

pH a measure of acidity or alkalinity; the pH scale ranges from 0 to 14, with 7 being neutral; low pH numbers indicate high acidity; high numbers indicate alkalinity

ecosystem an ecological community together with its environment

that nitrogen and phosphorus were negatively affecting some lakes and rivers. During the 1980s and 1990s dissolved oxygen levels declined in the Gulf of Mexico. By the late 1990s, a large area of the Gulf was almost devoid of aquatic life apparently due to nutrients transported by the Mississippi River. SEE ALSO AGRICULTURAL ECOSYSTEMS; ATMOSPHERE AND PLANTS; BIOCHEMICAL CYCLES; DECOMPOSERS; FERTILIZER; NITROGEN FIXATION; NUTRIENTS; SOIL, PHYSICAL CHARACTERISTICS OF.

M. Susan Erich

Bibliography

Brady, Nyle C., and Ray R. Weil. *The Nature and Properties of Soils*, 12th ed. Upper Saddle River, NJ: Prentice-Hall, 1999.

Foth, Henry D., and Boyd G. Ellis. *Soil Fertility*, 2nd ed. Boca Raton, FL: Lewis Publishers, 1997.

Moffat, Anne Simon. "Global Nitrogen Overload Problem Grows Critical." *Science* 279 (1998): 988–89.

Pierzynski, Gary, M., J. Thomas Sims, and George F. Vance. *Soils and Environmental Quality*. Boca Raton, FL: Lewis Publishers, 1994.

Soil, Physical Characteristics of

Soil physical properties are those related to the size and arrangement of solid particles, and how the movement of liquids and gases through soils is affected by the particles. Soil mineral particles are derived from the weathering of rocks and minerals. Soil organic matter is the product of microbial decomposition of the remains of plants and animals.

Soil Texture

Soil texture refers to a particular soil's distribution of mineral particles within certain size ranges. (Organic matter is removed before soil texture is determined.) Soil texture is an intrinsic property of a soil, which may be influenced by geologic processes such as erosion, but generally does not change appreciably within a human life span or as a result of human activities. Different groups use different classification schemes for particle sizes. A commonly used scheme is that of the U.S. Department of Agriculture (USDA). Although soil particles are rarely spherical, the USDA classification system is based on particle diameters.

Using the USDA classification system, gravel is between 2 and 75 millimeters, cobbles 75 to 254 millimeters, and stones greater than 254 millimeters. Soil is considered to consist of particles less than 2.0 millimeters in diameter. Sand-sized particles have diameters between 0.05 and 2 millimeters. The smallest sand particles are nearly invisible to the eye. Silt-sized particles range between 0.002 and 0.05 millimeter. Root hairs, nematodes, and fungi are also in this size range. Clay-sized particles are less than 0.002 millimeter in diameter. They are in the size range of bacteria and viruses.

In any soil analysis, the total amount of sand, silt, and clay in a soil always adds up to 100 percent. There are twelve soil textural classes defined by the percentages of these size groups. Along with an analysis of the percentages of sand, silt, and clay in a soil sample, a diagram called a soil textural triangle is used to determine a soil's textural class. For example, soils containing equal amounts of sand, silt, and clay are classified as clay loams. Although the term loam refers to a soil with a particular textural composition, loam is commonly used by nonsoil scientists to mean a fertile soil with a texture neither too sandy nor too clayey. Sandy soils are also called coarse-textured, clayey soils are referred to as fine-textured, and soils with a balance of sand, silt, and clay may be called medium-textured.

Soil Structure and Porosity

The arrangement of primary particles, particularly clays, into clumps or aggregates is referred to as soil structure. Soil organic matter is generally involved in binding particles into stable aggregates. The amount and arrangement of aggregates determines the total **porosity** of a soil. Total porosity of a soil can be determined from the soil's bulk density, the weight of a fixed volume of dried soil. The individual mineral particles in soil have

porosity openness

A U.S. Department of Agriculture researcher checks soil porosity using computer-enhanced images.

an average density of about 2.7 g/cm^3, and the organic matter has a much lower density in the range of 1.2 to 1.5 g/cm^3. A volume of dried soil contains mineral particles, organic matter, and pore space; although, of course, only the mineral and organic fraction contribute to the weight. The higher the bulk density, the lower the total pore space available for air and water within a soil. Soil bulk density ranges from about 0.1 to 0.7 g/cm^3 for highly organic soils and 0.9 to 1.8 for mineral soils. Sandy soils have higher bulk density values than those with more clay. Bulk density values higher than about 1.4 g/cm^3 indicate possible limitations to root growth and penetration; typical bulk densities for cultivated soils are 1.0 to 1.25 g/cm^3.

Porosity influences both gas diffusion and water movement in soil. As a generalization, a medium-textured soil with good aggregation contains about 50 percent pore space and 50 percent solid particles by volume. Porosity values can range from 25 percent in compacted soils to 60 percent in highly organic, well-aggregated soil. Macropores, also called aeration pores, are the larger pores between soil aggregates that allow relatively rapid water movement through a soil profile. More macropores in a soil means faster infiltration of water into the profile. Micropores are pores within aggregates; although they may represent a significant fraction of a soil's total porosity, water does not move rapidly through these small-diameter pores.

Porosity greatly influences water relations in soils. Soils with high clay content usually have a greater total porosity than sandy soils. However, a high percentage of the total pores are micropores that do not permit rapid water movement. Therefore water infiltrates slowly into, and out of, these high-clay soils. During a rain event, water may run off the surface of these soils more rapidly than it moves downward into them. Once they become wet, they dry out slowly. Sandy soils, with a higher percentage of macropores, have a high water infiltration rate. Water moves rapidly through the profile, and the soils generally dry out rapidly after rain.

Soil Tilth

Soil tilth, used more commonly by the general public than by soil scientists, is a general term for the physical condition of a soil. Soil tilth is influenced both by soil texture and soil structure. A soil with good tilth offers little resistance to penetration by plant roots during their growth. It also provides ample oxygen and water for plants. The presence of both macropores and micropores is important for good tilth. Macropores permit infiltration and drainage of water; micropores store water for future plant needs. Both the pore distribution and the amount of rainfall received influence whether the pores in any soil contain water or air. Capillarity refers to the ability of small pores to retain water against the force of gravity and results from the adhesive forces between water molecules and the particles in soil and from the cohesive forces between water molecules. Because small pores tend to be water-filled due to capillarity, fine-textured soils with little structure and large amounts of micropores may have inadequate oxygen for plant growth. Oxygen diffuses rapidly through air-filled pore space and slowly through water-filled pore space. Mechanized agricultural practices tend to destroy soil structure and compact soils, resulting in poor tilth. **Compaction** results from the pressure exerted on soils by heavy equipment moving over them. Agricultural practices also tend to destroy organic mat-

compaction compacting of soil, leading to loss of air spaces ter in soils that is needed to maintain structure. SEE ALSO AGRICULTURE, ORGANIC; COMPOST; DECOMPOSERS; PLANT COMMUNITY PROCESSES; ROOTS; SOIL, CHEMISTRY OF.

M. Susan Erich

Bibliography

Brady, Nyle C., and Ray R. Weil. *The Nature and Properties of Soils*, 12th ed. Upper Saddle River, NJ: Prentice-Hall, 1999.

Pierzynski, Gary, M., J. Thomas Sims, and George F. Vance. *Soils and Environmental Quality*. Boca Raton, FL: Lewis Publishers, 1994.

Plaster, Edward J. *Soil Science and Management*, 3rd ed. Albany, NY: Delmar Publishers, 1997.

Solanaceae

Although not large, the Solanaceae, or Nightshade family, is certainly one of the most economically important plant families. It includes about 2,500 species in 90 genera. The potato/tomato genus, *Solanum*, includes about one-half of the species. Many place the family third in worldwide importance to people, behind the grasses and the **legumes**. This ranking is based on the many food and drug plants found in this genus. Virtually all of the edible plants were prehistoric **domesticates** of Latin America, except eggplant (from India). Among the species that had dramatic effects on world cuisine and history are potatoes, tomatoes, and hot (chili) peppers. Prior to 1492, there were no hot peppers in China or Southeast Asia, no tomatoes in Italy, no potatoes in Ireland or Russia, and no tobacco in Europe. In addition, several minor domesticates from the New World have had a lesser impact: tamarillo, tomatillos (the "ground cherries" of North America), and pepinos. Pepinos are eaten fresh, whereas the other two are usually eaten cooked; tomatillos together with chile peppers constitute the salsa verde popular in the Southwest United States.

The family is sometimes referred to as the paradoxical nightshades because it includes so many domesticates of such importance—the modified stems that constitute the tubers of potatoes follow only corn, wheat, and rice in production as world crops—and at the same time, so many toxic plants. Although the family's origin and greatest diversity are in Latin America, the Nightshades first became notorious in written history based on the toxic **compounds** of Mediterranean plants. The strong tropane **alkaloids** like atropine and scopolamine that make henbane, belladonna, and mandrake so poisonous are used in medicine today. Atropine is used to promote pupil dilation in ophthalmology (the wider pupils the drug promotes were taken advantage of by Italian women to make their eyes more attractive—hence the name, belladonna). However, the most significant drug plant in the family is tobacco, from the New World.

In addition to direct economic importance, various members have been significant in plant **physiology** (studies of day length and flowering), biotechnology, and molecular biology. The family includes a number of ornamentals, most prominently, *Petunia*, *Salpiglossis*, and *Brunfelsia*.

The herbs, shrubs, trees, and lianas (climbing vines) in the family grow in habitats from deserts to tropical forests, from sea level to the Andes Moun-

legumes beans and other members of the Fabaceae family

domesticate an organism adapted to live with and to be of use to humans

compound a substance formed from two or more elements

alkaloids bitter secondary plant compounds, often used for defense

physiology the biochemical processes carried out by an organism

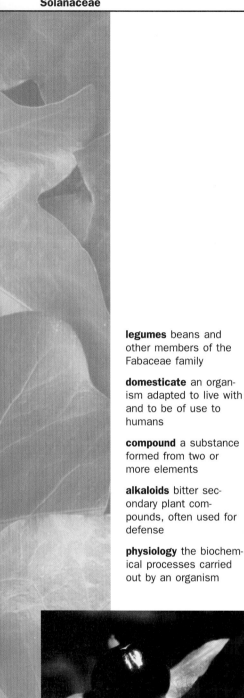

Belladonna, also known as deadly nightshade.

tains. The leaves are generally alternate, petiolate, and simple, although they can be lobed or compound, and are often covered with hairs and sometimes with prickles (trichomes). The unusual vascular tissue has internal phloem. The flowers, solitary or in **inflorescences**, are usually radially symmetrical, **pentamerous**, and have a calyx and corolla united in short or long tubes. Thus, the corolla can be tubular, rotate, or **campanulate**. The mostly hermaphroditic flowers bear stamens attached to the corolla tube with anthers that break open to release pollen, by longitudinal slits, or by terminal pores in *Solanum*. The **gynoecium** consists of a single **pistil** and generally has a superior two-carpellate, two-locular ovary with numerous ovules. Except in *Solanum*, a floral nectary is often present at the base of the ovary. The fruit is mostly a juicy berry or a dry capsule, characteristically with the calyx persistent. Many species are pollinated by insects, although some are pollinated by hummingbirds, perching birds, or bats. SEE ALSO POTATO; POTATO BLIGHT; PSYCHOACTIVE PLANTS; TOBACCO; TRICHOMES.

Gregory J. Anderson and Gabriel Bernardello

inflorescence group of flowers or arrangement of flowers in a flower head

pentamerous composed of five parts

campanulate bell-shaped

gynoecium the female reproductive organs as a whole

pistil the female reproductive organ

Soybean

Soybean, *Glycine max*, is an important crop throughout the world. Soybean is a source of food, oils—both culinary and industrial—and animal feed. In addition, soybean products can be found in plywood, particleboard, printing inks, soap, candy, cosmetics, and antibiotics.

Cultivated soybean and its wild ancestor, *Glycine soja*, are members of the legume family, Fabaceae. Legumes are particularly valuable because, in conjunction with symbiotic bacteria, they fix atmospheric nitrogen and they are excellent sources of protein, with soybeans containing the highest level of this nutrient.

The cultivated soybean plant is an erect, bushy annual. Plants produce clusters of three to fifteen purple or white flowers that develop into pubescent (fuzzy) pods, usually containing two to four seeds. Soybean seeds vary in size and are commonly yellow in color, but can also be green, black, or brown. Soybean varieties are classed into thirteen maturity groups according to their response to day length; the earliest group, 000, developed for far northern latitudes and the latest group, X, for tropical regions. Groups 000 through IX are grown across the central and eastern United States from Minnesota and North Dakota in the north to Florida and southern Texas in the south.

The soybean originated as a cultivated crop in northeast Asia about four thousand years ago. The earliest written record of the soybean plant is from China in 2838 B.C.E. Early farmers grew soy for their own food as well as for livestock feed. Soybean came to the United States in the late 1700s, but was used primarily as a forage crop until the beginning of the twentieth century.

Soybean is planted in the spring with row spacing averaging twelve inches using a grain drill. A skipped row system allows **cultivation** without damage from tractor tires. Nitrogen fixation by the symbiotic *Rhizobium* bacteria alleviates the need for nitrogen fertilizer, although soil testing may indicate other needed nutrients. Weed and insect pest controls are practiced

cultivation growth of crop plants, or turning the soil for this purpose

A soybean plant with pods in a field near Hutchinson, Kansas.

as needed. Soybean is harvested when the pods are dry and brown and the leaves have fallen, generally after the first freeze in the fall. The crop is harvested with combines that cut the plants and thresh the seed from the pods.

More soybeans are grown in the United States than in any other country in the world. Soybean is the second largest crop produced in the United States after corn. Over half of the soybeans produced in this country are exported to other parts of the world, making soybean an important part of the market economy of the United States.

Greater than half of the vegetable oil consumed in the United States is soy oil, a healthy vegetable oil high in unsaturated fats. Culinary soybean products include extracted soy protein, tofu (soybean curd), tempeh (fermented soybean mash), soy sauce, soy flour, edamame (green vegetable soybeans), soy sprouts, and soymilk. Other important soybean products are the animal feeds made from the meal that is one of the end products of oil extraction, and oil for light industrial purposes. SEE ALSO AGRICULTURE, MODERN; ECONOMIC IMPORTANCE OF PLANTS; FABACEAE; NITROGEN FIXATION.

Molly M. Welsh

Bibliography

Poehlman, John Milton. "Breeding Soybeans." In *Breeding Field Crops.* New York: Van Nostrand Reinhold, 1987.

A Short History of Soybeans. 1999. [Online] Available at http://www.cyberspaceag.com/soybeanhistory.html.

"Soybean Production." In *Ohio Agronomy Guide Bulletin 472.* 1999. [Online] Available at http://www.ag.ohio-state.edu/~ohioline/b472/soy.html.

Whigham, Keith. *Soybean History.* Department of Agronomy, Iowa State University. 1999. [Online] Available at http://www.agron.iastate.edu/soybean/history.html.

Speciation

Speciation can be defined, in a general way, as the various processes by which new species arise. Speciation mechanisms can be categorized in several ways. Some species arise by the divergence of two or more new species from a single common ancestral species (divergent speciation), while others arise from **hybridization** events involving two parental species (hybrid speciation). When a hybrid speciation event occurs, the newly derived species may have the same chromosome number as its parents (homoploid hybrid speciation), or it may have a higher number (polyploid hybrid speciation). In the latter case, the chromosome number of the newly derived species is usually the sum of those of its parents. In fact, polyploid hybrid speciation is one of the most frequent speciation mechanisms in plants.

hybridization formation of a new individual from parents of different species or varieties

Criteria for Recognizing Species

Because two major criteria for the recognition of species are in wide use in biology, any discussion of speciation processes should refer to the criteria under which species are recognized. Criterion 1 is known as the phylogenetic species concept. Criterion 2 is known as the biological species concept. Under either criterion (genetically distinct groups or reproductively isolated groups), species exist as one or more local **populations**. Most mating events involve individuals from just one population, and if local populations are small, all of the individuals within each one are closely related. However, there is often some degree of migration of individuals between populations by processes such as seed dispersal. Thus, the various local populations of a species may be loosely connected—by occasional interbreeding among them—into a larger population system, or reproductive community. Regardless of whether species are regarded as fully differentiated population systems (criterion 1), or population systems between which there is a genetically based barrier to reproduction (criterion 2), speciation processes involve the generation of two or more population systems from a common ancestor (divergent speciation) or the generation of a population system following one or more mating events involving individuals of different species (hybrid speciation). Because the two major species concepts recognize species on the basis of different criteria, a speciation event may be regarded as being complete when evaluated under criterion 1 while it is still in progress when evaluated under criterion 2.

population a group of organisms of a single species that exist in the same region and inter-breed

Allopatric Speciation

Divergent speciation events can be categorized as those in which the populations that are separating into different species are geographically separated from each other (allopatric speciation) and those in which they are in close proximity (sympatric speciation). An allopatric speciation event begins with a single species that has allopatric (other land) populations, that is, populations that are geographically separated from each other and therefore in little or no contact with each other. This situation may arise when a long-distance dispersal event results in the founding of a new population that is distant from other populations of the species. An example of this would be an allopatric distribution of a species on two islands following the dispersal of one or more airborne seeds of a species from one island to the other. Allopatric distributions also arise when a widespread population system becomes fragmented into two or more allopatric systems by the formation of barriers to dispersal or by changes in climate. The rise of the Rocky Mountains and the corresponding formation of deserts and prairies in the North American interior have created unsuitable habitats for many plant species of temperate forest environments. These species, which at one time had continuous distribution ranges across the continent, became restricted to the forests of eastern and western North America. Once a species comes to have an allopatric distribution, the separate populations begin to evolve independently, and eventually they may become differentiated from each other. This differentiation may have an adaptive basis, as the populations evolve in response to different environmental conditions. Alternatively, the differentiation may be nonadaptive and simply reflect the random origins (by mutation) and genetic fixation of new characteristics that have little or no adaptive value. This is particularly likely to occur when one of the populations is very small, as is likely to be the case when a new population is founded by a long-distance dispersal event. Although the newly formed population may grow quickly, all individuals are descended from the small number of individuals that founded the new population (possibly just one individual). A population of this sort is described as having experienced a founder event, in which it goes through a "genetic bottleneck" and characteristics that were rare in the ancestral population but happened to occur among the founding individuals of the new population may occur in all individuals of the new population under these various circumstances.

As differentiation of allopatric populations proceeds, the point is eventually reached at which two species are recognized. Under the phylogenetic species criterion (criterion 1), speciation can be regarded as having been completed as soon as there are one or more genetically determined differences between the two populations, such that all individuals of one population are distinct from all individuals of the other. For example, all individuals on one island may have teeth on the margins of their leaves, while all of those on another island may lack such teeth. An intermediate stage in this process could be recognized when a particular characteristic is present in only one of the populations (possibly having arisen as a new mutation in that population), but this characteristic does not occur in all individuals of that population.

Reproductive Isolating Barriers

In the example just presented, the two populations still may not be recognized as separate species under the biological species criterion (criterion

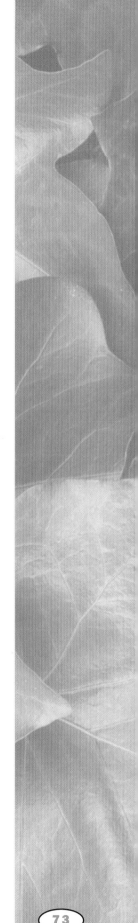

2) even after complete differentiation in one or more characteristics has occurred. Because criterion 2 involves the presence of a genetically determined reproductive isolating barrier (RIB), genetic differentiation in any number of characters, if maintained only by the geographic isolation of the populations, generally is regarded as an insufficient basis for the recognition of the two populations as separate species. Therefore, application of criterion 2 involves the assertion that genetically distinct and allopatric population systems may belong to the same species, and what is recognized as a speciation event under criterion 1 may be regarded as only the initial stages of a speciation event under criterion 2. However, if the two distinct populations later occur in sympatry—for example, following disperal of one of them into the range of the other—a test of sympatry occurs, and the presence or absence of RIBs can be evaluated. If these exist, criterion 2 is satisfied.

RIBs can be categorized in several ways. One useful distinction is between those that operate prior to fertilization (pre-fertilization RIBs) and those that operate afterward (post-fertilization RIBs). Fertilization is a critical point in the reproductive cycle of plants, because this is the point at which an ovule either begins to develop into a seed or is lost to the population. One example of a pre-fertilization RIB is the establishment of a different floral structure so that pollinating insects do not place the pollen from individuals of one plant species on the stigmas of individuals of another species, even if they visit plants of different species in succession. If a visit to the flower of one species results in the placement of pollen on the bee's back, but the stigma of another species is touched only by the underside of a visiting bee, cross-pollination and cross-fertilization will not occur. There are many cases of differing floral structure in the orchid family (Orchidaceae), in which natural pollinators do not cross-pollinate two closely related species, even when individuals of the two species grow side by side, but hybrids are easily generated when human investigators transfer the pollen from one species to the stigma of the other. In a natural setting, the two species are genetically isolated by a pre-fertilization RIB, and thus are recognized as separate species under criterion 2 as well as under criterion 1. Another form of pre-fertilization RIB is temporal isolation (isolation by time). In this case, two closely related plant species may flower at different

times of the year or day and cross-pollination therefore does not occur. However, under controlled environments, with appropriate day-lengths and temperatures, plants of two different species may be induced to flower at the same and cross-pollination may occur.

Hybridization

An example of a post-fertilization RIB is hybrid inviability. In this case, **interspecific hybridization** may occur under natural settings, but the offspring of such crosses may die soon after seed germination. Another example of a post-fertilization RIB is hybrid sterility. In this case, the hybrid individuals may be **viable** yet they fail to produce gametes, and therefore fail to reproduce. In this case, natural hybrids may be present and even abundant in natural settings, but the two parents of these hybrids are recognized as belonging to separate species under criteria 1 and 2. However, pollen and ovules are wasted by both species. This is a particular problem when two species occur in close proximity to each other and are isolated only by a post-fertilization RIB. In such cases, each of the two species is wasting some of its pollen and seeds and the reproductive potential of both species therefore is lessened. Furthermore, hybrid individuals, even if they are sterile, may compete with one or both of the parental species for habitat and pollinators. In such cases there will be selection against those individuals that cross with individuals of the other species, and any mutation that arises in one of the parental species and contributes to a pre-fertilization RIB is likely to become established in addition to the post-fertilization RIBs that already exist. In this manner, reproductive isolation can be reinforced between two species that are in geographic proximity yet are able to hybridize.

Hybrid speciation events must, of course, involve species that occur in sympatry. Although it may seem contradictory to speak of hybridization between species when (at least under criterion 2) species are reproductively isolated population systems, it is often the case that reproductive isolation is strong but not absolute, and in such cases viable, fertile hybrids may occasionally arise between sympatric species. In homoploid hybrid speciation events, hybridization occurs between two species and thereby generates plants with a combination of characteristics that does not occur in either of the parental species. The hybrids may be better adapted than either parental species to a particular habitat, and a new and successful **lineage** therefore may be initiated and may spread into a habitat that is unoccupied by the parental species. Eventually, if RIBs develop, a new species can be recognized under both criteria 1 and 2. At least three cases of homoploid hybrid speciation have been documented in native sunflowers of North America.

Polyploid hybrid speciation is extremely common in many plant groups, notably in ferns, the grass family (Poaceae), and the sunflower family (Asteraceae or Compositae). Like homoploid hybrid speciation, a polyploid speciation event is initiated by a hybridization event. However, reproductive isolation between the new species and both of its parents is usually established immediately, in the form of hybrid sterility, a post-fertilization RIB. Polyploid species usually have two complete sets of chromosomes from each parent, and any hybrids that are formed between the new species and either of the parental forms are likely to experience irregular meiosis and thus to be sterile. SEE ALSO EVOLUTION OF PLANTS; HYBRIDS AND HYBRIDIZATION; POLYPLOIDY; SPECIES.

Jerrold I. Davis

interspecific hybridization hybridization between two species

viable able to live or to function

lineage ancestry; the line of evolutionary descent of an organism

Bibliography

Avise, J. C. *Molecular Markers, Natural History, and Evolution.* New York: Chapman & Hall, 1994.

———. *Phylogeography: The History and Formation of Species.* Cambridge, MA: Harvard University Press, 2000.

Futuyma, D. J. *Evolutionary Biology.* Sunderland, MA: Sinauer Associates, 1997.

Grant, V. *Plant Speciation*, 2nd ed. New York: Columbia University Press, 1981.

Niklas, K. J. *The Evolutionary Biology of Plants.* Chicago: University of Chicago Press, 1997.

Stebbins, G. L., Jr. *Variation and Evolution in Plants.* New York: Columbia University Press, 1950.

Species

The term *species*, in the most general sense, refers to the various kinds of living things. Thus, species are generally recognized as distinct, fully differentiated groups of organisms. However, most modern definitions of species also recognize them as reproductive communities and acknowledge that mating occurs between members of each species but does not occur (or occurs only rarely) among members of different species. Species are therefore generally recognized as genetically differentiated, reproductive communities within which there is a pattern of ancestry and descent among organisms. Although most scientists accept this general definition, there are two somewhat different criteria that are often employed in the recognition of species, and the application of the two criteria does not always lead to the same conclusions.

The Role of Interbreeding

The first major criterion for the designation of species is the actual occurrence of interbreeding among the various organisms and **populations** within a species and the absence of such interbreeding between species. However, patterns of interbreeding are difficult to observe directly, particularly among plants that may live for hundreds of years. For this reason, indirect evidence regarding patterns of interbreeding is usually provided by the study of the patterns of differentiation among populations in genetically determined characteristics. In a trivial sense, oak trees and daisies are regarded as belonging to different species because they are distinguished by numerous characters and because hybrids between them are never observed. Thus, it is reasonable to conclude that they are not part of the same reproductive community. However, there are many recognized species of daisies, and many recognized species of oaks, and these species often are delimited by subtle differences. Consequently, one might examine several populations of daisies and observe that the plants are identical except for one character: the occurrence of a line of hairs along the undersides of the leaves. If all of the individuals in some populations have the line of hairs, and all of the individuals in other populations lack these hairs, there is evidence that two population systems exist and that there is no gene flow between them. In contrast, if each population that is examined includes individuals with the line of hairs and other individuals without the line of hairs, it can be concluded that this is simply a character that varies within a single species, like blood types in humans. Under this criterion, two species can be recognized even when the differences between them are not readily observable. For example, there are many documented cases in which two

population a group of organisms of a single species that exist in the same region and interbreed

or more population systems differ from each other by genetically determined differences that can only be detected by biochemical tests. Though they are difficult to distinguish, the species are recognized as distinct genetic communities.

Reproductive Isolating Barriers

The second major criterion of species status is the existence of a genetically determined barrier to gene flow between species. Such a barrier, known as a reproductive-isolating mechanism or a reproductive isolating barrier (RIB), prevents members of two different species from interbreeding, even if they occur in the same location. For example, the pollen that is produced by plants of one species may not germinate when placed on the stigmas of plants of another species and, thus, there can be no reproduction or gene flow between them. In this case, the RIB is the pollen/stigma incompatibility. Because this barrier is genetically determined, the two are regarded as reproductively isolated, and, as a result, two species are recognized.

Generally, any species boundary due to a reproductive isolating barrier also serves to prevent interbreeding as defined by the first criterion, but there are many instances in which the first criterion is satisfied while the second is not. The line of hairs on the underside of the leaves, which distinguishes two species of daisies under the first criterion in the example just described, does not by itself prevent interbreeding from occurring between the two kinds of daisies. The two daisy species may fail to exchange genes not because of a genetic mechanism but because they occur on different sides of a mountain range. Some biologists argue that if a RIB is not identified, the two kinds of daisies (one with the line of hairs, the other lacking it) should be grouped together and recognized as belonging to the same species. Others argue that the two populations are, indeed, persisting as separate and fully differentiated reproductive communities. Although they may have the potential to interbreed, the available evidence suggests that this does not occur, so they should be recognized as different species. Whatever position one takes on this matter, it should be noted that most species that have been recognized by science have, in fact, been delimited according the first criterion. SEE ALSO CULTIVAR; HYBRIDS AND HYBRIDIZATION; SPECIATION; TAXONOMY; VARIETY.

Jerrold I. Davis

Bibliography

Futuyma, D. J. *Evolutionary Biology.* Sunderland, MA: Sinauer Associates, 1997.

Grant, V. *Plant Speciation,* 2nd ed. New York: Columbia University Press, 1981.

Mayr, E. *The Growth of Biological Thought.* Cambridge, MA: Belknap Press of Harvard University Press, 1982.

Spice *See Herbs and Spices.*

Sporophyte

diploid having two of each type of chromosome; twice the haploid number

Sporophyte, which literally means "spore-bearing" plant, is the **diploid** multicellular phase of an organism that displays alternation of generations. The sporophyte phase develops from the fertilized egg, or zygote, by sim-

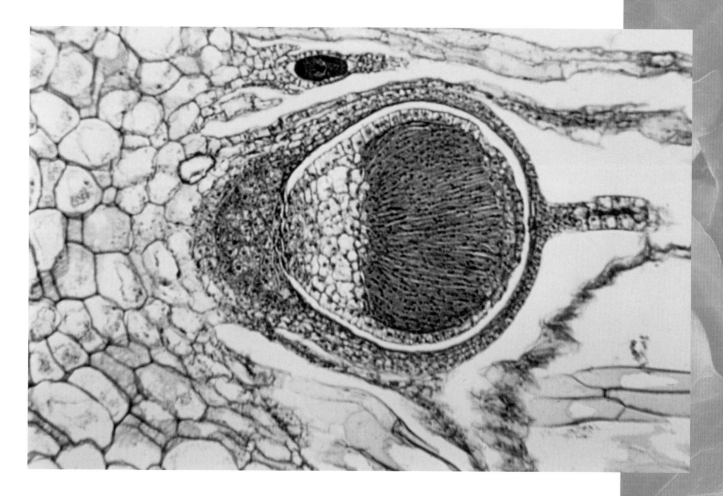

ple cell division and subsequent differentiation. Sporophytes occur in a few algae and aquatic fungi, and are universal in true plants. They differ greatly in size and level of complexity. In bryophytes the sporophyte is short-lived and permanently attached to the female parent, upon which it is nutritionally dependent. In all other plants, the sporophyte becomes independent of the female parent soon after embryological development is completed and remains as the dominant, photosynthetic stage of the plant. In the simplest case, a sporophyte can consist of only a capsule, or sporangium, as in the liverwort *Riccia*, but usually it will also possess one or more vegetative organs. For example, in mosses the sporophyte consists of a foot; a green, stemlike **seta**; and a single complex sporangium, while in pines it is a highly branched tree with roots, stems, leaves and thousands of sporangia. Within the sporangia, which are the reproductive organs of the sporophyte, **haploid** spores are produced by **meiosis**. Germination of these spores marks the beginning of the haploid, sexual phase of the life cycle. SEE ALSO BRYOPHYTES; GAMETOPHYTE; REPRODUCTION, ALTERNATION OF GENERATIONS AND; REPRODUCTION, ASEXUAL; REPRODUCTION; SEXUAL.

Barbara Crandall-Stotler

Bibliography

Graham, Linda. "The Origin of the Life Cycle of Land Plants." *American Scientist* 73 (1985): 178–86.

Sporophyte of a *Marchantia* liverwort, composed of three parts (from left to right): foot, seta, and sporangium.

seta a stiff hair or bristle

haploid having one set of chromosomes, versus having two (diploid)

meiosis division of chromosomes in which the resulting cells have half the original number of chromosomes

Stems

The body of a land plant is composed of a shoot system and a root system. The shoot includes the stem, leaves, and other reproductive systems. The stem is the axis or supporting column of the shoot system, providing support for the leaves and the reproductive structures. It is the channel through which water and mineral elements derived from the soil flow from the roots to the upper parts of the plant. It is also the route taken by organic products synthesized in the leaves when they are transported to other plant parts.

Anatomy

The structure of the stem is organized around the vascular or conducting system, which in seed plants consists of an interconnected pattern of bundles extending lengthwise in the stem. At each node, or site of leaf attachment, one or more of the bundles bends outward into the petiole (leaf stalk) to provide the vascular supply of the leaf, the leaf trace. Despite this constant loss of bundles into the leaves, the number remains constant because of branching within the stem. Each bundle consists of two tissues, the inner xylem, which is the channel for water and dissolved minerals, and the outer phloem, which transports the organic products of photosynthesis.

In dicotyledorous plants the bundles are arranged in a ring around a central pith composed of thin-walled **parenchyma**. The bundles themselves are surrounded by the cortex, which consists of parenchyma often with additional supporting tissues. The entire structure is bounded by the epidermis, which prevents excessive water loss. In many herbaceous plants the cells of the cortex contain chloroplasts and are photosynthetic, and the surrounding epidermis includes the **stomata** necessary for gas exchange. In the monocotyledons, such as lilies and grasses, the vascular bundles are not arranged in a ring but are distributed through the central region of the stem inside the cortex.

Growth

Unlike animals, which ordinarily reach a final stable size, plants continue to grow throughout their lives. This indeterminate growth is accomplished by means of meristems. Growth of the stem, and of the entire shoot, is accomplished through the activity of the shoot **apical meristem** located at the tip of the stem. This region of continued cell division gives rise to the tissues of the stem and also to the **primordia** of the leaves that the stem bears. The leaves are initiated in a regular pattern and develop to mature size along with the tissues of the stem. Although the tissues of the stem are initiated by the apical meristem, much of the growth takes place below the meristem as the tissues are acquiring their mature size and functional properties through the process of differentiation. When initiated by the apical meristem, the leaf primordia are very close together; the growth that occurs below the meristem is by expansion of the internodes (regions between the leaf attachment points). Elongation of the internodes separates the leaves to their final positions. In some plants the expansion of the internodes is limited so that the mature leaves are close together and the stem is very short. This is seen, for example, in rosette plants such as the dandelion.

parenchyma one of three plant cell types

stomata openings between guard cells on the underside of leaves that allow gas exchange

apical meristem region of dividing cells at the tips of growing plants

primordia the earliest and most primitive form of the developing leaf

A bundle of vascular tissue in the stem of a horsetail plant (*Equisteum max*) magnified two hundred times. In stems, monocots have scattered vascular bundles while dicots and gymnosperms have vascular bundles in a ring.

One further aspect of growth is very important for trees or shrubs; this is the formation of a woody secondary body. A meristem known as the vascular cambium develops between the xylem and the phloem in the bundles. Divisions of this cambium form a layer of xylem to the inside and of phloem to the outside. This secondary production of tissue may be limited if the life of the stem is short, but in long-lived trees it may build up a trunk of extensive dimensions. The development of the secondary body expands the stem **laterally.** If continued for any length of time, this lateral growth ruptures the protective epidermis. Continued protection is provided by the formation of the cork cambium, which lays down a layer of largely impervious cork tissue.

laterally away from the center

Branching

In many of the lower vascular plants the stem branches by the subdivision of the apical meristem into two portions each of which forms a branch stem. In the seed plants, however, branches are formed through the development of buds formed in leaf **axils**, that is, on the stem just above the point of attachment to the leaf. Typically a small portion of the apical meristem is detached, or left behind, in the axillary position as the apical meristem

axils the angle or crotch where a leaf stalk meets the stem

axillary bud the bud that forms in the angle between the stem and leaf

adventitious arising from secondary buds

propagate to create more of through sexual or asexual reproduction

succulent marked by fleshy, water-holding leaves or stems

advances and this forms a daughter apical meristem that initiates leaf primordia and forms an **axillary bud**. These often become arrested after a certain degree of development is attained, remaining suppressed by the apical meristem. When released, such a bud expands to form a branch, a replica of the main axis. In addition to this regular pattern of branching, many plants form buds capable of developing into new shoots in various locations other than leaf axils, including roots. Such buds are called **adventitious**.

Modified Stems

There are many ways in which the basic form of the stem deviates from the typical pattern just described, and some of these are of economic significance. In the strawberry, for example, branches called runners extend over the ground, take root at nodes and establish new plants. This natural means of reproduction is used to **propagate** the plant commercially. The same kind of structure but extending underground is called a stolon; when it is the main axis of the plant it becomes a rhizome. Rhizomes may become enlarged and serve as repositories for stored nutrients that may be economically important.

Another similar structure develops when the terminal portion of a stolon enlarges to form a tuber, as in the potato. A corm, seen in the gladiolus, is an upright underground stem that is greatly swollen with stored nutrients. The superficially similar bulb, as in the onion, has a much reduced stem and the stored materials are in fleshy leaf bases. In some cases stems may become broad and flattened to resemble leaves, and are called cladophylls. Many plants of desert or salty environments become very **succulent** or fleshy and bear reduced leaves. Stems may also assume a protective function by developing sharp, hardened tips as spines, while others form tendrils, which may help climbing stems to attach to their support. SEE ALSO ANATOMY OF PLANTS; GERMINATION AND GROWTH; MERISTEMS; PHYLLOTAXIS; POTATO; SHAPE AND FORM OF PLANTS.

Taylor A. Steeves

Bibliography

Esau, Katherine. *Anatomy of Seed Plants*, 2nd ed. New York: John Wiley & Sons, 1977.

Mauseth, James D. *Plant Anatomy*. Menlo Park, CA: Benjamin/Cummings Publishing Company, 1988.

Rudall, Paula. *Anatomy of Flowering Plants*, 2nd ed. Cambridge: Cambridge University Press, 1992.

Succulents

The term *succulent*, when applied to plants, refers to those organisms that have very fleshy leaves or stems, regardless of whether they are adapted to dry habitats (as are most true succulents). Specifically, succulent plants are those that are strongly adapted to life in water and/or heat-stressed habitats, and are typically represented by members of certain plant families (see accompanying table). Plants that have evolved in very hot, dry conditions, or those that experience these conditions at certain times of the year, have evolved various structures, habits, and metabolic mechanisms to cope with existence in stressed habitats.

FLOWERING PLANT FAMILIES CONTAINING SUCCULENTS

Family	Common Name	Geographic Distribution*	Number of Species (approximate)	Examples of Succulent Genera
Agavaceae	Agave family	North America, Africa	625	*Agave, Dasylirion, Nolina, Sanseiveria, Yucca*
Aloaceae	Aloe family	Africa	440	*Aloe, Gasteria, Haworthia*
Aizoaceae	Ice plant family	Africa	1,300	*Carpobrotus, Faucaria, Lithops, Pleiospilos*
Asclepiadaceae	Milkweed family	Africa	>2,000†	*Ceropegia, Huernia, Orbea, Piaranthus, Stapelia*
Cactaceae	Cactus family	North and South America	1,600	*Carnegiea, Ferocactus, Mammillaria, Opuntia*
Crassulaceae	Stonecrop family	Africa, Asia, Europe	1,500	*Crassula, Echevaria, Kalanchoe, Sedum*
Didiereaceae	Didieriea family	Madagascar, Africa	11	*Allauadia, Decaryia, Didierea*
Euphorbiaceae	Euphorbia family	Africa, North America	5,000‡	*Euphorbia, Jatropha, Monadenium*
Portulacaceae	Purslane family	Africa, Australia, North and South America	250	*Anacampseros, Ceraria, Portulaca*

* For succulent members of the family.
† Approximately 450 species are succulent.
‡ Approximately 750 species are succulent.

Most succulents are xerophytes, that is, plants that have developed adaptive features for life in dry, often hot, environments. In addition to some shared features with nonsucculent xerophytes, succulent plants have acquired additional specialized features, independently, in several different plant families. The general characteristic of plants that have evolved succulence is the presence of large **parenchyma** cells in leaves or stems (and occasionally in roots) that serve the purpose of water storage. Furthermore, these plants may also possess one or more of the following adaptations to reduce water loss during periods of heat or drought stress: the presence of epidermal cells with thickened outer walls; increased accumulation of the waxy **cuticle** layer covering the epidermis; and the evolution of **crassulacean acid metabolism** (abbreviated CAM; this process delays gaseous exchange through **stomata** until nighttime, when temperatures are lower and water lost by **transpiration** is decreased). SEE ALSO CACTI; DESERTS; DEFENSES, PHYSICAL; PHOTOSYNTHESIS, CARBON FIXATION AND.

Robert S. Wallace

Bibliography

Mauseth, J. D. *Botany: An Introduction to Plant Biology.* Boston: Jones and Bartlett, 1998.

Raven, Peter. H., Ray F. Evert, and Susan E. Eichhorn. *Biology of Plants*, 6th ed. New York: W. H. Freeman and Co., 1999.

Sugar

Sugar, from the Greek word *saccharis*, is a term with a variety of meanings. To the biochemist, sugar is a broad term covering a large group of related organic **compounds**, all of which are composed of carbon, hydrogen, and oxygen. Green plants utilize their chlorophyll to transform solar energy (sunlight) into chemical energy by converting carbon dioxide and water into plant sugars through the process of photosynthesis. Generally, when people speak of sugar, they are referring to sucrose, which is a disaccharide or double sugar composed of equal parts of glucose and fructose. Glucose and fructose are monosaccharides or single sugars, found in fruits and in honey (together with sucrose). There are hun-

parenchyma one of three types of plant cell

cuticle the waxy outer coating of a leaf or other structure, providing protection against predators, infection, and water loss

crassulacean acid metabolism water-conserving strategy used by several types of plants

stomata openings between guard cells on the underside of leaves that allow gas exchange

transpiration movement of water from soil to atmosphere through a plant

compound a substance formed from two or more elements

dreds of different sugars and these are only a small section of the vast family of carbohydrates, which includes cellulose at one end of the scale and simple alcohols at the other. Starches, also made by plants, are dense complexes of sugar molecules. Starches and sugars make up the group of foodstuffs known as carbohydrates. All carbohydrates are formed originally by photosynthesis.

Sources of Natural Sugar

Sucrose, fructose, dextrose, and glucose are the natural sugars most frequently used. Although many fruit-bearing plants like the date palm and the carob produce sugar as a product of photosynthesis, the world's major supply of sugar is obtained from the cultivated or managed crops of sugarcane, sugar beet, corn, sugar maple, and sweet sorghum. Sugarcane, corn, and sweet sorghum are cultivated grass plants that store sugar in their stalks or seed. Sugar beet is a broadleaf plant that stores sugar in its root. Sugar maple is a hardwood tree with sugar in its sap, and honey is produced by honey bees from the nectar of plant flowers that contains sugars.

Sugar, Calories, and Energy

In addition to its flavor, which was the original reason for its popularity, sugar supplies an important nutritional factor in the form of energy. Sugar contains four calories per gram and one teaspoon of white table sugar (sucrose) weighs about 3.5 grams. The basic calorie requirement for maintaining life (respiration, circulation, muscle tone) varies between 750 and 1,630 per day in a state of complete rest. Intense muscular effort may require upwards of 7,000 calories during the day. Carbohydrates are an essential component of the human diet, and Recommended Dietary Allowances (RDAs) for nutrients in the American diet have been established by the National Academy of Sciences. The RDAs suggest that the average dietary energy intake (in calories) should consist of 10 to 15 percent protein, 35 to 40 percent fat, and 45 to 50 percent carbohydrates. Carbohydrates, therefore, contribute the major part of the available energy in the human diet. In less-developed areas, it is not unusual to find 80 to 90 percent of available energy in the diet coming from carbohydrate sources.

To get the energy needed, humans reverse the process that plants utilize to make sugar. Digestion of sugars (carbohydrates) is accomplished by **enzymes** beginning in the mouth and continuing in the small intestine. In the cells of the human body, all usable carbohydrates are converted to the same basic fuel, **pyruvic acid**, which is then burned to release energy, stored as fat for future energy needs or converted to intermediates for growth or maintenance of body tissue. Although proteins and fats can also be used as sources of energy, only sugars can yield pyruvic acid. That is why sugar is the principal and preferred fuel for the body's energy cycle.

Social and Environmental Impact

During its long history, sugar has been the cause and prize of wars, as well as the object of political activity. There are logical reasons for this. Sugar is an attractive commodity and thousands of people throughout the world gain their livelihood from sugar. With a rapidly expanding world

enzyme a protein that controls a reaction in a cell

pyruvic acid a three-carbon compound that forms an important intermediate in many cellular processes

Sugar beets on a Nebraska farm about to be processed for their sugar.

population, this is important because sugarcane and sugar beet are, respectively, the most efficient plant fixers of solar energy among tropical and temperate-zone vegetation. Sugarcane is four times as effective as any tropical plant in terms of dry-matter production per unit of land, and sugar beet is twice as productive as any temperate-zone plant. It requires an average of only 0.07 hectare (0.17 acre) to fix solar energy to the equivalent of one million kilocalories of energy in the form of sugar. All other forms of edible energy require more. Beef is at the top end of the scale, needing 7.7 hectares (19 acres)—more than one hundred times as much land as needed for sugar.

Processing and Marketing

Crystallized sugar, which is the basic commodity of the international sugar trade, comes from sugarcane, grown in warm, moist climates, and sugar beet, grown in temperate climates. Juice containing sugar is extracted from the stalks of sugarcane and from the roots of sugar beet. The process of crystallization separates sugar out of a sugar-saturated solution. It begins by the formation of minute crystals that act as nuclei for the growth of larger ones. The size of the crystals is controlled by temperature. The uniform small crystals in table or white sugar are the result of controlled crystallization.

Sugar in the international market is under the review of members of the International Sugar Agreement. About 70 percent of the world's sugar supply is consumed in the areas in which it is grown. Twenty percent is marketed through agreements or some form of preference. The remaining 10 percent is world market or free market, and is sold at a price that has no relationship to the cost of production.

Total caloric sweetener consumption in the United States is about 130 pounds per capita each year. Use of refined sugars (from sugarcane and sugar beet) has declined from 67 percent of total caloric sweeteners (84 pounds) in 1980 to less than 49 percent (63 pounds) in 1999. The principal reason for this decline is the increased per capita consumption of corn sweeteners, especially high fructose corn syrup. The approval of the artificial sweetener aspartame (for example, Nutrasweet) for table and industrial use in 1982 is another reason for this decline. SEE ALSO CARBOHYDRATES; ECONOMIC IMPORTANCE OF PLANTS; GRASSES.

Garry A. Smith

Bibliography

Clark, Margaret A., and Mary Ann Godshall, eds. *Chemistry and Processing of Sugarbeet and Sugarcane.* New York: Elsevier, 1988.

Patura, J. M. *By-products of the Cane Sugar Industry,* 2nd ed. Amsterdam: Elsevier, 1982.

Smith, Garry A. "Sugar Myths and Majesties."*Sugar Journal* 61 (1998), nos. 2, 3, 4.

———. "Sugar Beet." *Principles of Cultivar Development,*Vol. 2, ed. Walter R. Fehr. New York: Macmillan, 1987.

———. "Sugar Crops." *CRC Handbook of Plant Science in Agriculture,* Vol. 2, ed. B. R. Christie. Boca Raton, FL: CRC Press, 1987.

Symbiosis

Symbiosis is simply defined as living together. Scientists use this term to describe intimate relationships between members of different species. By definition there are at least two species in a symbiotic relationship; it is unknown the maximum number of species that a symbiosis can sustain. This number may be very great; fungal partners (mycorrhizae) of plant roots link many photosynthetic plants of different species in one continuous networked symbiosis. Partners may belong to the same kingdom (for example, plants in symbiosis with other plant species) or may include partners from different kingdoms. A lichen symbiosis consists of partners from two or three kingdoms—a fungus, a **protist** (algae), and often a cyanobacterium (eubacteria). The smaller partner(s) are usually called the symbiont(s) and the larger partner the host. The host's cells, body, body surface, or even its home may be shared with its symbionts.

To what extent must two species live together be considered a symbiosis? A general rule is that the partners must spend a significant amount of time together (part or all of their life cycles). This sustained contact enables a relationship to develop that affects how both species adapt and evolve. The symbiotic relationship is usually classified as belonging to one of three types: mutualism (benefiting both partners), parasitism (one partner, the parasite, benefits at the expense of the host), or commensalism (one partner benefits while the other is unaffected). However, it is too simplistic to place symbioses into such restrictive categories since the environment and ecological interactions with other species may affect the nature of the relationship. Under one set of conditions a relationship may be characterized as mutualistic, while under different conditions it may be parasitic. For example, the relative benefit for plants to host ants as a way to defend them against **herbivores** depends on the degree of herbivory and must be weighed against the cost of synthesizing the nutritional **compounds** needed to support resident ants. Both of these are subject to external influences.

Symbiosis provides an important source of evolutionary novelty. Special symbiont capabilities include photosynthesis and the transfer of photosynthetic products from **cyanobacteria** and algae to animal and fungal hosts, and the supply of nutrients (nitrogen fixation by bacteria in **legumes** and

protist usually a single-celled organism with a cell nucleus, of the kingdom Protista

herbivore an organism that feeds on plant parts

compound a substance formed from two or more elements

cyanobacteria photosynthetic prokaryotic bacteria formerly known as blue-green algae

legumes beans and other members of the Fabaceae family

SYMBIOTIC ASSOCIATIONS INVOLVING PLANTS OR PHOTOSYNTHETIC ALGAE PARTNERS

Type of Symbiotic Relationship		Partners	Nature of Interaction
Symbionts Living in Host	Lichen	Symbionts: Algae, cyanobacteria	Algae provide photosynthetic sugars and cyanobacteria provide nutrients (nitrogen)
		Host: Fungus	Fungus provides protection against environmental extremes
	Coral (and anemones)	Symbionts: Algae	Algae provide photosynthetic sugars
		Host: Cnidarian (animal)	Animal host provides recycled nutrients (nitrogen and phosphorus) and protection
	Bacteria–plant	Symbionts: Nitrogen-fixing bacteria (*Rhizobium*, actinomycetes, cyanobacteria)	Bacteria provide nutrients (nitrogen)
		Host: Plant (legumes, alders, cycads, *Azolla* ferns)	Plant host provides photosynthetic sugars
Symbionts Living on or in Intimate Contact With Host	Ant–plant mutualisms	Symbionts: Ant colonies	Ants provide defense against herbivores, nutrients from colony wastes, protection
		Host: Plant (e.g., acacia trees)	Plant host provides nutrition (nectar, food bodies) and shelter (hollow thorns)
	Plant–plant	Symbionts: Parasitic plant (mistletoes, *Rafflesia*)	Gains photosynthetic sugars, water, and other nutrition from host
		Host: Plant	Harmed only
	Mycorrhizae	Symbionts: Fungus (ectomycorrhizae include many basidiomycete fungi; endomycorrhizae include many ascomycete fungi)	Absorption of nutrients and water from soil; transfer of photosynthetic sugars among different plant species
		Host: Plant (many partners)	Plant host provides photosynthetic sugars

by cyanobacteria in cycads) to plant hosts. Other novel capabilities in marine animal symbioses include light production (luminous bacteria in marine fishes and invertebrates) and chemosynthesis by sulfur-reducing bacteria in hydrothermal vent host animals. In exchange for these services, the host provides the symbiont shelter and/or nutrition. These exchanges allow symbiotic relationships to thrive in marginal environments where resources such as energy and nutrients are limiting. Lichens are able to **colonize** bare rocks because the fungus provides shelter and protection against **desiccation**, its algal partners provide nutritional energy through photosynthesis, and its cyanobacteria provide nitrogen to the algae and to the fungal host. In the coral reef **ecosystem**, symbiotic algae called zooxanthellae photosynthesize and provide energy-rich sugars to their host corals. In nutrient-poor and sunlit tropical seawater, this symbiosis forms the base of the food web and supports the high diversity of all coral reef organisms. Other examples of mutualistic symbioses include the relationship between fungi and the roots of higher plants. Mycorrhizae (the fungal symbionts) associate with roots of higher plants and increase the water and nutrient uptake capabilities of plants. In return, they receive photosynthetic products from their host plants. In 1997, Suzanne Simard and her colleagues found that mycorrhizae connect and transport photosynthetic products between plants and trees in different environments. Other symbionts such as parasitic orchids take advantage of this association by connecting to the fungal network and withdrawing nutrients for their own use.

In parasitic symbioses, the parasite must avoid host defenses and obtain nutrients while remaining in or on the host. In so doing, the parasite often loses the ability to live independently. Plants such as dwarf mistletoes and the largest flower in the world, *Rafflesia*, have lost the ability to photosynthesize; they must derive nourishment from their photosynthetic host plants. These are considered to be obligate symbioses (one or more partners is de-

colonize to inhabit a new area

desiccation drying out

ecosystem an ecological community together with its environment

A *Rafflesia* flower at Poring Hot Springs in Sabah, eastern Malaysia. *Rafflesia,* which lost the ability to photosynthesize, must derive nourishment from their photosynthetic host plants.

intracellular bacteria bacteria that live inside other cells

eukaryotic a cell with a nucleus (*eu* means "true" and *karyo* means "nucleus"); includes protists, plants, animals, and fungi

mitochondria cell organelles that produce ATP to power cell reactions

biodiversity degree of variety of life

pendent on another and cannot survive alone). Often these relationships include more than one partner, each with a different role in the symbiosis. For example, insect aphids specialized to suck plant juices from their hosts must rely on **intracellular bacteria** for essential amino acids not available in plant tissues.

The few examples of commensalistic symbioses are behavioral; one partner taking advantage of the activities of another to obtain food. It is unlikely that the unaffected partner is truly unaffected. If it is really unaffected, commensalism is difficult to define in the context of symbiosis. The definition of symbiosis usually assumes that an interaction is taking place, which means both partners must participate.

Flexibility in the type and amount of nutritional exchanges and in the roles of partners enables the symbiotic relationship to adapt and evolve over time to meet the different needs of the partners. A symbiont, host, or both may lose the ability to live independently because the partner has irrevocably assumed certain critical life functions. This concept is fundamental to the endosymbiotic theory of the origin of **eukaryotic** cells. Chloroplasts and **mitochondria** are the remnants of former symbionts that provided novel metabolic functions (photosynthesis and respiration) to their host cells.

Finally, symbiosis plays an important and often overlooked role in ecology. Nitrogen-fixing bacteria and mycorrhizal fungi provide nutrients to primary producers, and symbiotic associations like lichens are usually the first colonizers. Feeding interactions among symbiotic partners may increase the energy efficiency of food chains and promote nutrient recycling. When one thinks about saving species and **biodiversity**, the emphasis should be placed on understanding and preserving symbiotic relationships. If one partner is lost, all dependent partners will perish. It is rare that any species lives in isolation. SEE ALSO COEVOLUTION; ENDOSYMBIOSIS; INTERACTIONS, PLANT-FUNGAL; INTERACTIONS, PLANT-INSECT; INTERACTIONS, PLANT-PLANT; INTERACTIONS, PLANT-VERTEBRATE; LICHEN; MYCORRHIZAE; PARASITIC PLANTS.

Gisèle Muller-Parker

Bibliography

Douglas, A. E. *Symbiotic Interactions.* Oxford, England: Oxford University Press, 1994.

Margulis, Lynn. *Symbiosis in Cell Evolution,* 2nd ed. San Francisco: Freeman, 1993.

———, and Rene Fester, eds. *Symbiosis as a Source of Evolutionary Novelty.* Cambridge, MA: M.I.T. Press, 1991.

Paracer, Surinder, and Vernon Ahmadjian. *Symbiosis: An Introduction to Biological Associations,* 2nd ed. Oxford: Oxford University Press, 2000.

Simard, S. W., D. A. Perry, M. D. Jones, D. D. Myrold, D. M. Durall, and R. Molina. "Net Transfer of Carbon Between Ectomycorrhizal Tree Species in the Field." *Nature* 388 (1997): 579–82.

Systematics, Molecular

Molecular systematics is the use of molecules to determine classification systems and relationships. For hundreds of years botanists used **morphology**, or overall appearance, to identify and classify plants. Morphological systematics has been important for the basic understanding of plant evolution and relationships; however, it has limitations. One limitation to morphology in plants is homology. Homology assumes that two similar structures have the same evolutionary origin. In other words, the trait arose in an ancestor and was passed down to its descendants. Homology in plant morphology is frequently very difficult to resolve since plant structures can become modified into other forms (e.g., spines of cacti are modified leaves).

Just as a botanist may compare the shape of a leaf between two different plants, molecular **systematists** compare molecules. Molecules have an advantage over morphology in two aspects. First, homology is usually much easier to determine in molecules than in morphology. Second, molecules tend to provide many more pieces of information than can be gained from morphology. A scientist studying morphology may compare one hundred traits, but a scientist using molecules will compare several hundred to several thousand traits depending on the technique.

Early molecular systematics began with micromolecules. The earliest of these studies can be traced as far back as the 1880s, but much of the work was conducted between the 1950s and 1970s. Micromolecules are small molecules mostly responsible for colors, scents, and chemical defenses of plants. Chemicals found in different plants are identified and compared across species for similarities. Species sharing **compounds** are presumed to be more closely related. Later botanists used macromolecules, which are proteins and nucleic acids. Much of the work on proteins was conducted in the 1970s and consisted of determining the order of amino acids in specific proteins (protein sequencing) or determining whether different **populations** or species of plants had different forms of specific **enzymes** (isozyme variability). Other protein-based studies utilized principles of **serology** and created antibodies for protein extracts that were compared to extracts from a different species. The degree to which the **antibodies** of one plant matched the proteins of a another plant provides an estimate of how closely the two plants are related.

Studies began to use deoxyribonucleic acid (DNA) in the late 1960s and 1970s with DNA-DNA hybridization. This method uses the principle that DNA is a double-stranded molecule and that high temperatures (greater

morphology shape and form

systematists scientists who study systematics, the classification of species to reflect evolutionary relationships

compound a substance formed from two or more elements

population a group of organisms of a single species that exist in the same region and interbreed

enzyme a protein that controls a reaction in a cell

serology the study of serum, the liquid, noncellular portion of blood

antibodies proteins produced to fight infection

than 80°C) can cause all of the DNA to become single-stranded. When cooled, the DNA resumes its double-stranded nature (re-annealling) and the temperature at which it becomes completely double-stranded is an indication of how similar the strands of DNA are. In this method, DNA from two plants is combined and heated. If all of the DNA is from closely related plants, the re-annealling temperature is high. If the DNA is from two distantly related plants it is lower. The re-annealling temperature is an estimate of how similar the plants are. The closer the temperatures are to the re-annealling temperature of a single plant, the more closely the plants are assumed to be related.

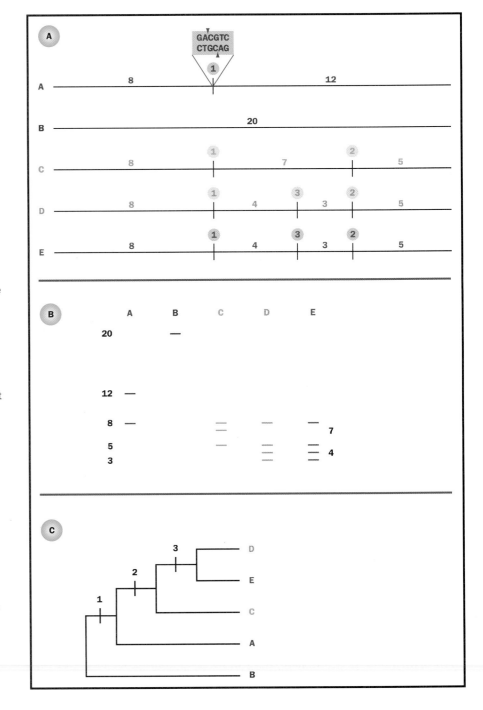

A. Restriction site map for five plants labeled A to E. The numbers above the bars represent the distance between restriction sites (in units of one thousand nucleotides), which are the numbers in the circles. For plant A, the nucleotide sequence that is recognized by this restriction enzyme is enlarged and the areas where the enzyme cuts the DNA are shown with black carats. **B.** A drawing of what a gel would look like after restriction enzymes had cut the DNA for the five plants in A. Each bar represents a fragment and the fragment sizes are shown on the sides. **C.** A phylogeny for the five plants based on the restriction site variation shown. The sites are marked on the tree, where they are present for all plants farther up the tree.

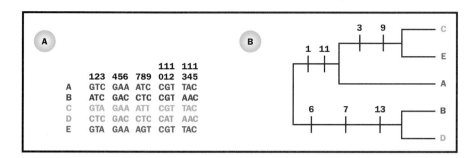

A. A portion of an aligned sequence showing fifteen consecutive nucleotides for five plants labeled A to E. **B.** The phylogenetic tree generated from the data in A. Bars along the branches indicate where changes in the DNA sequence serve to unite two or more plants together. For example, since only plants B and D have the nucleotide C at position 6, this serves to put theses two plants in the same group.

During the 1980s botanists made comparisons of DNA between plants using restriction site analysis. Scientists used restriction enzymes that cut DNA into fragments of various lengths. These enzymes cut the DNA at specific combinations of nucleotides every time this combination of sequences is encountered. The fragments are separated by size using **gel electrophoresis** and visualized by a probe that matches specific regions of the DNA. Comparing fragment sizes, it is possible to determine whether a specific restriction site is present or absent in any given species. The presence of a restriction site in two or more plants implies that the plants with the site have a more recent common ancestor. Restriction site data are capable of producing hundreds of sites depending on the numbers of enzymes that are used. Most botanists use the DNA from the **chloroplast** since it is smaller in comparison to other regions of the **genome** and a number of probes are available.

During the late 1980s and the 1990s molecular systematists made a shift to comparing DNA sequences. A specific gene or DNA region is selected and the order of nucleotides of that gene are determined (sequencing). DNA sequencing was made easier by the polymerase chain reaction (PCR), which allows millions of copies of a gene to be made (amplification) from a single copy. Once a gene is amplified, it is relatively easy to sequence. Nucleotide sequences generated from the same gene of different plants can be compared, or aligned. The traits that are compared are the nucleotides that occur at each aligned position in the gene. As with restriction sites, the shared presence of a specific nucleotide at a specific site in two or more plants is assumed to mean that these plants share a more recent common ancestor.

Many botanists utilize a gene called ribulose bis-phosphate carboxylast-oxygenase, large subunit, abbreviated rubisco, found in the chloroplast DNA. This gene is functionally important for plants as it encodes the enzyme that allows plants to make CO_2 into complex molecules. Because it is so important, changes in the gene sequence are infrequent, allowing botanists to use these changes to answer questions about relationships and origins of flowering plants. Recently, botanists have expanded the number of genes studied. Many genes are now used depending on the taxonomic level of interest. Genes with lesser, or no, function evolve quickly and are useful to compare species or populations. Genes with functional constraints are more useful to compare **genera** or families.

It is common for scientists to use several genes for a study. As more genes are added, it strengthens the results by adding more data, and from genes that may evolve differently. One important example of this is the com-

gel electrophoresis a technique for separating molecules based on size and electrical charge

chloroplast the photosynthetic organelle of plants and algae

genome the genetic material of an organism

genera plural of genus; a taxonomic level above species

parison of nuclear genes to chloroplast genes. Chloroplasts usually are inherited through a single parent (the mother), whereas nuclear genes are inherited from both parents. If a botanist studies only chloroplast genes, it is possible that only the maternal **lineage** will be resolved. This is especially critical in plant groups that are known to hybridize. To counter this potential error, many botanists look at chloroplast genes in conjunction with nuclear genes. Common nuclear genes that are used are the ribosomal ribonucleic acid (RNA) genes. SEE ALSO PHYLOGENY; PLANT IDENTIFICATION; SYSTEMATICS, PLANT; TAXONOMY.

James F. Smith

Bibliography

Donoghue, Michael J. "Progress and Prospects in Reconstructing Plant Phylogeny."*Annals of the Missouri Botanical Garden* 81 (1994): 405–18.

Judd, Walter S., Christopher S. Campbell, Elizabeth A. Kellogg, and Peter F. Stevens. *Plant Systematics: A Phylogenetic Approach.* Sunderland, MA: Sinauer Associates, Inc., 1999.

Soltis, Pamela S., Douglas E. Soltis, and Jeff J. Doyle, eds. *Molecular Systematics of Plants.* New York: Chapman & Hall, 1992.

———, eds. *Molecular Systematics of Plants II: DNA Sequencing.* Boston: Kluwer, 1998.

Stuessy, Tod F. *Plant Taxonomy.* New York: Columbia University Press, 1990.

Systematics, Plant

Plant systematics is a broad discipline that is often defined as the study of the kinds of organisms (both living and fossils), and of the relationships among these organisms. Thus, students and researchers in the area of systematics (termed systematists) study the diversity of all life, including bacteria, fungi, plants, and animals, with several major goals. Systematics includes the identification, naming, and classification of plants, as well as the investigation of evolutionary relationships (phylogeny) and of evolutionary processes. As such, some consider systematics the fundamental discipline upon which all other areas of biology must rely. That is, other areas of investigation all depend on a clear understanding of species names, species delimitation, and organismal relationships. Thus, systematics is a unifying discipline and operates in a highly similar fashion regardless of the major group of organisms investigated (e.g., plants, fungi, animals, or bacteria).

Research in systematics may involve the collection of organisms in the field and the study of these organisms in their natural setting, in museums, and in the laboratory; the latter may employ approaches also used in molecular biology. The sources of evidence used in systematics are also highly varied and may include morphology, chemistry (a subdiscipline often referred to as chemosystematics), **paleobotany**, **physiology**, ecology, **biogeography**, and various sources of deoxyribonucleic acid (DNA)/ribonucleic acid (RNA) data (an area referred to as **molecular systematics**). For several reasons, computer analysis is also an important aspect of systematics. The task of classifying all life (estimated at ten to one hundred million species) is a monumental undertaking, involving the comparative analysis of many organisms; hence, systematists have made significant use of computers to analyze large data sets and to store information so that it is easily retrievable.

Because the areas of study encompassed by systematics are so diverse, the tools or methods employed are also highly varied. One aspect of sys-

---

lineage ancestry; the line of evolutionary descent of an organism

paleobotany the study of ancient plants and plant communities

physiology the biochemical processes carried out by an organism

biogeography the study of the reasons for the geographic distribution of organisms

molecular systematics the analysis of DNA and other molecules to determine evolutionary relationships

METHODOLOGICAL APPROACHES USED IN PLANT SYSTEMATICS	
General Approach	Information Provided
Anatomy	Species relationships, phylogeny
Chemosystematics	Species relationships, medicinal plants
Cytogenetics	Species relationships, evolution
DNA markers	Species relationships, population genetics, evolution, phylogeny, conservation biology
Isozymes/allozymes	Species relationships, population genetics, evolution, conservation biology
Morphology	Species descriptions, phylogeny, preparation of technical keys and floras
Paleobiology	Critical information on now-extinct organisms and the evolutionary history of modern species
Palynology	Species relationships, past climates, fossil floras

tematics involves the collection, pressing, and identification of plant **specimens**, herbarium management, and archiving type specimens (the actual plant specimen upon which the name of a species is based). Some systematists are heavily involved in field research. These individuals explore many natural areas of our planet seeking to describe and catalog the diversity of life; they may also be interested in discovering potential new crops or medicinal plants. This aspect of systematics may also include the discovery and description of new species. Closely associated with this aspect of systematics is developing and refining methods of identifying plants. This is also a critical area of plant systematics that includes the writing and use of identification keys and floras.

specimen object or organism under consideration

Another important aspect of plant systematics includes the collection of evidence for determining relationships among species, that is, reconstructing phylogenies (the development of an hypothesis of evolutionary history; these are depicted as **phylogenetic** trees). Ultimately, these phylogenetic trees are used for revising classifications. Classifying organisms in a manner that reflects evolutionary history has been a longstanding goal of systematics since the work of Charles Darwin. An evolutionary biologist of the twentieth century, Theodosius Dobzhansky, stated that "Nothing in biology makes sense except in the light of evolution." Modern systematists feel that an important corollary of this famous statement is that "things make much more sense in light of phylogeny." That is, understanding the evolutionary history of organisms and their closest relatives is central to comparative biology.

phylogenetic related to phylogeny, the evolutionary development of a species

Finally, systematists are often involved in elucidating the processes of evolution. Through their study of plant diversity and natural **populations**, systematists may be involved in analyzing the levels and distribution of genetic variation within and among populations, estimating gene flow, analyzing isolating mechanisms and species origins, and investigating evolutionary mechanisms such as hybridization, **polyploidy**, and **apomixis**. As a result, one area of the broad discipline of systematics becomes intertwined with the field of evolutionary biology.

population a group of organisms of a single species that exist in the same region and interbreed

polyploidy having multiple sets of chromosomes

apomixis asexual reproduction that may mimic sexual reproduction

History of Systematics

Systematics is arguably the oldest biological discipline and has been practiced, in one form or another, for thousands of years. Prehistoric peoples knew and used almost all of the important crop plants we cultivate today,

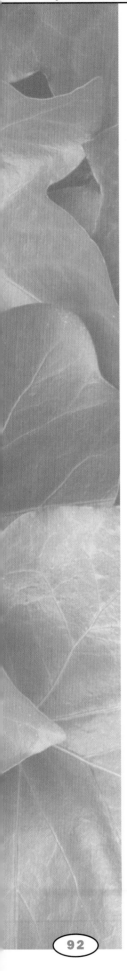

plus others specific to their geographic location. They selected plants with useful features for foods, medicines, fibers, and poisons. As civilizations developed throughout the world, people developed different ways of studying and classifying plants. Our systematics heritage traces back to early western civilizations where several men from Ancient Greece and later the Roman Empire made valuable contributions to our knowledge of plants. Theophrastus, a Greek philosopher who lived from 370 to 285 B.C.E., was a student of Aristotle and is regarded as the father of botany. Theophrastus wrote several hundred manuscripts describing and classifying plants. Many plant names used today are derived from those used by Theophrastus. In the first century A.D., Dioscorides, a Greek physician traveling with the Roman armies, wrote *De Materia Medica*, a book that described and classified more than five hundred species of plants based on their medicinal or other useful properties. This book served as the primary botanical text throughout Europe until the **Renaissance**, nearly fifteen hundred years.

Renaissance a period of artistic and intellectual expansion in Europe from the fourteenth to the sixteenth century

A fifteenth-century manuscript illumination of a marigold from Dioscorides's *De Materia Medica*, which described and classified more than five hundred species of plants based on their medicinal or other useful properties.

Hierarchical classification systems, such as those we use today, can be traced to the late 1600s and the work of Englishman John Ray. Ray developed a classification system for eighteen thousand species and introduced the concept of placing **morphologically** similar species together in a larger group, the genus. The most notable contributions during the 1600s and 1700s were those of Carl von Linné, a Swedish naturalist better known as Carolus Linnaeus. Linnaeus is considered the father of taxonomy, and is best remembered for developing the binomial system of **nomenclature**, that is, the use of a two-part name for each species; the species name consists of the genus name and the specific epithet. Linnaeus also wrote several major books, including his two-volume catalog for plant identification, *Species Plantarum*, which was published in 1753.

All of biology, including systematics, was changed by the publication of Charles Darwin's *The Origin of Species* in 1859. Darwin's theory of evolution had an important message for systematists: Species are dynamic, changing entities, and classification is a way to order the products of evolution. Through efforts to reflect evolutionary history in classifications, we see the first evidence of phylogenetic classifications in the latter part of the nineteenth century—these are the roots of those systems in use today. Throughout the 1900s, improved means of data gathering and improved knowledge of the world's flora contributed to improvements in plant classifications. As noted, current efforts in phylogeny reconstruction are being incorporated into classifications, and systematics has expanded to include studies of speciation as well as phylogeny and classification.

Systematics and Classification

As the branch of biology concerned with understanding phylogeny and with organizing biological diversity, systematics also encompasses the development of classification systems for storage and retrieval of information. The major categories (ranks) of the botanical classification system still in wide use today are, in descending order:

Kingdom

Division (or Phylum)

Class

Order

Family

Genus

Species

Each organism can be placed into such a hierarchical system. Biological systematists attempt to create classifications that reflect phylogeny; that is, a group of closely related species will be classified into a genus; closely related **genera** are placed in a family, and so on.

Recent analytical developments in inferring phylogeny have improved our estimates of evolutionary history: now, in many groups of organisms, we can identify specific **lineages**, or **clades**, of related species. Unfortunately, our classification systems have not kept pace with our improved understanding of phylogeny. For this reason, clades and formal classifications

morphologically related to shape or form

nomenclatural naming system

genera plural of genus; a taxonomic level above species

lineage ancestry; the line of evolutionary descent of an organism

clade a group of organisms composed of an ancestor and all of its descendants

93

do not always agree. For example, many textbooks follow the Five Kingdom approach to classification of life on Earth: Kingdoms Monera, Protista, Fungi, Plantae, and Animalia. However, although this approach was a vast improvement over previous Two Kingdom classifications (Plantae and Animalia), it does not accurately reflect what we know about the history of life on Earth. Other classification systems have been proposed, some recognizing as many as eight or ten kingdoms, in an attempt to include the various major lineages of life in a classification system. At present, none of these classifications adequately meets the challenge of representing current hypotheses of the phylogeny of life. Similar inconsistencies between estimates of phylogeny and classification can also be seen at other levels of the taxonomic hierarchy; thus systematists are torn between scientific reality and the tradition of classification. This inconsistency should not be viewed as a failure of systematics; instead, it should indicate that biological systematics is a dynamic area of biology, an unending synthesis that seeks to incorporate new information into our estimates of phylogeny and our classification systems that organize biological diversity. To improve the connection between our understanding of phylogeny and classification, some systematists are attempting to develop new methods of classification. One approach is to abandon the traditional Linnaean hierarchy in favor of a strictly phylogenetic system of classification.

Systematics and Society

Systematics plays a key role in benefiting human society, both directly and indirectly, and has been part of the human endeavor for millennia. To understand and appreciate the extent of human impact on either local communities or global **ecosystems**, it is first critical to know what species inhabit the community or area in question. Systematists also play a major role in conservation biology and in the study of invasive species, identifying those species that are endangered by human activities, as well as those being spread by humans from one part of the globe to another. Another aspect of systematics involves the careful study of relationships of domesticated plant and animal species and their nondomesticated wild relatives. For example, determination of the closest wild relatives of a particular crop may provide new sources of genetic variation for breeding programs and crop improvement. Such research has led to significant improvements in the yield and disease resistance of many of our food plants and domesticated animals. Systematists also play a critical role in the discovery of new drugs from medicinal plants through their field work and interactions with native peoples (**ethnobotany**) who have long used these plants for medicinal purposes. Furthermore, the use of systematic knowledge of evolutionary relationships between related plant groups can guide chemists in choosing the best species to test for potential new drugs. In addition, systematists often serve as consultants to poison-control centers in hospitals because doctors need rapid and correct identifications of poisonous mushrooms, plants, and other potentially poisonous organisms. Systematists may also be involved in studying the evolution of diseases. For example, recent systematic studies have tracked the evolution of the AIDS virus and, in some instances, the pattern of transmission and source of infection.

ecosystem an ecological community together with its environment

ethnobotany the study of traditional uses of plants within a culture

Because systematics is such a large, diverse field, a distinction is often made among subdisciplines or subareas of endeavor. For example, plant nomenclature is the application of names to **taxa** following a strict set of published rules (the International Code of Botanical Nomenclature). Another key aspect is classification, which involves the organization of plants into groups or categories. As noted above, classification traditionally has employed the taxonomic hierarchy of categories established by Linnaeus (e.g., kingdom, division, class, etc.), but the utility of this approach to classification has recently been questioned. Some would collectively consider nomenclature and classification to represent the field of taxonomy and thus make a distinction between this and systematics, the latter focusing on the study of phylogeny and evolutionary biology. An integral part of modern systematics is phylogeny reconstruction. Phylogenetic trees showing evolutionary relationships may be reconstructed by using characters from a number of different sources, including morphological, anatomical, chemical, and palynological (pollen). Cytogenetics involves the study of chromosome **morphology**, as well as the investigation of chromosome pairing at **meiosis**. This field of systematics has enjoyed a recent revival with the application of chromosome painting techniques that facilitate the study of chromosomal evolution. Chemosystematics is the application of chemical data in a comparative fashion to study problems in systematics and to infer relationships based on the presence or absence of certain chemical **compounds** in the organisms studied. Recently, deoxyribonucleic acid (DNA) sequence data have been employed to reconstruct phylogeny, and at present serves as a major source of information to establish evolutionary relationships.

Systematists are often broadly trained, having not only a knowledge of field biology, but also ecology, life history, plant chemistry, population biology, speciation, phylogenetics, and molecular biology. A modern systematist is often, therefore, a jack of all trades. The research of a systematist may involve field work and collection in the tropics, as well as extensive laboratory work involving DNA sequencing and gene cloning.

A fundamental goal of the field of systematics is understanding biological diversity and the organization of this knowledge into a classification system that reflects the evolutionary history of life. Hence, much of modern systematics is devoted to building evolutionary trees of relationships. The ultimate goal of this massive enterprise is the reconstruction of the "tree of life." Historically, most systematic research was based on morphological and anatomical similarities of organisms. Recently, however, the relative ease of DNA sequencing has provided another, very powerful approach to investigate relationships among species. DNA sequences and other molecular data not only are of enormous utility for inferring phylogenetic relationships, but also have other important applications. In much the same way that DNA markers can be used with human subjects to determine paternity, these same approaches can also be used for determining the parents of suspected plant and animal hybrids. This too is yet another aspect of the highly diverse field of systematics. SEE ALSO BIODIVERSITY; DARWIN, CHARLES; FLORA; HERBARIA; IDENTIFICATION OF PLANTS; PHYLOGENY; SYSTEMATICS, MOLECULAR; TAXONOMY.

Doug Soltis and Pam Soltis

taxa a type of organism, or a level of classification of organisms

morphology shape and form

meiosis division of chromosomes in which the resulting cells have half the original number of chromosomes

compound a substance formed from two or more elements

Bibliography

Judd, W. S., C. S. Campbell, E. A. Kellogg, and P. F. Stevens. *Plant Systematics—A Phylogentic Approach*. Sunderland, MA: Sinauer Associates, 1999.

Kenrick, P., and P. R. Crane. *The Origin and Early Diversification of Land Plants: A Cladistic Study*. Washington, DC: Smithsonian Institution, 1997.

Soltis, D. E., P. S. Soltis, and J. J. Doyle, eds. *Molecular Systematics of Plants II: DNA Sequencing*. Boston: Kluwer, 1992.

Taiga *See Coniferous Forest.*

Taxonomic Keys

Taxonomic keys are a written means of helping people to identify an unknown plant. Looking randomly through a flora that includes thousands of plants would take far too much time. A key provides a structure for sorting through a great deal of information, so that the user can quickly and automatically skip over many species that do not resemble the plant.

A key is written as a series of couplets. Each couplet consists of two opposing descriptions of some features of a plant. The user chooses the description that best fits the unknown plant, and is guided by that choice to another couplet or to an answer. The two halves of the couplet lead the user to different parts of the key, dealing with different subgroups of the plants included in the key. All of the plants in the half that was not chosen are instantly rejected. Because the key is constructed of pairs of contrasting choices, it is often referred to as a dichotomous key.

A taxonomic key begins by looking at large, important features that can divide the possible answers into a few large groups, thus quickly ruling out most of them. Later couplets, which divide those groups into smaller and smaller subgroups, use tiny details to help the user tell the difference between very similar species. SEE ALSO FLORA; PLANT IDENTIFICATION; SYSTEMATICS, PLANT; TAXONOMIST; TAXONOMY.

Wendy L. Applequist

Bibliography

Fernald, Merritt Lyndon. *Gray's Manual of Botany*, 8th ed. New York: American Book Company, 1950.

Taxonomist

Taxonomy, or systematics, is the study of the kinds of organisms and their evolutionary history and relationships. Plant taxonomists collect and study groups of plants, focusing on the ways species arise, relationships among them, and selective forces that have molded their characteristics. To understand patterns of variation and relationships among plants, taxonomists study plants in nature, museums, laboratories, greenhouses, and experimental gardens.

Taxonomists identify, name, and classify organisms. They explore areas to collect, identify, and press representatives of every plant species, in or-

---

EXAMPLE OF A TAXONOMIC KEY

This is a simple taxonomic key allowing the user to identify the following common grocery store fruits: apple, banana, orange, peach, tomato, and watermelon. To use the key, pick one of these as your unknown, then read both halves of the first couplet. Which half better describes your fruit? There will be a number after that half. Go to the couplet of that number, and deal with each couplet similarly until, instead of being led to another couplet, you find the name of your fruit.

1a. Skin of fruit is thin, soft or at least flexible, edible 2
1b. Skin of fruit is thick, leathery or hard, inedible 4

2a. Seeds in several liquid-filled chambers; fruit soft throughout . . . . Tomato
2b. Seeds in hard or papery structure in center of fruit 3

3a. Seed enclosed in hard, stonelike pit; flesh soft . . . . . Peach
3b. Seeds enclosed in papery core; flesh crisp . . . . . Apple

4a. Fruit weighs more than 1 pound (0.5 kg); skin does not peel off . . Watermelon
4b. Fruit weighs less than 1 pound (0.5 kg); skin can be peeled 5

5a. Fruit long and narrow, yellow; flesh not divided into sections . . . . Banana
5b. Fruit round, orange; inner flesh divided into several segments . . . . Orange

der to record **biodiversity** before the species are lost to extinction forever. Some explorations lead to conservation efforts or to the discovery of new species, an exciting experience that presents the taxonomist with the opportunity to name and publish a description of the newly discovered species. Basic to these tasks is the challenge of developing a classification for the myriad forms of life, based on differences and similarities such as form, chromosome number, behavior, molecular structure (especially deoxyribonucleic acid [DNA] sequences), and biochemical pathways. Recent advances in cladistics have made new gains in understanding how the world's plant species are related. Cladistics is a field in which taxonomists compare the most evolutionarily relevant traits among various related organisms in addition to the most obvious ones, using computer programs.

biodiversity degree of variety of life

Taxonomists may be found working at universities, herbaria and museums, government agencies, conservation organizations, industry, and botanical gardens. Universities hire taxonomists as professors to teach and conduct research. In herbaria and museums with large plant collections, taxonomists maintain these collections, add to them, and conduct research on them. Federal and state agencies employ taxonomists in many fields, from public health and agriculture to wildlife management and forestry. Taxonomists also help prepare environmental impact statements and work with conservation and natural heritage offices. Industries that employ taxonomists include agricultural processors, pharmaceutical firms, oil companies, and commercial suppliers of plants and seeds. Most jobs in government and industry are more taxonomic and ecological than evolutionary in nature. In general, availability of these jobs depends on the training and experience of the applicant. The higher the level of preparation, the greater the responsibility and independence the job will provide.

The typical plant taxonomist will major in botany or biology with supporting work in other sciences and math. After graduating from college, the student may begin graduate training immediately to earn a M.S. or Ph.D., or work as a research assistant at a university, herbarium, or other opportunity for a year or more. Working out of doors can be very exciting and rewarding for the adventurous. Assisting an established researcher in a herbarium, laboratory, or greenhouse can be fulfilling as one learns by working with the scientist. University teaching and research offers a very stimulating mix of experiences and sometimes administrative posts.

In 1999, salaries for taxonomists ranged from $40,000 to over $80,000. Persons interested in taxonomy follow their own interests in plants, earning satisfaction from doing interesting and worthwhile work. SEE ALSO CURATOR OF AN HERBARIUM; TAXONOMIC KEYS; TAXONOMY.

Elizabeth Fortson Wells

Bibliography

Anderson, G. J., and J. A. Slater. *Careers in Biological Systematics.* Laramie, WY: American Society of Plant Taxonomists, 1986.

Berg, L., M. Albertsen, H. Bedell, L. Debonte, J. Mullins, B. Saigo, R. Saigo, and W. Stern. *Careers in Botany.* Columbus, OH: Botanical Society of America, 1988.

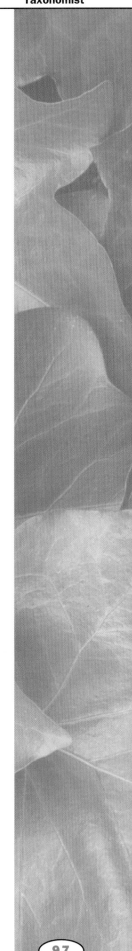

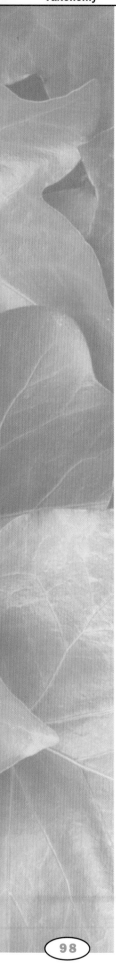

Taxonomy

Narrowly defined, plant taxonomy is that aspect of the study of plants having to do with taxa—that is, the naming of plant names (nomenclature) and the determination of the hierarchical relationships used to identify them or understand their relationships (identification and classification). More broadly defined, plant taxonomy includes areas of investigation from a variety of disciplines, including classification, nomenclature, phylogeny reconstruction, and investigation of evolutionary processes. Under this broader definition, the goal of taxonomy is to use comparative data to assess relationships between plants, define taxonomic boundaries between species and other ranks, provide means of identifying and communicating about the organisms, and understanding the patterns (and even the processes) in the evolution of the plants. Seen in this way, plant taxonomy overlaps and grades into the disciplines of plant systematics, **phylogenetics**, and evolution.

Distinguishing, classifying, and naming plant taxa is basic to any study of nature and for making use of plants. To have the name of a plant (or taxon) is the prerequisite to get further information about it. Taxonomy, therefore, is inevitably necessary for all further studies of plants in order to understand their structures, life histories, and distributions, as well as for making use of them for the benefit of humans (i.e., applied botany, comprising pharmacy [medicinal plants], crops and food production [agricul-

phylogenetic related to phylogeny, the evolutionary development of a species

Researchers experiment with different species of rice in an International Research Institute greenhouse in Los Banos, Luzon, Philippines.

HIERARCHY OF BOTANICAL TAXONOMIC RANKS

Rank	Suffix (or abbreviation of rank name)
domain	
kingdom	
subkingdom	
division	*-phyta, -mycota*
subdivision	*(-phytina)*
superclass	*(-phytina) (-phyceae, -mycetes)*
class	*-phyceae, -mycetes, -opsida, -atae*
subclass	*-idae*
superorder	*-anae*
order	*-ales*
family	*-aceae*
subfamily	*-oideae*
tribe	*-eae*
subtribe	*-inae*
genus	(usually *-us, -a, -um*)
subgenus	(subg.)
section	(sect.)
subsection	(subsect.)
series	(ser.)
species	(sp.)
subspecies	(subsp.)
variety	(var.)
forma	(fa.)

ture], forestry, production of plant raw material [fibers, gum, etc.], horticulture [ornamental plants], and conservation).

Taxonomy, therefore, is one of the oldest branches within the life sciences. But taxonomy is a synthetic science, as it uses and relies on data from all other fields of botany, including that from structural botany (**cytology** and anatomy, palynology and ultrastructure), **morphology** (including embryology), genetics (heredity), **physiology**, phytochemistry, ecology (habitats), and phytogeography (distribution of taxa).

cytology the study of cells

morphology shape and form

physiology the biochemical processes carried out by an organism

Plant Systems: Artificial and Natural

Variation among plants is not continuous—that is, there are discontinuities separating one type of plant from another. We distinguish different individuals of the same kind, and we distinguish different kinds of oaks, roses, dandelions, violets, and so on. Variations among taxa are of different quantity and quality, and as a result, they can be arranged in a hierarchical system. Those plants being almost alike and interbreeding belong to the same species. All similar species together form a genus, similar **genera** are put together as a family, and so forth. The tasks of taxonomy, therefore, are to describe the plants thoroughly (phytography) and to compare them in order to discover natural groups, and to classify (classification) and name them (nomenclature).

genera plural of genus; a taxonomic level above species

Other questions examined in evolutionary botany and phylogenetics include: How did the differences between taxa come about? And what are the reasons for their mutual hierarchical connections? To some authors, all these studies together are called (biological) systematics, and taxonomy is restricted to dealing only with classification.

In order to standardize terminology and promote effective communication among plant scientists, plant taxonomists have agreed to a set of formal guidelines to be used when naming plants. Known as the International Code of Botanical Nomenclature (ICBN), these guidelines were adopted in 1867 and serve as the official reference rules with which nomenclatural decisions about plants must be made. The Code is updated and modified periodically by an international committee on plant nomenclature and serves as the basis for all naming of plant ranks from infraspecific taxa (variety, subspecies, etc.) to species and to taxa of higher ranks (genus, family, order, etc.). There is also a separate code for the naming of cultivated plants, which has nomenclatural conventions very similar to that of the ICBN.

At its founding, the ICBN agreed that plant nomenclature would officially begin with the work by Linnaeus, *Species Plantarum*, published in 1753. To avoid unnecessary duplication of names for the same species or to stabilize the way plant names are applied to the various taxonomic hierarchies, a system of date priority was also instituted, so that the earliest correctly published name for a taxon must be used if the plants concerned are found to be the same. Taxonomic publications describing new species or proposing new genera, families, or other formal ranks are expected to follow the rules included in the ICBN. If these requirements are not met, the name proposed by the botanist may be rejected.

The Swedish botanist Carolus Linnaeus (1707–1778) was an excellent analytical observer, and his talent for methodical recording, concise summarizing, and systematic thinking enabled him to produce a synthesis, the Linnaean System, which was in use for almost one hundred years. It was easy to handle because it was mainly based on very few numerical flower characters (number of stamens and styles). A system using only one or very few characters is considered an artificial one, and the Linnaean System for the most part did not reflect natural (evolutionary) relationships.

Botanists who followed Linnaeus elaborated a natural system of classification, considering all organs of the plant. Important contributors included the Frenchmen M. Adanson, A. L. de Jussieu, and Jean Baptiste de Lamarck; their Swiss colleagues A. P. and Augustin de Candolle; the Scot Robert Brown; the Austrian S. Endlicher; and the Britons G. Bentham and J. D. Hooker. Their system was based on comparative morphology, a discipline arising in the beginning of the nineteenth century. It made use of the concept of **homology** and of crucial discoveries like the alternation of generations by the German W. Hofmeister. Their "natural system"—though subsequently modified in many ways—essentially persisted up to modern times, although it aimed at reflecting the natural order they believed to have been established by God the Creator rather than attempting to reveal evolutionary relationships.

Biological Kinship: Phylogenetic, Phenetic, and Evolutionary Systems

A revolution in biology was the discovery of evolution and its mechanisms by the English naturalists Charles Darwin and A. R. Wallace in the middle of the nineteenth century, presenting common descent and gradual changes in geological time scale as an explanation for the taxonomic hierarchy already established. No essential changes of the previous morphologically based system, therefore, proved necessary. However, the acceptance of evolution as a unifying concept in biology turned the attention of taxonomists to questions of ancestry and descent.

Toward the end of the nineteenth century, the connections among taxa were more carefully studied in order to answer the questions: Which are the older (i.e., more primitive) characters and taxa, and which are the younger and more advanced ones? How did specific adaptations evolve? A typical and important question concerned the evolution of pollination mechanisms. Are unisexual wind-pollinated flowers primitive (original) or advanced (derived, secondary) or vice versa?

The first attempts to answer these questions were by A. Engler and R. V. Wettstein and followers in the late nineteenth century. They considered the *Fagales* (beech and birch families), *Juglandaceae* (hickories), and *Salicaceae* (willows and cottonwoods) as the most primitive angiosperms because of their small, wind-pollinated, unisexual flowers arranged in **catkins**, thus forming a presumptive link between the more ancestral gymnosperms (including conifers like pines, spruces, firs, cedars, etc.) and the **angiosperms**, which often have showy, insect-pollinated, hermaphroditic flowers. However, subsequent research in the early part of the twentieth century, especially by C. E. Bessey, showed that the phylogenetic relations are just the other way around: angiosperms appear to be primarily hermaphroditic and insect-pollinated, these traits being

Pussy willow (*Salix discolor*) catkins are pollinated by the wind, dispersing their spores. Though *Salicaceae* (willows and cottonwoods) were once considered the most primitive angiosperms, subsequent research has shown that the catkin-bearing families evolved later, adapting to habitats in which wind pollination is advantageous.

responsible for one of their major advantages (more effective pollination) in contrast to **gymnosperms**. The catkin-bearing families are judged to have evolved later, adapting to habitats in which wind pollination is advantageous.

In the beginning of the twentieth century, the new field of genetics strongly improved our understanding of evolution. Many phylogenists, however, were skeptical because of the large number of empirically ill-based, speculative phylogenetic trees produced at the turn of the century. Toward the middle of the twentieth century, taxonomy at the specific and infraspecific (below species) levels was changed into the New Systematics, Biosystematics, and Experimental Systematics, strongly accelerated by knowledge from genetics, population genetics, breeding systems, cytogenetics, karyology (chromosome number), and ecology in combination with traditional data from morphology, embryology, anatomy, and distribution.

Despite these stimulating and largely successful efforts to combine understanding of evolutionary processes with the needs and challenges of taxonomy, the study of phylogeny (trees of evolutionary descent) and of systematics above the species level (macrosystematics) was not markedly improved because no data were available for establishing scientifically sound hypotheses. A pragmatic method was developed, therefore, that tried to overcome the difficulty of having classification based on phylogeny, but these were often burdened with intuitive and speculative hypotheses. Phenetic systems were designed in the late 1950s to resolve these problems.

Phenetics

Phenetics is a strictly empirical method. It avoids evaluating character states as ancestral versus derived and thus avoids any phylogenetic hypotheses. All characters are treated as equal (unweighted). The use of newly developed mathematical methods and of electronic data processing allowed calculation of large amounts of character data and classification based exclusively on overall similarity. The resulting phenetic system does not attempt to reveal kinship (relationships based on descent). As it is not biased by phylogenetic judgements, it can be considered, in some way, a multi-

homology a similarity in structure between anatomical parts due to descent from a common ancestor

catkin a flowering structure used for wind pollination

angiosperm a flowering plant

gymnosperm a major group of plants that includes the conifers

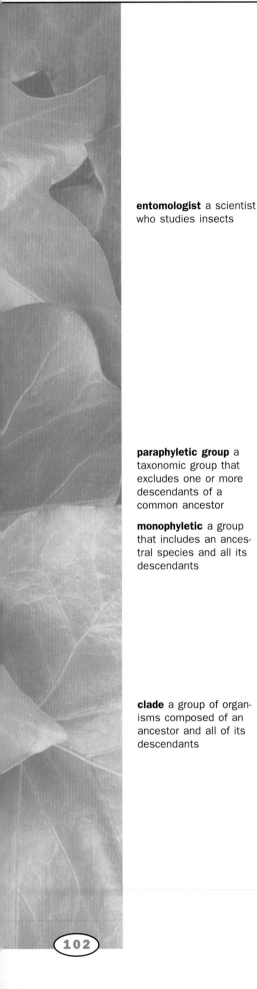

purpose system allowing a maximum of predictability. Convergences (i.e., similarities caused by evolutionary adaptation to the same environmental factors), however, may not become apparent in a phenetic system.

Not all workers were satisfied with phenetics, however, and starting in the late 1960s the method called cladistics was developed for handling taxonomic characters and exploring relationships between taxa. Cladistics, which was strongly opposed to phenetics, developed rapidly and successfully.

Cladistics

entomologist a scientist who studies insects

Using and developing the ideas and concepts of the German **entomologist** Willi Hennig, cladistics is an effective tool for studying and describing phylogenetic relationships and reconstructing a truly phylogenetic system. It constructs conceptually strict phylogenetic branching patterns by evaluating character states as ancestral (plesiomorphic) or derived (apomorphic). The basic assumption is that speciation takes place mainly by bifurcation: one ancestral species splits into two sister species, which are to be treated as having equal taxonomic rank, both characterized by newly developed (apomorphic) characters.

The big advantage of cladistics is the use of clear assumptions and procedures, in contrast to intuitive phylogenetic trees devised by earlier generations of phylogenetic taxonomists. An important conceptual change is the more restrictive definition of monophyly, meaning a group containing all descendants of a certain taxon. But if, say, one or more descendants are excluded, the remaining group forms a **paraphyletic group** because it does not contain all descendants from the common ancestor. In pre-cladistic phylogenetic systems, however, a paraphyletic group has been accepted as being **monophyletic** because all its members share a common ancestor. This, however, has not been accepted by cladistic practitioners.

paraphyletic group a taxonomic group that excludes one or more descendants of a common ancestor

monophyletic a group that includes an ancestral species and all its descendants

These simple concepts, seemingly formalistic and of no empirical value, have, however, major effects on defining phylogenetic taxa and constructing a phylogeny-based system. Through this type of work, the understanding of relationships in the plant kingdom has recently undergone a major revision.

clade a group of organisms composed of an ancestor and all of its descendants

There is much evidence, accumulated for many decades and including modern molecular investigations, that all plants in the strict sense (the so-called *Embryophyta*, the bryophytes and the vascular plants) are offspring of the green algae (*Chlorophyta* s.l.) because they share a combination of common features that would have been unlikely to have evolved several times independently. Both together form a single big branch (**clade**) of the phylogenetic tree and, therefore, are united into one monophyletic taxon, the *Chlorobionta*. This big and highly heterogenous taxon, comprising unicellular algae together with all the land plants, has the same rank in the phylogenetic system as the red algae, comprising a number of seaweeds only. In a cladistic sense, you cannot unite the green algae with the red algae (and other algal groups) to form the taxon algae. Such a group, which mixes organisms from different branches, is called a polyphyletic group. SEE ALSO ALGAE; BESSEY, CHARLES; CANDOLLE, AUGUSTIN DE; FAMILY; FLORA; HERBARIA; HOOKER, JOSEPH DALTON; IDENTIFICATION OF PLANTS; LINNAEUS, CAROLUS; PHYLOGENY; SPECIES; SYSTEMATICS, MOLECULAR; SYSTEMATICS, PLANT; TAXONOMIC KEYS; TAXONOMIST.

Manfred A. Fischer

Bibliography

Greuter, W., et al., eds. *International Code of Botanical Nomenclature*. Berlin: *Regnum Veg*, 1988.

Stuessy, T. F. *Plant Taxonomy*. New York: Columbia University Press. 1990.

Taxonomy, History of

The origin of plant taxonomy goes back centuries, and there are thought-provoking parallels between folk classifications and those produced in more recent times. The Swedish botanist Carolus Linnaeus (1707–1778) provided the first widely used framework, the basis of our current classification. He placed all plants in a genus and species, giving each a **binomial** (such as *Taraxacum officinale* for the dandelion), allowing botanists worldwide to communicate.

binomial two-part

Linnaeus was not very successful in recognizing larger groupings of plants, but in 1786 Antoine-Laurent de Jussieu put all **genera** in families. Jussieu believed that nature could be represented as a single, continuous series of relationships, and he made his families (and genera) of convenient sizes. There was much debate during the ensuing century and a half as to whether all characters should be used in classification or only in the most important ones. The issue was never resolved, but in practice the human mind cannot compute relationships using all characters. Another issue was less contentious: It had been realized that prominent characters used for the identification of plants (in keys) might be different from the most fundamental ones used in deciding on the same plant's relationships.

genera plural of genus; a taxonomic level above species

The Nineteenth Century

The late eighteenth and the nineteenth centuries saw many new developments in the area of plant taxonomy. Voyages of discovery and colonization yielded a stream of unknown plants needing names. Plants of economic importance like quinine, breadfruit, rubber, and tea were moved to colonies where they could best be exploited. Herbaria, collections of flattened and dried plants attached to paper, were developed. By the middle of the nineteenth century most large herbaria such as those at Washington, D.C., Kew (London), and Paris were owned by the state or, less frequently, universities. Systematic work was largely based on the dried plants there, with botanical gardens or field studies being of less importance. This practice persisted through much of the twentieth century.

Darwin's ideas on evolution, published in 1859, had little effect on the practice of taxonomy, although many workers used the ideas to explain the classifications they produced—using techniques very similar to those of Jussieu. Systematists like Asa Gray were among Darwin's staunchest supporters. Darwin himself was very interested in genealogies, ancestor-descendant sequences. Most botanists thought that without fossils such genealogies could not be recognized, but nonetheless when they talked about relationships it was most often in terms of living group A giving rise to living group B—just as if they were talking about genealogies.

Along with professional taxonomists, there was a flourishing group of amateurs. Botany was particularly popular among women. In the later nine-

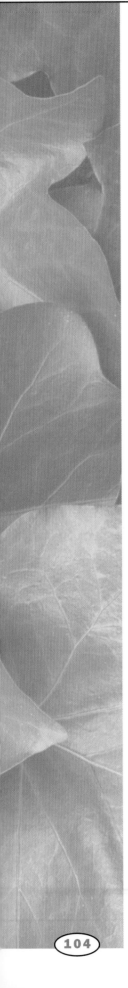

physiology the biochemical processes carried out by an organism

morphology shape and form

cytology the study of cells

phylogenetic related to phylogeny, the evolutionary development of a species

biogeography the study of the reasons for the geographic distribution of organisms

biodiversity degree of variety of life

teenth century, first in Germany and later in the United States, reaction against classificatory botany set in. **Physiology**, anatomy, ecology, and the study of lower plants were thought to be more exciting, particularly among those who worked at universities. Charles Bessey was a forceful proponent of this "new Botany" in the United States, and although he was not particularly against taxonomy, the popularity of the new approach led to a decline in the status of taxonomic botany and of taxonomists. In the sometimes bitter arguments, taxonomic botany was often portrayed as an old-fashioned subject practiced by women and children and of no scientific interest.

In the 1930s emphasis came to be placed on the study of living plants both in the wild and the greenhouse, particularly in the area of species and speciation. G. Ledyard Stebbins, one of the most influential botanists of his time, was a founder, along with Ernst Mayr, Gaylord Simpson, and others, of the "evolutionary synthesis," an integration of evolutionary theory, systematics, and **morphology**. However, taxonomists working in herbaria—where most taxonomic work was still carried out—were little affected by such developments.

Since the late nineteenth century, new disciplines such as anatomy, **cytology**, and plant chemistry had been promoted as likely to solve the difficult problem of understanding the limits and relationships of groups like genera and families. Progress, however, was painfully slow. In the latter part of the twentieth century, a system of relationships that built on those of earlier works was proposed by Arthur Cronquist.

Phenetics and Cladistics

However, changes were afoot. In the 1960s phenetics, or numerical taxonomy, was very popular. By looking at many characters and using early computers to analyze the data, botanists hoped to produce classifications of maximum usefulness, stability, and objectivity. Such botanists were less interested in evolutionary relationships, and problems became evident both in the goals of phenetics and in some analytical techniques. Nevertheless, many of their techniques remain useful, particularly when working at the level of species. In the late 1970s the cladistics approach of Willi Hennig became widely known, and this led to the development of new ways of producing treelike diagrams depicting hypothesized **phylogenetic** relationships. In such phylogenies, genera and species were not linked directly but by way of their common ancestors. After much debate, Hennig's principles, somewhat modified, have been accepted by most botanists, allowing taxonomists to justify their work much more clearly.

In the 1990s the advent of molecular techniques, combined with the practice of phylogenetic analysis and the use of computers, led to a rapid improvement in our understanding of relationships among the main groupings of plants. This has become perhaps the most common kind of systematic work in universities and is notable for being highly collaborative, contrasting with the individuality of classic taxonomic work. Studies on **biogeography**, evolution, and diversification have been greatly facilitated as a result. However, morphological studies have tended to stagnate, and there has been relatively little emphasis on studies at the species level. Furthermore, interest in conservation and **biodiversity** has made it clear how little we understand about most species that have been described, how many species—particularly in groups like fungi—remain to be described, and how few systematists remain engaged in this kind of work. SEE ALSO BESSEY, CHARLES; BRITTON, NATHANIEL; CANDOLLE, AUGUSTIN DE; GRAY, ASA; LINNAEUS, CAROLUS; PHYLOGENY; TAXONOMIC KEYS; TAXONOMIST; TAXONOMY; TORREY, JOHN.

Peter F. Stevens

Bibliography

Judd, Walter S., Christopher S. Campbell, Elizabeth A. Kellogg, and Peter F. Stevens. *Plant Systematics: A Phylogenetic Approach.* Sunderland, MA: Sinauer Associates, Inc., 1999.

Tea

In the broadest sense, tea is a water extract of leaves, blossoms, roots, bark, or other parts of plants. The extraction can be done by soaking, boiling, and steeping (soaking in water below the boiling point). The extract can be an ordinary beverage or a medication.

The most common tea is from the leaves of the plant known as *Camellia sinensis*. Chinese legend attributes the accidental discovery (around 2700 B.C.E.) of drink made from this plant to King Shen Nong, who noticed tea leaves had blown into his kettle of boiling water. The tea that Shen Nong most probably drank is green tea, which quickly became the most popular beverage in China, Japan, Korea, and the countries of Southeast Asia. (Its popularity has continued, and in fact, tea brewed from *Camellia sinensis* is second only to water as the world's most popular beverage.) Unlike orange pekoe (a black tea, which is most identified as tea by consumers in the United States), fresh green tea beverage is tinted apple green, hence its name. Other teas from *Camellia sinensis* are broadly termed black, red, and yellow according to the appearance of either the dried leaf or its extract.

Tea Processing

All *Camellia sinensis* teas are from the growing ends and buds (called the flushes) of the tea tree or shrub. Flushes that undergo a process called fermentation become black, red, or yellow teas. This process is not the one in

Workers harvest tea leaves on a plantation in Assam, India.

TEN LARGEST TEA-PRODUCING AND EXPORTING COUNTRIES, 1998		
Principal Producers	Quantity Produced (in metric tons)	Quantity Exported (in metric tons)
India	870,400	225,000
China	687,675	219,325
Kenya	294,165	263,685
Sri Lanka	280,056	267,726
Indonesia	152,063	67,219
Turkey	120,300	17,526
Japan	91,000	752
Myanmar	66,808	N/A
Vietnam	51,000	33,000
Bangladesh	50,575	25,049

SOURCE: Food and Agriculture Organization of the United Nations.

enzyme a protein that controls a reaction in a cell

which microbes are added to make alcohol-containing beverages, cheese, sauerkraut, and other foods. Rather, an **enzyme** (catalyst) changes molecules called polyphenols that are green into more complex polyphenols that are red and yellow. Both the enzyme and the polyphenols are in (and not added to) the tea leaf, and leaf fermentation is activated first by withering (slow drying of the leaves) and then by rolling (pressing the leaves so that the sap comes to the surface). Black tea is made when the fresh tea leaves are allowed to totally ferment (100 percent). Partial fermentation of 10 to 15 percent and 20 to 30 percent yields yellow and red (sometimes known as oolong) teas, respectively. Steaming or roasting the leaves to inactivate the enzymes soon after harvest prevents fermentation, and these are the first steps in green tea manufacture.

Health Benefits

Tea has been called an elixir of life and is commonly used as an antidote to mental fatigue. This effect may in fact be caffeine-induced. Although there is less in tea than in coffee, enough caffeine is present in a cup of tea to dilate the brain's blood vessels. Tea seems to have a wide range of health benefits, as a survey of the scientific literature between 1998 and 2000 attests. The two principal active ingredients are the tea polyphenols (a group of six chemically and structurally related molecules) and theanine (an unusual amino acid found in green but not black tea beverage). (Amino acids are the building blocks of proteins.) Like vitamins C and E, the tea polyphenols are **antioxidants** that may slow the onset of atherosclerosis, some forms of cancer, and the onset and severity of arthritis. Nonantioxidant properties of tea polyphenols also may contribute to their overall effectiveness in disease prevention. Evidence is mounting to suggest theanine can help anticancer chemicals (such as doxorubicin) kill tumor cells more specifically, but how it does this is still unknown.

antioxidant a substance that prevents damage from oxygen or other reactive substances

Economic Importance of Tea

Worldwide tea production was over 3 million metric tons (worth about $8 billion to growers) in 1998. India and China produced about half of this output, most of it for internal consumption. Whereas China and Japan produce mainly green and partially fermented teas, the other growers supply mainly black teas. The world's largest importers of tea are the United King-

TEN LARGEST TEA-IMPORTING COUNTRIES, 1998	
Principal Consumers	Quantity Imported (in metric tons)
United Kingdom	175,829
Russian Federation	150,225
Pakistan	111,559
United States	96,646
Egypt	65,457
Japan	45,442
Iran	40,000
Germany	38,664
Poland	36,569
Sudan	23,843

SOURCE: Food and Agriculture Organization of the United Nations.

dom, the Russian Federation, Pakistan, and the United States. However, Ireland, the United Kingdom, Turkey, Syria, and Iran are the world's leading consumers on a per-capita basis.

The estimated wholesale value of the U.S. tea industry has risen from $1.84 billion in 1990 to $4.60 billion in 1999 and continues to rise, according to the U.S. Tea Association. The largest segment of that growth was due to the increased consumption of ready-to-drink teas, which rose from $0.2 billion to $1.65 billion dollars during this period.

Herbal Tea

Herbal teas, like regular tea, have been consumed for eons and for the same calming, stimulating, or medicinal reasons. Tea made from chamomile flowers steeped for more than thirty minutes in boiling water is said to be a sedative that also soothes indigestion. Tea made from the rootstock of comfrey was believed to heal broken bones and be a good gargle for sore throat and cure bleeding gums. Tea made from sassafras root bark or leaves may have the pleasant taste of root beer but will cause the drinker to perspire and urinate. This tea has been used for everything from a blood-thinner to a cure for rheumatism and syphilis. Indeed, teas can be made from many plants and may contain thousands of active **compounds**. The U.S. Food and Drug Administration recommends that herbal tea drinkers use caution. Chamomile can cause a severe allergic reaction in people with sensitivity to ragweed, asters, or chrysanthemums. Liver disease has been reported in drinkers of large amounts of comfrey tea (ten or more cups a day), and comfrey contains a chemical that causes cancer in rats. The major chemical components of sassafras tea, once used to flavor root beer, were banned thirty years ago because they caused cancer in rats. The use of caution means moderation—daily consumption of any particular herbal tea for not more than two to three days at a time—and avoidance—by children, pregnant women, or nursing mothers. SEE ALSO COFFEE; ECONOMIC IMPORTANCE OF PLANTS; HERBALS AND HERBALISTS; HERBS AND SPICES; MEDICINAL PLANTS.

Robert Gutman

compound a substance formed from two or more elements

Bibliography

Gutman, Robert L., and Beung-Ho Ryu. "Rediscovering Tea: An Exploration of the Scientific Literature." *HerbalGram* 37 (1996): 33–48.

Snider, S. "Herbal Teas and Toxicity." *FDA Consumer* 25, no. 4 (1991): 30–33.

Tyler, Varro. *The Honest Herbal: A Sensible Guide to the Use of Herbs and Related Remedies.* New York: Pharmaceutical Products Press, 1993.

Willson, Kenneth C., and Michael N. Clifford, eds. *Tea: Cultivation and Consumption.* London: Chapman & Hall, 1992.

Terpenes

compound a substance formed from two or more elements

hemiterpene a half terpene

pigments colored molecules

carotenoid a colored molecule made by plants

Terpenes (terpenoids) are a very large family of plant **compounds** that play a variety of roles in many different plants. All terpenes are constructed from isoprenoid units by biochemically unusual pathways involving highly reactive intermediates. The **hemiterpene** isoprene, which contains five carbons (one isoprene unit), is a gas emitted into the atmosphere by many plant species, where it plays a role in the chemistry of ozone production. A monoterpene (monoterpenoid) contains ten carbons (two isoprene units); a sesquiterpene, fifteen carbons (three isoprene units); a diterpene, twenty carbons (four isoprene units). Triterpenes (thirty carbons) are important structural components of plant cell membranes. Many plant **pigments**, including the yellow and red **carotenoids**, are tetraterpenes (forty carbons). Natural rubber is a polyterpene containing many isoprene units. The monoterpenes and sesquiterpenes are common components of the essential oils of herbs and spices (peppermint, lavender), of flower scents (rose), and of turpentine derived from the resin of evergreen trees.

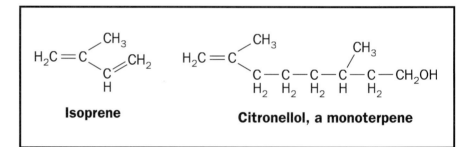

Isoprene

Citronellol, a monoterpene

The bark on a Western yew tree in Washington's Mount Rainier National Park. The cancer-fighting drug taxol was first isolated from yew bark.

These compounds have important uses as flavorings and perfumes, as well as intermediates in the production of other commercial products like solvents and adhesives. Many terpenes play roles as plant hormones and in the chemical defenses of plants against microbial diseases and insect **herbivores**; many others have important medicinal properties. Artemisinin is a sesquiterpene drug derived from traditional Chinese herbal medicine that is useful for treating malaria, and taxol obtained from yew trees is a diterpenoid that is highly effective in treating cancer. Recent advances in molecular biology have made it possible to genetically engineer terpene metabolism in plants for agricultural, industrial, and pharmaceutical purposes. SEE ALSO ATMOSPHERE AND PLANTS; FLAVOR AND FRAGRANCE CHEMIST; HORMONES; MEDICINAL PLANTS; OILS, PLANT-DERIVED; PIGMENTS; POISONOUS PLANTS.

Rodney Croteau

herbivore an organism that feeds on plant parts

Bibliography

Cane, David E., ed. *Comprehensive Natural Products Chemistry*, Vol. 2: *Isoprenoids Including Carotenoids and Steroids*. Oxford: Elsevier, 1999.

Croteau, Rodney B. "The Discovery of Terpenes." In *Discoveries in Plant Biology*, Vol. I, eds. Shain-Dow Kung and Shang-Fa Yang. Singapore: World Scientific, 1998.

Langenheim, Jean H. "Higher Plant Terpenoids: A Phytocentric Overview of Their Ecological Roles." *Journal of Chemical Ecology* 20 (1994): 1223–80.

Tissue Culture

For a variety of purposes, plant cells, tissues, organs, and whole plants can be grown in labware containing a medium composed of defined molecules. Tissue culture media provide water, minerals, vitamins, hormones, carbon sources, and antibiotics depending on the plant material being cultured. Since most living plant cells are **totipotent,** scientists can manipulate the medium to regenerate whole plants from even a single genetically engineered plant cell or from a cluster of cells from a rare plant. Hormones in the medium determine what plant parts form from the cells (callus) in the culture: Auxins stimulate root formation and cytokinins stimulate shoot formation. The medium may contain agar, agarose, phytagel, or other **polysaccharides** to form a semisolid gel to support the plant tissue. The container must be colorless if photosynthesis is to be supported, and the light source should not be too intense to avoid the greenhouse effect inside the container. If the container is not ventilated, a carbon source such as sucrose will have to be used. Tissues must be subcultured periodically to avoid **solute** concentration buildup if the container is ventilated. Antibiotics may be used to keep the culture clear of bacteria, fungi, or other contaminants or to select for genetically engineered cells. Tissue culture techniques are also used to generate large numbers of genetically identical plants for agricultural applications, or to generate additional plants of rare or endangered species. SEE ALSO GENETIC ENGINEERING; PROPAGATION; REPRODUCTION, ASEXUAL; TRANSGENIC PLANTS.

Ross Koning

totipotent capable of forming entire plants from individual cells

polysaccharide a linked chain of many sugar molecules

solute a substance dissolved in a solution

A petri dish of Venus's-flytrap tissues.

Bibliography

Hopkins, W. G. *Introduction to Plant Physiology*, 2nd ed. New York: John Wiley & Sons, 1999.

Raven, Peter. H., Ray F. Evert, and Susan E. Eichhorn. *Biology of Plants*, 6th ed. New York: W. H. Freeman and Co., 1999.

Tissues

Plants are a composite of cells organized into tissues. Every cell within these tissues has a unique size and shape and is surrounded by a wall composed of a complex carbohydrate called cellulose. Plant cells are attached to each other by a gluelike substance, pectin, that cements them together.

All plant tissues originate in meristems, which are unique tissues of the plant body. They are the sites of new cell production and of the genetic events necessary for cellular specialization. Meristems can be categorized by their locations. **Apical meristems** are composed of groups of dividing cells at the tips of shoots (branches) and roots. When meristematic cells produced by apical meristems begin elongating, they are classified as primary meristems. There are three types of primary meristems: protoderm, ground meristem, and procambium. As primary meristem cells stop dividing and begin differentiating, their classification changes to primary tissues. There are four primary tissues: the epidermis derived from protoderm, the ground tissues (parenchyma, sclerenchyma, and collenchyma) derived from ground meristem, and two types of vascular tissue—xylem and phloem—derived from procambium. Primary tissues have specific positions in the plant body and specific functions.

As the organs of the plant body age, the stems and roots often grow wider. Growth in width is called lateral growth and is initiated by secondary meristems. There are two types of secondary meristems: the vascular cambium and the cork cambium. The vascular cambium is located near the outside of stems and roots. Its function is to produce new cells that become part of the secondary xylem and secondary phloem tissues. The cork cambium is located near the outer edge of older stems and roots, and it produces the periderm, which is part of the bark.

The Concept of the Tissue System

In 1875, German scientist Julius von Sachs introduced a scheme that is still used today: the tissue systems. A tissue system is composed of tissues with a common position and function. The plant body has three tissue systems: dermal, ground, and vascular.

The dermal tissue system forms the outer, protective covering of the plant body. In young plants, the dermal tissue system consists of epidermis tissue. In some plants and plant organs, the epidermis remains intact

apical meristem region of dividing cells at the tips of growing plants

---

PLANT TISSUE SYSTEMS

Tissue System	Tissue	Meristem Origin	Primary or Secondary?	Function
Dermal	Epidermis	Protoderm	Primary	Protect against pathogen entry and inhibit water loss
	Periderm	Cork cambium	Secondary	Protect against pathogen entry and inhibit water loss
Ground*	Parenchyma	Ground meristem†	Both	Storage of food products and water, photosynthesis, and other basic processes
	Collenchyma	Ground meristem	Both	Structural support of leaves and young stems
	Sclerenchyma	Ground meristem	Both	Structural support of plant organs
Vascular	Xylem	Procambium and vascular cambium	Both	Movement of water and dissolved materials throughout the plant
	Phloem	Procambium and vascular cambium	Both	Movement of sugars throughout the plant

* The gound tissues are located mostly in the cortex and pith of stems, roots, and fruits and in the mesophyll of leaves.

† These tissues can also appear as component parts of other complex tissues, e.g., parenchyma cells are an important part of the xylem.

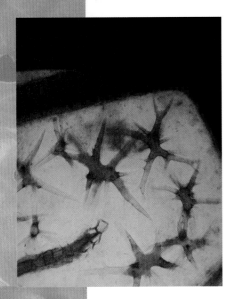

A *Trochodendron* leaf whose tissues have been cleared to reveal the elaborate sclereids.

polyhedral in the form of a polyhedron, a solid whose sides are polygons

succulent marked by fleshy, water-holding leaves or stems

chloroplast the photosynthetic organelle of plants and algae

polymer a large molecule made from many similar parts

throughout the life of the plant. However, in some aging plants the epidermis is torn and an underlying secondary meristem, the cork cambium, produces a secondary tissue, the periderm. The periderm, which consists of stacks of cells with waxy cell walls, then takes over the protective function. Although both the epidermis and the periderm occupy the same outer position and perform the same protective functions, they are derived from different meristems.

The ground tissue system consists of tissues that are produced by the ground meristem, one of the primary meristems. It is responsible for functions such as photosynthesis and storage and is comprised of the following tissues: parenchyma, collenchyma, and sclerenchyma.

The vascular tissue system is composed of the water- and mineral-conducting tissue, xylem, and the food-conducting tissue, phloem. Primary vascular tissue is produced by the primary meristem, procambium, and secondary vascular tissue is produced by the vascular cambium.

The Ground Tissue System

The ground meristem produces the primary ground tissue of stems, leaves, roots, flowers, and fruits. The three ground tissues are parenchyma, collenchyma, and sclerenchyma. In stems and roots, ground tissues are located in the cortex and pith. The cortex lies between the epidermis and vascular tissue; the pith, when it is present, is located in the center of the organ. In leaves, the ground tissue is called mesophyll and is located between the upper and lower epidermis.

Parenchyma Tissue. Typically the cortex of roots, the pith of stems, the mesophyll of leaves, and the edible parts of fruits are composed entirely of parenchyma tissue. Although parenchyma cells making up this tissue vary in size, shape, wall structure, and function, generally they are living at maturity, are **polyhedral** in shape, have thin cell walls, and perform many of the basic physiological functions of the plant. Parenchyma tissue in the cortex and pith regions of roots and stems are often specialized for storage of carbohydrates, proteins, fats, and oils. Water is stored in the mesophyll of **succulent** plants. Cells in the mesophyll of leaves contain **chloroplasts** and are specialized for photosynthesis. There are two types of leaf mesophyll: palisade mesophyll is composed of columnar-shaped cells near the upper surface of the leaf, and branched spongy mesophyll is next to the lower surface.

Collenchyma Tissue. Collenchyma is a supporting tissue found in the leaves and young stems. This tissue provides strong but flexible support. Collenchyma cells are living at maturity and have plastic walls that can expand with the growing organ. Collenchyma cells are elongated and have a thick cell wall containing large amounts of pectins and water. The unevenly thickened cell wall is a definitive feature of collenchyma cells. Strands of collenchyma tissue often occur just beneath the epidermis in stems and petioles and between vascular bundles and the epidermis in leaves.

Sclerenchyma Tissue. Sclerenchyma is also supporting tissue, but its cells are generally dead at maturity. Sclerenchyma cells have thick cell walls that are usually lignified. Lignin is a complex **polymer** that is impervious to water. Supporting sclerenchyma tissue is common in plant organs that have completed elongation growth. Lignification of the cell walls of sclerenchyma cells not only makes them harder and stronger, it also makes them resistant to decay. There are two major categories of sclerenchyma cells: sclereids and fibers. Generally sclereids are short and irregular in shape, while fibers are long and narrow. Sclereids often have massively thick lignified cell walls. Columnar-shaped sclereids form the outer seed coat tissue of bean seeds; clusters of sclereids give pear fruits their gritty texture; branched sclereids are sometimes present in the mesophyll of leaves; and strands of elongate fibers are important structural components in the cortex, associated with vascular tissue, or extending from vascular bundles to the epidermis in leaves. Extremely long fibers from flax and ramie plants, and other plant species, are commercially important sources of fibers used in the manufacture of ropes and fabrics.

The Dermal Tissue System

The dermal tissue system consists of the epidermis and the periderm. The epidermis is a primary tissue derived from the protoderm, and the periderm is a secondary tissue derived from the cork cambium.

The Epidermis. The epidermis is a complex tissue and is the outermost covering of the primary plant body. It provides a protective barrier between the internal tissues of the plant and the outside. Although the epidermis is generally one cell layer thick, it is made up of several different cell types. From the surface, epidermal cells appear slightly elongated in stems and leaf petioles and irregular in outline like jigsaw puzzle pieces. Epidermal cells generally lack chloroplasts and their outer surfaces are covered by a waxy layer, the **cuticle**. The cuticle reduces water loss from the plant surface. Another common epidermal cell type, the guard cell, contains chloroplasts. Guard cells are always present in pairs surrounding a pore. A pair of guard cells and its pore is called a stoma (plural, **stomata**). The exchange of gases essential for photosynthesis, such as the uptake of carbon dioxide, and the loss of water vapor through **transpiration** occur through stomata. Stomata are common in photosynthetic leaves and other photosynthetic organs, such as herbaceous stems and aerial roots. In many plants, stomata are surrounded by cells that differ from ordinary epidermal cells; these are called subsidiary cells. Another common type of epidermal structure is the trichome. Trichomes may be single-celled outgrowths, such as root hairs, or they may be simple or complex multicellular structures.

The Periderm. The periderm forms the outer covering over most older stems and roots. It may have a few to several cell layers. During the first year of secondary growth, the cork cambium produces tabular-shaped cork cells to the outside, and the epidermis is crushed and destroyed. Additional cork cambia may arise deeper within the plant body in subsequent years. In some plants, cylinders or arcs of cork cambia activate, resulting in multiple layers of periderm tissue. Suberized (waxy) cork cells form an impervious outer plant tissue.

The Vascular Tissue System

Xylem and phloem are complex tissues comprising the vascular tissue system. Vascular tissue is present in all stems, roots, leaves, flower parts, seeds, and fruits.

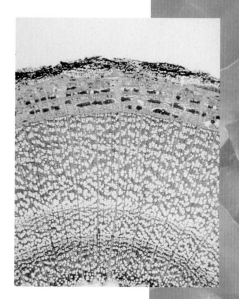

Cross-section of a three-year-old elderberry (*Sambucus*) stem. The vascular cambium is visible at the boundary between the greenish phloem and the brownish secondary xylem. The cork cambium is just inside the dark cells at the stem surface.

cuticle the waxy outer coating of a leaf or other structure, providing protection against predators, infection, and water loss

stomata openings between guard cells on the underside of leaves that allow gas exchange

transpiration movement of water from soil to atmosphere through a plant

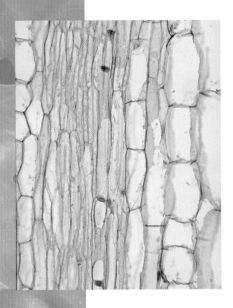

Cucumber (*Cucurbita*) stem section. Strands of phloem are shown in at the center; the cells have red-stained end walls.

Xylem Tissue. Xylem is a complex tissue specialized to transport water and dissolved minerals. In young organs, xylem is formed from a primary meristem, the procambium, and is a primary tissue. In older stems and roots it continues to form as a secondary tissue from a secondary meristem, the vascular cambium.

The two cell types specifically charged with water transport are vessel members and tracheids. These cell types are fundamentally similar in that both are dead at maturity and tend to have thickened cell walls with openings called pits. A pit is a thin region in the wall that extends between two adjacent cells. Pits allow water to pass freely, but air bubbles are trapped. Differences are apparent in the end walls of these cells. The end walls of tracheids are tapered and cells connected end-to-end communicate through pits. The end walls of vessel members are completely open. The open area is called a perforation plate. When two vessel members are connected end-to-end they form an open tube called a vessel, which is typically composed of several vessel members connected end-to-end. The end walls of vessel members at opposite ends of a vessel have non-perforated end walls, so a vessel is like a length of tube with closed ends. The non-perforated end walls do have pits, allowing water and minerals to easily pass from one vessel to another, but restricting air bubbles to a single vessel. Because air bubbles block the movement of water, any that form inside tracheids and vessel members create conducting problems. Isolating air bubbles and restricting their movement improves conducting efficiency of tracheids and vessels.

Xylem is composed of several different cell types. In addition to vessel members and tracheids, parenchyma cells and fibers are commonly found in xylem tissue. Parenchyma cells and fibers contribute to the transport and support function of this tissue.

Phloem Tissue. The complex phloem tissue transports sugars from leaves to the other plant organs. It is a primary tissue in young organs, and in older stems and roots it is a secondary tissue formed from the vascular cambium.

Within phloem tissue, cells that collect and transport sugars are called sieve-tube members (STMs). STMs are living cells joined end-to-end to form a tubelike structure called a sieve tube. Each STM has a unique attachment to another important phloem cell type called a companion cell. Companions cells help regulate cellular functions inside STMs and assist in loading and unloading sugars into STMs. Other cells in the phloem include parenchyma cells and fibers. Fibers act to strengthen and support the weight of the phloem and surrounding tissues, and phloem parenchyma cells store water and help with loading and unloading sugars. SEE ALSO ANATOMY OF PLANTS; CELLS, SPECIALIZED TYPES; MERISTEMS; SACHS, JULIUS VON; VASCULAR TISSUES.

Thomas L. Rost and Deborah K. Canington

Bibliography

Esau, Katherine. *Anatomy of Seed Plants*, 2nd ed. New York: John Wiley & Sons, 1977.

Mauseth, James D. *Plant Anatomy*. Menlo Park, CA: Benjamin/Cummings Publishing Company, Inc., 1988.

Rost, Thomas L., Michael G. Barbour, C. Ralph Stocking, and Terence M. Murphy. *Plant Biology*. Belmont, CA: Wadsworth Publishing Company, 1998.

Tobacco

Tobacco, *Nicotiana tabacum* (family Solanaceae), is grown in over one hundred countries around the world, in both temperate and tropical climates. It is a stout, rapidly growing annual, 1 to 2 meters tall. It has large, ovate to oblong leaves and produces numerous white-pinkish flowers with corollas about 2 centimeters long. Tobacco seeds are minute, so in commercial production seedlings are generally produced in plant beds or in greenhouses and transferred to the field. Production and harvesting methods differ widely depending on the type of tobacco being produced, but most tobacco types require significant inputs of time, labor, and pest management. Both underfertilization and overfertilization may cause inferior quality leaves. Commonly, whole plants of air-cured tobaccos are cut off just above the ground and hung in barns for several months until cured. Leaves of bright, flue-cured tobaccos are typically harvested individually as they ripen. These leaves are cured by heating them up slowly through yellowing, drying, and stem-drying steps. Piles of cured tobacco leaves are generally sold at auction in large, well-lighted warehouses.

Tobacco is believed to have originated in northwestern Argentina and adjacent Bolivia. Native peoples undoubtedly used it for centuries before Europeans colonized the Americas. Christopher Columbus was introduced to tobacco by the Arawaks on October 11, 1492, when he first visited the Caribbean islands. Tobacco smoking spread throughout Europe in the second half of the sixteenth century. Tobacco soon became the most important commercial crop in Colonial America, and the tobacco trade directly contributed to the success of the first permanent English settlement at Jamestown, Virginia.

Differences in cultural practices and diverse climatic and soil conditions produce several different types of tobacco that are used in various smoking and chewing products. The major types of tobacco are bright (flue-cured), light air-cured (burley), dark air-cured, fire-cured, oriental, cigar wrapper, and cigar filler. Burley and flue-cured tobaccos are the primary tobacco types

A Zimbabwean man working in a tobacco field. During harvest, tobacco is cut and placed on sticks and later taken to cure in drying barns.

used in the manufacture of cigarettes, and they account for most of the U.S. production. Over 90 percent of the tobacco grown in the United States is from North Carolina and Kentucky, but Maryland, South Carolina, Virginia, Georgia, Florida, Ohio, and Tennessee also produce substantial amounts of this crop.

Tobacco leaves are covered with trichomes (hairs) that have multicellular glands on their tips. These glandular trichomes produce a sticky resinous material that contains many of the flavor and aroma components. Tobacco also produces many internal, secondary components, including pyridine **alkaloids**. The most important alkaloid is nicotine, which acts as a stimulant to the user and is addictive. Nicotine is quite toxic, and products containing nicotine were used as early insecticides. The adverse health effects of smoking, including nicotine addiction and the increased risks of cancer, emphysema, and heart attack, are well documented.

Tobacco has been extensively used as a model system in many basic scientific studies. Pioneering work in **quantitative** genetics, tissue culture techniques, plant **physiology**, and genetic engineering have utilized the unique characteristics of tobacco, which has been referred to as "the white rat of the plant world." SEE ALSO ALKALOIDS; ECONOMIC IMPORTANCE OF PLANTS; POISONOUS PLANTS; PSYCHOACTIVE PLANTS; SOLANACEAE.

D. Michael Jackson

alkaloids bitter secondary plant compounds, often used for defense

quantitative numerical, especially as derived from measurement

physiology the biochemical processes carried out by an organism

Bibliography

Goodspeed, T. H. *The Genus Nicotiana*. Waltham, MA: Chronica Botanica Co., 1954.

Tso, T. C. *Production, Physiology, and Biochemistry of the Tobacco Plant*. Beltsville, MD: Ideals, Inc., 1990.

Torrey, John

American Botanist and Chemist
1796–1873

John Torrey was one of the major botanists in the United States in the nineteenth century. As a youth he chose medicine as a career and in 1816 entered the College of Physicians and Surgeons in New York City. Before graduation he joined with his professors to become one of the founders of the Lyceum of Natural History of New York (now the New York Academy of Sciences). In 1818, he received his medical degree (M.D.). His first academic position was as an Assistant Surgeon and Professor of Chemistry and Mineralogy at West Point, New York. A few years later he was invited to return to his alma mater, and there he taught chemistry from 1827 to 1855. He also taught at Princeton from 1830 to 1854.

From 1820 until his death in 1873, Torrey was recognized as the major botanist of the innumerable plant collections by the many military expeditions sent by the U.S. government into the western lands of the Louisiana Purchase. Torrey assorted, arranged, named, diagnosed, and described new species by thousands. His life is in many ways a bibliography of early North American botanical exploration and discovery.

Torrey's first expedition papers analyzed plants collected during the Major Long Expedition in 1820 to the Platte River. Torrey's third paper

PROF. JOHN TORREY.

John Torrey.

on the tundra plants of the Rocky Mountains used the Natural System of classification, which had been recently introduced from Europe and had jarred many American traditionalists who still followed the Sexual System of classification as developed by Linnaeus. This shift was a major step forward in the American scientific community.

In 1832, Torrey met Asa Gray, a medical doctor. They commenced on a fruitful working relationship, and eventually Gray became one of America's greatest botanists, and, ultimately, Torrey's successor. "Torrey and Gray" were soon a kind of botanical statement as today "Watson and Crick" are.

In 1839, Torrey was named State Botanist of New York, and in 1843 he published the first *Flora of New York State*.

Retired from Columbia College in 1855, Torrey, then a trustee of the college, offered the administration his huge, well-known herbarium, asking to remain on campus as the curator. The college accepted and he lived on the campus until his death in 1873. Also a known mineralogist, Torrey was hired as the **assayer** of the New York Mint, which he continued until his death.

assayer one who performs chemical tests to determine the composition of a substance

In 1860, with the looming danger of the Civil War, Torrey volunteered to take temporarily the Smithsonian Herbarium to his New York Columbia Herbarium, where it was assumed to be safer. Torrey kept the materials for nine years, greatly increasing the number of **specimens** and working hard to improve the collection. The National Herbarium owes much to Torrey.

specimen object or organism under consideration

In 1867, a Manhattan botanical club, which was assisted by Torrey and which held its meetings in his herbarium, was renamed The Torrey Botanical Club (now Society). Today it is a national scientific society and holds its meetings in the New York Botanical Garden's Torrey Room. Torrey's herbarium is now the heart of the world-class Herbarium of the New York Botanical Garden. SEE ALSO GRAY, ASA; LINNAEUS, CAROLUS; TAXONOMIST; TAXONOMY, HISTORY OF.

Lawrence J. Crockett

Bibliography

Rodgers, Andrew Denny III. *John Torrey: A Study of North American Botany*. Originally published in 1942. New York: Hafner Pub. Co., 1965.

Transgenic Plants

Transgenic plants are produced when a gene from one plant is inserted into the **genome** of another. For the gene to work properly in the transgenic plant, it must be engineered to have a promoter before its start codon (to turn it on) and a terminator after its end (to turn it off). Generally the gene also needs some deoxyribonucleic acid (DNA) at either end that will allow it to be inserted into the host genome. The transfer DNA (tDNA) from the bacterial microbe *Agrobacterium* is used routinely for this purpose. Also required is an antibiotic resistance gene that will allow the transgenic plant cells to be recovered from a mixture with untransformed cells. In a typical project, the desired gene is engineered with the correct elements, placed in

genome the genetic material of an organism

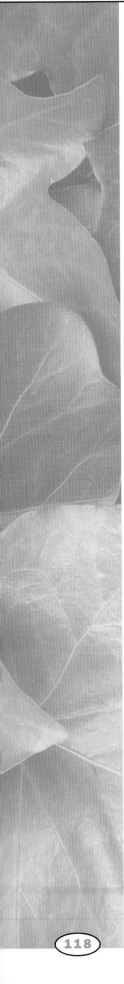

vector carrier, usually a carrier who is not affected by the thing carried

a plasmid **vector**, and then inserted into *Agrobacterium* cells. *Agrobacterium* is then used to infect the plant cells with the plasmid vector. The tDNA allows the desired gene and the antibiotic resistance gene to be incorporated into the plant cell's genome. The transgenic cells are selected using the antibiotic in a tissue culture medium; only cells having antibiotic resistance as a result of transformation will survive on this medium. Finally, the transgenic cells are manipulated with the hormones in the tissue culture medium to regenerate whole transgenic plants. To be sure that the gene is inserted and is functioning, botanists will check for the presence of inserted DNA using a **Southern blot** and will confirm the presence of modified ribonucleic acid (RNA) with a **Northern blot**. Development of an expected phenotype in mature plants can also confirm the insertion. SEE ALSO BREEDING; GENETIC ENGINEER; GENETIC ENGINEERING; MOLECULAR PLANT GENETICS; TISSUE CULTURE.

Ross Koning

Southern blot a technique for separating DNA fragments by electrophoresis, and then identifying a target fragment with a DNA probe

Northern Blot a technique for separating RNA molecules by electrophoresis, and then identifying a target fragment with a DNA probe

Bibliography

Hopkins, W. G. *Introduction for Plant Physiology*, 2nd ed. New York: John Wiley & Sons, 1999.

Raven, Peter. H., Ray F. Evert, and Susan E. Eichhorn. *Biology of Plants*, 6th ed. New York: W. H. Freeman and Co., 1999.

Watson, J. D., M. Gilman, J. Witkowski, M. Zoller. *Recombinant DNA*, 2nd ed. New York: W. H. Freeman and Company, 1992.

Translocation

solute a substance dissolved in a solution

Translocation is the process within plants that functions to deliver nutrients and other molecules over long distances throughout the organism. Translocation occurs within a series of cells known as the phloem pathway, or phloem transport system, with phloem being the principal food-conducting tissue in vascular plants. Nutrients are translocated in the phloem as **solutes** in a solution called phloem sap.

The predominant nutrients translocated are sugars, amino acids, and minerals, with sugar being the most concentrated solute in the phloem sap. Various cell types utilize these nutrients to support their requirements for life or store them for future use. Because translocation is responsible for the delivery of nutrients to developing seeds and fruits, this process is critical to the achievement of optimal crop yield. It also accounts for the ultimate nutritional composition of plant foods important to humans.

ions charged particles

compound a substance formed from two or more elements

pathogen disease-causing organism

Various plant hormones, proteins, and nucleic acids are also moved throughout the plant via translocation. Hormones act as cues, or signals, to stimulate distant cells to alter their pattern of growth or to adjust various cellular machinery. Examples of such signaling events would be the conversion of vegetatively growing cells into reproductive tissues (i.e., flowers); an enhancement in the ability of root cells to absorb needed mineral **ions** from the soil (e.g., iron, zinc); or the synthesis of specific **compounds** in distant leaves to deter **pathogens** (e.g., insect feeding, fungal infections). Thus, the translocation of information molecules makes it possible for plants to correctly sense and respond to varying conditions or challenges in their environment.

Pathway of Translocation

The movement of sugars and other molecules generally follows a path that originates in plant organs where sugars (the primary solute) are made and terminates in regions where these nutrients are utilized. The organs where the pathway begins are called source regions, or sources, and the ends of the pathway are referred to as sink regions, or sinks. The predominant organ for the manufacture of sugars is the leaf, which can take in carbon dioxide and light energy to produce sugars through the process of photosynthesis. These sugars can be used locally by the leaf or can be translocated to the rest of the plant. Leaves are generally considered the primary source regions, but it should be noted that only fully expanded, mature leaves can act as sources. Newly emerging leaves are unable to fully nourish themselves with their own sugar production, and thus they act as sink regions until they reach full maturity.

Other sink tissues include root systems, which cannot carry out the process of photosynthesis and must be fed by the leaves, and developing reproductive tissues, such as seeds and fruit, which store nutrients for future use. Additional storage organs that are translocation sinks and which are important human food crops include tubers (e.g., potatoes and yams) and tap roots (e.g., carrots and beets).

Plant structures that lie between terminal source and sink tissues, such as the stem of an herbaceous plant, the trunk and branches of a tree, or the petiole of a leaf, make up the translocation pathway. All of these structures contain numerous living cells that require nourishment and, thus, these pathway tissues can also function as sinks. In certain cases, however, they serve dual roles, because in some plants (e.g., cereals such as rice and wheat) the stems act as temporary storage organs for nutrients. At late stages in the plant's life cycle, these stems are converted to source regions that provide nutrients for the developing seeds. Various non-leafy green tissues that can conduct photosynthesis also can serve as sources; pea pods, for instance, can translocate sugars and other nutrients to the developing pea seeds.

Structure of Phloem Cells

The translocation of molecules via the phloem pathway is dependent on the functioning of specialized cells that are distributed in an organized manner throughout the plant. The cells that conduct nutrients over long distances are called sieve elements, of which there are two types: sieve cells, which are found in **gymnosperms** (e.g., conifers and cycads), and sieve-tube members, which are found in **angiosperms** (i.e., monocots and dicots). Sieve elements are narrow, elongated cells that are aligned in long columns that extend from source to sink regions within the plant. Sieve elements are living cells and thus possess a plasma membrane at their periphery, just inside the cell wall. However, they do not contain a nucleus at full maturity, and possess only a few cellular **organelles** (e.g., **mitochondria**, **endoplasmic reticulum**). The lack of a nucleus and most other cellular structures means that the cell interior is rather open. This serves to make sieve elements good conduits for long-distance solution flow.

The term *sieve* in the various names refers to the clusters of pores, or sieve areas, that perforate the common cell walls between adjoining sieve

gymnosperm a major group of plants that includes the conifers

angiosperm a flowering plant

organelle a membrane-bound structure within a cell

mitochondria cell organelles that produce ATP to power cell reactions

endoplasmic reticulum membrane network inside a cell

Micrograph of phloem fibers and sieve tubes from the stem of a bryony plant (*Bryonia*), through which nutrients are transported.

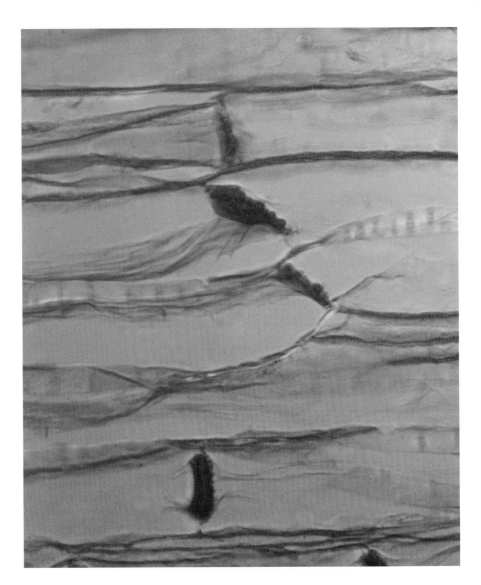

elements and which interconnect these cells. The interconnection is possible because the plasma membrane of each sieve element is extended as a tube through each sieve pore. In sieve cells, the pores are narrow and the structure of the sieve areas is fairly uniform on all walls of the cell. Sieve cells are usually arranged with long, tapering, overlapping ends, and most of the sieve areas are concentrated on these overlapping regions. In sieve-tube members, narrow-pored sieve areas exist, but some walls also possess much larger pores. The areas with larger pores are called sieve plates, and are usually located on the end walls. These end walls tend to be less obliquely oriented than the ends of sieve cells, and in many species can be situated almost perpendicular to the long, side walls. Sieve-tube members are organized end-to-end in columns of cells called sieve tubes, thus forming a long tubular network throughout the plant. Their larger end-wall pores means that the phloem sap can be more readily translocated over long distances.

The cell walls of sieve elements are considered primary walls, as they are composed chiefly of cellulose. The pores of the sieve areas and sieve plates are additionally lined with a substance called callose, which is a **poly-saccharide** consisting of glucose units. The role of callose in the vicinity of

polysaccharide a linked chain of many sugar molecules

pores is to act as a sealing agent in the case of injury to the phloem pathway. When a plant structure is damaged by mechanical stress, such as wind, or by biological attack, such as feeding by an insect, the plant could lose nutrients if these were to "bleed" from the cut end of the sieve elements. This usually does not happen, because following injury callose is rapidly deposited within the wall region of sieve pores. This deposition constricts the interconnecting tube of plasma membrane and thereby blocks the pore. With time, the plant can generate new sieve elements around the cut area to reestablish translocation within that column of phloem cells.

As mentioned earlier, sieve elements do not contain a nucleus in their mature state, yet in some species sieve elements are known to live for decades. How is this possible? Sieve elements are always found to be associated with specialized accessory cells that contain all the components commonly found in living plant cells, including a nucleus. For sieve-tube members, these specialized cells are called companion cells, and the specialized association is referred to as the sieve element-companion cell complex. Companion cells are very densely filled with organelles, and thus they are not structurally suited for the long-distance translocation of nutrients. Functionally, however, companion cells are extremely important, as they are responsible for the coordinated movement of molecules into and out of the sieve-tube members. These molecules include not only substances translocated throughout the plant, but also proteins and nucleic acids that are needed to maintain the life and functions of the sieve-tube member. The movement of these molecules occurs through elaborate channels called plasmodesmata that interconnect companion cells and sieve-tube members. Less specialized plasmodesmata also exist between certain other cell types. Although very important, the movement of molecules through plasmodesmata is poorly understood, and scientists are currently focusing much attention on this area of plant biology.

Accessory cells are also found associated with the sieve cells of gymnosperms, where they are called **albuminous** cells. The albuminous cells are structurally comparable to and perform a role similar to that of companion cells.

albuminous gelatinous, or composed of the protein albumin

Loading and Unloading of Sugars and the Pressure-Flow Mechanism

With the presence of a continuous, membrane-bound pathway, phloem sap can flow from source to sink regions within the plant. But how do the components of the phloem sap get in to or out of the pathway, and what is the mechanism, or driving force, that moves the solution? As noted earlier, the predominant solute in phloem sap is sugar, and in many species the translocated sugar is sucrose. For these species, sucrose is manufactured primarily in the photosynthetic mesophyll cells of the leaf, from where it must be transported to the minor veins of the phloem system. Sucrose can move to the minor veins using an **intracellular** pathway, referred to as symplastic movement, or it can diffuse through a path along the cell walls, a process known as apoplastic movement. In either case, sucrose is eventually pumped into sieve elements through an active, energy-requiring process called phloem loading. The amino acids and mineral ions found in phloem sap also are said to be "phloem loaded."

intracellular remaining inside cells

osmosis the movement of water across a membrane to a region of high solute concentration

What phloem loading accomplishes is to create a very high concentration of solutes within the interior of the sieve elements in a source region. Because the sieve element interior is surrounded by a largely nonpermeable plasma membrane, it is able to retain these solutes within the cell. On the other hand, the plasma membrane also contains special channels that make it highly permeable to water molecules and water molecules enter by **osmosis.** This is critical because the movement of water into sieve elements increases the hydrostatic pressure (i.e., the water pressure) of phloem sap within these cells. The end result is that the interior of the sieve element becomes pressurized with respect to other cells of the source region.

At the sink end of the pathway, an opposite chain of events is occurring. Sugars and other solutes are moved out of the sieve elements through a process called phloem unloading, as these solutes are used by other cell types for growth, metabolism, or storage. In response to this release of solutes water molecules move out of the sieve element, and the result is a localized decrease in the sieve element hydrostatic pressure. The lowered pressure within the sieve elements of the sink region in conjunction with the higher pressure within the sieve elements of the source region creates a **gradient** of pressure along the length of the interconnected phloem pathway. Because of this pressure gradient, a bulk flow of phloem sap occurs from high to low pressure, or from source to sink tissues. The pressure gradient remains in place, even as flow proceeds, as long as solutes are continuously loaded into and unloaded from the pathway. This translocation process is known as the pressure-flow mechanism.

gradient difference in concentration between two places

It should be noted that the larger the gradient in pressure between two points in the pathway, the greater the potential for translocation of phloem sap. Thus, actively photosynthetic tissues have the ability to load more sugars into the pathway, creating higher localized sieve element pressures in these regions. Similarly, an actively growing sink tissue, which is consuming/removing large quantities of sugars and other solutes from the pathway, will create lower localized sieve element pressures in this region, which will help sustain translocation flow to the sink.

Ways to Determine the Chemical Nature of Phloem Sap and the Rate of Translocation

Scientists have been interested in studying the composition of phloem sap for many years because of its importance to plant growth and development. Unfortunately, access to pure phloem sap is difficult for a number of reasons: sieve elements are very narrow cells (approximately 10^{-8} meters in diameter), they are embedded within other tissues of the plant, and most plants have a sealing mechanism that prevents the loss of phloem sap upon cutting. Certain techniques do exist, however, that get around these problems. One approach involves the use of aphids, which are insects that feed selectively upon the contents of sieve elements but do not induce a sealing reaction. Scientists allow an aphid to insert its stylet, a long tube-shaped mouth part, into the side of a sieve element within a stem or leaf. The insect is then sacrificed and removed, with its stylet still inserted in the plant tissue, either by using a razor blade or a laser burst. Because the phloem sap is pressurized, phloem sap will flow out the cut end of the stylet for a short period of time and it can be collected for analysis. Standard analytical chemistry techniques are then used to determine carbohydrate and mineral composition of the phloem sap, or more modern techniques of protein chemistry and molecular biology are used to quantify and characterize the protein and nucleic acid composition of the collected solution.

The rate of translocation in different plants, especially in response to various environmental conditions, is also of interest to scientists who study phloem function. Because sugars are the predominant component of the phloem sap, researchers have used radioactively labeled sugars to monitor and quantify phloem translocation. A source leaf, for instance, can be exposed to radioactive carbon dioxide within a sealed glass chamber, allowing it to convert the carbon dioxide to radioactive sugars via the process of photosynthesis. These sugars are phloem loaded and can be monitored as they move throughout the plant using external radiation detectors, or sink regions can be harvested and analyzed for radioactivity following some period of translocation. In either case, rates of translocation can be quantified, and the effect of various physical or biological factors on translocation rate can be determined. These types of studies help scientists determine ways to improve plants, both in terms of yield and nutritional quality. SEE ALSO LEAVES; PHOTOSYNTHESIS, CARBON FIXATION AND; STEMS; VASCULAR TISSUES.

Michael A. Grusak

Bibliography

Baker, Dennis A., and John A. Milburn. *Transport of Photoassimilates.* Essex, England: Longman Scientific and Technical, 1989.

Evans, Lloyd T. *Crop Evolution, Adaptation and Yield.* Cambridge: Cambridge University Press, 1993.

Lucas, William J., Biao Ding, and Chris van der Schoot. "Plasmodesmata and the Supracellular Nature of Plants." *New Phytologist* 125 (1993): 435–76.

Zamski, Eli, and Arthur A. Schaffer. *Photoassimilate Distribution in Plants and Crops: Source-Sink Relationships.* New York: Marcel Dekker, 1996.

Transpiration *See Water Movement.*

Tree Architecture

Most people are familiar with the shoot systems of trees but few people know much about their root systems; fewer still know much about how the architecture of trees helps them stand up against the major natural force threatening to topple them: the wind.

Trees typically have a single woody trunk that projects many meters vertically from the ground. Only toward the top of the tree does repeated branching form ever-narrower branches and twigs, which together make up the compact crown where most of the leaves are held.

It is a commonly held fallacy that the root systems of trees belowground are mirror images of the shoot systems aboveground. The roots do branch, and they extend radially about the same distance from the trunk as the crown, but here the resemblance ends. There is no belowground equivalent of the trunk because the central tap roots of most trees grow very slowly as the tree matures. Instead the system is dominated by several woody **lateral** roots, which grow horizontally away from the tap root, before branching into smaller, more

lateral to the side of

distal further away from

fibrous, **distal** roots. The vast majority of the root system therefore grows within a meter of the soil surface where the distal roots obtain resources from the nutrient-rich topsoil. Only the tap root and a few sinker roots that grow vertically down from the woody laterals penetrate down to the subsoil.

Mechanics of Wood

The form of the woody parts of trees, both above and belowground, is strongly influenced by their mechanical function of raising the leaves above other plants, and so outcompeting them for the light. The material of which trees are made—wood—is apparently well designed to withstand the overturning forces caused both by the weight of the tree itself and, more importantly, the wind. Whenever the crown of a tree is blown by the wind the branches and trunk are both bent. This results in longitudinal **tensile forces** being set up along the windward side, and longitudinal compressive forces being set up on the leeward side. Both forces are efficiently resisted by the walls of the wood cells, which are arranged longitudinally like densely packed drinking straws.

tensile forces forces causing tension, or pulling apart; the opposite of compression

Mechanics of the Shoot System

The aboveground architecture also plays a key part in preventing toppling. The single trunk is better at holding up the crown against strong wind forces than many separate trunks with the same total diameter. This is because the rigidity of a beam is proportional to the fourth power of its radius, whereas its weight is only proportional to the square of the radius. Hence a single trunk will be twice as stiff as two trunks with the same combined mass, and will be able to hold up the crown even in high winds. The

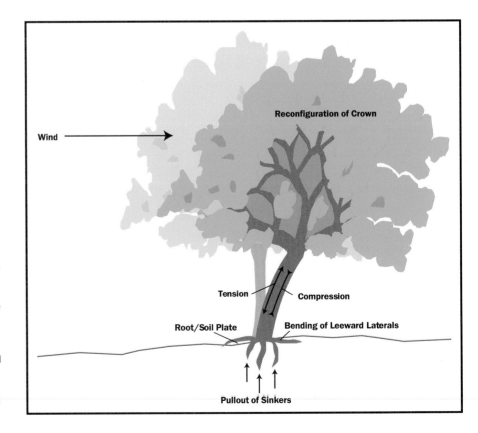

Mechanical changes that occur when a tree is blown by the wind. Above ground the trunk is bent, putting the leeward side into compression and the windward side into tension, while the crown reconfigures. Meanwhile, below ground the leeward laterals are bent and a root/soil plate is levered out of the ground, pulling up the sinker roots.

much thinner branches and twigs from which the crown is formed, meanwhile, are much better able to bend away from the wind. This reconfiguration helps to streamline the crown and reduce the forces it experiences. This streamlining can be improved by two other mechanisms. First, the leaves themselves reconfigure, folding up together with others along the same branches to reduce drag, while the lobed and pinnate leaves of some broad-leaved trees can each individually roll up into a streamlined tube. Second, in exposed areas wind forces reduce growth on the windward side of the crown and bend branches permanently to leeward. This produces a crown with a permanently streamlined "flagged" shape that presents less drag to the prevailing wind.

Mechanics of the Root System

Even with all of these drag-reducing mechanisms, overturning forces are still transmitted to the trunk and hence to the root system. Fortunately this is also well designed to resist failure. The extensive woody laterals prevent the leeward side of the root system from being pushed into the ground. Instead, the likely mode of failure is for a windward root/soil plate to be levered out of the ground. This movement is resisted strongly by the weight of the soil plate and the resistance of the leeward roots to bending. But the greatest component of anchorage is provided by the sinker and tap roots, which must be pulled out of the ground; their vertical orientation, reminiscent of that of tent pegs, is ideal to resist this movement. The result is that a fairly small woody root system can effectively anchor a large tree.

Growth Responses of Trees

The genetically determined architecture of trees is therefore ideally suited to resist mechanical failure. Their mechanical efficiency is further improved by a growth response called thigmomorphogenesis. The higher the mechanical stresses imposed on trees by the wind, the more wood they lay down to strengthen their structure; consequently trees growing in exposed areas develop shorter but thicker trunks, branches, and roots. In contrast, if a tree grows in a sheltered wood it will grow taller and thinner, improving its chances of reaching the light. A further refinement, which was first suggested by Claus Mattheck, is that the growth response is locally controlled. Wood is laid down fastest in the areas subject to the highest stress and these areas are consequently strengthened. This response ensures that there are no weak areas in the tree, and it also improves the mechanical design. It automatically ensures that branches are joined to the trunk with smooth fairings and that the vulnerable sides of wounds heal fastest. Research also suggests that it might be responsible for the growth of one of the most bizarre features of rain forest trees: the platelike buttresses that join the superficial lateral roots to the trunk like angle brackets.

The combination of efficient material design, good above and below-ground architecture, and adaptive growth responses have ensured that trees can survive even in the face of terrible gales. Moreover, they are the largest and most spectacular of all biological structures. Giant redwoods can grow well over 100 meters tall, weigh over 1,000 tons, and live for over 1,000 years. SEE ALSO ANATOMY OF PLANTS; ROOTS; TREES.

Roland Ennos

Bibliography

Ennos, A. Roland. "The Function and Formation of Buttresses" *Trends in Ecology and Evolution* 8 (1993): 350–51.

Mattheck, Claus. *Trees: The Mechanical Design* Berlin: Springer-Verlag, 1991.

Vogel, Steven. *Life's Devices.* Princeton, NJ: Princeton University Press, 1987.

Trees

Trees are plants with an erect perennial stem at least 4 meters (13 feet) tall, a diameter measured at breast height (1.3 meters or 4.5 feet) of at least 7.5 centimeters (3 inches), and a distinct crown of leaves or leafy branches. This definition is widely used by foresters and forest ecologists to divide woody plants into trees, shrubs (smaller plants, often with clustered stems), and vines (plants not self-supporting and usually without a distinct crown). However, plant species are not constrained to fit definitions, thus plants of the same species may grow as trees in some areas and as shrubs in others, especially at the edge of the species' range where growing conditions are harsh. Thus lodgepole pine, valued by Native Americans for its tall, straight "lodge poles," becomes a sprawling shrub near timberline in the Rocky Mountains and on sandy beach dunes of the Pacific Coast.

Trees are usually woody; that is, their stems are composed largely of densely packed, elongated, thick-walled cells (secondary wood) produced by a cylindrical growing center, the vascular cambium, that surrounds the stem underneath the bark. Typically the secondary cambium adds new wood throughout the life of the tree, gradually increasing the trunk diameter as the crown grows larger and taller. Notable exceptions occur in tree ferns, cycads, palms, and a few other plants that reach tree dimensions while producing little or no secondary wood. In these plants neither trunk diameter nor crown size increases much with age once the single apex of large compound leaves reaches mature size. However, mechanical support by the stem is often aided by an encircling band of tightly packed roots (e.g., tree ferns) or persistent leaf bases (e.g., cycads and palms).

Trees are regularly associated with certain plant groups such as the oak (oak, beech, chestnut) and pine (pine, spruce, fir, hemlock, etc.) families; however, most families of **vascular plants** contain some tree species. Residents of temperate climates are often surprised to find that tomatoes, violets, shrubby sumacs, and even grasses have close tropical relatives that are trees. Today's diminutive club mosses, spike mosses, and quillworts (order Lycopodiales) and horsetails (order Equisetales) are the remaining relatives of huge scale-trees (Lepidodendrales) and giant horsetails (Calamitales) that dominated swampy forests in the Carboniferous (coal-forming) period of Earth's history three hundred million years ago.

Trees are the giants of the plant world. Among the tallest ever measured was a Douglas-fir (*Pseudotsuga menziesii*) in Washington that measured 117 meters (385 feet) tall. California claims the tallest living tree, a coast redwood (*Sequoia sempervirens*) 112.6 meters tall, but competing for this distinction are trees of *Eucalyptus* in Australia, which are perhaps a few meters

vascular plants plants with specialized transport cells; plants other than bryophytes

taller. In total weight or **biomass**, probably no other species has ever produced larger trees than the Big Tree redwoods (*Sequoiadendron giganteum*) of the California Sierra Nevada Mountains. These colossal giants (to 88 meters) maintain their basal diameter of 5 to 10 meters with little taper to the base of their crown over 40 meters high.

Big Tree redwoods are also among the oldest known trees, reaching ages of more than three thousand years. However, the oldest trees in North America and perhaps in the world are quite modest in size (10 × .6 meters). These belong to a species called bristlecone pine (*Pinus aristata*). The oldest bristlecone pines (more than forty-six hundred years) grow in dry rocky soils near timberline in southern California where the harsh growing season is very short and annual growth in trunk diameter is often less than 0.2 millimeters. Age estimates of bristlecone pines are obtained by counting annual growth rings in studies collectively termed dendrochronology. The science of dendrochronology uses tree-ring information to reconstruct long records of climatic history and to date prehistoric wooden structures.

biomass the total dry weight of an organism or group of organisms

Trees and Forest Types

Trees greatly modify the habitat in which they live, by their shade and by their litter of fallen leaves. Typically light-loving tree species occupy the highest section of the forest, the overstory or canopy, with shade-tolerant species below. Species inhabiting these forest layers differ according to geographic and **topographic** location and associated climate and soils. Forest composition may also differ with age, and to some degree, by chance, that is, which species managed to get its seeds to the area first or survived the longest. Despite these causes of forest differences, it is possible to recognize common associations of particular plant species with particular habitats. For example, ecologists and foresters usefully refer to Oak–Hickory forests as tending to occur on dry upland areas in the east central United States, with Beech–Maple forests tending to occur on more moist north-facing slopes. Many such forest communities are recognized across the country and are often named for their two most common overstory trees.

Perhaps the greatest contrast between forest types in temperate regions is between deciduous broad-leaved and evergreen coniferous forests. In deciduous forests light penetrating to the forest floor in early spring supports a diverse array of spring wildflowers and ferns whereas the perennially dark floor of a dense coniferous forest supports many fewer species.

Tree Uses

It is hard to overestimate the importance of trees in their many uses for lumber, landscaping, shade, ornamental plantings, and windbreaks. In all of these uses diversity among trees is important. Wood types differ in strength, weight, hardness, color, figure, and other characteristics. Even taste can be important where cooking utensils or food storage is the use. Usually fast-growing trees such as cottonwood produce light, soft wood relative to that produced by slow-growing trees such as oaks and hickories. Conifers (often called softwoods) are preferred for construction lumber where ease of cutting, carrying, and nailing is important. The heavier, stronger, tougher wood of flowering trees (hardwoods) is preferred for railroad ties, strong crates, hardwood floors, tool handles, and sports equipment. Because of their attractive color and grain, hardwoods are also favored for fine furniture, cabinetry, and wall panels. All species and all sizes of trees are used for pulp and wood flakes for paper products and synthetic lumber.

Tree Diversity

To meet the need for diverse wood products, naturally diverse forests must be maintained. More than 600 species of native trees occur in North America north of Mexico, but much greater diversity occurs in tropical forests. A single hectare (2.5 acres) of Amazon forest may contain more than 200 different species whereas the most diverse U.S. forests contain about 20 species per hectare. In addition to variety in wood products, tree diversity aids forests in resisting diseases and pests and promotes wildlife diversity through the variety of foods, dens, and perching and nesting sites they maintain. Tropical rain forests' tree canopies support an array of epiphytic mosses, ferns, and flowering plants and hundreds of insect and larger animal species that scientists are just beginning to explore.

topographic related to the shape or contours of the land

Tree Identification

Tree identification is necessary for forest and tree management and a rewarding hobby enjoyed by many nonprofessionals. Books aiding identification and describing trees, tree uses, and tree care are available for nearly all areas, ranging in coverage from local regions to entire countries and continents. Leaf size, shape, and arrangement on the stem are often sufficient to identify a tree, but twigs, bark, fruits, cones, and sometimes flowers may be required. Winter identification of deciduous trees by twigs and bark presents a special challenge, but one that can be mastered by the dedicated student. SEE ALSO CHESTNUT BLIGHT; CONIFEROUS FORESTS; CONIFERS; DECIDUOUS FORESTS; DENDROCHRONOLOGY; DUTCH ELM DISEASE; FORESTER; FORESTRY; GYMNOSPERMS; PALMS; RAIN FOREST CANOPY; RAIN FORESTS; RECORD-HOLDING PLANTS; SEQUOIA; TREE ARCHITECTURE; WOOD ANATOMY; WOOD PRODUCTS.

Donald R. Farrar

Bibliography

Brockman, C. Frank. *Trees of North America.* New York: Golden Press, 1986.

Farrar, John Laird. *Trees of the Northern United States and Canada.* Ames, IA: Iowa State University Press, 1995.

Harlow, William. M., Donald J. Leopold, and Fred M. White. *Harlow and Harrar's Textbook of Dendrology*, 9th ed. New York: McGraw-Hill Inc., 1996.

Little, Elbert L. *The Audubon Society Field Guide to North American Trees.* New York: Chanticleer Press, 1980.

Preston, Richard J., Jr. *North American Trees*, 4th ed. Ames, IA: Iowa State University Press, 1989.

Trichomes

Trichomes are single or multicellular outgrowths of the plant epidermis and collectively constitute the pubescence (hairiness) of the plant surface. These epidermal hairs in many plant species are specialized for defense against attack by insects and mites. The mode of defense used by trichomes is determined by whether they are nonsecretory or glandular, as well as their density, length, shape, and degree of erectness. When present on the plant surface at high densities, **nonsecretory** trichomes create a physical barrier to insect feeding on the underlying surface or internal tissues. Barrier defense is an important element of resistance to leafhoppers in cultivated crop plants such as alfalfa (*Medicago*), cotton (*Gossypium*), and soybean (*Glycine*). Although not defensive, similar but downward-pointing trichomes in the upright tube of the carnivorous pitcher plant (*Sarracenia*) create a "lobster pot" effect preventing the escape of prey. Beans (*Phaseolus*) have evolved fish-hook-shaped trichomes that help to anchor their climbing vines but the hooked feature is also defensive because leafhopper and aphid pests are impaled and captured by these hairs. The most elegant specializations of plant hairs for defense are glandular trichomes, which secrete adhesive materials that physically entrap and immobilize insects and mites or which contain toxic or deterrent substances. Trichomes of this type are common in the nightshade family (Solanaceae) and plant breeders have created new varieties of potatoes (*Solanum*) and tomatoes (*Lycopersicon*) that resist insect pests because of glandular hairs on their leaves and stems. Other crop plants in

nonsecretory not involved in secretion, or release of materials

A praying mantis perched atop a pitcher plant. Trichomes in the upright tube of the carnivorous pitcher plant (*Sarracenia*) create a "lobster pot" effect, preventing prey from escaping.

which glandular trichomes are being used to breed for pest resistance include alfalfa, strawberry (*Fragaria*), sunflower (*Helianthus*), and tobacco (*Nicotiana*). SEE ALSO CARNIVOROUS PLANTS; DEFENSES, CHEMICAL; DEFENSES, PHYSICAL; HALOPHYTES; LEAVES.

Ward M. Tingey

Bibliography

Juniper, Barrie E., and T. Richard E. Southwood, eds. *The Plant Surface and Insects.* London: Edward Arnold Ltd., 1986.

Tropisms and Nastic Movements

Unlike animals, plants cannot move to more favorable locations. Instead, plants survive by adjusting their growth to their local environment. A major way this is done is by sensing the directions of environmental signals such as light and gravity. This sensory information is then used to orient the direction of growth toward or away from a stimulus in a process called a tropism. By these mechanisms, shoots grow up from the ground and into the light. This enhances photosynthesis and biomass by increasing the amount of sunlight absorbed by chlorophyll. The raised stature of the plant also promotes pollination and seed dispersal, and increases plant competitiveness.

Tropisms are different from nastic movements. Like tropisms, these plant movements are influenced by environmental cues. But the direction of a nastic movement is independent of where the signal comes from, and most such movements are temporary. Nastic movements are more specialized in function and distribution than tropisms. For example, some **insectivorous** plants capture prey by moving trap organs together.

insectivorous insect-eating

Tropisms should not be confused with tactic movements found in many microorganisms, such as a unicellular green alga that moves toward the light (phototaxis). Because plants are not **motile**, only part of their body grows in the direction of a stimulus.

motile capable of movement

Tropisms

In tropisms, the growth of a plant organ is oriented by an environmental signal. Usually the organ grows toward or away from the stimulus. The former is considered to be a positive tropism, whereas growth away from a stimulus is a negative tropism. Houseplants on a windowsill grow toward the light by positive phototropism. Stems that emerge from seeds buried in the soil grow upward away from gravity by negative gravitropism. Tropisms can also occur at other angles with respect to a stimulus. Modified stems, called rhizomes, grow along the surface of the soil at right angles to gravity, such as in iris plants. Phototropism and gravitropism are by far the most important and widespread of tropisms in plants. In some plants and organs, other physical stimuli, including touch, temperature, and water, can orient growth as well.

Tropisms allow plants to adjust the direction of growth when their environment changes. For example, when a seedling is turned on its side, the root grows gradually downward creating a curvature, an example of positive gravitropism. This occurs in the growing region of the root, a region located close to the root tip. Once the root tip points downward again, the root stops curving and the subsequent growth is straight. After a region responds to a stimulus its orientation is usually permanent. For example, the curvature remains for the life of the root.

In most cases, only the growing regions of the plant are capable of tropisms. There are many such regions in a plant. The tips of stems and roots contain meristems, regions where new growth occurs. Cell divisions in meristems contribute to the elongation of stems and roots, and form new stem branches. Each stem branch is capable of phototropism and gravitropism. Their collective responses help determine the overall shape of the shoot.

By definition, a tropism involves a stimulus that contains some directional information. With gravity, both the direction and strength of the stimulus are uniform. In contrast, the direction of illumination constantly changes, and even heavily shaded plants receive at least some light from all directions. Two conditions must be fulfilled for a tropism to occur in such situations. First, the stimulus must exist in a **gradient** with respect to the plant. Thus the light is brighter on one side of a shoot, or there is more

gradient difference in concentration between two places

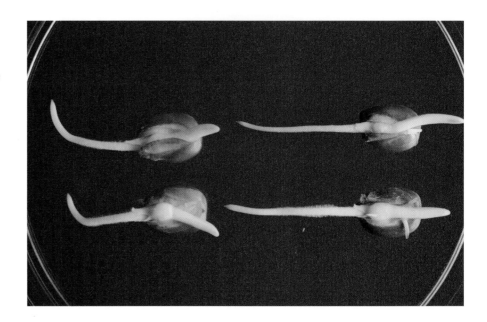

Form corn seedlings sprouting in a petri dish. When seedlings are turned on their sides, their roots grow gradually downward and create a curvature, an example of positive gravitropism.

water on one side of a root. Second, this gradient must last long enough to influence growth. Because a tropism results in a permanent change in position, it would be wasteful for plants to respond to short-lived changes in the environment.

All tropisms include two major stages, sensing and the growth response. The direction of the signal must first be sensed. Sensing means that physical information in the environment is somehow converted into biological information in the plant. This biological information is then interpreted in the growing zone resulting in guided growth. When a root is placed on its side, it curves downward because the upper side of the root grows faster than the lower side. The end result is that directional information about a physical signal is translated into different rates of elongation to produce directional growth.

Much of the research done on tropisms tries to understand how sensing and differential growth take place. Although scientific understanding of these processes is still incomplete, there have been some important advances, especially since the late 1980s and the development of genetic analytical techniques.

Phototropism. Phototropism is one of the most significant tropisms for plant survival because it positions shoots where more light for photosynthesis is available. It is especially important during seedling emergence and when plants are shaded unequally.

Sensing. One of the first important studies of plant tropisms was of phototropism by Charles Darwin and his son Francis over a century ago. They tried to determine where light is sensed in the coleoptile, which is a leaflike sheath that covers and protects emerging grass seedlings. As in current phototropism experiments, they exposed the seedling to light from just one side. Coleoptiles whose tips were cut off or were kept dark by a hood did not grow toward the light. However, if the tips were covered by transparent material or if the base of the coleoptile was kept dark, then the coleoptiles grew towards the light. They concluded that the tip of the coleoptile is largely responsible for sensing the light during phototropism.

However, coleoptiles are an unusual organ found only in grasses. In stems, the most common phototropic organ, the site of sensing seems to be more spread out. Even stems whose tips were covered and darkened were capable of bending toward a light from the side.

One reason why the precise site of stem sensing is unclear is that the pigment responsible was unknown for many years. Light acts when it is absorbed by a pigment-containing molecule. For many years, scientists knew that blue light is the most effective color in causing phototropism. Green or red light were either ineffective or caused only slight bending. Scientists tried to find pigments isolated from plants that especially absorbed blue light, but that did not absorb green or red light. Two types of **pigments** had these characteristics, **carotenoids** and flavin-containing molecules. But this information was not enough to identify the particular molecule responsible. One reason for this is that there are many types of blue-light responses in plants in addition to phototropism.

As in so many other areas in plant biology, recent studies using the model plant *Arabidopsis* resulted in rapid progress in phototropism. A mutant was isolated, non-phototropic 1 (nph1), which fails to grow towards blue light. The affected gene was found to code for a protein that binds to a flavin molecule. It is likely that the combination of this protein and a flavin pigment molecule is responsible for phototropism. The identification of this molecule provides an important foundation for future research.

Growth response. The Darwins showed that light sensing takes place in the tip of the oat coleoptile and that phototropic curvature occurs several millimeters below the tip. This separation suggests that there is communication between these two regions. Subsequent studies provided evidence for a chemical signal that moves from the tip to the base. This signal can move through the water in a gelatin block. In 1926 Fritz Went isolated this chemical and named it "auxin." In the 1930s, auxin was identified as the molecule indoleacetic acid (IAA). IAA was found to cause many effects in plants in addition to phototropism, and auxin is now recognized as a major plant hormone.

Auxin moves from the tip of a coleoptile towards the base. Under some circumstances, auxin can also move from one side of the organ to the other. A major effect of auxin is to stimulate stem elongation. When coleoptiles are illuminated, auxin moves from the lighted side to the dark side. This **lateral** movement occurs in or close to the tip of the coleoptile. The auxin then moves down to the growing part of the coleoptile. The presence of more auxin in the dark side causes that side to grow more than the illuminated side. This causes the coleoptile to curve towards the light. Similar events appear to occur in stems.

In summary, a light gradient is sensed by a flavo-protein pigment molecule. Light absorption somehow increases the amount of auxin on the dark side of the growing zone, which causes more growth on that side and curvature towards the light.

Phototropism and solar tracking. It is often easy to detect the effects of phototropism in nature. It can be seen when stems emerge from the

pigments colored molecules

carotenoid a colored molecule made by plants

lateral away from the center

ground, or when part of a plant is more shaded than another. Unequal shading can be produced by other plants, or by objects such as rocks, logs, and walls. In contrast, phototropism is rare in a mature plant that is growing in an open, sunny area. This is because the movement of the sun during the day and the season is too fast and variable to allow phototropism to develop.

However, in a few plants, the leaves do follow the sun during the day. The leaf stalk twists during the day so that the leaf blade keeps facing the sun. The result is an increase in photosynthesis. This phenomenon, known as solar tracking, is not a tropism because there is no permanent change in the direction of growth.

Gravitropism. Gravitropism helps plants flourish. The importance of gravitropism can be illustrated by the maize (corn) plant. The upward growth of the stem raises the leaves up. The base of each leaf is also oriented by gravitropism at a set angle. The result is that the leaves become located in the position that exposes them to the most light. The raised stature also allows the plant to compete with other plants for sunlight. The upward growth also positions the pollen-producing flowers at the top of the plant where it can be carried by the wind to pollinate the female flowers (the silks). Some roots grow straight down, but others only do so after the roots reach a certain length. The result is well-branched root system that is distributed throughout the soil in a coordinated manner. This positions the roots near new supplies of water and minerals. It also anchors the plant to prevent it from falling over. Gravitropism helps optimize the growth of all of parts of this maize plant.

Gravitropism has a profound effect on the shape and form of many plants in addition to maize. Its influence is obvious in plants with pronounced vertical stems such as pine trees. Careful observation will also reveal subtler effects of gravitropism in other plants. Many stems and branches that are not vertical still grow at a more or less set angle with respect to gravity. This angle may vary with age and lengthwise position, but if a regularity is observed, it is likely to represent gravitropism. Indeed, gravitropism probably shapes plant life more than any other tropism.

Sensing. How might a plant sense the direction of gravity? Unlike light, gravity cannot be absorbed by a molecule. Instead it must act on some dense structure. A century ago, German scientist Gottlieb Haberlandt observed that gravitropic organs contain heavy starch-filled bodies that fall or sediment. These bodies are **organelles** called amyloplasts. They are a type of plastid, special organelles in plants that include **chloroplasts**. Starch is dense and thus amyloplasts are heavy. Amyloplasts are found in many different locations in plants. But they only sediment in specific locations, such as the rootcap at the tip of roots and the starch sheath in the growing zone of stems. Haberlandt proposed that the falling of amyloplasts triggers gravity sensing. Most data support Haberlandt's hypothesis. For example, all natural, gravitropic organs have sedimented amyloplasts. And stems of the *Arabidopsis* "scarecrow" mutant are not gravitropic probably because they lack both a starch sheath and sedimented amyloplasts.

But this hypothesis was challenged when several mutants were found that do not have any starch but that are still gravitropic. This shows that starch is not necessary for gravitropism. However, the gravitropism in these

organelle a membrane-bound structure within a cell

chloroplast the photosynthetic organelle of plants and algae mutants is defective, and they are much less sensitive to gravity than normal plants. This suggests that starch normally plays a role. But how might starchless mutants sense gravity, albeit poorly? Even these mutants still have plastids. Perhaps the starchless plastids can still function mechanically in sensing, but more poorly because they are lighter. When starch is present, there is more mass and probably a stronger signal as well.

Growth response. The mechanisms of gravitropic curvature are thought to be similar to that of phototropic curvature. The lower side of a stem probably has more auxin than the upper side, resulting in faster growth on the lower side and upward curvature. In roots it is thought that a higher concentration of auxin inhibits rather than stimulates growth. Thus more auxin on the lower side would cause it to grow more slowly than the upper side, causing downward curvature. The involvement of auxin in gravitropism is strongly supported by the isolation of two different types of mutants in *Arabidopsis* whose roots are not gravitropic. In each case, the mutated gene was found to disrupt the function of proteins that are probably necessary for auxin transport.

Thigmotropism. Thigmotropic organs grow around an object that touches them. When a tendril on a pea leaf or the stem of a vine come in contact with an object, they cling to and wrap around it. Thigmotropic shoots avoid the expense of making their own support tissue. Instead, they depend on an object to help them climb and position their leaves into the light. Vines and tendrils typically locate a support through slow sweeping movements. These movements stop when contact is made with a support. Pea tendrils respond to contact in two stages. They first quickly coil around the object through changes in water pressure of the cells. The outer part of the tendril then grows much faster than the inner part. The mechanism of sensing is not known. But in some plants, contact induces a wave of electrical signals down the organ. And thigmotropic organs might contain specialized stretch receptors such as membrane proteins that allow **ions** to pass through them when they are mechanically stimulated. Roots are also capable of thigmotropism. This probably helps them grow around hard objects in the soil.

ions charged particles

Roots also exhibit hydrotropism and electropism, which are growth responses to gradients in water and voltage. Electropism probably does not operate in nature, but scientists have used it to study root growth, including on NASA's Space Shuttle. Hydrotropism is obviously adaptive to guide root growth towards water. But root growth is much more affected by gravitropism, and in some plants by negative phototropism, than by hydrotropism.

Nastic Movements

In tropisms the direction of the stimulus controls the orientation of growth, and the effect is more or less permanent. In nastic movements, the direction of the response results from the structure of the organ, and it is only the quality, rather than the direction, of the stimulus that triggers a response. Most nastic movements are reversible. Unlike tropisms, which are found in virtually all plants, nastic movements are mostly found in specialized plants and organs.

Nyctinasty and Photonasty. The quality and intensity of light can cause organ movements. In many plants, such as legumes (members of the bean

An open sensitive plant (*Mimosa*).

family), the leaves move downward or fold at the end of the day. In other plants such as tulips, it is the flowers that close as night approaches. These nyctinastic or "sleep" movements are triggered by changes in the color and intensity of sunlight at the end of the day. The organs open up again around dawn.

The "light-off" and "light-on" signals interact with internal rhythms in plants. The light signals are used to set the internal clock, but are not actually required for movement. Once the rhythm is set, the leaves open and close in the dark at the correct times for several days.

Sleep movements help protect leaves and flowers from damage at night, but many plants survive quite well without such movements. Some plants that grow in the shade show photonastic movements. The leaves of wood sorrel (*Oxalis*) fold up during the day if the sun gets too strong This protects the pigments in the leaves from sun-induced damage. Leaves can also curve downwards in response to other signals (epinasty) such as when roots are flooded. Although light and dark can cause nastic movements in plants, there are no gravinastic movements. Gravity is not useful as a signal of changes in the environment because it is constant in presence and extent.

Thigmonasty and Seismonasty. Organ movements can also be induced by touch (thigmonasty) or shaking (seismonasty). These two types of nastic movements are related but distinct. The leaves of the sensitive plant, mimosa, fold up when they are touched by a falling object or an animal. They also close when they are shaken such as by the wind. This closing may reduce evaporation from the leaf in a strong wind, or discourage an animal from eating it.

In contrast, the closing of the specialized leaves of the Venus's-flytrap plant is only triggered by touch, not shaking. The inner surface of this trap has several trigger hairs. These hairs will only activate the closing of the trap if they are touched several times in rapid succession. One touch has no effect. In this way, the trap is only likely to close if an insect is exploring the leaf, but not if the insect flies away after a single contact. Trap clo-

A closed sensitive plant. In an example of thigmonasty, the leaves of the mimosa fold up when they are touched by an animal, perhaps to discourage the animal from eating it.

sure in turn triggers the release of **enzymes** that break down the prey in the trap. Many insectivorous plants grow in bogs where little combined nitrogen (nitrate, nitrite, or ammonia) is available because the water is so acidic that decomposition is slowed. The digestion of the prey in traps is important to the plant because it provides a source of combined nitrogen for protein synthesis.

enzyme a protein that controls a reaction in a cell

The rapid movements of the sensitive plant and the Venus's-flytrap share similar mechanisms. Stimulation causes a wave of electrical signals called action potentials that are similar to, but slower than, nerve impulses in animals. These signals change the **turgor** (water) **pressure** inside cells causing some cells to expand and other cells to contract. After a certain amount of time without any further stimulation, the turgor changes again and the organs open up.

turgor pressure the outward pressure exerted on the cell wall by the fluid within

Thigmonastic movements also help spread seeds. When ripe fruits of touch-me-not plants (impatiens) are touched, they snap open with such force that they spread seeds into areas where the new seedlings will not be shaded by the parent plant. SEE ALSO CARNIVOROUS PLANTS; FLAVONOIDS; HORMONAL CONTROL AND DEVELOPMENT; HORMONES; PLASTIDS; RHYTHMS IN PLANT LIFE.

Fred D. Sack

Bibliography

Chen, Rujin, Elizabeth Rosen, and Patrick Masson. "Gravitropism in Higher Plants." *Plant Physiology* 120 (1999): 343–50.

Hart, James W. *Tropisms and Other Plant Growth Movements.* London: Unwyn Hyman Ltd., 1990.

Motchoulski, Andrei, and Emmanuel Liscum. "*Arabidopsis* NPH3: A NPH1 Photoreceptor-Interacting Protein Essential for Phototropism." *Science* 286 (1999): 961–64.

Taiz, Lincoln, and Eduardo Zeiger. *Plant Physiology*, 2nd ed. Sunderland, MA: Sinauer Associates, 1998.

Wilkins, Malcolm. *Plant Watching.* New York: Facts on File, 1988.

COMMON PLANT SPECIES FOUND IN TUNDRA

Sedges (Cyperaceae family)
Carex aquatilis
Carex bigelowii
Eriophorum vaginatum
Eriophorum scheuchzeri

Grasses (Poaceae family)
Poa arctica
Poa alpina
Alopecurus alpinus
Arctophila fulva
Deschampsia caespitosa
Arctagrostis latifolia
Trisetum spicatum

Willows (Salicaceae family)
Salix arctica
Salix rotundifolia
Salix reticulata

Blueberries and Heaths (Ericaceae family)
Vaccinium uliginosum
Vaccinium vitis-idaea
Arctostaphylos alpina
Arctostaphylos uva-ursi
Ledum palustre
Cassiope tetragona
Empetrum nigrum

(continued on page 139)

ecosystem an ecological community together with its environment

angiosperm a flowering plant

aeration introduction of air

Tundra

Tundra is treeless vegetation found at high elevation in mountains and in many landscapes of the Arctic. Collectively, **ecosystems** with tundra vegetation are grouped into the tundra biome. A distinction is usually made between Arctic tundra, which exists beyond the northern limit of tree growth, and alpine tundra, which exists above the elevational limit of tree growth in mountains. In mountains of the far north this distinction becomes blurred as tree lines descend to meet the northern limits of trees. Tundra is dominated by low-growing, perennial **angiosperms** and by mosses and lichens. Larger plants include grasses, sedges, herbs, and dwarf shrubs, but it is the lack of trees that most characterizes tundra. Plant species commonly found in tundra include sedges; grasses, including many of the genus *Poa*; willows, blueberries, dwarf birch, and other deciduous and evergreen shrubs or other low-growing woody plants; a host of herbaceous perennials, including many species of the genus *Saxifraga*, many members of the buttercup family, and several members of the rose family.

Climates of tundra regions are generally cold, and temperatures are commonly below freezing for much of the year, limiting the period of plant growth to a briefly thawed period during summer. Annual precipitation in tundra regions includes snow, although the amount of snow and total precipitation varies tremendously among different areas of tundra. Tundra regions are snow-covered much of the year, but the depth and duration of snow cover differs between locations. The tundra of the Sierra Nevada of California is characterized by heavy winter snow and little summer precipitation, while tundra in the Rocky Mountains generally has less snow but dependable summer rains. Precipitation in tundra regions of the Arctic is generally extremely low, often less than that found in many desert regions, but most soils nonetheless remain moist and may be waterlogged.

It may seem paradoxical that Arctic regions may have less precipitation than many deserts, yet they are covered by moist or wet tundra with numerous ponds and lakes. Low temperatures explain this apparent contradiction, limiting effects of evaporation and contributing to the formation of frost. Soils and materials beneath tundra are considered to be in a permafrost (perennially frozen) condition when they remain frozen for periods of two or more years. Permafrost is a condition generally characteristic of Arctic tundra soils but is also descriptive of isolated portions of the soils of alpine tundra regions. The top of the permafrost layer occurs a few inches to several feet below the surface and can extend downward for many feet. Permafrost soils drain poorly since the frozen soil is as impermeable as rock, and because much of the Arctic landscape is flat. A small amount of precipitation in the Arctic may be held in the thawed soil near the tundra surface, creating a moist landscape dotted with ponds and lakes. The flat Arctic plain is also patterned with irregularly shaped ridges and depressions, called polygons.

Soils of tundra regions are slow to develop due largely to low temperatures and limited periods of thaw. A variety of soil types may develop with time, depending primarily upon moisture or the degree of saturation. Wet tundra, with poor **aeration** and slow decomposition of plant roots, mosses, and other organic matter, produces highly organic soils, while well-drained tundra is characterized by mineral soils. The soil supply of nitrogen, phosphorus, or other elements needed by plants is often low and limits plant growth, and thus tundra regions generally support fewer animals than grasslands and other biomes. Despite low net primary productivity (plant growth potentially available to grazing animals), tundra regions support a variety of mammals, birds, and insects. Arctic tundra herbivores (plant eaters) include caribou, musk ox, lemmings, insects, hares, ground squirrels, and ptarmigan. Carnivores (eaters of insects or other animals) include many birds, especially waterfowl and shorebirds (that appear only in summer), snowy owls, jaegers, and ravens. Other important Arctic carnivores include Arctic fox, wolves, brown bears, and mosquitoes. The fauna of alpine tundra is variable but commonly includes various species of mountain sheep and/or mountain goats, voles and other rodents, bears, eagles, insects, and a variety of animals characteristic of the adjacent forests that sporadically use tundra habitats.

Within both Arctic and alpine regions exist extremes of vegetation considered atypical of tundra. Many areas within the Arctic are true desert; vegetation scientists classify these areas as polar desert. Tropical high mountains exhibit treeless zones at high elevations, sharing many similarities with the alpine tundra of temperate regions, but the lack of seasons, the large **diurnal** temperature variations, and the presence of distinct plant growth forms are clear differences. Tropical alpine vegetation commonly includes one plant life form not found in other tundra regions: the tall columnar rosette. In the tropical alpine of Africa this life form is represented by members of the genus *Lobelia*, in the Andes of South America by members of the genus *Espeletia*, and in high mountains of Java it is represented by tree ferns. The absence of this life form in Arctic and temperate alpine tundra probably reflects the importance of wind in shaping plants of these ecosystems. **Floristic** similarities between tropical alpine and temperate alpine or even Arctic tundra regions include **genera** or species of mosses, lichens, and occasionally **vascular plants** that are held in common.

During glacial periods of the past, much of the area now covered by the Bering Sea was a land mass. This Bering land bridge, connecting North America and Eurasia, allowed plant and animal **populations** to migrate between Northern Hemisphere continents of Eurasia and North America. Today many tundra genera, including both plants and animals, have circumpolar distributions (surrounding the northern parts of the world). Since species migrations were made possible during the cold periods of the Pleistocene with lowered sea levels due to great masses of ice on land, tundra-like vegetation formed over great expanses in the Northern Hemisphere. Today isolated alpine regions show remarkable similarities in flora and fauna to those of the Arctic echoing a common tundra heritage. SEE ALSO BIOGEOGRAPHY; BIOME.

Kim Moreau Peterson

Bibliography

Archibold, O. W. *Ecology of World Vegetation.* London: Chapman & Hall, 1995.

Billings, William Dwight. "Alpine Vegetation." In *North American Terrestrial Vegetation*, 2nd ed., ed. Michael G. Barbour and William Dwight Billings. Cambridge: Cambridge University Press, 2000.

Bliss, Lawrence C. "Arctic Tundra and Polar Desert Biome." In *North American Terrestrial Vegetation*, 2nd ed., ed. Michael G. Barbour and William Dwight Billings. Cambridge: Cambridge University Press, 2000.

COMMON PLANT SPECIES FOUND IN TUNDRA

(continued from page 138)

Dwarf birch *Betula glandulosa*
Herbaceous perennials
Saxifrage family
    Saxifragra oppositifolia
    Saxifragra cernua
    Saxifragra caespitosa
Ranunculaceae (Buttercup family)
    Ranunculus nivalis
    Anemone parviflora
    Caltha leptosepala
Rosaceae (Rose family)
    Geum Rosii
    Dryas integrifolia
    Potentilla species
    Rubus species
Brassicaceae (Mustard family)
    Draba species
Artemisia species
Lupinus species
Castilleja species
Pedicularis species
Senecio species
Silene species

diurnal daily, or by day

floristic related to plants

genera plural of genus; a taxonomic level above species

vascular plants plants with specialized transport cells; plants other than bryophytes

population a group of organisms of a single species that exist in the same region and interbreed

Sedges on the tundra in Brooks Rouge, Alaska.

Chapin, F. Stuart III, Robert L. Jefferies, James F. Reynolds, Gaius R. Shaver, and Josef Svoboda, eds. *Arctic Ecosystems in a Changing Climate: An Ecophysiological Perspective.* San Diego, CA: Academic Press, 1992.

Wielgolaski, F.E., ed. "Polar and Alpine Tundra." In *Ecosystems of the World*, Vol. 3. New York: Elsevier Science Ltd., 1997.

Turf Management

Careers in turf management involve working outdoors with plants, people, and Mother Nature. Turf managers are employed at various turfgrass facilities worldwide. Although advancement into a management position normally requires a two- or four-year college degree, there are various nonmanagement positions for those who choose not to attend college. Below are various career opportunities in the turf management industry.

A golf course superintendent supervises the maintenance of a golf course. Depending on the course, the superintendent may oversee two to more than fifty employees with a budget ranging from $100,000 to over $1,000,000. Some superintendents enjoy the challenge of hosting a professional golf tournament or building a new course, while others enjoy the more relaxed atmosphere of a daily-fee public course. Salary range for head superintendents was $35,000 to $150,000 in 1999. Graduates with a two- or four-year degree in turf management start their careers as a first or second assistant superintendent. Starting salaries ranged from $25,000 to $35,000 in 1999. Advancement to head superintendent can occur within one to five years.

A sports turf manager oversees the maintenance of one athletic field or an entire sports complex. Professional sports facilities need educated turf managers to maintain the fields used by professional baseball, football, and soccer teams. Universities, colleges, high schools, community parks, horse tracks, polo clubs, tennis clubs, and cricket clubs are beginning to recognize the need for a professional turf manager to maintain their athletic complexes. A well-maintained field reduces injuries and offers better playing conditions. Graduates with a two- or four-year degree in turf management usually start their careers as an assistant field manager. Some may even start as head field manager. In 1999 salaries ranged from $25,000 to $80,000.

Lawn care managers often work as supervisors, consultants, or technicians for professional lawn care franchises. Many start their own company. Responsibilities can include mowing, fertilization, pest control, renovation, sales, and evaluation of home lawns. College graduates normally start as technicians or managers. Lawn care is the largest sector of the turf industry. Homeowners in the United States spend about $15 billion on their lawns and landscape each year.

A grounds manager maintains an institutional site landscaped with turf, trees, flowers, buildings, and roads. They can be hired by colleges, universities, municipalities, park and recreation facilities, office parks, residential communities, hotels, resorts, theme parks, and cemeteries. Education in turf management, landscaping, ornamentals, and business is helpful.

Sod producers grow, harvest, and sell mature turfgrass to various customers. Customers include homeowners, landscapers, golf courses, and athletic fields. Many producers own and operate their own sod farms. Sales and service people also sell and/or service the materials and equipment that turf managers use. Indeed, there are sales and service representatives associated with just about anything purchased in the turf industry—mowers, fertilizer, pesticides, seed, sprayers, and **amendments**. Education and experience in turf management and related fields is helpful.

amendment additive

Researchers and educators develop the grass or fertilizer of the future. They teach turf management at a technical school, college, or university as well. Consultants give turf advice in exchange for money. Clients include homeowners, golf courses, athletic fields, institutions, and landscape management companies. SEE ALSO ECONOMIC IMPORTANCE OF PLANTS; GRASSES.

Douglas T. Linde

Vacuoles

Vacuoles are **organelles** of plant, fungal, and algal cells. They are part of the internal membrane system and are separated from the rest of the cytoplasm by a membrane called the **tonoplast**. A single large vacuole occupies more than 80 percent of the volume of most plant cells, mature fugal hyphae, and some algal cells. Many smaller vacuoles are found in expanding plant cells and in the tips of growing fungal **hyphae**. These vacuoles can be less than one micrometer in diameter. As the cell in which they reside matures, smaller vacuoles fuse to produce larger vacuoles.

Vacuoles are multifunctional organelles, and individual cells may contain more than one kind of vacuole, each kind having a different function. Vacuoles play crucial roles in cell expansion, serve as storage compartments for nutrients, and function as **lytic** organelles that contain digestive **enzymes**. **Compounds** contained within vacuoles also protect cells against environmental damage and deter attack by **herbivores**.

organelle a membrane-bound structure within a cell

tonoplast the membrane of the vacuole

hyphae the threadlike body mass of a fungus

lytic breaking apart, by the action of enzymes.

enzyme a protein that controls a reaction in a cell

compound a substance formed from two or more elements

herbivore an organism that feeds on plant parts

turgor pressure the outward pressure exerted on the cell wall by the fluid within

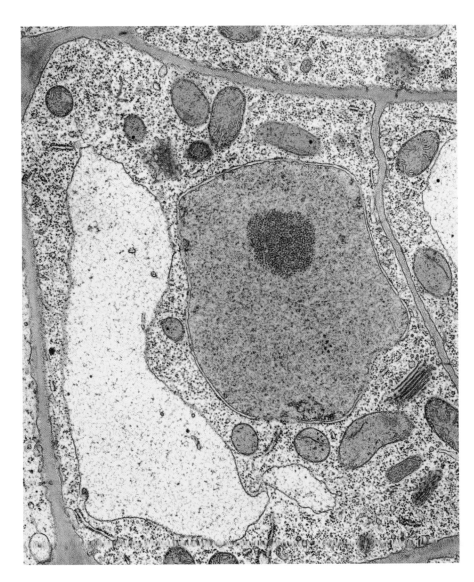

An electron micrograph of a young cell from the root-tip meristem of *Arabidopsis thaliana.* The nucleus (pink) contains a nucleolus (dark) and granular nucleoplasm; the cytoplasm contains mitochondria (blue), proplastids (juvenile chloroplasts; green), and Golgi bodies (red). The large L-shaped body on the left (gold) and the smaller body to the right at its base are vacuoles.

Vacuoles take up water through specialized membrane transporters called aquaporins. The hydrostatic pressure that develops within each cell, known as **turgor pressure**, is required for cell expansion and growth. Turgor pressure is carefully regulated in plants, fungi, and many algae by controlling rates of water and ion movement through the tonoplast. In fresh water algae and fungi lacking cell walls, **contractile** vacuoles fill with excess water from the cytosol and their contents are expelled from the cell through specialized pores.

The vacuole is an acidic organelle, and the **pH** of most vacuoles is around 5 to 6. Vacuole acidity is important for its lytic function since many vacuolar enzymes work most efficiently at or near pH 5. Acidification of vacuoles is brought about by transporters embedded in the tonoplast. These transporters use the energy stored in adenosine triphosphate (**ATP**), or in some cases, pyrophosphate, to pump protons from the cytosol into the vacuole. In extreme cases, such as in the lemon fruit juice sac, the pH of the vacuole can be as low as 2.

Vacuoles store organic acids, carbohydrates, proteins, and minerals. Some of these compounds are important for human nutrition. These include proteins stored in the cotyledons of beans and peas or the grains of cereals; simple sugars such as sucrose found in many fruits, the stems of sugarcane and the roots of sugar beets; and minerals such as potassium. In the leaves and stems of forage grasses, vacuoles store complex **polysaccharides** that are the principal energy source for herbivores.

Many other compounds accumulate in vacuoles. These include the water-soluble anthocyanin **pigments** that give the blue or red color to red beets, grapes, and peonies. Anthocyanins are also contained in the vacuoles of leaves and stems and are important **photoprotectants** that absorb excess light. **Alkaloids**, enzyme inhibitors, and **toxins** are contained in some vacuoles. Although these compounds may deter herbivory, some have been used to produce medicines. Aspirin and morphine are two examples. Waste products and **xenobiotics**, including herbicides, are often shuttled into vacuoles by specialized membrane transporters. Once in the vacuole, these compounds are digested or detoxified. SEE ALSO ANTHO-CYANINS; CELLS.

Paul Bethke and Russell Jones

van Helmont, Jan

Flemish Physician and Chemist
1579–1644

Renowned physician and chemist Jan van Helmont was born into the Flemish gentry in 1579. He received his medical degree at the age of twenty, then proceeded to revolutionize the field of plant nutrition. As a young university student first in Belgium, then in Switzerland, France, and England, van Helmont openly rejected the mysticism and superstition prevalent in academia at the time, being especially skeptical of natural magic and magnetic cures.

Jan van Helmont.

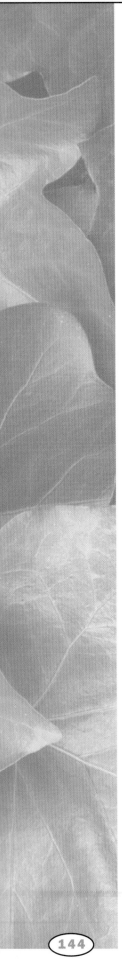

In all of his attempts to understand "the small things" that at the time were treated with "magic" and magnetism and today are studied with microscopes, van Helmont relied on the principles of balance, experiment, and quantification. Van Helmont applied chemical analysis to smoke, which he produced by burning a variety of solids and fluids. He observed that the vapors that formed when solids were burned were very different from "just air"; these vapors had distinct and unique properties depending on the solid from which they had been derived.

Van Helmont called this class of vapors by the term "gas." He referred to gas as being "wild," stating that this new type of substance "could not be contained by vessels nor reduced into a visible body." Van Helmont described and identified a variety of gases and therefore is credited as the "discoverer" of gas.

quantitative numerical, especially as derived from measurement

Van Helmont's desire to understand the composition of water initially motivated his experiments on plant nutrition. He was the first to use a **quantitative**—and ingenious—experimental approach to show that plants obtain nutrition from the chemicals in water. Van Helmont planted a young willow plant in a container. The willow shoot weighed 5 pounds and the container (including earth) had a dry weight of 200 pounds. For five years, van Helmont attended his willow plant with great care, watering it as often as necessary. Once those five years were up, van Helmont weighed the shoot. It had gone from 5 pounds to 169 pounds. Meanwhile, the dry weight of the soil had decreased by only 2 ounces. As van Helmont concluded: "Therefore 164 pounds of wood, bark, and root have arisen from water alone." Van Helmont thus demonstrated that the main source of plant nutrition was not the soil, thus countering a widely held belief among his contemporaries.

Ironically, van Helmont, even though he was extremely interested in the air, overlooked the role that air plays in plant nutrition. He had the right idea, but came to the wrong conclusion. It is known now that plants need to get nutrients from water and air in order for carbon fixation to occur.

Van Helmont's radical thinking would eventually land him in some trouble with the Spanish government and Catholic church. In 1625 the General Inquisition of Spain condemned a treatise he had published in 1621, citing van Helmont for 157 counts of heresy, impudence, and arrogance, as well as for association with Lutheran doctrine. He was kept under house arrest for years, and, perhaps because of this experience, published little of his work. When he was dying in 1644, he asked his son to edit and publish his works. SEE ALSO PHYSIOLOGIST; PHYSIOLOGY; PHYSIOLOGY, HISTORY OF; WATER MOVEMENT.

Hanna Rose Shell

Bibliography

Isley, D. "Helmont." *One Hundred and One Botanists*. Ames, IA: Iowa State University Press, 1994.

Morton, A.G. "J. B. Van Helmont." *History of Botanical Science*. London: Academic Press, 1981.

Pagel, W. "J. B. Van Helmont." *Dictionary of Scientific Biography* 6 (1972): 253–59.

van Niel, C. B.

Dutch Microbiologist and Educator
1897–1985

Cornelis Bernardus van Niel was a Dutch microbiologist whose experiments with bacteria helped explain how photosynthesis occurs in plants. Sulfur bacteria particularly interested van Niel, because there was a controversy in the early 1900s concerning the bacteria. Scientists were not sure if the bacteria got their energy from chemicals in their environment or from sunlight. They knew that the bacteria used sulfur **compounds** and did take in carbon dioxide to create more complex carbon compounds, and van Niel wanted to determine which energy source the bacteria used to do this.

compound a substance formed from two or more elements

One problem was that previous scientists had usually studied cultures of bacteria that contained several different species. They knew that the bacteria needed light and also needed and stored sulfur compounds, but the interactions between different species in the cultures made experimentation difficult. Van Niel decided he would have to do his work on pure cultures. He began the labor of isolating and studying pure cultures of purple and green sulfur bacteria in the Netherlands and he continued this work after he transferred to the Hopkins Marine Station in California, in 1929.

Van Niel carefully examined his cultures, using very specific growing conditions. He measured as accurately as possible the amounts of carbon, sulfur, and other chemicals that the bacteria used up or released. In this way, he saw that in the light, the amount of carbon dioxide the bacteria could convert into other carbon compounds depended precisely on how much hydrogen sulfide was available. He worked out a formula for this bacterial photosynthesis and he noticed it was very similar to the formula known for plant photosynthesis. The only difference was that the bacteria used hydrogen sulfide in the reaction where plants used water, and the bacteria produced sulfur compounds where the plants produced oxygen. This led him to make a general formula for the reactions of photosynthesis in both bacteria and plants that is still used today.

The most striking part of van Niel's ideas about photosynthesis was that light was used to split water or hydrogen sulfide. The energy and hydrogen released would then be used to reduce carbon dioxide into more complex compounds. This was new and interesting at the time, because it meant that the oxygen given off by plants during photosynthesis came from the split water molecule, and not from carbon dioxide as previously thought. Later researchers confirmed van Niel's theory by doing experiments using heavy isotopes of oxygen to label the oxygen and observe its origins in photosynthesis. Van Niel's research originated the study of the electron transport chain involved in transferring the energy in photosynthesis.

Other van Niel studies became the foundation for studying bacterial evolution and for the classification of organisms as **prokaryotes** or eukaryotes. Van Niel died in 1985. SEE ALSO PHOTOSYNTHESIS, LIGHT REACTIONS AND; PHYSIOLOGIST; PHYSIOLOGY; PHYSIOLOGY, HISTORY OF.

prokaryotes single-celled organisms without nuclei, including Eubacteria and Archaea

Jessica P. Penney

Bibliography

Kluyver, A. J., and C. B. van Niel. *The Microbe's Contribution to Biology.* Cambridge, MA: Harvard University Press, 1956.

Variety

population a group of organisms of a single species that exist in the same region and interbreed

Plant species maintain different levels of variation within and among **populations**, much of which is genetically determined. As such, variation in form below the taxonomic rank of species, called infraspecific variation, is widely recognized in plants. In contrast to zoological taxonomy, three categories have been applied to recognize this variation in plants. In order of decreasing taxonomic rank, these are: subspecies, variety, and forma. Additionally, the category of cultivar is used to recognize horticultural varieties not typically found in naturally occurring populations. The subspecies, which is the most inclusive of the three categories, is usually applied in recognition of population variation that is correlated with geography. By definition, populations of subspecies differ from other such populations. Furthermore, subspecies are expected to interbreed more freely than species, which may comprise two or more subspecies. The category of variety is similarly applied to recognize variation below the level of subspecies. Unfortunately, the two categories are not distinct, and application of the taxonomic rank of variety is more frequently encountered. Forma, the least-inclusive category, is applied to recognize minor infraspecific variation that is presumably due to variation at a single gene and, as such, may vary within populations. Flower color variants are typically recognized at this level. SEE ALSO CLINES AND ECOTYPES; CULTIVAR; SPECIES; TAXONOMY.

Leo P. Bruederle

Bibliography

Stuessy, Tod F. *Case Studies in Plant Taxonomy: Exercises in Applied Pattern Recognition.* New York: Columbia University Press, 1994.

Vascular Tissues

All living cells require water and nutrients. If an organism is a single cell or if its body is only a few cells thick, water and nutrients are easily moved through the organism by diffusion. However, diffusion is generally too slow for even small plants to meet their water and nutrient needs. In plants, this problem was solved with the evolution of a specialized system for fast and efficient long-distance transport of water and nutrients. This specialized cellular network is the vascular tissue system; plants with vascular tissues are referred to as vascular plants.

The vascular tissue system is composed of two different types of tissues: xylem and phloem. Although both xylem and phloem form a continuous tissue system throughout the plant body, the two tissues have different functions. Xylem is the primary water- and mineral-conducting tissue, and phloem is the primary food-conducting tissue.

Unlike the circulatory system in animals, the vascular tissue in plants does not recirculate water. Instead, water takes a one-way journey from the

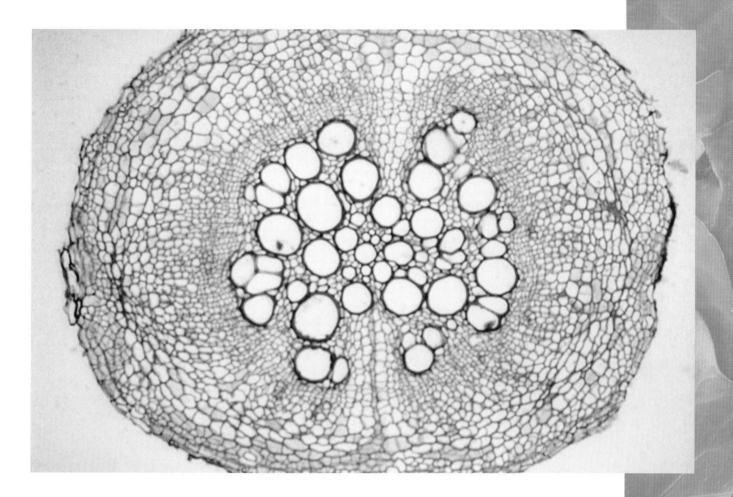

soil upward through the plant body to be lost to the atmosphere through evaporation. The watery journey occurs within the xylem tissue. In contrast, phloem tissue transports dissolved sugars (food) from regions where sugars are made or stored (sources) to regions where sugars are required for metabolic processes (sinks). Phloem transports sugars from source to sink. Source sites include photosynthetic tissue, usually leaves, where sugars are manufactured, and storage organs (thickened stems or roots, such as the root of a sugar beet).

Cross-section of a carrot root tissue, showing xylem, phloem, and cortex cells.

Vascular Plants

Freed from the requirement to hug a moist soil surface, plants with vascular tissue can grow tall, extending their complex stems and leaves into the dry air. Vascular tissue, along with several other important plant features, allowed plants to colonize Earth's surface. Today, our planet hosts an enormous diversity of vascular plant life, including such different forms as ferns, redwood trees, oak trees, and orchids.

Vascular tissue develops in all organs—root, stem, and leaf—of the plant body. In the primary plant body, vascular tissue differentiates from a primary meristem, the procambium. Xylem and phloem tissues that differentiate from procambial tissue are called primary xylem and primary phloem. In plants with secondary growth, vascular tissue differentiates from a lateral meristem, the vascular cambium, producing secondary xylem and secondary phloem. Secondary xylem is a familiar product: wood.

The xylem bundles of a cross-section of teak wood magnified fifty times.

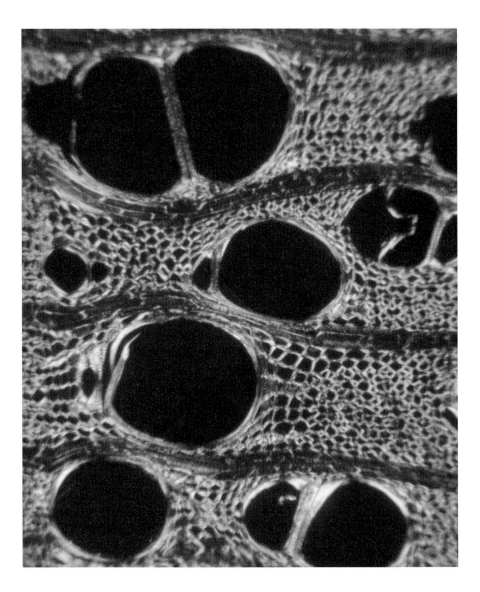

parenchyma one of three types of cells in ground tissue

tracheid a type of xylem cell for water transport

Xylem: The Water-Conducting Vascular Tissue

Xylem is a complex tissue composed of several different cell types. This tissue includes **parenchyma** cells, fibers, and two cell types specializing in water and mineral transport: **tracheids** and vessel members. Collectively tracheids and vessel members are called tracheary elements.

The tracheid evolved first, appearing in the fossil record about 420 million years ago, long before vessel members. Most seedless vascular plants, such as ferns, and cone-bearing seed plants, such as pines, have tracheids only. Although vessel members evolved independently several times and are present in a few seedless vascular plants, vessel members are usually associated with flower-bearing seed plants.

Tracheids are less specialized than vessel members. Tracheids appear first in the fossil record; vessel members and fibers are thought to have derived from tracheids. The less-specialized tracheid provides both water-conducting and strenghtening traits in one cell. In plants with fibers and vessel members, fibers specialize in strengthening plant tissue and vessel members specialize in water conduction.

Development. Mature tracheary elements are dead, tubelike cells. Only cell walls remain intact at the end of the differentiation process; the **protoplast** is completely eliminated, leaving a hollow cell. Whether tracheary elements arise from **meristematic** cells of the procambium or later in development from the vascular cambium, the pattern of tracheary element development and maturation is similar.

One of the first indications that a meristematic cell will become a tracheary element is cell elongation; mature tracheary elements are longer than they are wide. The elongating cells have thin, primary cell walls; but, as the cells elongate, additional cell wall **compounds** are deposited to the inside of the primary wall. The additional wall deposition forms the secondary cell wall. One of the secondary wall compounds is a complex **polymer** called lignin. A **lignified** cell wall is impermeable to water. To allow for water transport from cell to cell, numerous regions of the primary cell wall remain free of secondary wall deposition. The regions lacking secondary walls are called pits. Pit structure and the pattern of pitting on the walls of tracheary elements are specific for different plant species and are useful traits in plant identification.

Water Flow in Tracheary Elements. The pits of adjacent cells are aligned with one another, allowing water to pass from tracheary element to tracheary element. Water passes through aligned pits because the two adjacent primary walls, and the middle **lamella** cementing the two cells together, are composed of complex carbohydrates permeable to water, such as cellulose and pectin. An aligned pair of pits is called a pit pair, and the primary walls and middle lamella of the pit pair are called a pit membrane.

Although pit membranes are permeable to water, they do offer some resistance to the flow of water between cells. In vessel members, the maturation process includes dissolution of the end walls to form perforation plates. Perforation plates are cell wall regions that are completely open, offering no resistance to water flow. Vessel members are connected end-to-end, forming tubes called vessels. Water taken into a vessel from surrounding parenchyma cells, tracheids, or other vessels must pass through pits in the lateral walls of the vessels; but, once inside a vessel, water can flow unimpeded for the length of that vessel.

Because vessel members lack end walls, moving water with less resistance, they are thought to be more efficient water-conductors than tracheids. However, there is a tradeoff. If an air bubble forms in a vessel, it can expand and fill the entire vessel. An air-filled vessel can no longer function in water transport. Because water must pass through the pit membranes of pit pairs when traveling from tracheid to tracheid, air bubbles cannot pass between adjoining tracheids. Pit membranes are effective barriers to air bubbles, trapping bubbles within a single tracheid.

Secondary Wall Reinforcement. In primary xylem, selective secondary wall deposition creates different cell wall patterns in tracheary elements. In the first formed tracheary elements of the primary xylem, secondary wall deposition tends to occur in ringlike (called annular) or helical (spiral) bands around the cell. As the primary plant body continues to lengthen, cells with annular or helical thickenings stretch. These cells are often stretched beyond functional usefulness. Later, but still during primary growth, ladder-

protoplast the portion of the cell within the cell wall

meristematic related to cell division at the tip

compound a substance formed from two or more elements

polymer a large molecule made from many similar parts

lignified composed of lignin, a tough and resistant plant compound

lamella a thin layer or plate-like structure

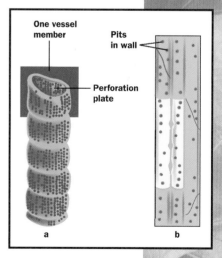

Xylem conducting cells. (a) A vessel composed of several vessel members; pits occur in the lateral walls and a perforation plate is visible in an end wall of one of the vessel members. (b) Adjacent tracheids; pits occur on lateral and end walls. Redrawn from Rost et al., 1998, Figure 4.11.

like (scalariform), netlike (reticulate), or pitted secondary wall patterns may develop. With increasing amounts of secondary wall deposition, tracheary elements become stronger and less resistant to stretching. Therefore, scalariform, reticulate, and pitted tracheary elements are generally found in organs that have ceased elongation.

The lignified secondary walls and pit pairs of tracheary elements and the perforation plates of vessel members provide for efficient water-conduction through vascular tissue. Water and dissolved minerals taken in from the external environment—usually wet soil—move upward through the xylem tissue of roots into stems and finally into leaves. Within leaves, water evaporates from cell surfaces and is lost to the environment as water vapor. Water evaporation from a plant surface is called transpiration. Water is literally pulled up tracheary elements during transpiration. The evaporation-generated pulling stretches hydrogen bonds between connected water molecules, resulting in a column of water that is under tension (negative pressure). The lignified cell walls of tracheary elements are strong enough to resist the tension, preventing inward cell collapse during water movement.

Phloem: The Food-Conducting Vascular Tissue

Phloem tissue is a complex tissue consisting of parenchyma cells, fibers, and one of two types of food-conducting cells. Sieve-tube members and sieve cells are food-conducting cells and are collectively called sieve elements. Sieve-tube members connected end-to-end form a sieve tube. Sieve cells evolved before sieve-tube members and are less specialized. Cone-bearing seed plants have sieve cells, and the more advanced flowering seed plants have sieve-tube members.

Sieve elements are long, narrow cells with primary cell walls. During differentiation, a sieve element undergoes major **protoplasmic** changes, including loss of its nucleus and vacuolar membrane. In addition, the cell loses ribosomes, the Golgi complex, and the cytoskeleton system, but the cell membrane remains intact. Next to the cell membrane, a network of smooth **endoplasmic reticulum** lines the cell, and a few plastids and **mitochondria** remain intact.

Sieve Areas. The defining feature of sieve elements are sieve areas. A sieve area is a cluster of pores in the wall of a sieve element. These pores allow materials to flow from cell to cell. In sieve cells, end walls overlap and, although sieve areas are found on all wall surfaces, they are concentrated on overlapping wall regions. Sieve-tube members have two types of sieve areas. Sieve plates are a specialized type of sieve area with relatively large pores. Most sieve plates occur on end walls of sieve-tube members with relatively smaller-pored sieve areas on the lateral cell walls. Sieve plate complexity is variable. Some sieve-tube members have compound sieve plates with several sieve areas on a steeply inclined end wall. Sieve-tube members with compound sieve plates are considered less specialized than sieve-tube members with simple sieve plates and horizontal end walls. The pores of simple sieve plates are relatively wider than the pores of compound plates, and wider pores increase cell-to-cell connection.

Unlike tracheary elements of the xylem, the fluid contents of sieve elements in the phloem are under positive pressure, and the movement of sugars and other substances through sieve elements is directed by pressure dif-

protoplasmic related to the protoplasm, cell material within the cell wall

endoplasmic reticulum membrane network inside a cell

mitochondria cell organelles that produce ATP to power cell reactions

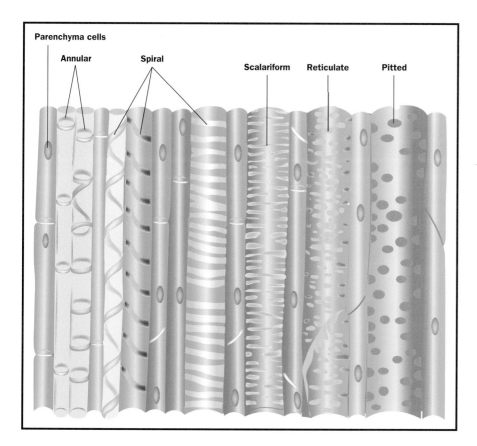

Parenchyma cells

Annular Spiral Scalariform Reticulate Pitted

Patterns of secondary wall deposition in tracheary elements. Cells with annular and spiral secondary wall thickenings can stretch during organ elongation. As organ elongation slows and then ceases, the wall thickening patterns tend to grade from scalariform and reticulate to pitted. Redrawn from Rost et al., 1998, Figure 4.9.

ferences. Because cell contents are under pressure, sieve elements require a method of sealing cells to prevent the loss of cellular contents upon sieve element injury or death. One blocking substance is callose. Callose is a carbohydrate that lines the pores of sieve areas and sieve plates; it can rapidly expand, filling pores and blocking the loss of cell contents. A few flowering plant sieve-tube members contain a protein substance called P-protein. (The "P" is for phloem.) P-protein appears to line sieve plate pores in living cells and to plug pores of damaged cells. Although the function of P-protein is not known, it may serve as an additional method of blocking sieve pores and preventing the loss of cell contents upon injury.

Companion Cells and Albuminous Cells. There are two types of specialized cells associated with sieve elements. Sieve-tube members are always associated with companion cells. Both cells arise from the same meristematic cell and are joined by numerous, well-developed **plasmodesmatal** connections. Companion cells probably provide a delivery and support system for the nonnucleated sieve-tube members. Associated with sieve cells are specialized parenchyma cells called albuminous cells. Albuminous cells may perform the same function for sieve cells as companion cells do for sieve-tube members.

Nonvascular Plants

Most organisms that we automatically classify as plants, such as roses and corn, have a vascular tissue system and are called vascular plants. However, plants such as mosses lack this highly developed transport system and are classified as nonvascular plants.

albuminous gelatinous, or composed of the protein albumin

plasmodesmata cell-cell junctions.

Informally, nonvascular plants are called bryophytes, and include three groups of plants: liverworts, hornworts, and mosses. Nonvascular plants specialize in absorbing moisture by efficiently moving water over their surfaces through capillary action. In many of these small plants, there is an additional internal conducting tissue that allows for efficient water and food conduction. When present, bryophyte-conducting tissue consists of two specialized cell types: water-conducting hydroids and food-conducting leptoids. Hydroids are elongated cells with thin primary cell walls and no protoplast at maturity. Leptoids are elongated cells, but their lateral cell walls are thick. The end walls of leptoids contain numerous plasmodesmata that may enlarge to form small pores. At maturity, the nuclei of leptoids degenerate. Because bryophyte conducting tissue apparently lacks lignin, it is not considered true vascular tissue. SEE ALSO ANATOMY OF PLANTS; CELLS, SPECIALIZED TYPES; ROOTS; TISSUES; TRANSLOCATION; WATER MOVEMENT.

Deborah K. Canington and Thomas L. Rost

Bibliography

Cutter, E. G. *Plant Anatomy. Part I: Cells and Tissues,* 2nd ed. Menlo Park, CA: Addison-Wesley Publishing Company, 1978.

Esau, K. *Anatomy of Seed Plants,* 2nd ed., New York: John Wiley & Sons, 1977.

Fahn, A. *Plant Anatomy,* 4th ed., Oxford: Pergamon Press, 1990.

Mauseth, James D. *Plant Anatomy.* Menlo Park, CA: Benjamin/Cummings Publishing Company, 1988.

Vavilov, N. I.

Russian Geneticist
1887–1943

Nikolay Ivanovich Vavilov was a geneticist and **phytogeographer** in Russia. He is best known for his attempts to apply the new science of genetics to improve agriculture in Russia, for his novel theory to determine the centers of origin of cultivated plants, and for his tireless efforts to organize science in Russia. Vavilov is also known as one of the outstanding victims of Soviet oppression during the regime of Josef Stalin. He openly opposed the teachings of the antigeneticist Trofim Lysenko. As a result Vavilov was unjustly imprisoned for supporting the very same work in genetics that had made him famous.

Early Life and Career

Vavilov was born in Moscow on November 25, 1887. He was the oldest of four children born to a wealthy Moscow merchant family. His younger brother, Sergey, shared some of his scientific interests and became a well-known physicist and president of the Soviet Academy of Sciences.

From an early age, Vavilov had an interest in applied botany and agriculture. In 1906 he graduated from a commercial high school and entered the Moscow Agricultural Institute. Following graduation in 1911, Vavilov remained with the head of the department of special agriculture to prepare for an academic career. In 1912 he moved to St. Petersburg, where he worked at the Bureau of Applied Botany of the Ministry of Agriculture and at the

N. I. Vavilov.

phytogeographer a scientist who studies the distribution of plants

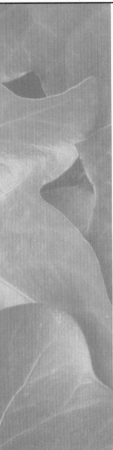

Bureau of Mycology and Phytopathology. The pivotal moment in his early career came when he was sent to study genetics in England. He left for England in 1913 to study with the eminent geneticist William Bateson. He also worked with the geneticist R. C. Punnett and cereal breeder R. D. Biffen. He returned to Russia just after the outbreak of World War I to complete the thesis for his master's degree titled "Plant Immunity to Infectious Diseases." In 1917 he became professor of agriculture, botany, and genetics at the University of Saratov.

Vavilov rose to prominence shortly following the Russian Revolution. He drew the favorable attention of Lenin and was placed in charge of the Bureau of Applied Botany in St. Petersburg. Under his direction, it became one of the world's most active research institutions. By 1934 it had a staff of approximately twenty thousand persons and was known as Lenin's All-Union Academy of Agricultural Sciences. His success was recognized both at home and abroad. Though he was never a Communist, he was made a member of the Soviet Central Executive Committee. He occupied many important international positions including being named President of the International Congress of Genetics in 1939.

Vavilov's Scientific Work

Vavilov's actual contributions to science were unusual. He did not make any new discoveries or formulate new scientific principles but was instead actively concerned with the application of the new genetics to problems of systematics and agriculture. His work fell into three distinct areas, which had in common a concern with cultivated plants.

His earliest work was concerned with the manner in which plants developed immunity to disease. He developed the concept of degree of specialization. This was based on his observation that the wider the range of hosts of a parasitic fungus, the less likely it is that there will be resistant varieties in any of the host species. In other words, the more hosts that were available, the less likely resistance could develop in any one species. In understanding the mechanism by which this happens, Vavilov sought out new varieties of wheat to test for disease resistance. In the process he discovered an important new disease-resistant wheat species, *Triticum timopheevi*, which is still used in breeding for disease resistant stocks. The techniques that Vavilov developed for testing disease-resistance are still important tools for plant disease specialists, or plant pathologists.

His second area of research led to the formulation of the law of homologous series in variation. This law held that genetic and **morphological** regularities existed in the differentiation of species, **genera**, and families. Such parallel variations, he argued, could be found in all categories of classification. Vavilov recognized that the study of similarities in related species and genera could lead to a valuable analytical tool because it could determine if and where any gaps in series of forms existed. Once this was determined, it was then possible to search for the organism that would fit into such a gap. Vavilov closely studied the parallel variation in many forms, especially the cereals, and in the process amassed an enormous amount of data on this economically important group. He was also able to locate many "missing" forms that were expected if his law held true.

morphologically related to shape or form

genera plural of genus; a taxonomic level above species

cytology the study of cell structure

Vavilov was best known for his third area of research into the origin and distribution of cultivated plants. He built on the earlier work of the French geographer Augustin de Candolle, which had used a novel combination of archaeological, historical, linguistic, and botanical evidence to trace the location of origin of cultivated plants. Vavilov additionally applied the insights and methods from two new sciences, **cytology** and genetics, and traveled extensively to examine and collect close relatives of important cultivated plants. From this work, he derived his own theory of the origin of cultivated plants, which postulated that there were eight principal "centers of origin." According to Vavilov these regions had a broad range of environmental conditions that gave rise to diverse natural floras. Cultivated plants in these regions also had many diverse varieties. Vavilov's novel insight here was to determine that cultivated plants in his centers of origin showed a marked increase in the frequencies of dominant genes compared to plants outside these centers. This, in fact, became his principal criterion for fixing centers of origin. In contrast, cultivated plants outside the centers of origin tended to have much less genetic variability.

Vavilov's centers of origin was a provocative and influential theory for its day. Although the specifics of the theory and the actual centers of origin have been called into question, it opened the way for subsequent research. In the process much was understood about the genetics of cultivated plants and many new varieties were collected and introduced.

specimen object or organism under consideration

Much of Vavilov's research over his life was based on close study of geographic distribution and variation. He traveled widely all over the world, but especially in Asia both to examine and collect usually wild relatives of cultivated plants. His expeditions were organized on a grand scale and led to the collection of an enormous range and number of plant **specimens**. Many of his collections of cultivated plants were without counterpart and still remain unsurpassed in quality and number. For his research into the origin of wheat alone, he amassed over twenty-five thousand specimens of different varieties of wheat and its wild relatives. With good reason, Vavilov had been called the most widely traveled biologist of his day.

Vavilov and Stalinist Science

Vavilov rose to such prominence that he was the most visible promoter of science in the Soviet Union. He was an advocate of international collaboration and sought to bring the methods and insights of the new science of genetics from Britain and the United States to improve agriculture in the new Soviet system. Unfortunately, this made him an easy target of anti-Western ideology that gained strength under Stalin's regime. Vavilov's support of Western science generally, and genetics in particular, were openly challenged by Trofim Lysenko, one of the most destructive influences in Soviet science. Although he had no training in the field, Lysenko pretended to be an authority in agricultural genetics. He was opposed to Mendelian genetics and Darwinism but instead was an advocate on **Lamarckian inheritance**, which was more compatible with Soviet ideology. Beginning in the late 1920s, Lysenko and his supporters began to systematically purge the Soviet Union of geneticists who they viewed as slaves to foreign science, as well as anyone who opposed Soviet ideology. Many of the leading geneticists in the Soviet Union were exiled, imprisoned, dispersed, or exe-

Lamarckian inheritance the hypothesis that acquired characteristics can be inherited

cuted. By the late 1930s Vavilov had been relieved of his administrative duties and was openly targeted by Lysenko.

On August 6, 1940, while he was on a collecting trip in the western Ukraine, Vavilov was arrested by Soviet agents. He was subsequently found guilty of trumped-up charges, including conducting sabotage on Soviet agriculture on behalf of Western powers. He was sentenced to death, but through the efforts of his brother, Sergey, he was instead imprisoned for ten years. He died while in prison on January 16, 1943, as a result of malnutrition.

Vavilov's case was examined closely after Stalin's death. He was subsequently rehabilitated, his scientific work was republished, and his contributions fully noted. He remains one of the most tragic figures in the history of science and his plight serves as a grim lesson against the ideological control of science. SEE ALSO AGRICULTURE, HISTORY OF; BIOGEOGRAPHY; BREEDING; CANDOLLE, AUGUSTIN DE; EVOLUTION OF PLANTS, HISTORY OF; FABACEAE.

Vassiliki Betty Smocovitis

Bibliography

Adams, Mark B. "Nikolay Ivanovich Vavilov." In *Dictionary of Scientific Biography*, ed. Charles Coulston Gillispie. New York: Scribner's Sons, 1970.

Krementsov, N. *Stalinist Science.* Princeton, NJ: Princeton University Press, 1997.

Mangelsdorf, Paul C., and Nikolai Ivanovich Vavilov, 1887–1942. *Genetics* 38 (1953): 1–4.

Popovsky, Mark. *The Vavilov Affair.* Hamden, CT: Archon Books, 1984.

Soyfer, V. *Lysenko and the Tragedy of Soviet Science.* New Brunswick, NJ: Rutgers University Press, 1994.

Vegetables

The term *vegetables* can have three distinct meanings when applied to plants. The first as in "animal, vegetable, or mineral" refers to the entire kingdom of green plants: algae, mosses, ferns, and flowering plants, and maybe including nongreen fungi and bacteria. The botanical sense of vegetables refers to all plant parts such as roots, stems, and leaves excluding the reproductive structures of flowers, fruits, and seeds, so that there is a vegetative phase of plant growth and a reproductive phase that is quite distinct. The third usage and the one most commonly understood refers to plant structures that are predominately water, edible without much woody fiber (cellulose), easily eaten raw, and low in sugar. This "kitchen sense" of the word vegetable as in "eat your vegetables" refers to botanical vegetables such as roots (e.g., radishes, parsnips, and carrots), underground stems or tubers (e.g., potatoes), young stems (e.g., asparagus and bamboo shoots), short stems with surrounding fleshy leaves (e.g., onions), leaf stalks (e.g., celery and rhubarb), leaves (e.g., lettuce and parsley), buds (e.g., cabbage and palm hearts), and extends into reproductive structures such as unopened flowers (e.g., broccoli and artichokes), fruit (e.g., tomatoes, okra, bell peppers, green beans, eggplants, and cucumbers), and seeds (e.g., green peas). "Kitchen-sense" vegetables are generally excellent sources of vitamins A and C, as well as

The common bean plant (*Phaseolus vulgaris*).

minerals, while being low in overall calories. Mushrooms are also considered vegetables in this sense. They are the reproductive structure of fungi.

Vegetables are consistently high in water and eaten when young and immature before much plant fiber has developed. Many vegetables are biennials, which grow the first year and accumulate materials in the root or other vegetative part to use in flowering the second year. Examples are carrots, beets, parsnips, and rutabaga, which are harvested the first year before the root turns woody. Many fruits are eaten immature before the enclosed seeds develop fully, such as zucchini, crookneck squash, sweet corn, snow pea, and chayote. Some vegetables are 91 to 95 percent water (cabbage, tomato, spinach), others are 85 to 95 percent water (carrots, artichoke, brussels sprouts) and some are 70 to 80 percent water (sweet corn, peas, sweet potato, parsnips, potato). The later are high in starch. The high water content explains why most vegetables are low in calories.

The most-consumed vegetable across cultures is the tomato, much of it being processed for sauces and other tomato-based products. Originally from Mexico, this fruit, which is used as a vegetable, has been adopted by almost every cooking style. The onion and its various pungent lily relatives are the vegetables with the highest sugar content and are found in cooking (which brings out the sugar) worldwide. The vegetable with the most forms from a single species, *Brassica oleraceo*, are the Mediterranean cabbage relatives: kale, collards, broccoli, and cauliflower known from Greek and Roman times, headed cabbage from the Middle Ages to brussels sprouts and kholrabi from the time of the **Renaissance**. The potato is the world's number-one vegetable by tonnage harvested but is seldom eaten raw and is more often classified as a starchy tuber. SEE ALSO ECONOMIC IMPORTANCE OF PLANTS; FRUITS; POTATO.

Garrison Wilkes

Renaissance a period of artistic and intellectual expansion in Europe from the fourteenth to the sixteenth century

Bibliography

Camp, Wendell H., Victor R. Boswell, and John R. Magness. *The World in Your Garden.* Washington, DC: National Geographic Society, 1959.

Masefield, G. B., Michael Wallis, S.G. Harrison, and B. E. Nicholson. *The Oxford Book of Food Plants.* London: Oxford University Press, 1969.

Warming, Johannes

Danish Botanist
1841–1924

Johannes Warming was a Danish botanist who is regarded as the founder of plant ecology. The term ecology had been used before, but Warming was the first to describe the fundamental questions that must be addressed in a study of plant ecology and the first to popularize detailed research into the ways plants relate to their environments.

Warming was born November 3, 1841, in Mandø, Denmark. His father was a Lutheran minister there on one of the northern Frisian Islands. Warming loved living there on the coast and he later wrote about his homeland's marshlands and dunes. From his early observations there, he compiled written records that are still important for the study of the ecology of the area's plants today.

Early Research on Structure and Adaption

In his early twenties, while he was a student, Warming became the secretary for a Danish zoologist, P. W. Lund, who was studying fossils in Brazil. Warming accompanied him to Minas Gerais, Brazil, and he spent three years there from 1863 until 1866. While there, Warming carefully studied the environment in that tropical savanna climate. He compiled writings and observations that would be the most thorough examination of a tropical environment at that time. It took Warming nearly twenty-five years to complete the organization and publication of his descriptions of the Brazilian environment. His outstanding work was a detailed record of the plants there; it carefully explained the range of plant geography in the area. At that time, before the study of plant ecology as Warming later introduced it, plant geographers were only beginning to document the regional differences between plants and the effects the surrounding environment might have on plants. Warming then studied plant geography, but he would soon begin the study of plant ecology.

Warming left Brazil to study with respected botanists, first in Munich and then in Bonn, Germany, in 1871. At this time he began detailed research into plant **morphology**, which was then a popular branch of botany. In studying morphology, he made observations about the functions and origins of different plant structures, particularly floral structures. His work was important to the understanding of the development of the stamen and the ovule, and to research into the general morphology of the flower. He did interesting work with carnivorous plants such as *Drosera*, which catches insects in its many sticky tentacles. Warming carefully observed these tentacles, trying to determine the mechanism of their movement.

morphology shape and form

In the late 1870s, Warming became interested in evolution, as had recently been described by Darwin and Lamarck. Warming became a dedicated proponent of the Lamarckian ideas about the causes of evolution. With these ideas in mind, Warming published several more papers about the structure and morphology of different plants and flowers. He classified these plants morphologically and paid special attention to the features of these plants that might help them adapt to their environment. Most of the plants he described were Scandinavian, and he was able to present them in a very clear and easily understood way in his texts. In these early studies, Warming had proved himself to be a careful and thoughtful botanist, and in 1886 he became a professor of botany at the University of Copenhagen. He stayed working there for twenty-five years, until 1911.

Foundations of Plant Community Ecology

Warming went on to develop his interest in plant adaptations, and it led to the publication in 1895 of his work *Ecology of Plants* or *Plantesamfund*, as it was originally published. This work was the first plant ecology text and it laid the foundations for the new ecological branch of botanical research, inspiring many botanists to study plant ecology. In it, Warming described his ideas about the types of questions one should ask when examining **populations** of plants. He wanted to know why each plant had a particular habitat, why different plant species would often occur in communities, and why these communities would have specific characteristic growth patterns. The book was sensational among botanists at the time. It proposed a new way to group and describe associations between plants. Warming's ideas about

population a group of organisms of a single species that exist in the same region and interbreed

plant communities had come out of his study of plant geography and the idea of a community of plants was a new term in botany and plant geography. It applied to a group of different species that interacted together to form a well-defined unit, such as a lake or meadow. Warming divided plant communities into four types. These types were based on whether the plants lived in wet, dry, salty, or moderate environments. Water figured closely in his descriptions, as Warming generally considered it to be the most important factor influencing plant communities.

His idea about communities of plants being influenced as units was a brilliant new way to look at plants in general. Warming suggested that botanists examine all the environmental factors that effect the growth of a plant. These factors would affect individual plants, but they would also affect others plants in the area. Together these influences would then affect the ways that the different plants interacted with each other in the community.

Among all his publications, *Plantesamfund* was probably the most important, as it started a whole new field of study. Warming's ability to discern the details of plants' relationships with their environments influenced all of his writings, but in his book on ecology it brought the desire of ecological research to many other botanists. In the following years, numerous ecology publications appeared. The next century saw the development and growth of the ecological movement, as people began to understand the interactions not just between plants, but between plants, their environments, and the animals (including humans) that encounter them. Warming had seen an explosion of ecological awareness begin by the time he died in Copenhagen on April 2, 1924, and he will be remembered as the founding pioneer of ecological research. SEE ALSO ECOLOGY; ECOLOGY, HISTORY OF; PLANT COMMUNITY PROCESSES; ODUM, EUGENE.

Jessica P. Penney

Bibliography

Ewan, Joseph. *A Short History of Botany in the United States.* New York: Hafner Publishing Company, 1969.

Green, J. Reynolds. *A History of Botany, 1860–1900.* New York: Russel and Russel, 1967.

Morton, A. G. *History of Botanical Science.* New York: Academic Press, 1981.

Reed, Howard S. *A Short History of the Plant Sciences.* New York: Ronald Press Company, 1942.

Water Movement

Plants that grow on land (terrestrial plants) find the materials they require for life in two different locations. The soil is the source of water and minerals to be used for a variety of functions, while the atmosphere provides carbon dioxide for photosynthesis. The root system takes up water and minerals from the soil, while the shoot system, consisting of leaves and stems, carries out photosynthesis. As larger plants evolved, the roots and shoots became increasingly distant from each other, and long-distance transport systems (xylem and phloem) became necessary for survival. Clearly, one of the most important functions of the root system is the absorption of water.

How does the root absorb water? Once inside the plant, how do water and dissolved minerals move from the root to the shoot? What happens to the water once it is delivered to the leaves by the xylem? To answer these questions, it is useful to discuss the end of the transport process first, since it is there that the driving force is found.

Transpiration

Nearly 99 percent of the water taken up by plants is lost to the atmosphere through small pores located mainly on the lower surface of leaves. Estimates of water loss by a single corn plant exceed 200 liters (53 gallons) over a growing season. This loss of water by the shoots of plants is called transpiration. Transpiration provides the driving force for the movement of water up the plant from the roots to the leaves. This movement ultimately results in further uptake of water from the soil.

Of course, the water taken up by the plant serves functions within the plant as well. Water is the environment in which life and its reactions occur. Water, and the materials dissolved or suspended in it, make up the cytoplasm of cells and the interior of cellular compartments. It is the uptake of water that drives the growth of plant cells. Water enters into many reactions or chemical changes in cells, including the reactions that capture light energy during photosynthesis.

The Causes of Transpiration. The small pores through which shoots lose water to the atmosphere are called stomata. These pores, which allow carbon dioxide into the plant from the surrounding air, are actually spaces between the cells that make up the "skin," or epidermis, of the shoot. Stomata can be open or closed, depending on the action of a pair of cells, called guard cells, surrounding the pore.

Stomata open in response to the plant's requirement for carbon dioxide in photosynthesis. The carbon dioxide cannot move directly into the shoot cells because the outside of the shoot is covered with an impenetrable waxy coating, the **cuticle**. This coating prevents the plant from drying

cuticle the waxy outer coating of a leaf or other structure, providing protection against predators, infection, and water loss

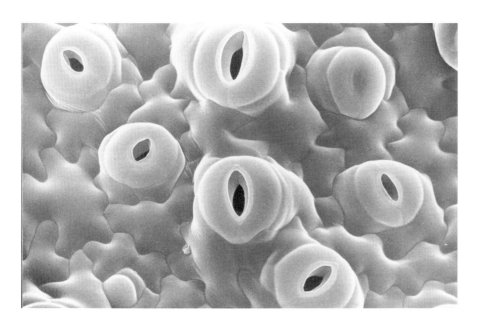

Scanning electron micrograph of the stomata on the surface of a tobacco leaf.

out but also prevents the movement of carbon dioxide into the leaves. The presence of the stomata allows for sufficient carbon dioxide to reach the leaf cells mainly responsible for photosynthesis.

Not only does carbon dioxide move into the plant when the stomata are open, but water in the form of water vapor also moves out of the plant, driven by the difference in water concentration between the plant and the atmosphere. The opening and closing of the stomatal pores maximize the uptake of carbon dioxide and minimize the loss of water by the shoot. Thus, two of the major signals that cause the stomata to open are the absorption of light and the low concentration of carbon dioxide in the leaves. As a result of these signals, most plants open their stomata during the day, when light energy is available for photosynthesis, and close them at night. Water stress, that is, a water deficit sufficient to prevent normal functioning, can override these signals and cause the pores to close in order to prevent excess water loss. For a plant, taking up carbon dioxide for growth is secondary when further water loss might threaten survival.

While transpiration is often described as a necessary evil, it does serve to cool leaves under conditions of high light absorption. The evaporation of water from leaves thus serves the same purpose for plants as sweating does for humans. Transpiration also speeds up the flow of water and dissolved minerals from the roots to the shoots. In the absence of transpiration, however, other mechanisms would cool the leaves, and water would continue to flow, though at a much lower rate, as it was used in the leaves.

The Nature of Transpiration. Transpiration is an example of diffusion, the net movement of a substance from a region of high concentration to a region of lower concentration. Diffusion accounts for transpiration because the air inside the plant is very moist, while the atmosphere surrounding the plant almost always contains less water vapor than the inside of the plant. The relative humidity of the air inside a leaf usually ranges from 98 to 100 percent, while the atmosphere rarely approaches such high values. (Relative humidity [RH] is the amount of water in the air compared to the maximum amount that could be held at that temperature.) These differences in relative humidity reflect differences in water vapor concentration, the driving force for diffusion. For example, assume that both the leaf and the atmosphere are at the same temperature of 20°C (68°F) and that the atmosphere is at a relative humidity of 50 percent. Then the air inside the leaf holds 10.9 grams of water per cubic meter, and the atmosphere holds only 5.5 grams of water per cubic meter. If the leaf is warmer than the atmosphere, a common occurrence, the difference in water vapor concentration will be even higher.

The Transpiration-Cohesion-Tension Mechanism for the Transport of Water in the Xylem

The problem of how water moves upward in plants from roots to shoots is most extreme in the tallest trees, where distances to be traveled are the greatest. Some of the tallest trees are at least 120 meters (394 feet) tall. If a hypothesis or model can explain water movement in these tallest plants, then the model can also explain it in smaller examples. Much of the research on the mechanism of water transport has been performed on relatively tall trees.

Since around the 1960s one mechanism has been the most widely accepted explanation for how water moves in the xylem. This mechanism is intimately connected to the process of transpiration described above.

Xylem Transport Cells. The xylem has a number of kinds of cells and so is called a complex tissue. The xylem vessels are the cells that actually transport water and dissolved minerals from the root. Two types of xylem vessels exist: vessel members and tracheids.

While vessel members and tracheids differ in a number of respects, they share one prominent structural feature: both are dead when transporting water. For xylem vessels, the production of strong secondary walls and the death of the cell are key characteristics that must be taken into account by any proposed mechanism. Also significant is the fact that cell walls are permeable to the flow of water, though they do offer some resistance to the flow.

Inadequate Explanations for the Movement of Water from Roots to Shoots. Ideas to explain the uptake and transport of water are of two basic types. Either water can be pushed (pumped) from the bottom of the plant, or it can be pulled to the top. Early experimenters attempted to explain water movement in terms of pumps, which were thought to be located either in the roots or all along the path of water movement. Pumping water requires energy, and only the living cells in the plant expend energy. So, in 1893 a German researcher named Eduard Strasburger tested the hypothesis that living cells in the plant push water up the stem. He cut twenty-

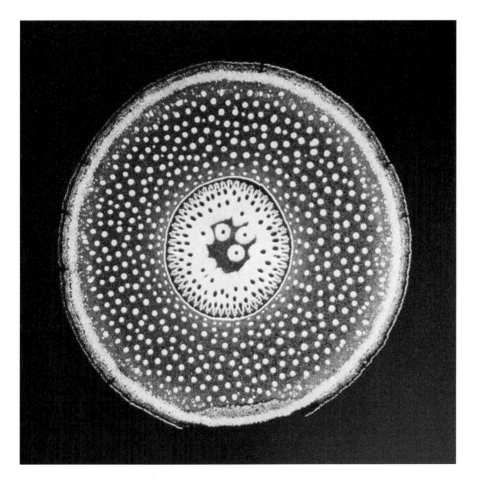

Cross-section micrograph of a root of a species of *Pandanus* conifer showing xylem, phloem, and cortex cells.

161

meter-tall trees off at the base and placed the cut stumps in buckets of poisons that would kill any living cells that were contacted. The trees continued to transport water despite the death of the living cells in the trunks. This experiment demonstrated that living stem cells are not required for transport of water through the stem. Further, the experiment showed that the roots are not necessary for the transport of water.

One "pull" model for water transport in the xylem is capillarity, the rise of some liquids in small tubes that are made of materials to which the liquid is attracted. However, capillarity can only pull water to a height of less than half a meter (ten and a half feet) in tubes the size of xylem vessels. This mechanism is clearly inadequate to explain water transport in tall trees.

The Transpiration-Cohesion-Tension Mechanism

An alternative pull model, the transpiration-cohesion-tension mechanism, is accepted as the best explanation thus far for water movement. The hypothesis has several components, as the name implies. Transpiration, the loss of water by the above-ground or aerial parts of the plant, has already been described. Cohesion refers to an attraction between molecules that are alike, in this case, water molecules. When water molecules interact, they are attracted to each other, the partial negative charge on the oxygen of one molecule being attracted to the partial positively charged hydrogen of another. These attractions, called hydrogen bonds, are quite important in the transpiration-cohesion mechanism.

Another important but less familiar idea is tension, or negative pressure. When a substance is compressed, a positive pressure higher than atmospheric pressure is generated. When a substance is being pulled from both ends, rather than compressed, a negative pressure, or tension, results that is lower than atmospheric pressure. One way to visualize a tension is to think about liquid in a syringe, which has the needle end sealed. When the plunger is pulled toward the back of the barrel, the liquid is pulled and is under a tension.

The transpiration-cohesion-tension mechanism can be explained as a series of sequential steps:

1. The first step is the diffusion of water from the leaf through the stomatal pores. This is transpiration, and it provides the force driving the transport of water.

2. As water exits the leaf, more water evaporates from the cell walls of the leaf into the extensive air spaces within the leaf.

3. As water evaporates from the cell walls, this loss pulls more liquid water from the xylem of the leaf. This flow occurs because the water in the tiny pores and crevices in the cell walls is continuous with the water in the xylem vessels and because the continuous water molecules are held together by the high cohesion of water.

4. Cohesion also accounts for the flow of the column of water from the xylem of the root to the xylem of the leaves, as water is lost through the stomata.

5. As water flows upward in the root, water influx from the soil fills the void.

The flow of water and dissolved minerals in the xylem is an example of bulk flow, the movement of a solution as a whole rather than as individual molecules. A more common example of bulk flow is the streaming of water with its dissolved minerals in the pipes of a house. One difference between the house and xylem examples is that the pressures in plumbing are positive pressures, and water is pushed out the faucet. The pressures in the xylem are negative pressures, and water is pulled up the plant. In both cases transport occurs from a region of higher pressure to lower pressure. The transport cells in the xylem are also unlike the living cells of the plant, which have positive pressures on the order of five to ten times atmospheric pressure.

Evidence for the Transpiration-Cohesion-Tension Mechanism. According to the transpiration-cohesion-tension mechanism, the process of water transport in the xylem is purely physical, with no energy input from living cells of the plant. This is consistent with the structure of the xylem vessels, which are nonliving. The cell walls of the xylem vessels are strong secondary walls, which can withstand the very negative pressures in the xylem stream. In order to pull water to the top of the tallest trees, the tensions at the top must be around negative thirty atmospheres.

Experimental evidence supports the transpiration-cohesion-tension mechanism as well. If the pressures in the xylem were positive and higher than atmospheric pressure, cutting through a xylem vessel would open the cut end to atmospheric pressure, and water would exude from the cut end. Since the pressures in the xylem are negative and lower than atmospheric, air is actually sucked into the cut end when the xylem vessels are cut, and water retreats into the xylem vessels. (Recutting cut flowers under water is good advice, since this refills the xylem vessels with water and keeps the flowers fresh longer.)

The retreat into the xylem vessels allows the tensions in the xylem to be measured by a device called a pressure bomb or pressure chamber. A leaf or twig is cut from the plant, and the blade is sealed into a strong metal chamber with the leaf stalk (petiole) or stem extending into the air. The chamber is pressurized until the contents of the xylem are forced back to their original position at the cut surface. The positive pressure required to restore the water to its original position is equal to, but opposite in sign, to the tension that existed in the xylem before it was cut. Tensions measured in the xylem higher up a tree are more negative than lower in the tree, in keeping with the proposed mechanism.

Questions About the Mechanism. The main controversy surrounding transpiration-cohesion-tension mechanism questions whether water columns in the xylem can withstand the tensions required for transport. In a large pipe a column of water can withstand very little tension before the column breaks and an air bubble forms. Bubble formation (cavitation) stops the flow of water in a xylem vessel in much the same way that vapor lock stops the flow of gasoline in the fuel line of a car. However, the tension that a liquid can sustain increases as the diameter of the vessel decreases, and xylem vessels are very small (twenty to several hundred micrometers in trees, for example), and as a result the tension they can sustain without cavitation is very high.

HENRY DIXON

Henry Dixon, an early researcher important in developing the cohesion theory, actually devised the pressure chamber in 1914, but made his chambers out of glass, with explosive results. Per Scholander first successfully used the pressure chamber in 1965 to measure the xylem tensions in tall Douglas-fir trees. He obtained his twig samples with the help of a sharpshooter who shot them down with a rifle.

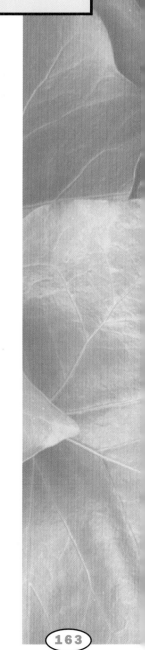

Even so, bubbles do form in the xylem under various conditions such as drought, when very negative tensions are required to transport water. Using sensitive microphones, researchers can detect individual cavitation events as clicks that occur when the water column breaks. Although bubbles do form, water can move around a blocked xylem vessel, and plants can restore the continuity of the water columns in various ways. Researchers continue to investigate and question the cohesion mechanism, particularly new methods to measure tensions in the xylem.

Uptake of Water by Roots and the Movement of Water Into the Xylem

The mechanism for water uptake into roots differs from that for transpiration (diffusion) and for the flow of sap in the xylem (bulk flow). In order for water and dissolved minerals from the soil to enter the xylem of the root, cell membranes must be crossed. Osmosis is the movement of water across membranes that allow water to move freely but that control the movement of dissolved substances, such as mineral ions.

parenchyma one of three types of cells in ground tissue

Why must water cross living cells as it moves across the root? Why can't water simply flow around the cells in the cell walls and enter the root xylem directly? The primary roots of plants generally consist of three concentric rings of tissue. On the outside is the epidermis, a single layer of cells usually lacking a thick waxy coating, suiting the root well for its role in water absorption. Next toward the center are layers of **parenchyma** cells that make up the cortex of the root. At the center of the root is the vascular tissue, including the xylem. The innermost layer of the cortex, the endodermis or "inner skin," has a special feature that prevents water movement through the cell walls of this layer. The walls that are perpendicular to the surface of the root contain waxy deposits called Casparian strips. The Casparian

ions charged particles

strips are impermeable to water and dissolved substances like mineral **ions** and thus block transport in the cell walls at the endodermis. Both water and minerals must enter the cytoplasm of the endodermal cells by crossing cell membranes. The water and minerals then cross into the vascular tissue by moving through living cells and cytoplasmic connections between them, finally exiting into the xylem by crossing yet another membrane.

The role of the Casparian strips is probably related more to the movement of mineral ions into the plant than to the movement of water. Mineral ions must cross membranes by means of special proteins in the membrane. Sometimes these proteins concentrate ions and other substances inside the cells by using cellular energy. By forcing mineral ions to cross membranes, the Casparian strips allow the plant to control which minerals will enter and to accumulate these ions to levels higher than in the soil water. SEE ALSO ANATOMY OF PLANTS; CELLS, SPECIALIZED TYPES; LEAVES; PHOTOSYNTHESIS, CARBON FIXATION AND; PHOTOSYNTHESIS, LIGHT REACTIONS AND; ROOTS; STEMS; VASCULAR TISSUES.

Susan A. Dunford

Bibliography

Campbell, Neil A., Jane B. Reece, and Lawrence G. Mitchell. "Transport in Plants." *Biology*. Menlo Park, CA: Benjamin Cummings, 1999.

Canny, Martin J. "Transporting Water in Plants." *American Scientist* 86 (1998): 152–59.

Pockman, William T., John S. Sperry, and James W. O'Leary. "Sustained and Significant Negative Water Pressure in Xylem." *Nature* 378 (1995): 715–16.

Raven, Peter. H., Ray F. Evert, and Susan E. Eichhorn. *Biology of Plants*, 6th ed. New York: W. H. Freeman and Co., 1999.

Ryan, Michael G., and Barbara J. Yoder. "Hydraulic Limits to Tree Height and Tree Growth." *Bioscience* 47 (1997): 235–42.

Steudle, Ernst. "Trees Under Tension." *Nature* 378 (1995): 663–64.

Zimmerman, Martin H., and Claud L. Brown. "Transport in the Xylem." In *Trees: Structure and Function*. New York: Springer-Verlag, 1971.

Weeds

Weeds represent the most important pest complex affecting humans throughout the world. In the United States, weeds are estimated to cost the economy more than $20 billion annually. Weeds negatively affect food and fiber production, human and animal health, and the quality of life for the world population. For instance, weeds impact humankind by causing crop failures, triggering allergic reactions, and reducing the esthetic quality of lawns. Interestingly, of the thousands of plant species in the world, less than 250, or approximately one-tenth of a percent, are considered important weeds.

There are a number of definitions for weeds. The Weed Science Society of America in 1994 defined weeds simply as "plants that are objectionable or interfere with the activities or welfare of man." However, an ecological definition describing the characteristics that allow some plants to be weeds is more useful. These characteristics include: the ability to establish in disturbed habitats; the ability to grow and reproduce across a wide range of climatic conditions; seed dormancy; nonspecific germination requirements; rapid growth; high seed production; and unspecialized pollination. Weeds can improve their success by releasing metabolic **compounds** that interfere with neighboring plants. These compounds are allelotoxins, and the resulting allelopathic response on other plants may represent a future weed management opportunity.

compound a substance formed from two or more elements

Weeds growing in a North Dakota wheat stubble field.

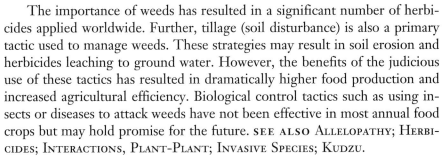

The importance of weeds has resulted in a significant number of herbicides applied worldwide. Further, tillage (soil disturbance) is also a primary tactic used to manage weeds. These strategies may result in soil erosion and herbicides leaching to ground water. However, the benefits of the judicious use of these tactics has resulted in dramatically higher food production and increased agricultural efficiency. Biological control tactics such as using insects or diseases to attack weeds have not been effective in most annual food crops but may hold promise for the future. SEE ALSO Allelopathy; Herbicides; Interactions, Plant-Plant; Invasive Species; Kudzu.

Micheal D. K. Owen

Bibliography

Baker, H. G. "The Evolution of Weeds." In *Annual Review of Ecology and Systematics*, Vol. 5, eds. R. F. Johnston, P. W. Frank, and C. D. Michener. Palo Alto, CA: Annual Review, Inc., 1974.

Bridges, D. D. "Impact of Weeds on Human Endeavors." *Weed Technology* 8 (1994): 392–95.

Wetlands

Wetlands are habitats characterized by saturated (waterlogged) soils for at least part of the year and plants that are adapted to grow under wet conditions. They may be completely covered by water or the water may be just below the ground. There are many different types of wetlands, such as swamps (wetlands dominated by trees), marshes (wetlands dominated by nonwoody plants such as grasses and sedges), wet meadows, bogs, fens, floodplain forests, lakes, and ponds.

Wetlands are to a large extent the product of the topography of the land. They develop wherever there is a depression in the land that brings the **water table** (groundwater) close to or even above ground. The type of wetland that will develop in a particular area depends on the rate of water flow, the length of the season of soil saturation, latitude (polar versus temperate versus tropical), proximity to the coast (marine versus freshwater wetlands), and the surrounding geology.

water table level of water in the soil

Plant Adaptations to Wetlands

It is challenging for a plants to grow in constantly damp conditions. The saturated soil contains little or no oxygen compared to upland soil, therefore the roots of wetland plants require special adaptations to enable them to survive. Water lilies have air channels that run from their leaves, which are in constant contact with the air, to their roots under water. Water lilies also have their **stomata** only on the upper surface of their leaves (most plants have stomata on the lower surface) so that water can not enter when these pores open to allow carbon dioxide in for photosynthesis. Salt marsh grasses (*Spartina* species) also transport oxygen to their roots, where it may be excreted into the surrounding soil and create a small oxygenated zone around their roots. Plants that grow completely underwater, such as seagrasses and pondweeds, use the oxygen created as a by-product of photosynthesis to aerate their roots. Most wetland plants have also adapted to wet conditions through changes in their metabolism. Non-wetland plants, for example, typically produce an alcohol (ethanol) as a breakdown product of sugar me-

stomata openings between guard cells on the underside of leaves that allow gas exchange

Wetlands develop wherever there is a depression in the land that brings the water table close to or even above ground.

tabolism when the soil is saturated with water. Ethanol is toxic to plants. Wetland plants have different **enzymes** that prevent the formation of the alcohol.

enzyme a protein that controls a reaction in a cell

Although only a limited number of species can thrive in the constantly saturated soils of wetlands, those plants that have adapted are often extremely productive. As anyone who has planted a garden knows, one of the major factors limiting the growth of terrestrial plants is water. Having adapted to life in constantly damp conditions, wetland plants never have to worry about getting water. As a result, their growth rates can be very high.

The Value of Wetlands to Humans

Wetlands are very important features in the landscape and provide humans with some tangible benefits. They act like a sponge helping to reduce the impacts of floods by absorbing water and serving as a reservoir for groundwater. As water flows through a wetland, pollutants such as excess silt and harmful nutrients are trapped; thus, the wetland acts as a filter of pollutants and helps to maintain clean water. Wetlands serve as a vital habitat to many different species of wildlife, including many that are very rare and in danger of extinction.

The value of wetlands has not always been appreciated. A conservative estimate is that over 30 percent of the original wetlands in the United States have been lost forever. These were filled in the past to make way for farms, houses, highways, businesses, and other human activity. Since the early 1970s, the attitude toward wetlands has changed. Not only are there now strong efforts in most states to protect the remaining wetlands, many environmental agencies and land conservation groups are working to restore wetlands damaged by past human activities.

Current Threats to Wetlands

Even with a greater sense of the value of wetlands among much of the public, there are still pressures on these habitats. The ability of wetlands to

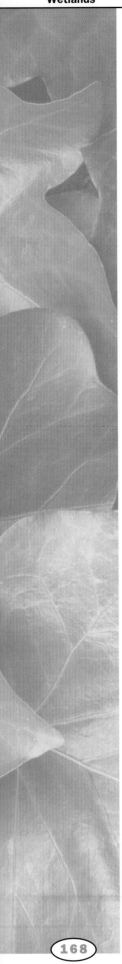

GROWTH HABITS OF WETLAND PLANTS

Growth Habit	Examples
Completely submerged	Sea grasses, pondweeds, water plantain, water milfoil, elodea
Floating plants, unrooted in substrate	Duckweeds, bladderworts, water hyacinth
Floating leaves, rooted in substrate	Water lilies, lotus, floating hearts, water chestnut
Emergent perennials: roots in substrate under water, leaves and stems above water	Cattails, common reed, purple loosestrife, salt marsh grasses, tule, saw grass, wild rice
Emergent shrubs	Buttonbush, alders, leather leaf, sweet gale
Trees: constantly submerged	Mangroves, bald cypress, black spruce
Trees of floodplains: tolerate periodic flooding	Cottonwood, willow, silver maple, black ash

community a group of organisms of different species living in a region

absorb pollutants is not unlimited. Excessive amounts of pollution entering a wetland over a long period of time is likely to cause long-term changes in the wetland. One of the world's most famous wetlands, the Everglades of southern Florida, has suffered for years from pollution from fertilizers used by farms upstream from it. The pollution has resulted in some major changes in the plant **community** and suspected declines in the diversity of animals it supports.

Another major threat to wetlands is changes in hydrology (the flow of water). Water is the lifeblood of wetlands. If too much water is removed for human consumption or to irrigate cropland, the wetland may be degraded into a less-valuable habitat or even disappear completely. The Florida Everglades has to compete with the farms and rapidly growing cities of southern Florida for this precious resource and has suffered as a result. Not only is the quantity of water important to maintaining wetlands, but so is the timing. Many wetlands depend on seasonal flooding followed by a dry period. This type of natural cycle may be altered by dams, which may hold back the water during the wet season.

Direct filling of wetlands, although less common than it was twenty years ago, still occurs, particularly with smaller wetlands that may be perceived as less valuable than larger ones. Some small wetland types contain rare species of animals precisely because they are too small and temporary in existence to support fish predators, pointing out that size is not always a good indicator of value.

Finally, many wetlands throughout the world are threatened by invasions of nonnative plant species. Purple loosestrife, a European garden plant, has taken over many freshwater marshes in the northeastern United States. West Coast salt marshes are threatened with being overrun by tall cordgrass, an East Coast salt marsh species. These are only two examples of a very widespread problem. SEE ALSO AQUATIC ECOSYSTEMS; AQUATIC PLANTS; CARNIVOROUS PLANTS; ENDANGERED PLANTS; INVASIVE SPECIES; PEAT BOGS.

Robert Buchsbaum

Bibliography

Mitsch, William J., and James G. Gosselink. *Wetlands,* 3rd ed. New York: John Wiley & Sons, 2000.

Niering, William A., and Charles Elliot, eds. *Wetlands.* National Audubon Society Nature Guides, 1983.

Tiner, Ralph W. *In Search of Swampland: A Wetland Sourcebook and Field Guide.* New Brunswick, NJ: Rutgers University Press, 1998.

Wheat

Common wheat (*Triticum aestivum*) is an annual cool season grass that is grown across a wide range of environments around the world. It has the broadest range of adaptation of all the cereals and more land is devoted to wheat than any other commercial crop. Wheat is the number-one food grain consumed directly by humans, and its production leads all crops, including rice, maize, and potatoes.

Wheat is a typical grass in that it forms several leafy shoots that grow about one meter in height. Each shoot has five to seven nodes and produces an **inflorescence** that is a thick condensed spike. Each spike has a main axis bearing spikelets separated by short internodes with two to five florets within each spikelet. Wheat normally has thirty to forty kernels per spike and is self-pollinated. The moisture content of the seed is about 10 percent, which makes wheat grain easy to store and transport.

This crop is the most important source of carbohydrates in the majority of countries in the temperate zone. Wheat is an excellent food, even though the grain is deficient in some essential amino acids (it is particularly low in lysine). Wheat starch is easily digested, as is most wheat protein. The grain contains minerals, vitamins, and fats (lipids), and when wheat products are complemented by small amounts of animal or **legume** protein, the combination is highly nutritious. A predominantly wheat-based diet is higher in fiber and lower in fats than a meat-based diet.

Most of the wheat marketed is used to manufacture flour from which bread, cakes, cookies, crackers, and pastries are made. Wheat grain is an excellent livestock feed, as are many of the by-products from the milling of the grain into flour. Normally about 70 percent of the grain can be made into flour and the rest into very useful by-products. Also, the green plants can be used for livestock forage.

Wheat has unique baking properties, the most important of which is the elasticity of its gluten protein. The amount and quality of the gluten pro-

inflorescence an arrangement of flowers on a stalk

legumes beans and other members of the Fabaceae family

More land is devoted to wheat than to any other commercial crop.

duced by any particular type are prime factors in determining the quality of the flour that can be obtained from the milling process. Unlike any other grain or plant product, wheat gluten enables dough to rise through the formation of small gas cells that retain the carbon dioxide formed during yeast fermentation or chemical leavening. This is what gives bread its porous structure. Bread has been a basic food for humans throughout recorded history, and probably for a much longer period: it remains the principal food product made from wheat.

Wheat is divided into several classes based on the level of the gluten protein. Hard wheats are high in protein (13 to 15 percent) with strong gluten strength and are used primarily for bread making. Soft wheats are low in protein (10 to 12 percent) with weak gluten strength and are used for cakes, cookies, and other pastries.

There are also two types of wheat based on the season they are grown. Winter wheat is fall planted and is harvested in early summer. Spring wheat is planted in the early spring and harvested in the summer. Winter wheat is quite winter hardy and actually requires cold temperatures in order to head out and produce a grain crop, whereas spring wheat is not winter hardy and does not have a cold requirement to produce grain.

A crop of wheat is harvested somewhere in the world during every month of the year. Most of the global harvest, however, occurs between April and September in the temperate zone of the Northern Hemisphere; considerably less wheat is grown in the Southern Hemisphere, where harvest occurs from October to January.

The culture of wheat is highly mechanized with large grain drills used to plant and large combines to harvest. A single person can grow hundreds of acres since it is not labor intensive. Wheat does not require as much fertilizer as most other crops and only occasionally requires pesticides such as fungicides, herbicides, or insecticides. Wheat is less profitable on a per-acre basis than many other crops and to date no genetically transformed wheat has been grown on a commercial scale. A great deal of research is being done with wheat and it is probable that genetically engineered wheat will be available in the near future. SEE ALSO AGRICULTURE, HISTORY OF; AGRICULTURE, MODERN; ECONOMIC IMPORTANCE OF PLANTS; GRAINS; TRANSGENIC PLANTS.

Ronald D. Barnett

Bibliography

Briggle, L. W. "Origin and Botany of Wheat." In *Wheat*, ed. E. Hafliger. Basel, Switzerland: Documenta Ciba-Geigy, 1980.

———, and B. C. Curtis. "Wheat Worldwide." In *Wheat and Wheat Improvement*, ed. E. G. Heyne. Madison, WI: American Society of Agronomy, Inc., 1987.

Buskuk, W., and C. W. Wrigley. "Proteins: Composition, Structure, and Function." In *Wheat: Production and Utilization*, ed. G. E. Inglett. Westport, CT: AVI Publishing Co., 1974.

Johnson, V. A., L. W. Briggle, J. D. Axtell, L. F. Bouman, E. R. Leng, and T. H. Johnston. "Grain Crops." In *Protein Resources and Technology*, eds. M. Milner et al. Westport, CT: AVI Publishing Co., 1978.

Leonard, W. H., and J. H. Martin. *Cereal Crops*. New York: Macmillan, 1963.

Wood Anatomy

Woody trees such as the giant sequoia of California and the blue gum of Australia are among the world's largest organisms. Despite the tremendous bulk of their stems, only a relatively thin layer of tissue between the bark and the wood is actually alive and continues to produce new layers of wood throughout the life of the tree. How the **meristematic** tissue that produces these layers remains active for hundreds or even thousands of years is one of the major unanswered questions of plant biology.

meristematic related to cell division at the tip

Meristematic Regions and Growth Patterns of Woody Plants

Plant embryos inside the seed are tiny rudimentary individuals that have the potential to produce the entire adult plant. This potential for growth rests in specialized areas of the embryo called the **apical meristems**. Upon seed germination, the root apical meristem at the basal end of the embryo starts to grow and to produce the root system of the plant. The shoot apical meristem at the opposite end of the embryo produces the shoot system. These apical meristems extend the length of the stem-root axis and, through cell proliferation, produce all the primary tissues of the plant body (epidermis, vascular tissues, and ground tissues). Plants belonging to the monocot group have only apical meristems. While some monocot stems become thick through primary thickening growth and become large trees like the date palm, monocots are never truly woody plants because they lack a vascular cambium.

apical meristem region of dividing cells at the tips of growing plants

In contrast, almost all plants belonging to the dicot group have two types of lateral meristems that increase the girth of the stems and roots: vascular cambium and cork cambium. The vascular cambium arises within the tissues of the stem and root. It first appears between the xylem and phloem of the vascular bundles and then extends between the vascular bundles to form a continuous sheet of cells around the stem. The defining feature of the vascular cambium is its distinctive plane of cell division: vascular cambium cells called cambial initials divide periclinally (that is, in a plane that is parallel with the surface of the stem and root). Cells derived from divisions of the cambial initials are called derivatives. Derivatives formed toward the inside of the stem and root become xylem cells, while derivatives formed toward the outside become phloem cells. The tissues formed by a lateral meristem are called secondary tissues, so the vascular cambium produces secondary xylem (wood) and secondary phloem.

The cells of secondary xylem tissue have hard, rigid cell walls and do not compress easily. Therefore, as the cambial initials produce increasingly more secondary xylem derivatives and the stem or root increase in girth, the cambium and all other tissues to the exterior begin to be stretched. This is often the signal for the formation of the second kind of lateral meristem, the cork cambium. In the stem, the cork cambium usually arises just under the epidermis, while in the root the cork cambium arises closer to the vascular tissue, from the pericycle. In each case, the initials of the cork cambium divide periclinally, like the vascular cambium, but the cork cambium produces derivative cells only toward the outside. These derivatives mature as cork tissue, a compact, waterproof, and airtight layer that protects internal cells.

A magnified transverse section of a piece of wood reveals its growth rings.

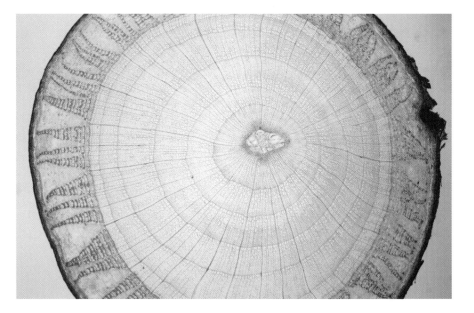

Many common wild and garden plants such as roses, sunflowers, and asters have both vascular and cork cambiums that produce secondary vascular and cork tissues. These plants live for a relatively short time and their lateral meristems produce only a moderate amount of secondary tissue. Other plants live for decades or centuries, and their lateral meristems produce secondary tissues year after year, building up massive volumes of wood and bark. These are the true woody plants, and most produce a large main stem or trunk, with smaller lateral branches.

Anatomy of a Woody Stem

Many features of wood and bark can be identified in a tree stump without a microscope's magnification. Growth rings reflect the annual activity of the vascular cambium. Early in the growing season, the cambium produces xylem derivatives that mature as wide, thin-walled cells, forming a visible light layer of wood called the earlywood. Later in the growing season, xylem derivatives mature as narrower, thicker-walled cells, forming a darker layer in the wood called latewood. In temperate climates, each pair of earlywood and latewood layers form a recognizable annual ring. In years when conditions for tree growth are good, the vascular cambium divides actively and produces a wide annual ring. When growth conditions are poor, the cambium divides slowly, and the annual ring is narrow. The distinctive pattern of wide and narrow annual rings in a tree trunk provides clues about tree growth rates in the past, often for periods that extend for hundreds of years. **Dendrochronologists** use this information to make deductions about past climatic conditions and, in some cases, can determine the exact dates that a piece of wood from an ancient building was part of a living tree.

Many trees have a darker region of wood at the center of the trunk or root called heartwood. The coloration arises from **tannins** and other substances that retard decay created by xylem **parenchyma** cells before they die. Since the conducting cells (vessel elements and **tracheids**) and the sup-

dendrochronologist a scientist who uses tree rings to determine climate or other features of the past

tannins compounds produced by plants that usually serve protective functions; often colored and used for "tanning" and dyeing

parenchyma one of three types of plant cell

tracheid a type of xylem cell for water transport

porting cells (sclerenchyma fibers) are already dead, the entire heartwood is nonliving. The lighter wood toward the outside of the trunk is called sapwood. Sapwood contains living parenchyma cells that function in storage and to recover nutrients from the sap. Although the entire sapwood region is moist, usually only the outer growth rings nearest the vascular cambium actually transport water from the roots to the leaves.

Another conspicuous feature of woody stems and roots are the panels of parenchyma tissue called rays that extend radially from the center of the heartwood, across the cambium, and into the bark. The ray parenchyma cells are produced by specialized cambium initials called ray initials and function as other xylem parenchyma cells. In some kinds of wood such as oak, the rays are very wide; in others such as pine, the rays are very narrow.

The bark found at the exterior of woody stems and roots is a composite structure. The secondary phloem that conducts the products of photosynthesis from leaves to roots is located directly adjacent to the vascular cambium. In most trees, the sieve elements of the secondary phloem are able to **translocate** for only one year. As the phloem ages, it becomes nonfunctional. Before all the phloem cells die, some of the parenchyma cells give rise to a new cork cambium that produces a new layer of cork tissue. Thus, bark is composed of alternating layers of dead phloem and cork tissues, with the only living cells found toward the inside. Thus woody stems have a thick insulating layer that protects the delicate vascular cambium within.

translocate to move, especially to move sugars from the leaf to other parts of the plant

Differences Between Hardwood and Softwood

Hardwood is the term used for the strong, dense wood of **angiosperm** trees such as maple, oak, and mahogany. Usually more than 50 percent of the volume of the wood is composed of sclerenchyma fibers, cells with extremely thick, lignin-impregnated walls, which give the wood its great physical strength. The remainder of the wood consists of conducting cells, the vessel elements and tracheids, and parenchyma cells. Hardwood trees vary in the arrangement of these cells within the annual ring. Some, like oak and elm, have wide, thin-walled vessel elements in the earlywood and much narrower vessel elements in the latewood, accentuating the differences between the two parts of the annual growth ring. This pattern is referred to as ring porous wood. Other hardwoods such as maple and willow have vessel elements of more uniform diameter scattered across the growth ring. This pattern is called diffuse porous wood.

angiosperm a flowering plant

The term softwood is used for the wood of conifers such as pines, firs, and spruces. The wood tends to be softer and less dense because it lacks the specialized sclerenchyma fibers of the hardwoods. Most of the volume of conifer wood is occupied by tracheids, cells that both conduct water and provide mechanical support. Because they carry out both functions, tracheids have relatively thin cell walls. The parenchyma tissue of softwoods often contains resin-filled ducts; these are part of the tree's defense system against insects and fungal diseases. SEE ALSO ANATOMY OF PLANTS; CONIFERS; CORK; DENDROCHRONOLOGY; TREES; VASCULAR TISSUES; WOOD PRODUCTS.

Nancy G. Dengler

Bibliography

Carlquist, Sherwin. *Ecological Strategies of Xylem Evolution.* Los Angeles: University of California Press, 1975.

Esau, Katherine. *Anatomy of Seed Plants.* New York: John Wiley & Sons, 1977.

Raven, Peter. H., Ray F. Evert, and Susan E. Eichhorn. *Biology of Plants,* 6th ed. New York: W. H. Freeman and Co., 1999.

Zimmerman, Martin H. *Xylem Structure and the Ascent of Sap.* New York: Springer-Verlag, 1983.

Wood Products

Wood is one of the most significant structural materials used throughout human history. As documented by the earliest **artifacts** of human activity, wood has been associated with activities of hunting and gathering, early development of agriculture, and the foundations of civilization, as well as its obvious use as a fuel for fire. Archaeological studies of virtually every known civilization confirm the use of wood for a wide range of items and attest to wood's intimate involvement with human evolution and its progress through time.

artifacts pots, tools, or other cultural objects

As a structural material, wood has some rather remarkable properties. Despite its relatively low density (most woods float), it has physical characteristics that make it highly suitable for the building of structures that require resistance to bending, limited compressibility, relative ease of forming the members, and reliable means of attaching the structures together. In addition, properly prepared wood also possess aesthetic and physical beauty due to its color, strength, and grain characteristics that are highly valued in the fabrication of fine furniture and architectural components.

Dimensional Lumber

Among the many uses of wood products, the production of dimensional lumber ranks as one of the most significant, particularly in the construction of residential dwellings. The majority of timber species used for dimensional lumber are conifers (**gymnosperms**), which are typically evergreen (nondeciduous) trees, and come from areas where these plants are the major component of the flora in their habitats (e.g., coniferous forests). The wood produced from them is called softwood despite the fact that for many species it is quite hard and durable. This term is used in contrast to hardwood, a term applied to the wood obtained from **angiosperm** trees, which are typically (but not always) deciduous, and have slightly different cellular characteristics of their xylem. In North America, three major groups of conifers are used for the majority of dimensional lumber: spruce (*Picea* spp.), pine (*Pinus* spp.), and fir (*Abies* spp. or *Pseudotsuga* spp.). The woods of these species are very similar in appearance and have similar construction properties. The lumber industry identifies wood produced from them as SPF lumber (spruce–pine–fir), and this forms the bulk of the wood used for the construction of houses.

gymnosperm a major group of plants that includes the conifers

angiosperm a flowering plant

In the building trades, dimensional lumber is typically referred to as "2-by" material, alluding to the thickness dimension (in inches) of the rough lumber as it is sawn at a mill. A 2 × 4 when rough-sawn is nominally 2 inches (5 centimeters) in thickness by 4 inches (10 centimeters) in width and is supplied in standard lengths of 8, 10, 12, 14, 16, and 20 feet, depending on the

The wood frame of a new house being erected in Lone Pine, California.

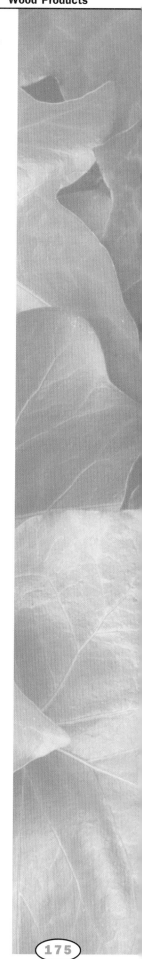

length of the felled log before sawing. After drying the wood and surfacing the faces, a 2 × 4 actually measures 1.5 × 3.5 inches (3.7 × 8.8 centimeters) in width. Other commonly used dimensions are 2 × 3, 2 × 6, 2 × 8, 2 × 10, and 2 × 12, each of which are actually one-half to three-quarters of an inch thinner than the given dimensions. Dimensional lumber forms the major structural elements of floors, walls, joists, and rafters in home construction. Recently, the use of factory-made roof trusses built from dimensional wood materials provides for quick and easy construction of roof systems that are structurally strong and provide for free spans without the need for additional structural support from within the building. Construction workers or carpenters who erect the wooden frame of the building are called framers, and dimensional lumber is the material these people rely on for their livelihood.

Hardwoods

Woods that are used for building furniture, cabinetry, millwork, or other architectural features are typically hardwoods, although some conifer woods are also used for these items. Woods that are valued for furniture and cabinetry typically have aesthetically pleasing characteristics of uniform color, interesting patterns of earlywood and latewood in cut and surfaced lumber (this characteristic is termed grain or figure), and also possess desirable properties of hardness and durability. There are literally thousands of different species of hardwood (angiosperm) trees from around the world that have the potential for use in fine furniture and cabinetry; however, there are only relatively few species that are used commercially for this purpose. This is due to the requirement of having a reliable local source for adequate amounts of lumber (which differs in various parts of the world), the wood's machineability and finishing properties to provide a pleasing end-product, and consumers who favor certain wood species over others. In North America, the three major species used for furniture production are oak (*Quercus* spp., in particular, red oak), walnut (*Juglans* spp.), and cherry (*Prunus* spp.), which are more or less

A worker carving teak furniture at a factory in Chiang Mai, Thailand.

commonly available throughout the region. Many other species of hardwoods have similarly desirable properties, and furniture made from them is also valued; their use may reflect regional availability. Certain species of woods are also best suited to specific applications given their physical attributes. The strength and shock resistance of white ash (*Fraxinus americana*) makes it the wood of choice for the manufacture of baseball bats; rake, shovel, and other tool handles; and certain parts of chairs and other heavy-use furniture. Various species of maple (*Acer* spp.) are used for butcher blocks, bowling alley surfaces, bowling pins, the backs of violins, and various parts in the construction of pianos—all relying on maple's hard and durable characteristics.

Hardwoods are harvested in nearly every country capable of supporting a lumber industry. Thus, a considerable variety of wood species is available on the world lumber market. Those woods originating within the country of intended use are called domestic lumber, versus wood from those species obtained from foreign countries, which are called exotic woods. Hundreds of hardwood species are traded globally and have a diversity of color, grain, hardness, machineability, and finishing characteristics. One of the softest and lightest woods, balsa (*Ochroma lagopus*), a tropical species from South and Central America, is technically a hardwood, although it is much softer than most coniferous softwoods. Despite this fact, it is remarkably strong for its light weight, and modern uses for this wood include model building, insulation, and flotation devices. In contrast, one of the world's heaviest hardwoods is lignum vitae (*Guaiacum officinale*), another tropical tree species from the same general region as balsa. This wood has a specific gravity of 1.3 and will not float in water. The wood of lignum vitae is very heavy, and up to 30 percent of its weight is in the form of resins and oils. This wood resists decay very well and can withstand pressures of greater than 2,000 pounds per square inch. These characteristics make lignum vitae a very useful wood for various industrial, manufacturing, and marine applications. Some hardwoods are in plentiful supply, while others are uncommon or rare due to the relative scarcity of the species in natural forests. While many of these woods possess beautiful figure and color in their grain patterns and are highly sought by furniture builders, their continued harvest may pose problems in maintaining the tree species in its habitat, since many grow slowly and reproduce infrequently.

One way of using rare or uncommon hardwoods in furniture-making is through the process of veneering. Thin slices of highly desirable hardwoods are prepared and carefully dried. The dried wood slices (veneers) are glued to the surfaces of more common, structurally stable materials (such as plywood or fiberboard), and the veneer is protected with a suitable finish such as lacquer or varnish. The use of veneer saves valuable timber resources while enabling the enjoyment of beautiful grain and color characteristics of these hardwoods.

Lumber Production and Preparation

All production of wood products begins with the logging of timber by a number of methods (e.g., clear-cutting versus selective cutting). In intensively managed forest stands, softwood lumber (particularly dimension lumber or pulp lumber) can be produced quite efficiently. In contrast, the inherently slow growth of hardwood species restricts the methods of harvest primarily to selective methods from naturally occurring timber stands. Once logs have been felled and are ready for transport, they are moved from the timber stands by vehicle or by using waterways to float them to a milling operation. At the sawmill, the logs are sawn to optimize the quantity and quality of the lumber. The sawyer needs to know the characteristics of the wood being cut and how the lumber will respond to drying and further milling operations. When cut, live timber is very wet; the cell spaces in the xylem are filled with water (a moisture content of approximately 100 percent). This water (free water) must be removed; any remaining water within the cell wall complexes (bound water) must be removed so that the final moisture content of the wood is brought down to approximately 6 to 12 percent of the total weight of the dried wood.

Two main forms of drying wood are used. If an air-drying method is used, the rough-cut lumber is stacked with spacer boards (stickers) between the pieces of wood to promote air circulation around the boards. The lumber is then set out in open areas to allow the water to evaporate slowly from the cut surfaces of the wood, which eventually reduces the moisture content to an acceptable level. The other method uses a drying kiln—essentially a very large, forced-air oven in which temperature and air movement can be carefully controlled. The wet (or partially air-dried) stickered lumber is placed in the kiln, and the temperature and air circulation is increased to evaporate the water from within the wood; this process takes much less time than air-drying. When wood dries, it tends to shrink (particularly across the grain of the wood), so the kiln operator must be aware of the drying properties of each species of wood. If dried too quickly, the lumber can split, twist, or become damaged. When the wood has been sufficiently dried, it will remain relatively stable and is less likely to be attacked by wood rotting fungi when compared to wet woods. The dry, rough-cut lumber is then planed to final dimensions and is transported to distribution centers and lumber yards for use. Further processing of some woods is done with special rotary cutters to produce millwork, architectural trim pieces commonly used around doors and windows and along floors and ceilings. Other millwork items include railings, banisters, balusters, doors, and window frames—all essential components found in most traditionally built homes and other buildings.

Manufactured Wood Products

Some wood products are actually manufactured; that is, constructed from raw wood materials, but utilizing adhesives or other filler components to create new products useful to the construction industry. Perhaps the most important of these is plywood, a wood product made of several layers or plys of thinly cut wood. The grain patterns are normally oriented at right angles to one another prior to their lamination with various forms of adhesives. The result is a sheet stock product that is very dimensionally stable, maintains its flatness when installed properly, and can be used for a wide variety of applications: flooring, sheathing for the outer shell of framed buildings, and roofing. Development of plywood has revolutionized the home construction industry, which previously relied upon sawn and processed lumber planks for these purposes. Other manufactured wood products make use of chips, coarse wood particles, and, in some cases, wood fibers or sawdust, all of which were previously discarded as waste by-products of the lumber processing industry. Advances in wood technology have permitted the use of these materials with the addition of modern adhesives to produce products such as oriented strand board (OSB), particle board, and medium-density fiberboard (MDF). These are sheet-stock materials used in home construction, furniture manufacturing, and other industrial applications.

Other Wood Products

In addition to wood's uses for construction and furniture/cabinetry manufacture, other significant uses for wood products include the harvesting of wood for use by the pulp and paper industry, production of fibers for use in industry, conversion of raw wood materials into charcoal, extraction of turpentine and similar **compounds** for use as solvents and paint additives, and the use of cork in the beverage and manufacturing industries. Even the material previously stripped from the logs and discarded prior to transport to the mill is now used. Tree bark is a valued commodity for use in the landscaping/horticultural industry, and in some cases forms an organic component to artificial soil mixes. It is encouraging to note that today none of the parts of harvested trees are wasted—the technology of wood processing is sufficiently advanced to ensure that one of the world's most valuable and sustainable resources is used as efficiently as possible. Management of forests and natural habitats as sources of wood products is essential to provide for increasing needs of wood by humans. SEE ALSO CONIFERS; CORK; FIBER AND FIBER PRODUCTS; FORESTRY; PAPER; TREES; WOOD ANATOMY.

Robert S. Wallace

compound a substance formed from two or more elements

Bibliography

Constantine, Albert, Jr. *Know Your Woods.* New York: Albert Constantine and Son, Inc., 1969.

Forest Products Laboratory. *Wood Handbook: Wood as an Engineering Material.* Madison, WI: U.S. Forest Products Laboratory, 1974.

Hoadley, R. Bruce. *Identifying Wood—Accurate Results with Simple Tools.* Newtown, CT: Taunton Press, Inc., 1995.

———. *Understanding Wood—A Craftsman's Guide to Wood Technology.* Newtown, CT: Taunton Press, Inc., 1997.

Jackson, Albert, and David Day. *Good Wood Handbook.* Cincinnati, OH: Betterway Books, 1996.

Lincoln, William A. *World Woods in Color.* Fresno, CA: Linden Publishing Co., Inc., 1986.

Yeast   *See Fungi.*

Photo and
Illustration Credits

Volume 1

Ted Spiegel/Corbis: **2, 17, 96**; JLM Visuals: **4, 107**; Bojan Brecelj/Corbis: **6**; Tom Bean/Corbis: **9, 49**; Thomas Del Brase/The Stock Market: **11**; Chinch Gryniewicz; Ecoscene/Corbis: **13**; Charles O'Rear/Corbis: **19**; Steve Raymer/Corbis: **21**; Alex Rakoey/Custom Medical Stock Photo, Inc.: **28**; Wolfgang Kaehler/Corbis: **30, 100**; Field Mark Publications: **44**; Lester V. Bergman/Corbis: **50, 158**; Julie Meech; Ecoscene/Corbis: **53**; Raymond Gehman/Corbis: **55**; Dr. Kari Lounatmaa; Science Photo Library/Photo Researchers, Inc: **57**; Roger Tidman/Corbis: **58**; The Purcell Team/Corbis: **60**; David Muench/Corbis: **63, 114**; Adrian Arbib/Corbis: **67**; Barry Griffiths; National Audubon Society Collection/Photo Researchers, Inc.: **76**; Kopp Illustration, 81; Prof. Jim Watson; Science Photo Library/Photo Researchers, Inc: **85**; Michael S. Yamashita/Corbis: **87**; Pallava Bagla/Corbis: **88**; Bettmann/Corbis: **90, 116**; Richard T. Nowitz/Corbis: **92, 94**; UPI/Corbis–Bettmann: **109**; Owen Franken/Corbis: **112**; Bill Lisenby/Corbis: **119**; Hans & Cassady: **124, 136**; Fritz Polking; Frank Lane Picture Agency/Corbis: **128**; Ron Watts/Corbis: **130**; UPI/Bettmann Newsphotos: **131**; David Spears; Science Pictures Limited/Corbis: **138, 143**; Dr. Dennis Kunkel/Phototake NYC: **141**; Dr. Jeremy Burgess/Photo Researchers, Inc.: **146, 155**; Andrew Brown; Ecoscene/Corbis: **148**; Richard Cummins/Corbis: **162**.

Volume 2

Arne Hodalic/Corbis: **2**; Gregory G. Dimijian/Photo Researchers, Inc.: **5**; Michael & Patricia Fogden/Corbis: **9**; Dean Conger/Corbis: **11, 76**; Joseph Sohm; ChromoSohm, Inc./Corbis: **16**; Darrell Gulin/Corbis: **18, 61**; Galen Rowell/Corbis: **23**; Courtesy of the Library of Congress: **24, 40, 143**; Charles O'Rear/Corbis: **26, 157**; Liba Taylor/Corbis: **29**; Richard Hamilton Smith/Corbis: **31, 32**; Bojan Brecelj/Corbis: **35**; Lester V. Bergman/Corbis: **39, 119, 166, 175**; Robert Estall/Corbis: **48**; William A. Bake/Corbis: **52**; Rosemary Mayer/Photo Researchers, Inc.: **54**; George Lepp/Corbis: **56**; Michael S. Yamashita/Corbis: **58, 114**; Raymond Gehman/Corbis: **62, 93**; Wayne Lawler; Ecoscene/Corbis: **64**; Dr. William M. Harlow/Photo Researchers, Inc.: **66**; William Boyce/Corbis: **74**; David Spears; Science Pictures Limited/Corbis: **82**; Roger Tidman/Corbis: **84**; Hans & Cassady: **86**; Roger Ressmeyer/Corbis: **103**; Susan Middleton and David Liitschwager/Corbis: **107**; Robin Foster/Conservation International: **108**; John Durham/Photo Researchers, Inc.: **112**; Jaime Razuri; AFP/Corbis: **116**; Courtesy of Linda E. Graham: **122, 125**; Buddy Mays/Corbis: **136**; Michael Freeman/Corbis: **142**; Field Mark Publications: **146, 186**; David Cumming; Eye Ubiquitous/Corbis: **149**; Bob Krist/Corbis: **152**; Gunter Marx/Corbis: **154**; Jim Sugar Photography/Corbis: **156**; Courtesy of Dr. Orson K. Miller, Jr.: **162, 163, 164**; Lowell Georgia/Corbis: **167, 170**; William James Warren/Corbis: **169**; Patrick Johns/Corbis: **178**; Eric and David Hosking/Corbis: **180**; Thomas Bettge,

National Center for Atmospheric Research/ University Corporation for Atmospheric Research/National Science Foundation: **182, 183**; Philip Gould/Corbis: **184**; Roy Morsch/ The Stock Market: **188**; Tom Bean/Corbis: **190**; Archive Photos, Inc.: **194**; JLM Visuals: **199, 200**.

Volume 3

Courtesy of the Library of Congress: **1, 30, 61, 73**; JLM Visuals: **3, 49, 106**; Corbis: **4**; Anthony Cooper; Ecoscene/Corbis: **9**; Photo Researchers, Inc.: **11**; Archive Photos, Inc.: **12**; Ed Young/Corbis: **23, 147**; Kansas Division of Travel and Tourism: **26**; Asa Thoresen/Photo Researchers, Inc.: **28**; Ted Streshinsky/Corbis: **32**; Michael S. Yamashita/Corbis: **35**; Patrick Johns/Corbis: **38, 96, 104, 125, 187**; Cumego/Corbis/ Bettmann: **39**; David Spears; Science Pictures Limited/Corbis: **41, 54, 114, 129**; W. Wayne Lockwood, M.D./Corbis: **42**; Field Mark Publications: **44, 57, 71, 169, 171, 175**; Michael & Patricia Fogden/Corbis: **46**; Phil Schermeister/Corbis: **52**; Judyth Platt; Ecoscene/Corbis: **59**; Courtesy of Hunt Institute for Botanical Documentation, Carnegie Mellon University, Pittsburgh, PA: **62**; UPI/Bettmann: **66**; Eric Crichton/Corbis: **72**; Biophoto Associates; National Audubon Society Collection/Photo Researchers, Inc.: **88**; Adam Hart-Davis/Photo Researchers, Inc.: **92**; Lester V. Bergman/Corbis: **94, 108, 167**; Patrick Field; Eye Ubiquitous/Corbis: **103**; Michael Boys/Corbis: **105**; Sally A. Morgan; Ecoscene/Corbis: **110**; Kevin Schafer/Corbis: **112**; Jim Zipp; National Audubon Society Collection/Photo Researchers, Inc.: **117**; Richard T. Nowitz/ Corbis: **120**; Wayne Lawler; Ecoscene/ Corbis: **122**; Bob Krist/Corbis: **123**; Tom and

Pat Lesson/Photo Researchers, Inc.: **158**; Raymond Gehman/Corbis: **164**; George Lepp/Corbis: **177**; Richard Hamilton Smith/Corbis: **181**; Nigel Cattlin; Holt Studios International/Photo Researchers, Inc.: **185**; Owen Franken/Corbis: **189**; Alison Wright/Corbis: **193**.

Volume 4

Kevin Schafer/Corbis: **2, 42**; Wolfgang Kaehler/Corbis: **5, 7**; E. S. Ross: **9**; Galen Rowell/Corbis: **14, 127**; David Spears; Science Pictures Limited/Corbis: **17, 20, 79, 120, 161, 172**; Robert Pickett/Corbis: **19, 101**; Dr. Jeremy Burgess/Photo Researchers, Inc.: **21, 159**; Biophoto Associates/Photo Researchers, Inc.: **22, 142**; JLM Visuals: **25, 26, 40, 140, 155, 169**; Owen Franken/ Corbis: **27**; Philip Gould/Corbis: **30, 70**; Corbis: **39, 152**; Steve Raymer/Corbis: **49**; Mark Gibson/Corbis: **57**; James Lee Sikkema: **58**; Field Mark Publications: **62, 130, 167**; Wayne Lawler/Corbis: **63**; Richard T. Nowitz/Corbis: **66**; Photo Researchers, Inc.: **68**; Karen Tweedy-Holmes/Corbis: **73**; Lester V. Bergman/Corbis: **77, 147**; Craig Aurness/Corbis: **83**; John Holmes; Frank Lane Picture Agency/Corbis: **86**; Archivo Iconografico, S.A./Corbis: **92**; Paul Almasy/Corbis: **98**; Tiziana and Gianni Baldizzone/Corbis: **105**; Darrell Gulin/ Corbis: **108**; Lynda Richardson/Corbis: **110**; Courtesy of Thomas L. Rost and Deborah K. Canington: **112, 113, 114**; Laure Communications: **115**; Archive Photos, Inc.: **116**; Jim Sugar Photography/Corbis: **132**; Hugh Clark; Frank Lane Picture Agency/Corbis: **136, 137**; Ron Boardman; Frank Lane Picture Agency/ Corbis: **148**; Richard Hamilton Smith/Corbis: **165**; Joseph Sohm; ChromoSohm, Inc./ Corbis: **175**; Dave G. Houser/Corbis: **176**.

Glossary

abiotic nonliving

abrade to wear away through contact

abrasive tending to wear away through contact

abscission dropping off or separating

accession a plant that has been acquired and catalogued

achene a small, dry, thin-walled type of fruit

actinomycetes common name for a group of Gram-positive bacteria that are filamentous and superficially similar to fungi

addictive capable of causing addiction or chemical dependence

adhesion sticking to the surface of

adventitious arising from secondary buds, or arising in an unusual position

aeration the introduction of air

albuminous gelatinous, or composed of the protein albumin

alkali chemically basic; the opposite of acidic

alkalinization increase in basicity or reduction in acidity

alkaloid bitter secondary plant compound, often used for defense

allele one form of a gene

allelopathy harmful action by one plant against another

allopolyploidy a polyploid organism formed by hybridization between two different species or varieties (*allo* = other)

alluvial plain broad area formed by the deposit of river sediment at its outlet

amended soils soils to which fertilizers or other growth aids have been added

amendment additive

anaerobic without oxygen

analgesic pain-relieving

analog a structure or thing, especially a chemical, similar to something else

angiosperm a flowering plant

anomalous unusual or out of place

anoxic without oxygen

antenna system a collection of protein complexes that harvests light energy and converts it to excitation energy that can migrate to a reaction center; the light is absorbed by pigment molecules (e.g., chlorophyll, carotenoids, phycobilin) that are attached to the protein

anthropogenic human-made; related to or produced by the influence of humans on nature

antibodies proteins produced to fight infection

antioxidant a substance that prevents damage from oxygen or other reactive substances

apical meristem region of dividing cells at the tips of growing plants

apical at the tip

apomixis asexual reproduction that may mimic sexual reproduction

appendages parts that are attached to a central stalk or axis

arable able to be cultivated for crops

Arcto-Tertiary geoflora the fossil flora discovered in Arctic areas dating back to the Tertiary period; this group contains magnolias (*Magnolia*), tulip trees (*Liriodendron*), maples (*Acer*), beech (*Fagus*), black gum (*Nyssa*), sweet gum (*Liquidambar*), dawn redwood (*Metasequoia*), cypress (*Taxodium*), and many other species

artifacts pots, tools, or other cultural objects

assayer one who performs chemical tests to determine the composition of a substance

ATP adenosine triphosphate, a small, water-soluble molecule that acts as an energy currency in cells

attractant something that attracts

autotroph "self-feeder"; any organism that uses sunlight or chemical energy

auxin a plant hormone

avian related to birds

axil the angle or crotch where a leaf stalk meets the stem

axillary bud the bud that forms in the angle between the stem and leaf

basipetal toward the base

belladonna the source of atropine; means "beautiful woman," and is so named because dilated pupils were thought to enhance a woman's beauty

binomial two-part

biodirected assays tests that examine some biological property

biodiversity degree of variety of life

biogeography the study of the reasons for the geographic distribution of organisms

biomass the total dry weight of an organism or group of organisms

biosphere the region of the Earth in which life exists

biosynthesis creation through biological pathways

biota the sum total of living organisms in a region of a given size

biotic involving or related to life

bryologist someone who studies bryophytes, a division of nonflowering plants

campanulate bell-shaped

capitulum the head of a compound flower, such as a dandelion

cardiotonic changing the contraction properties of the heart

carotenoid a yellow-colored molecule made by plants

carpels the innermost whorl of flower parts, including the egg-bearing ovules, plus the style and stigma attached to the ovules

catastrophism the geologic doctrine that sudden, violent changes mark the geologic history of Earth

cation positively charged particle

catkin a flowering structure used for wind pollination

centrifugation spinning at high speed in a centrifuge to separate components

chitin a cellulose-like molecule found in the cell wall of many fungi and arthropods

chloroplast the photosynthetic organelle of plants and algae

circadian "about a day"; related to a day

circumscription the definition of the boundaries surrounding an object or an idea

cisterna a fluid-containing sac or space

clade a group of organisms composed of an ancestor and all of its descendants

cladode a modified stem having the appearance and function of a leaf

coalescing roots roots that grow together

coleoptile the growing tip of a monocot seedling

collenchyma one of three cell types in ground tissue

colonize to inhabit a new area

colony a group of organisms inhabiting a particular area, especially organisms descended from a common ancestor

commensalism a symbiotic association in which one organism benefits while the other is unaffected

commodities goods that are traded, especially agricultural goods

community a group of organisms of different species living in a region

compaction compacting of soil, leading to the loss of air spaces

complex hybrid hybridized plant having more than two parent plants

compound a substance formed from two or more elements

concentration gradient a difference in concentration between two areas

continental drift the movement of continental land masses due to plate tectonics

contractile capable of contracting

convective uplift the movement of air upwards due to heating from the sun

coppice growth the growth of many stems from a single trunk or root, following the removal of the main stem

cortical relating to the cortex of a plant

covalent held together by electron-sharing bonds

crassulacean acid metabolism water-conserving strategy used by several types of plants

crop rotation alternating crops from year to year in a particular field

cultivation growth of plants, or turning the soil for growth of crop plants

crystallography the use of x-rays on crystals to determine molecular structure

cuticle the waxy outer coating of a leaf or other structure, which provides protection against predators, infection, and water loss

cyanide heap leach gold mining a technique used to extract gold by treating ore with cyanide

cyanobacteria photosynthetic prokaryotic bacteria formerly known as blue-green algae

cyanogenic giving rise to cyanide

cytologist a scientist who studies cells

cytology the microscopic study of cells and cell structure

cytosol the fluid portion of a cell

cytostatic inhibiting cell division

deductive reasoning from facts to conclusion

dendrochronologist a scientist who uses tree rings to determine climate or other features of the past

dermatophytes fungi that cause skin diseases

desertification degradation of dry lands, reducing productivity

desiccation drying out

detritus material from decaying organisms

diatoms hard-shelled, single-celled marine organisms; a type of algae

dictyosome any one of the membranous or vesicular structures making up the Golgi apparatus

dioicous having male and female sexual parts on different plants

diploid having two sets of chromosomes, versus having one set (haploid)

dissipate to reduce by spreading out or scattering

distal further away from

diurnal daily, or by day

domestication the taming of an organism to live with and be of use to humans

dormant inactive, not growing

drupe a fruit with a leathery or stone-like seed

dynamical system theory the mathematical theory of change within a system

ecophysiological related to how an organism's physiology affects its function in an ecosystem

ecosystem an ecological community and its environment

elater an elongated, thickened filament

empirical formula the simplest whole number ratio of atoms in a compound

emulsifier a chemical used to suspend oils in water

encroachment moving in on

endemic belonging or native to a particular area or country

endophyte a fungus that lives within a plant

endoplasmic reticulum the membrane network inside a cell

endosperm the nutritive tissue in a seed, formed by the fertilization of a diploid egg tissue by a sperm from pollen

endosporic the formation of a gametophyte inside the spore wall

endosymbiosis a symbiosis in which one organism lives inside the other

Enlightenment eighteenth-century philosophical movement stressing rational critique of previously accepted doctrines in all areas of thought

entomologist a scientist who studies insects

enzyme a protein that controls a reaction in a cell

ephemeral short-lived

epicuticle the waxy outer covering of a plant, produced by the epidermis

epidermis outer layer of cells

epiphytes plants that grow on other plants

escarpment a steep slope or cliff resulting from erosion

ethnobotanist a scientist who interacts with native peoples to learn more about the plants of a region

ethnobotany the study of traditional uses of plants within a culture

euglossine bees a group of bees that pollinate orchids and other rain-forest plants

eukaryotic a cell with a nucleus (*eu* means "true" and *karyo* means "nucleus"); includes protists, plants, animals, and fungi

extrafloral outside the flower

exudation the release of a liquid substance; oozing

facultative capable of but not obligated to

fertigation application of small amounts of fertilizer while irrigating

filament a threadlike extension

filamentous thin and long

flagella threadlike extension of the cell membrane, used for movement

flavonoids aromatic compounds occurring in both seeds and young roots and involved in host-pathogen and host-symbiont interactions

florigen a substance that promotes flowering

floristic related to plants

follicle sac or pouch

forbs broad-leaved, herbaceous plants

free radicals toxic molecular fragments

frugivous feeding on fruits

gametangia structure where gametes are formed

gametophyte the haploid organism in the life cycle

gel electrophoresis a technique for separating molecules based on size and electrical charge

genera plural of genus; a taxonomic level above species

genome the genetic material of an organism

genotype the genetic makeup of an organism

germplasm hereditary material, especially stored seed or other embryonic forms

globose rounded and swollen; globe-shaped

gradient difference in concentration between two places

green manure crop planted to be plowed under to nourish the soil, especially with nitrogen

gymnosperm a major group of plants that includes the conifers

gynoecium the female reproductive organs as a whole

gypsipherous containing the mineral gypsum

hallucinogenic capable of inducing hallucinations

haploid having one set of chromosomes, versus having two (diploid)

haustorial related to a haustorium, or food-absorbing organ

hemiterpene a half terpene

herbivore an organism that feeds on plant parts

heterocyclic a chemical ring structure composed of more than one type of atom, for instance carbon and nitrogen

heterosporous bearing spores of two types, large megaspores and small microspores

heterostylous having styles (female flower parts) of different lengths, to aid cross-pollination

heterotroph an organism that derives its energy from consuming other organisms or their body parts

holistic including all the parts or factors that relate to an object or idea

homeotic relating to or being a gene that produces a shift in structural development

homology a similarity in structure between anatomical parts due to descent from a common ancestor

humus the organic material in soil formed from decaying organisms

hybrid a mix of two varieties or species

hybridization formation of a new individual from parents of different species or varieties

hydrological cycle the movement of water through the biosphere

hydrophobic water repellent

hydroponic growing without soil, in a watery medium

hydroxyl the chemical group -OH

hyphae the threadlike body mass of a fungus

illicit illegal

impede to slow down or inhibit

inert incapable of reaction

inflorescence a group of flowers or arrangement of flowers in a flower head

infrastructure roads, phone lines, and other utilities that allow commerce

insectivorous insect-eating

intercalary inserted; between

interspecific hybridization hybridization between two species

intertidal between the lines of high and low tide

intracellular bacteria bacteria that live inside other cells

intraspecific taxa levels of classification below the species level

intuiting using intuition

ionic present as a charged particle

ions charged particles

irreversible unable to be reversed

juxtaposition contrast brought on by close positioning

lacerate cut

Lamarckian inheritance the hypothesis that acquired characteristics can be inherited

lamellae thin layers or plate-like structure

land-grant university a state university given land by the federal government on the condition that it offer courses in agriculture

landrace a variety of a cultivated plant, occurring in a particular region

lateral to the side of

legume beans and other members of the Fabaceae family

lignified composed of lignin, a tough and resistant plant compound

lineage ancestry; the line of evolutionary descent of an organism

loci (singular: locus) sites or locations

lodging falling over while still growing

lytic breaking apart by the action of enzymes

macromolecule a large molecule such as a protein, fat, nucleic acid, or carbohydrate

macroscopic large, visible

medulla middle part

megaphylls large leaves having many veins or a highly branched vein system

meiosis the division of chromosomes in which the resulting cells have half the original number of chromosomes

meristem the growing tip of a plant

mesic of medium wetness

microfibrils microscopic fibers in a cell

micron one millionth of a meter; also called micrometer

microphylls small leaves having a single unbranched vein

mitigation reduction of amount or effect

mitochondria cell organelles that produce adenosine triphosphate (ATP) to power cell reactions

mitosis the part of the cell cycle in which chromosomes are separated to give each daughter cell an identical chromosome set

molecular systematics the analysis of DNA and other molecules to determine evolutionary relationships

monoculture a large stand of a single crop species

monomer a single unit of a multi-unit structure

monophyletic a group that includes an ancestral species and all its descendants

montane growing in a mountainous region

morphology shape and form

motile capable of movement

mucilaginous sticky or gummy

murein a peptidoglycan, a molecule made up of sugar derivatives and amino acids

mutualism a symbiosis between two organisms in which both benefit

mycelium the vegetative body of a fungus, made up of threadlike hyphae

NADP⁺ oxidized form of nicotinamide adenine dinucleotide phosphate

NADPH reduced form of nicotinamide adenine dinucleotide phosphate, a small, water-soluble molecule that acts as a hydrogen carrier in biochemical reactions

nanometer one billionth of a meter

nectaries organs in flowers that secrete nectar

negative feedback a process by which an increase in some variable causes a response that leads to a decrease in that variable

neuromuscular junction the place on the muscle surface where the muscle receives stimulus from the nervous system

neurotransmitter a chemical that passes messages between nerve cells

node branching site on a stem

nomenclature a naming system

nonmotile not moving

nonpolar not directed along the root-shoot axis, or not marked by separation of charge (unlike water and other polar substances)

nonsecretory not involved in secretion, or the release of materials

Northern Blot a technique for separating RNA molecules by electrophoresis and then identifying a target fragment with a DNA probe

nucleolar related to the nucleolus, a distinct region in the nucleus

nurseryman a worker in a plant nursery

obligate required, without another option

obligate parasite a parasite without a free-living stage in the life cycle

odorant a molecule with an odor

organelle a membrane-bound structure within a cell

osmosis the movement of water across a membrane to a region of high solute concentration

oviposition egg-laying

oxidation reaction with oxygen, or loss of electrons in a chemical reaction

paleobotany the study of ancient plants and plant communities

pangenesis the belief that acquired traits can be inherited by bodily influences on the reproductive cells

panicle a type of inflorescence (flower cluster) that is loosely packed and irregularly branched

paraphyletic group a taxonomic group that excludes one or more descendants of a common ancestor

parenchyma one of three types of cells found in ground tissue

pastoralists farming people who keep animal flocks

pathogen disease-causing organism

pedicel a plant stalk that supports a fruiting or spore-bearing organ

pentamerous composed of five parts

percolate to move through, as a fluid through a solid

peribacteroid a membrane surrounding individual or groups of rhizobia bacteria within the root cells of their host; in such situations the bacteria have frequently undergone some change in surface chemistry and are referred to as bacteroids

pericycle cell layer between the conducting tissue and the endodermis

permeability the property of being permeable, or open to the passage of other substances

petiole the stalk of a leaf, by which it attaches to the stem

pH a measure of acidity or alkalinity; the pH scale ranges from 0 to 14, with 7 being neutral. Low pH numbers indicate high acidity while high numbers indicate alkalinity

pharmacognosy the study of drugs derived from natural products

pharmacopeia a group of medicines

phenology seasonal or other time-related aspects of an organism's life

pheromone a chemical released by one organism to influence the behavior of another

photooxidize to react with oxygen under the influence of sunlight

photoperiod the period in which an organism is exposed to light or is sensitive to light exposure, causing flowering or other light-sensitive changes

photoprotectant molecules that protect against damage by sunlight

phylogenetic related to phylogeny, the evolutionary development of a species

physiology the biochemical processes carried out by an organism

phytogeographer a scientist who studies the distribution of plants

pigments colored molecules

pistil the female reproductive organ of a flower

plasmodesmata cell-cell junctions that allow passage of small molecules between cells

polyculture mixed species

polyhedral in the form of a polyhedron, a solid whose sides are polygons

polymer a large molecule made from many similar parts

polynomial "many-named"; a name composed of several individual parts

polyploidy having multiple sets of chromosomes

polysaccharide a linked chain of many sugar molecules

population a group of organisms of a single species that exist in the same region and interbreed

porosity openness

positive feedback a process by which an increase in some variable causes a response that leads to a further increase in that variable

precipitation rainfall; or the process of a substance separating from a solution

pre-Columbian before Columbus

precursor a substance from which another is made

predation the act of preying upon; consuming for food

primordial primitive or early

progenitor parent or ancestor

prokaryotes single-celled organisms without nuclei, including Eubacteria and Archaea

propagate to create more of through sexual or asexual reproduction

protist a usually single-celled organism with a cell nucleus, of the kingdom Protista

protoplasmic related to the protoplasm, cell material within the cell wall

protoplast the portion of a cell within the cell wall

psychoactive causing an effect on the brain

pubescence covered with short hairs

pyruvic acid a three-carbon compound that forms an important intermediate in many cellular processes

quadruple hybrid hybridized plant with four parents

quantitative numerical, especially as derived from measurement

quid a wad for chewing

quinone chemical compound found in plants, often used in making dyes

radii distance across, especially across a circle (singular = radius)

radioisotopes radioactive forms of an element

rambling habit growing without obvious intended direction

reaction center a protein complex that uses light energy to create a stable charge separation by transferring a single electron energetically uphill from a donor molecule to an acceptor molecule, both of which are located in the reaction center

redox oxidation and reduction

regurgitant material brought up from the stomach

Renaissance a period of artistic and intellectual expansion in Europe from the fourteenth to the sixteenth century

salinization increase in salt content

samara a winged seed

saprophytes plants that feed on decaying parts of other plants

saturated containing as much dissolved substance as possible

sclerenchyma one of three cell types in ground tissue

sedimentation deposit of mud, sand, shell, or other material

semidwarf a variety that is intermediate in size between dwarf and full-size varieties

senescent aging or dying

sepals the outermost whorl of flower parts; usually green and leaf-like, they protect the inner parts of the flower

sequester to remove from circulation; lock up

serology the study of serum, the liquid, noncellular portion of blood

seta a stiff hair or bristle

silage livestock food produced by fermentation in a silo

siliceous composed of silica, a mineral

silicified composed of silicate minerals

soil horizon distinct layers of soil

solute a substance dissolved in a solution

Southern blot a technique for separating DNA fragments by electrophoresis and then identifying a target fragment with a DNA probe

spasticity abnormal muscle activity caused by damage to the nerve pathways controlling movement

speciation the creation of new species

specimen an object or organism under consideration

speciose marked by many species

sporophyte the diploid, spore-producing individual in the plant life cycle

sporulate to produce or release spores

sterile not capable or involved in reproduction, or unable to support life

sterols chemicals related to steroid hormones

stolons underground stems that may sprout and form new individuals

stomata openings between guard cells on the underside of leaves that allow gas exchange

stratification layering, or separation in space

stratigraphic geology the study of rock layers

stratigraphy the analysis of strata (layered rock)

strobili cone-like reproductive structures

subalpine a region less cold or elevated than alpine (mountaintop)

substrate the physical structure to which an organism attaches, or a molecule acted on by enzymes

succession the pattern of changes in plant species that occurs after a soil disturbance

succulent fleshy, moist

suckers naturally occuring adventitious shoots

suffrutescent a shrub-like plant with a woody base

sulfate a negatively charged particle combining sulfur and oxygen

surfaced smoothed for examination

susceptibility vulnerability

suture line of attachment

swidden agriculture the practice of farming an area until the soil has been depleted and then moving on

symbiont one member of a symbiotic association

symbiosis a relationship between organisms of two different species in which at least one benefits

systematists scientists who study systematics, the classification of species to reflect evolutionary relationships

systemic spread throughout the plant

tannins compounds produced by plants that usually serve protective functions, often colored and used for "tanning" and dyeing

taxa a type of organism, or a level of classification of organisms

tensile forces forces causing tension, or pulling apart; the opposite of compression

tepal an undifferentiated sepal or petal

Tertiary period geologic period from sixty-five to five million years ago

tetraploid having four sets of chromosomes; a form of polyploidy

thallus simple, flattened, nonleafy plant body

tilth soil structure characterized by open air spaces and high water storage capacity due to high levels of organic matter

tonoplast the membrane of the vacuole

topographic related to the shape or contours of the land

totipotent capable of forming entire plants from individual cells

toxin a poisonous substance

tracheid a type of xylem cell that conducts water from root to shoot

transcription factors proteins that bind to a specific DNA sequence called the promoter to regulate the expression of a nearby gene

translocate to move materials from one region to another

translucent allowing the passage of light

transmutation to change from one form to another

transpiration movement of water from soil to atmosphere through a plant

transverse across, or side to side

tribe a group of closely related genera

trophic related to feeding

turgor pressure the outward pressure exerted on the cell wall by the fluid within

twining twisting around while climbing

ultrastructural the level of structure visible with the electron microscope; very small details of structure

uniformitarian the geologic doctrine that formative processes on earth have proceeded at the same rate through time since earth's beginning

uplift raising up of rock layers, a geologic process caused by plate tectonics

urbanization increase in size or number of cities

vacuole the large fluid-filled sac that occupies most of the space in a plant cell. Used for storage and maintaining internal pressure

vascular plants plants with specialized transport cells; plants other than bryophytes

vascular related to the transport of nutrients, or related to blood vessels

vector a carrier, usually one that is not affected by the thing carried

vernal related to the spring season

vesicle a membrane-bound cell structure with specialized contents

viable able to live or to function

volatile easily released as a gas

volatilization the release of a gaseous substance

water table the level of water in the soil

whorl a ring

wort an old English term for plant; also an intermediate liquid in beer making

xenobiotics biomolecules from outside the plant, especially molecules that are potentially harmful

xeromorphic a form adapted for dry conditions

xerophytes plants adapted for growth in dry areas

zonation division into zones having different properties

zoospore a swimming spore

zygote the egg immediately after it has been fertilized; the one-cell stage of a new individual

Topic Outline

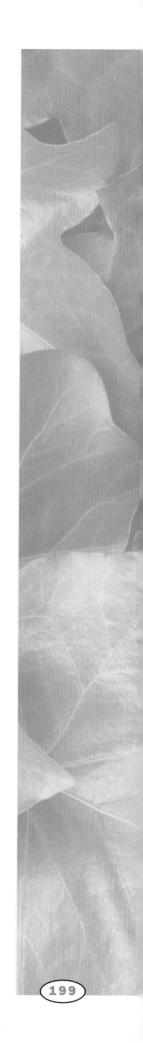

ADAPTATIONS

Alkaloids
Allelopathy
Cacti
Cells, Specialized Types
Clines and Ecotypes
Defenses, Chemical
Defenses, Physical
Halophytes
Lichens
Mycorrhizae
Nitrogen Fixation
Poisonous Plants
Seed Dispersal
Shape and Form of Plants
Symbiosis
Translocation
Trichomes

AGRICULTURE

Agriculture, History of
Agriculture, Modern
Agriculture, Organic
Agricultural Ecosystems
Agronomist
Alliaceae
Asteraceae
Biofuels
Borlaug, Norman
Breeder
Breeding
Burbank, Luther
Cacao
Carver, George W.
Coffee
Compost
Cork

Corn
Cotton
Economic Importance of Plants
Ethnobotany
Fertilizer
Fiber and Fiber Products
Food Scientist
Fruits
Fruits, Seedless
Genetic Engineer
Genetic Engineering
Grains
Grasslands
Green Revolution
Halophytes
Herbs and Spices
Herbicides
Horticulture
Horticulturist
Hydroponics
Native Food Crops
Nitrogen Fixation
Oils, Plant-Derived
Pathogens
Pathologist
Polyploidy
Potato
Potato Blight
Quantitative Trait Loci
Rice
Seed Preservation
Soil, Chemistry of
Soil, Physical Characteristics
Solanaceae
Soybeans
Sugar
Tea
Tissue Culture

Tobacco
Transgenic Plants
Vavilov, N. I.
Vegetables
Weeds
Wheat
Wine and Beer Industry

ANATOMY

Anatomy of Plants
Bark
Botanical and Scientific Illustrator
Cell Walls
Cells
Cells, Specialized Types
Cork
Differentiation and Development
Fiber and Fiber Products
Flowers
Fruits
Inflorescence
Leaves
Meristems
Mycorrhizae
Phyllotaxis
Plants
Roots
Seeds
Shape and Form of Plants
Stems
Tissues
Tree Architecture
Trichomes
Vascular Tissues
Vegetables
Wood Anatomy

BIOCHEMISTRY/PHYSIOLOGY

Alcoholic Beverage Industry
Alkaloids
Anthocyanins
Biofuels
Biogeochemical Cycles
Bioremediation
Carbohydrates
Carbon Cycle
Cells
Cellulose
Chlorophyll
Chloroplasts

Cytokinins
Defenses, Chemical
Ecology, Energy Flow
Fertilizer
Flavonoids
Flavor and Fragrance Chemist
Halophytes
Herbicides
Hormones
Lipids
Medicinal Plants
Nitrogen Fixation
Nutrients
Oils, Plant-Derived
Pharmaceutical Scientist
Photoperiodism
Photosynthesis, Carbon Fixation
Photosynthesis, Light Reactions
Physiologist
Pigments
Poisonous Plants
Psychoactive Plants
Soil, Chemistry of
Terpenes
Translocation
Vacuoles
Water Movement

BIODIVERSITY

Agricultural Ecosystems
Aquatic Ecosystems
Biodiversity
Biogeography
Biome
Botanical Gardens and Arboreta
Chapparal
Clines and Ecotypes
Coastal Ecosystems
Coniferous Forests
Curator of a Botanical Garden
Curator of an Herbarium
Deciduous Forests
Deforestation
Desertification
Deserts
Ecology
Ethnobotany
Global Warning
Herbaria
Human Impacts
Invasive Species

Plant Prospecting
Rain Forest Canopy
Rain Forests
Savanna
Taxonomist
Tundra
Wetlands

BIOMES

Aquatic Ecosystems
Atmosphere and Plants
Biodiversity
Biogeography
Biome
Cacti
Chapparal
Coastal Ecosystems
Coniferous Forests
Deciduous Forests
Deforestation
Desertification
Deserts
Ecology
Ecosystem
Global Warning
Grasslands
Human Impacts
Invasive Species
Peat Bogs
Plant Prospecting
Rain Forest Canopy
Rain Forests
Savanna
Tundra
Wetlands

CAREERS

Agriculture, Modern
Agriculture, Organic
Agronomist
Alcoholic Beverage Industry
Arborist
Botanical and Scientific Illustrator
Breeder
Breeding
College Professor
Curator of a Botanical Garden
Curator of an Herbarium
Flavor and Fragrance Chemist
Food Scientist
Forester

Forestry
Genetic Engineer
Genetic Engineering
Horticulture
Horticulturist
Landscape Architect
Pathologist
Pharmaceutical Scientist
Physiologist
Plant Prospecting
Taxonomist
Turf Management

CELL BIOLOGY

Algae
Biogeochemical Cycles
Cell Cycle
Cell Walls
Cells
Cells, Specialized Types
Cellulose
Chloroplasts
Cork
Differentiation and Development
Embryogenesis
Fiber and Fiber Products
Germination
Germination and Growth
Leaves
Meristems
Molecular Plant Genetics
Mycorrhizae
Nitrogen Fixation
Physiologist
Plastids
Reproduction, Fertilization
Roots
Seeds
Stems
Tissues
Translocation
Trichomes
Tropisms and Nastic Movements
Vacuoles
Vascular Tissues
Water Movement
Wood Anatomy

DESERTS

Biome
Cacti

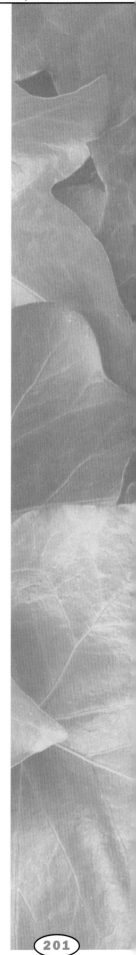

201

Desertification
Deserts
Ecosystem
Halophytes
Native Food Crops
Photosynthesis, Carbon Fixation and
Tundra

DISEASES OF PLANTS

Acid Rain
Chestnut Blight
Deforestation
Dutch Elm Disease
Fungi
Interactions, Plant-Fungal
Interactions, Plant-Insect
Nutrients
Pathogens
Pathologist
Potato Blight

DRUGS AND POISONS

Alcoholic Beverage Industry
Alcoholic Beverages
Alkaloids
Cacao
Cannabis
Coca
Coffee
Defenses, Chemical
Dioscorea
Economic Importance of Plants
Ethnobotany
Flavonoids
Medicinal Plants
Pharmaceutical Scientist
Plant Prospecting
Poison Ivy
Poisonous Plants
Psychoactive Plants
Solanaceae
Tea
Tobacco

ECOLOGY

Acid Rain
Agricultural Ecosystems
Aquatic Ecosystems
Atmosphere and Plants
Biodiversity
Biogeochemical Cycles

Biogeography
Biome
Carbon Cycle
Chapparal
Clines and Ecotypes
Coastal Ecosystems
Coniferous Forests
Deciduous Forests
Decomposers
Defenses, Chemical
Defenses, Physical
Deforestation
Desertification
Deserts
Ecology
Ecology, Energy Flow
Ecology, Fire
Ecosystem
Endangered Species
Global Warning
Grasslands
Human Impacts
Interactions, Plant-Fungal
Interactions, Plant-Insect
Interactions, Plant-Plant
Interactions, Plant-Vertebrate
Invasive Species
Mycorrhizae
Nutrients
Pathogens
Peat Bogs
Pollination Biology
Rain Forest Canopy
Rain Forests
Savanna
Seed Dispersal
Shape and Form of Plants
Soil, Chemistry of
Soil, Physical Characteristics
Symbiosis
Terpenes
Tundra
Wetlands

ECONOMIC IMPORTANCE OF PLANTS

Acid Rain
Agricultural Ecosystems
Arborist
Agriculture, History of
Agriculture, Modern
Agriculture, Organic

Alcoholic Beverage Industry
Alcoholic Beverages
Bamboo
Biofuels
Bioremediation
Breeder
Cacao
Cannabis
Chestnut Blight
Coffee
Coniferous Forests
Cork
Corn
Cotton
Deciduous Forests
Deforestation
Economic Importance of Plants
Fiber and Fiber Products
Flavor and Fragrance Chemist
Fruits
Fruits, Seedless
Food Scientist
Forensic Botany
Forester
Forestry
Genetic Engineer
Global Warning
Grains
Green Revolution
Herbs and Spices
Horticulture
Horticulturist
Human Impacts
Hydroponics
Landscape Architect
Medicinal Plants
Oils, Plant-Derived
Ornamental Plants
Paper
Peat Bogs
Pharmaceutical Scientist
Plant Prospecting
Potato Blight
Rice
Soybeans
Sugar
Tea
Turf Management
Wheat
Wood Products
Vegetables

EVOLUTION

Algae
Angiosperms
Archaea
Biodiversity
Biogeography
Breeding Systems
Bryophytes
Clines and Ecotypes
Curator of an Herbarium
Darwin, Charles
Defenses, Chemical
Defenses, Physical
Endangered Species
Endosymbiosis
Evolution of Plants, History of
Eubacteria
Ferns
Flora
Fungi
Global Warming
Hybrids and Hybridization
Interactions, Plant-Fungal
Interactions, Plant-Insect
Interactions, Plant-Plant
Interactions, Plant-Vertebrate
McClintock, Barbara
Molecular Plant Genetics
Mycorrhizae
Palynology
Phylogeny
Poisonous Plants
Pollination Biology
Polyploidy
Reproduction, Alternation of Generations
Seed Dispersal
Speciation
Symbiosis
Systematics, Molecular
Systematics, Plant
Warming, Johannes

FOODS

Alcoholic Beverage Industry
Alliaceae
Bamboo
Cacao
Cacti
Carbohydrates
Coffee
Corn

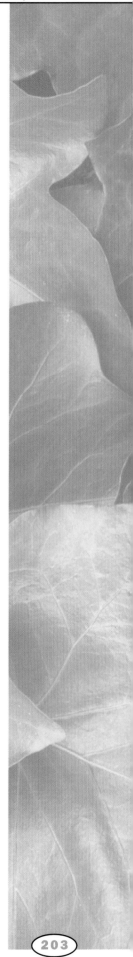

Fruits
Fruits, Seedless
Grains
Herbs and Spices
Leaves
Native Food Crops
Oils, Plant-Derived
Rice
Roots
Seeds
Solanaceae
Soybeans
Stems
Sugar
Tea
Wheat

GARDENING

Alliaceae
Compost
Flowers
Fruits
Herbicides
Horticulture
Invasive Species
Landscape Architect
Ornamental Plants
Vegetables

GENETICS

Breeder
Breeding
Breeding Systems
Cell Cycle
Chromosomes
Fruits, Seedless
Genetic Engineer
Genetic Engineering
Genetic Mechanisms and Development
Green Revolution
Hormonal Control and Development
Molecular Plant Genetics
Polyploidy
Quantitative Trait Loci
Reproduction, Alternation of Generations
Reproduction, Asexual
Reproduction, Fertilization
Reproduction, Sexual
Transgenic Plants

HISTORY OF BOTANY

Agriculture, History of
Bessey, Charles
Borlaug, Norman
Britton, Nathaniel
Brongniart, Adolphe-Theodore
Burbank, Luther
Calvin, Melvin
Carver, George W.
Clements, Frederic
Cordus, Valerius
Creighton, Harriet
Darwin, Charles
de Candolle, Augustin
de Saussure, Nicholas
Ecology, History of
Evolution of Plants, History of
Gray, Asa
Green Revolution
Hales, Stephen
Herbals and Herbalists
Hooker, Joseph Dalton
Humboldt, Alexander von
Ingenhousz, Jan
Linneaus, Carolus
McClintock, Barbara
Mendel, Gregor
Odum, Eugene
Physiology, History of
Sachs, Julius von
Taxonomy, History of
Torrey, John
Van Helmont, Jean Baptiste
van Niel, C. B.
Vavilov, N. I.
Warming, Johannes

HORMONES

Differentiation and Development
Genetic Mechanisms and Development
Herbicides
Hormonal Control and Development
Hormones
Meristems
Photoperiodism
Physiologist
Rhythms in Plant Life
Senescence
Shape and Form of Plants
Tropisms and Nastic Movements

HORTICULTURE

Alliaceae
Asteraceae
Bonsai
Botanical Gardens and Arboreta
Breeder
Breeding
Cacti
Curator of a Botanical Garden
Horticulture
Horticulturist
Hybrids and Hybridization
Hydroponics
Landscape Architect
Ornamental Plants
Polyploidy
Propagation
Turf Management

INDIVIDUAL PLANTS AND PLANT FAMILIES

Alliaceae
Asteraceae
Bamboo
Cacao
Cacti
Cannabis
Coca
Coffee
Corn
Cotton
Dioscorea
Fabaceae
Ginkgo
Grasses
Kudzu
Opium Poppy
Orchidaceae
Palms
Poison Ivy
Potato
Rice
Rosaceae
Sequoia
Solanaceae
Soybeans
Tobacco
Wheat

LIFE CYCLE

Breeder
Breeding Systems
Cell Cycle
Differentiation and Development
Embryogenesis
Flowers
Fruits
Gametophyte
Genetic Mechanisms and Development
Germination
Germination and Growth
Hormonal Control and Development
Meristems
Pollination Biology
Reproduction, Alternation of Generations
Reproduction, Asexual
Reproduction, Fertilization
Reproduction, Sexual
Rhythms in Plant Life
Seed Dispersal
Seed Preservation
Seeds
Senescence
Sporophyte
Tissue Culture

NUTRITION

Acid Rain
Biogeochemical Cycles
Carbon Cycle
Carnivorous Plants
Compost
Decomposers
Ecology, Fire
Epiphytes
Fertilizer
Germination and Growth
Hydroponics
Mycorrhizae
Nitrogen Fixation
Nutrients
Peat Bogs
Physiologist
Roots
Soil, Chemistry of
Soil, Physical Characteristics
Translocation
Water Movement

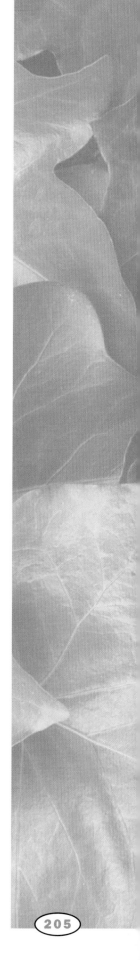

PHOTOSYNTHESIS

Algae
Atmosphere and Plants
Biofuels
Carbohydrates
Carbon Cycle
Carotenoids
Chlorophyll
Chloroplasts
Flavonoids
Global Warming
Leaves
Photosynthesis, Carbon Fixation
Photosynthesis, Light Reactions
Physiologist
Pigments
Plastids
Translocation

RAIN FORESTS

Atmosphere and Plants
Biodiversity
Deforestation
Endangered Species
Global Warning
Forestry
Human Impacts
Plant Prospecting
Rain Forest Canopy
Rain Forests
Wood Products

REPRODUCTION

Breeder
Breeding
Breeding Systems
Cell Cycle
Chromosomes
Embryogenesis
Flowers
Fruits
Fruits, Seedless
Gametophyte
Genetic Engineer
Hybrids and Hybridization
Invasive Species
Pollination Biology
Propagation
Reproduction, Alternation of Generations
Reproduction, Asexual

Reproduction, Fertilization
Reproduction, Sexual
Seed Dispersal
Seed Preservation
Seeds
Sporophyte
Tissue Culture

TREES AND FORESTS

Acid Rain
Allelopathy
Arborist
Atmosphere and Plants
Bark
Biodiversity
Biome
Botanical Gardens and Arboreta
Carbon Cycle
Chestnut Blight
Coffee
Coniferous Forests
Curator of a Botanical Garden
Deciduous Forests
Deforestation
Dendrochronology
Dutch Elm Disease
Ecology, Fire
Forester
Forestry
Interactions, Plant-Fungal
Landscape Architect
Mycorrhizae
Paper
Plant Prospecting
Propagation
Rain Forest Canopy
Rain Forests
Savanna
Shape and Form of Plants
Tree Architecture
Wood Products

WATER RELATIONS

Acid Rain
Aquatic Ecosystems
Atmosphere and Plants
Bark
Cacti
Desertification
Deserts

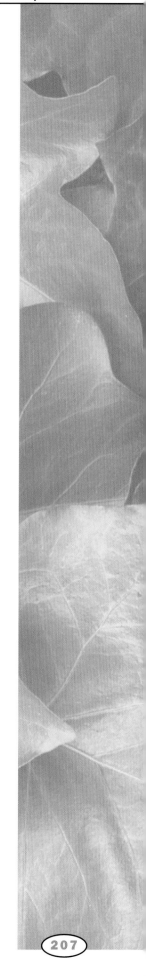

Halophytes
Hydroponics
Leaves
Mycorrhizae
Nutrients
Peat Bogs
Photosynthesis, Carbon Fixation
Photosynthesis, Light Reactions
Rain Forests

Rhythms in Plant Life
Roots
Stems
Tissues
Tundra
Vascular Tissues
Water Movement
Wetlands
Wood Anatomy

Cumulative Index

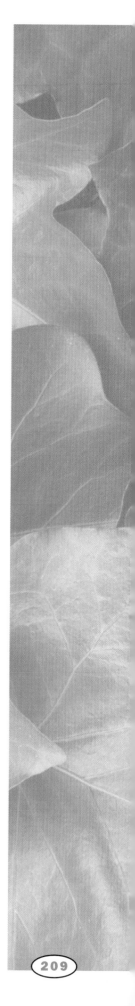

Page numbers in boldface indicate article titles. Those in italics indicate illustrations. The boldface number preceding the colon indicates the volume number.

A

ABA. *See* Abscisic acid
Abacá *(Musa textilis)*, **2:***138*, 139
Abbott, John, **2:**101
ABC genes, **2:**173–174, *174*
Abies (fir), **2:**19, *22*, **4:**59, 173, 174
Abiotic, defined, **1:**73, **3:**157, **4:**1 and Glossary
Abrade, defined, **2:**74, **4:**33 and Glossary
Abrasion, defined, **2:**26, **4:**33 and Glossary
Abscisic acid (ABA), **1:**53, **2:**57, 158, **3:***17*, 153, 155
  biosynthesis, **3:**14
  effects, **3:**19–20, **4:**56
  germination, **2:**176, 177
  interactions, **3:**20
  seed dormancy and, **3:**19, **4:**54
  stomatal closure and, **3:**16, 17, 19–20
Abscission, **3:**18, 20
  defined, **2:**49, **3:**20 and Glossary
Abscission layer, abscission zone, **2:**49, 51–52
Acacia, **2:**60, **3:**180, **4:**39, 40
  caven, **2:**48
ACC (1-amino-cyclopropane-1-carboxylic acid), **3:**14
Accelerated growth, **2:**61
Accession, defined, **1:**91, **2:**36, **4:**49 and Glossary
Accessory fruits, **2:**158, 160
Acer. See Boxelder; Maple
Acetobacter, **3:**92
Acetyl-coenzyme A, **3:**150, 151
Achenes, **2:***159*, 160, **4:**35
  defined, **4:**35 and Glossary
Acidic environments, **1:**56–57
Acidity. *See* pH
Acid rain, **1:1–3**, 60, 61, 72, 75, **4:**31, 64
Acid soils, **4:**64

Acorns, **2:**160, **4:**153
Acquired characters, **1:**110, **2:**128
Acremonium, **3:**40
Actaea (baneberry), **3:***171*
Actinomorphic flowers, **2:**146
Actinomycetes, **2:**162, 164, **3:**91
  defined, **2:**162, **3:**91 and Glossary
Actinorhizal symbiosis, **3:**94
Action potentials, **4:**137
Adanson, M., **4:**100
Adaptations, **1:**163, **4:***25–26*
  competitive, **3:**163
  Darwin's studies of, **2:**45, 129
  deciduous habit, **1:**47, 149, **2:**49, 130
  epiphytes, **2:**113–114, **3:**43
  fire, **1:**64, 149, **2:**93, **4:**39–40
  halophytes, **3:**2
  hydrophytes, **3:**57
  Lamarck's theory of, **2:**128
  leaves, **2:**52, 126, **4:**6
  physical defenses, **2:60–62**
  to promote out-crossing, **4:**23
  rain forest canopy, **4:**3
  wetlands plants, **4:**166–167
  xerophytic. *See* Xerophytic adaptations
  See also Clines and ecotypes
Adenine, **3:**17, 81, *148*
Adenosine diphosphate (ADP), **3:**130
Adenosine phosphate, **3:**14
Adenosine triphosphate. *See* ATP
Adenostoma fasciculatum (chamise), **1:**148
Adhesion, defined, **2:**60 and Glossary
Adnation, flowers, **2:**146
ADP (adenosine diphosphate), **3:**130
Adventitious, defined, **2:**78, **3:**187, **4:**80 and Glossary
Adventitious buds, **4:**80
Adventitious root systems, **2:**78
Aeration, defined, **1:**20, **2:**15, **4:**138 and Glossary
Aeration pores (macropores), **4:**67
Aerenchymatous tissues, **1:**52
Aerial roots, **3:**43, **4:**34
Aerobic bacteria, **3:**91
Aerosols, **1:**1

Aesculus (horsechestnut), **4:**61
Aflatoxins, **2:**164, **3:**173
Africa
  alpine plants, **4:**140
  deserts, **2:**64, *71, 72, 74, 75*
  grasslands, **4:**38–41, *40*
  origins of agriculture, **1:**6
  species diversity, **1:***68*
  See also specific countries
Agamospermy, **4:**18, 19
Agar, **1:**29
Agathis (kauri), **2:**1–2
Agave, **4:***81*
  fourcroydes (henequen), **2:***138*, 139
  sisalana (sisal), **1:***143*, **2:***138*, 139
  tequiliana, **1:***23*
Age
  record-holding plants, **4:**15, *127*
  of trees, **3:**160–161 (*see also* Dendrochronology)
Agent Orange, **3:**10
Aggregate fruits, **2:**158, *159*, 160
AGI (*Arabidopsis* Genome Initiative), **3:***85*
Aging, **4:**56
  See also Senescence
Aglycone, **3:**172
Agoutis, **4:**43
Agricultural economics, **1:**17
Agricultural ecosystems, **1:3–5**, **2:**12–13
Agricultural engineering, **1:**17
Agricultural Research Service, USDA, **4:**48
Agricultural yields, **1:**7–8, 10
  air pollution and, **1:**61
  Green Revolution and, **1:**9, 89, **2:**197
  improvement through breeding, **1:**9, 99
  increases, **1:**7–10, 88–89
  organic vs. conventional farming, **1:**13–14
Agriculture
  conventional and organic compared, **1:***14*
  desertification of agricultural lands, **2:**72
  energy crops, **1:**79–80

Agriculture (continued)
fiber crops. *See* Fiber and fiber products
food crops. *See* Food crops; Grains; *specific crop plants*
forest conversion, **1**:7, 125, **2**:50, 63, **3**:26
grasslands conversion, **1**:7, 71, **2**:189, 193–194, **3**:26
herbicide use, **3**:9
history of, **1:5–10**
hydroponics, **3:35–36**
impacts of, **1**:7–8, **3**:25–27
income from, **1**:14–15
land use statistics, **1**:125
marketing of agricultural products, **2**:100–102
modern, **1:10–12**
native food crops, **3**:91, **4**:*50*
nurse plants, **3**:44
organic, **1:12–16**, *14*, **2**:16, 33
permaculture, **2**:65
plant-insect interactions, **3**:42–43
and population growth, **1**:7–8, **3**:26
seed dormancy and, **4**:55
soil impacts, **1**:11, 12, 15, **2**:71, **4**:67–68
subsistence farming, **2**:99
sustainability, **1**:13
swidden, defined, **2**:63 and Glossary
swidden/slash-and-burn, **2**:63, **3**:*28*, 102, **4**:12
water use, **1**:12
yields. *See* Agricultural yields
See also Agricultural ecosystems; Agricultural yields; Breeding; Crop plants; Fertilizers; Forestry; Green Revolution; Horticulture; Plant domestication; *specific crops*
Agrobacterium, **2**:169, **3**:117, **4**:117–118
Agroecologists, **1**:3, 5
Agroecology, **1**:3
Agroecosystems. *See* Agricultural ecosystems
Agroforestry, **2**:65, 153
See also Forestry
Agronomists, **1**:10, **16–18**
AI (atherogenicity index), **3**:*101, 102*
AIDS virus, **4**:94
Ailanthus altissima (tree-of-heaven), **3**:*48, 50*
Air bubbles, water transport and, **4**:149, 163–164
Air pollution, **1**:60–61, 72, **3**:60, 61, 105
ALA (5-aminolevulinic acid), **1**:152
Albuminous, defined, **4**:121 and Glossary
Albuminous cells, **4**:121, 151
Alcoholic beverage industry, **1:18–22**
Alcoholic beverages, **1:22–26**, *23*, **2**:30, 164, 189
beer, **1**:20, *23*, 24–25, **2**:164, 189

spirits, **1**:*23*, 26, **2**:164, 189
wine, **1**:18–20, 22–24, *23*, **2**:59, 164, **3**:152
Alcohols, **3**:172, **4**:82
See also Ethanol; Methanol
Aldehydes, **1**:121
Alders, **3**:122
Alerce (*Fitzroya*), **2**:21–22, *23*
Aleurone layer, **4**:54
Alexiades, Miguel N., **2**:117–118
Alfalfa (*Medicago sativa*), **1**:135, **3**:93, **4**:129, 130
pests, **3**:112
polyploidy, **1**:97, **3**:181
Algae, **1:26–31**, 49–50, *50*, 105
ancestors of land plants, **1**:29, 31
blue-green. *See* Cyanobacteria
brown, **1**:29, 31, 156, **2**:80, **3**:141, 165, **4**:17
cellulose synthesis, **1**:146–147
charophycean, **1**:29, 31, **2**:*122*, 122–124, 127
chlorophylls in, **1**:152, **3**:165
defined, **1**:27 and Glossary
diatoms, **1**:27, 29, 31, 156, **3**:165
dinoflagellates, **1**:27, 29–30, 31, 156
divisions, **1**:27, 30–31
economic importance, **1**:29
evolution, **1**:26–27, 30–31, **2**:113, **3**:145–146
as food source, **1**:29
in food web, **1**:29, **2**:86, 87
green. *See* Green algae
Ingenhousz's research, **3**:39–40
parasitic, **1**:29
phytoplankton, **1**:*50*, **2**:2
vs. plants, **3**:165
plastids in, **1**:156, **2**:112–113
rain forests, **4**:6
red, **1**:29, 31, 156, **2**:112, **3**:165, **4**:17, 102
reproduction, **2**:166, **4**:16, 17, 77
seaweeds, **1**:29, 31, 50, **2**:2, 123, **4**:102
symbioses. *See* Corals; Lichens
taxonomy, **1**:26–29, 30–31, 93, **3**:166
vacuole function, **4**:143
yellow-green, golden brown, or golden, **1**:27, 156, **3**:165
See also Aquatic plants
Algal blooms, **1**:29–30, 49–50, 72, **4**:64–65
Alginates, **1**:29
Alien species. *See* Exotic species; Invasive species
Alismatidae, **1**:45
Alkaline soils, **4**:64
Alkalinity. *See* pH
Alkaloids, **1:32–34**, **2**:55, **3**:11, 69, 70, 152, **4**:143
atropine, **1**:32, *33*, **3**:*70*, 174, **4**:68
in cacao/chocolate, **1**:113
in cacti, **1**:115
caffeine, **1**:*32, 33*, 113, **2**:59, **3**:172, 194, **4**:106

cathinone, **3**:194
chemical structures, **1**:*33, 34*
cocaine, **1**:*33*, **2**:4–6, 59, **3**:194
codeine, **2**:59, **3**:103, 165
coniine, **1**:*32, 33*, **3**:153
defined, **3**:171, **4**:10 and Glossary
function, **1**:32
harmaline, **3**:193
harmine, **3**:193
human uses, **1**:32–33, **2**:59
in legumes, **2**:55, 130
mescaline, **2**:59, **3**:192
morphine, **1**:32, *33*, **3**:103, 153, 174, 195, **4**:143
narcotine, **3**:103
in nectar, **2**:148
nicotine, **1**:32–33, *34*, **2**:59, **3**:192, 194, **4**:116
in opium poppy, **1**:*32, 33*, **3**:103
papaverine, **3**:103
in potatoes, **1**:*32, 34*, **3**:171
pyridine alkaloids, **4**:116
quinine, **1**:*33*, 64, **2**:10, **3**:*70*, 165
rain forests, **4**:10
scopolamine, **3**:*70*, 194, **4**:68
solanine, **1**:*32, 34*
strychnine, **1**:33, *34*, **3**:103
synthesis and structure, **1**:32, **2**:55, 58, **3**:171–172
taxol, **1**:*33, 34*, **2**:24, 202, **3**:*70*, 174, **4**:108, *109*
thebaine, **3**:103
theobromine, **1**:113, **3**:194
theophylline, **1**:113, **3**:194
xanthine alkaloids, **3**:194
Allard, Henry A., **3**:125
Alleles, **1**:33, 34, 184
defined, **3**:33 and Glossary
Allelochemicals, **1**:35, **4**:165
Allelopathy, **1**:35, 150, **2**:7–8, **3**:45, 163, **4**:165
defined, **3**:45 and Glossary
See also Chemical defenses
Allen, Timothy, **3**:159
Allergens, **3**:169, 174
Allergies to plants, **3**:174
Alliaceae (onion family), **1:35–36**
Allium, **1**:36
Allometric growth, **3**:57
Allopatric speciation, **4**:72
Allopolyploidy, **1**:97–98, **3**:33–34, 181–182
Allorhizobium, **3**:93
Alluvial plain, defined, **1**:148 and Glossary
Almonds, **4**:35
Alpha-amylase, **3**:15–16, 19
Alpha-carotene, **1**:129
Alpha diversity, **1**:66
Alpha-ketoglutaric acid, **3**:150
Alpine sorrel (*Oxyria digyna*), **3**:128
Alpine tundra, **4**:138
Alpine vegetation, **4**:140
Alternation of generations, **1**:158–159, **2**:123, **4:16–18**, 20, 45, 100

See also Diploid stage; Gameto-
phytes; Haploid stage; Sporo-
phytes; *specific plant groups*
Aluminum, **4**:63, 64
Amanita
  muscaria (fly agaric), **2**:164, **3**:*175*
  toxic species listed, **3**:175
  virosa, **2**:*163*, 164, **3**:175
Amaranth, **3**:91
Amatoxins, **2**:164
Amazonia
  forest, **1**:59, **4**:4, 12
  seed dispersal, **3**:46
  species diversity, **4**:7, 128
Amborella, **1**:45, **2**:126
Ambrosia beetles, **2**:61
Amended soils, defined, **3**:105 and
  Glossary
Amendment, defined, **1**:48, **4**:141
  and Glossary
American Association for the Ad-
  vancement of Science, **1**:65, **2**:34
American Chemical Society, **2**:141
American Code of Botanical
  Nomenclature, **1**:103
American Naturalist (journal), **1**:65
American Orchid Society, **3**:104
American Society of Perfumers,
  2:141
Amines, **3**:153
Amino acids, **1**:155, **3**:152, **4**:10
  ACC, **3**:14
  in alkaloid formation, **1**:32
  aspartic acid, **3**:132
  chlorophyll precursors, **1**:152
  components, **3**:98
  deficiency in corn, **2**:30
  hydroxyproline, **1**:136
  legume seeds, **2**:130
  lysine, **2**:30, **4**:169
  in nectar, **2**:148
  in protein synthesis, **3**:81, 83,
    149, 150
  in tea, **4**:106
  tryptophan (tryptophane), **2**:30,
    3:14
Amino-cyclopropane-1-carboxylic
  acid (ACC), **3**:14
5-aminolevulinic acid (ALA), **1**:152
Ammonia, **1**:74, **3**:150
  anhydrous, **2**:136
Ammonium nitrate, **2**:136
Ammonium polyphosphate, **2**:136
Ammonium thiosulfate, **2**:136
Amorphophallus, **3**:178
Amphibians, **4**:7
Amylases, **1**:25, **3**:15–16, 19, 119
Amylopectin, **3**:149
Amyloplasts, **1**:140, **3**:168, **4**:134
Amylose, **3**:149
Anabaena, **2**:39
Anabolism, **3**:148, 150, *151*, 152
Anacardiaceae, **3**:170
Anaerobic, defined, **1**:22, **3**:91 and
  Glossary
Anaerobic bacteria, **3**:91
Anaerobic digestion, **1**:80

Anaerobic fermentation, **1**:22
Analgesic, defined, **1**:33 and Glossary
Analgesic alkaloids, **1**:33
Analog, defined, **2**:59 and Glossary
Analogous characters, **3**:144
Anaphase, **1**:133–134
Anastral cell division, **1**:133–134
Anatomy of plants, **1**:36–42, **4**:29
  aquatic plants, **1**:52
  bryophytes, **1**:42
  cells, **1**:36, 42
  classifications based on, **1**:118
  ferns, **1**:42
  fruits, **1**:38
  leaves, **1**:39–40, *40*, 42
  monocots vs. dicots, **1**:39, 40
  phyllotaxis, **3**:56, **140–143**
  reproductive organs, **1**:38, 39
  roots, **1**:*37*, 38, 42
  seeds, **1**:38
  stems, **1**:38, 40–42, *41*
  tissues, **1**:37–38, 42
  *See also specific plant groups and
    plant parts*
Anderson, Edgar, **3**:33
Anderson, Ernest Gustof, **3**:67
Andes mountains, **1**:7, 69, 111,
  3:184, **4**:140
Androecium, **2**:144, 145, 147
Androsthenes, **4**:25
Angel's trumpet (*Brugmansia*),
  3:193–194
Angiosperms, **1**:43–48, **2**:127, 156
  coevolution with animals, **1**:48,
    2:126–127, 144, 147–148,
    3:112, **4**:8
  defined, **1**:38, **2**:25, **3**:76, **4**:17
    and Glossary
  evolution and adaptations,
    1:45–48, 65, **2**:79, 147–148,
    201, **3**:111–112, *144*
  features, **2**:144
  floral evolution in, **4**:100–101
  gametophytes, **1**:43, **2**:166, **4**:21
  major groups, **1**:*43*
  meristems, **3**:76–77
  mycorrhizal associations, **3**:88–89
  origins, **1**:44–45, **2**:126–127
  as pathogens, **3**:113, 116
  phloem structure, **4**:119, 150
  reproduction, **1**:43–44, 47, **2**:166,
    4:17, 20–22
  rise of, **2**:122
  seeds, **2**:197, **4**:51, 53
  specimen preparation, **3**:7, 37
  taxonomy, **1**:45–47, 65, **2**:78–79
  See also Dicots; Flowers; Flower
    structure; Monocots; *specific
    families and genera*
Angostura bitters, **1**:46, 64
Anhydrous ammonia, **2**:136
Animal fats, **3**:*101*
Animalia, **4**:94
Animal manures, as fertilizer,
  2:136–137
Animals
  carnivorous plant prey, **1**:126

  carotenoids in, **1**:130–131, **3**:157
  coastal ecosystems, **2**:1
  coevolution with angiosperms,
    1:48, **2**:126–127, 144, 147–148,
    3:112, **4**:8
  exotic, threat to native plants, **1**:71
  extinction rates, **1**:71
  grasslands, **2**:192–193
  nutrient transport by, **1**:74
  in organic agriculture, **1**:13, 15
  photoperiodism, **3**:127
  plant and animal cells compared,
    1:*139*
  plants poisonous to, **3**:173
  relationship to fungi, **3**:165
  responses to plant pigments,
    3:157
  savannas, **4**:40
  seed dispersal by, **2**:19–20, **3**:46,
    4:8, 43–44
  tropical rain forests, **4**:3, 6, 7–9
  tundra, **4**:139
  See also Herbivores and her-
    bivory; Insects; Interactions,
    plant-animal; *specific animals and
    animal groups*
Animal science, **1**:17
Annonaceae (sweetsop or custard-
  apple family), **1**:46
Annual ryegrass (*Lolium multiflo-
  rum*), **1**:150
Annuals, desert, **2**:76
Anomalous, defined, **3**:68 and Glos-
  sary
Anoxic, defined, **1**:56, **2**:38 and
  Glossary
Antagonism, **2**:50
Antarctic hair grass (*Deschampsia
  antarctica*), **2**:187
Antenna system, **3**:*135*, 136
  defined, **3**:135 and Glossary
Ant gardens, **4**:3
Antheridia, **1**:105, **2**:*134–135*, 134,
  166
Anthers, **2**:144, 147, **4**:22
Anthoceros, **2**:125
Anthocerotophyta. *See* Hornworts
Anthocyanins, **1**:48–49, 130, **2**:52,
  140, **3**:152, 156
  function, **3**:153, 157
  occurrence, **1**:139, 140, 143,
    4:143
  structure, **1**:*48*
  synthesis, **4**:56
Anthophyta. *See* Angiosperms
Anthropogenic, defined, **1**:1, **2**:73
  and Glossary
Anthropologists, ethnobotanical
  research by, **2**:116
Anthurium, **3**:142, **4**:43, 61
Antibiotics, **1**:36, **2**:59, 164, **3**:61
Antibodies, defined, **4**:87 and
  Glossary
Anticancer agents, **1**:33, 107, **2**:24,
  3:70, 71, 165
  taxol, **1**:33, *34*, **2**:24, 202, **3**:70,
    174, **4**:108, *109*

Anticancer agents (continued)
tea, **4:**106
vincristine and vinblastine, **3:***70,*
165, 174
See also Cancer protection
Antioxidants
defined, **2:**55, **4:**106 and Glossary
glucosinolates, **2:**56, 59
in nectar, **2:**148
phenolics, **2:**55–56, 58, 59
in tea, **4:**106
See also Carotenoids
Antirrhinum (snapdragon), **2:**146,
148, 161, 173
Ants, **1:**32, **4:***9,* 43
ant-plant symbioses, **2:**115, **4:**84,
85
rain forests, **2:**115, **4:**3, 7, 8, *9,*
10
Apatite, **1:**73, 74
Aphids, **2:**60, **3:**42, **4:**85, 122, 129
Apical, defined, **1:**37, **2:**10, **3:**18 and
Glossary
Apical buds, **2:**179, **3:**18, *141*
Apical dominance, auxins in, **3:**18
Apical growth, **2:**178
defined, **1:**105 and Glossary
Apical meristems, **3:**76–77, *77,*
4:111, 171
bryophytes, **2:**123
defined, **4:**58 and Glossary
differentiation and function,
1:37, **2:**105–106, 178–179,
3:76–77
leaf differentiation, **1:**39, **3:**56,
76–77, **4:**78
See also Root apical meristems;
Shoot apical meristems
Apico-basal patterning, in embryo-
genesis, **2:**105–106, *106*
Apomixis, **4:**18
defined, **4:**91 and Glossary
See also Asexual reproduction
Apomorphy, **3:**144, 145, **4:**102
Apoplastic movement, **4:**121
Apoptosis, **2:**57
Appalachian Mountains, **1:**69
Appendages, defined, **1:**38, **2:**146,
3:178, **4:**43 and Glossary
Apples, **1:**6, 8, **3:**172, 181, 189, **4:**35
Appressorium, **3:**118
Apricots, **3:**172
Aquaporins, **4:**143
Aquatic ecosystems, **1:49–52,** **2:**87
cyanobacteria in, **2:**38
forest canopy (tank epiphytes),
2:115
monocots in, **3:**86
threats to, **1:**52, 54, **2:**109,
4:64–65
zones, **1:***51*
See also Coastal ecosystems; Estu-
aries; Freshwater ecosystems;
Marine ecosystems; Oceans;
Wetlands
Aquatic fungi, **2:**163
Aquatic plants, **1:**49–50, **52–54,** 72,

127, **4:***168*
adaptations, **1:**52, **4:**166–167
duckweeds, **1:**43, **3:**53, **4:**15, 31
monocots, **3:**86, 87
quillworts, **4:**45, 46, *47,* 126
roots, **1:**52, **4:**31, 32, 166
weeds, **1:**53–54, **2:**109, **3:**9
See also Algae; Rice; *specific genera*
Arabidopsis, **3:***84–85,* **4:***142*
cell cycle, **1:**132–133, 135
chromosomal structure, **3:**180
embryogenesis, **2:**106
floral differentiation, **2:**148, 173,
3:84
hormone signaling experiments,
3:15, 16
root hair development, **2:**81–82
tropism experiments, **4:**133–135
Arabidopsis Genome Initiative (AGI),
3:85
Arable, defined, **1:**8 and Glossary
Araceae. *See* Aroids
Arachis. See Peanuts
Arales, **4:**6
Araucaria, **2:**18, 21, *22,* **3:**142
heterophylla (Norfolk Island pine),
2:24
Araucaria family, **2:**22
Arbinogalactans, **3:**150
Arboreta, **1:91–93**
See also Botanical gardens
Arboriculture, **1:**54–56, **3:**22
Arborists, **1:54–56**
Arbuscules, **3:**40, 89
Arceuthobium (dwarf mistletoe),
3:112, 116, **4:**85
Archaea, **1:56–57,** *57,* **2:**120
Archegonia, **2:***134–135,* 134, 135,
166, **4:**20
Archeopteris, **2:**126
Arctic tundra, **4:**138
Arctostaphylos. See Manzanita
Arcto-Tertiary geoflora, **1:**77–78
defined, **1:**77 and Glossary
Arecaceae. *See* Palms
Arecidae, **1:**45
Areoles, **1:**113
Argentina, **1:**24, **2:**18, 48
Argids, **2:**75
Aridisols, **2:**75
Aridization, **2:**71
See also Desertification
Aril, **2:**130
Aristida, **3:**187
Aristolochia, **3:**178
Aristolochiaceae (wild-ginger fam-
ily), **1:**46
Aristotle, **2:**127, **4:**92
Arnon, Daniel, **3:**154
Aroids (Araceae), **2:**114, **3:***87,* 178,
179
Aroma components, **1:**46, **2:**57, 59,
3:152, **4:**108
Arrowroot, **1:**7
Arsenic, **1:**85
Artemisia, **4:***139*
sagebrush, **1:**58, 149, 150

Artemisinin, **4:**108
Artery disease, **3:***101,* 194
Arthropods, **2:**54, **4:**3, 7, 8, 10
See also Insects; Mites; Spiders
Artichoke *(Cynara scolymus),* **1:**58
Artifacts, defined, **2:**67, **3:**107, **4:**174
and Glossary
Arum family, **3:**172
Ascomycetes, **3:**58, 89, 113
Ascospores, **3:**113
Asexual propagation, **3:**186–191
cuttings, **3:**187–188
grafting and budding, **3:**188–
190
pest and pathogen susceptibility,
3:118–119, 187
runners, **4:**18, 59, 80
tissue culture, **2:***170,* **3:**190–191,
4:109–110
Asexual reproduction, **1:**38, 53,
4:18–19, 24
Ash *(Fraxinus),* **2:**160, **4:**41, 176
Asia
deserts, **2:***71,* 72, 73, 75, 76
early agriculture, **1:**6, 7
forests, **2:**18, 19, 47–48, **4:**4, 5
See also specific countries
Aspartame, **4:**83–84
Aspartate, **3:**132
Aspartic acid, **3:**132, 150
Aspergillus, **1:**26, **2:**164, **3:**172–173
Aspidium, **3:**142
Aspirin, **2:**57, **4:**143
Assayer, defined, **4:**117 and Glossary
Associations. *See* Plant communities;
specific ecosystem types
Asteraceae (Compositae) (sunflower
family), **1:57–58,** 67, 77, **2:**55,
78, **3:**178
speciation, **4:**74
Asteridae (asterids), **1:**45–47, **2:**78,
79
Asteroid impacts, **2:**107
Asters, **4:**172
Aster yellows, **3:**115
Asymmetric cell divisions, **2:**81,
104
Atherogenicity index (AI), **3:***101,*
102
Athlete's foot, **2:**164–165
Atlantic cord grass *(Spartina alterniflora),* **3:**47
Atmosphere and plants, **1:59–61**
ancient atmospheric changes,
2:38, 121
oxygen consumption by plants,
1:59, 123
oxygen production by photosynthetic bacteria, **2:**120, **3:**25
oxygen production by plants and
algae, **1:**29, 59, **2:**64, 120, 185,
3:22, 39
plants' effects on climate, **1:**59,
4:1
role of forests, **1:**59, **2:**64
volatile organic compounds,
1:59–60, 61

See also Air pollution; Carbon cycle; Climate; Global warming; Greenhouse effect; Photorespiration; Transpiration
Atomic Energy Commission, **3**:100
ATP (adenosine triphosphate), **1**:56, 154, **3**:98, **4**:143
  in cell elongation, **3**:15
  defined, **1**:56, **3**:15, **4**:143 and Glossary
  in photosynthesis, **3**:130, 132, 134, 137, *140*, 151
ATP synthase, **3**:139
Atrazine, **3**:10
Atropa belladonna. See Belladonna
Atropine, **1**:32, *33*, **3**:70, 174, **4**:68
Aubreville, A., **2**:70
Aurones, **3**:157
Australia
  agriculture, **2**:31
  deserts/desertification, **2**:*71*, 72, 73, 75
  endemism, **1**:67
  grasslands, **4**:38–40
  rain forest, **4**:4
  species diversity, **1**:66, *68*, 69
  wine industry, **1**:24
Austria, **1**:13
Austrobaileya, **1**:45
Autoallopolyploidy, **3**:182
Autogamy, **1**:100, 101
Autopolyploidy, **1**:97–98, **3**:181, 182, 184
Autotrophic bacteria, **3**:91
Autotrophs (primary producers), **2**:86, 90–91
  coastal ecosystems, **2**:1, 2
  defined, **1**:27, **2**:86, **3**:91, **4**:51 and Glossary
Autumn crocus (*Colchicum autumnale*), **3**:70
Auxins (IAA), **2**:158, 161, **3**:*17*, 118, 153
  biosynthesis, **3**:14
  in cell elongation, **3**:15
  in cell polarity, **2**:80
  defined, **2**:80, **3**:10 and Glossary
  discovery, **3**:17, 154
  effects, **3**:18–19, **4**:109, 133
  in gravitropism, **4**:135
  hormone interactions, **3**:19, 20
  in phototropism, **4**:133
  seedling growth, **2**:179
  senescence and, **4**:56
  synthetic, **3**:10, 17
  tissue culture media, **4**:109
  transport, **3**:14–15
Avena sativa. See Oats
Avian, defined, **3**:46 and Glossary
Avicennia (black mangrove), **4**:34
  See also Mangroves
Awns, **2**:187
Axillary (lateral) buds, **2**:179, **3**:18, 19, 76, 77, **4**:80
  defined, **3**:188, **4**:80 and Glossary
Axils, defined, **4**:60 and Glossary
Ayahuasca, **2**:*116*, **3**:*193*

Azorhizobium, **3**:93
Azotobacter, **3**:91, 92
Aztec herbal, **3**:5

B

Babylon, **1**:24
Bacillariophyceae. *See* Diatoms
Bacillus, **3**:91
  thuringiensis, **2**:171
Backcrossing. *See* Introgression
Bacteria (eubacteria), **2**:119–121, *119*, **3**:91, **4**:65
  cell structure, **1**:56, **2**:120
  as decomposers, **1**:128, **2**:53, *54*, 121
  in genetic engineering, **2**:169, 171
  intracellular, **4**:86
  luminous, **4**:85
  nitrogen fixation, **3**:91–92, **4**:31, 32, 84–85 (*see also* Rhizobia)
  as pathogens, **2**:120, **3**:113, 114, *115*
  phytoplasmas, **3**:113, *115*, 117
  sulfur bacteria, **1**:*85*, **4**:85, 145
  See also Cyanobacteria; Photosynthetic bacteria; Soil bacteria
Bacterial diseases, **2**:169, **3**:114–119
Bacteriochlorophylls, **1**:152
Bacteriorhodopsin, **1**:56
Bacteroids, **3**:44
Badiano, Juan, **3**:5
Badianus manuscript, **3**:5
Bailey, Liberty Hyde, **3**:21
Bailey, Robert, **1**:84
Balanophora family (Balanophoraceae), **3**:*111*
Bald cypress (*Taxodium*), **1**:77, **2**:17, 18, *22*
Balsa (*Ochroma*), **3**:179, **4**:177
Bamboo palm (*Raffia taedigera*), **4**:13
Bamboos, **1**:62–63, *63*, **2**:187, 189, **3**:87, 109
  record-holding, **4**:15, 16
Bambusa arundinacea, **4**:15
Bambuseae, **1**:62–63
Banana family. *See* Musaceae
Bananas, **1**:6–8, **2**:158, 160–161, **3**:87, 181, 183
Baneberry (*Actaea*), **3**:*171*
Bangladesh, **4**:27, *106*
Banisteriopsis caapi. See Ayahuasca
Banyan tree, **4**:34
Baobab, **4**:*39*, 40
Barber's itch, **2**:164
Barbour, Michael, **1**:84, **3**:159
Bark, **1**:64, **2**:25–26, 61, *62*, **3**:154
  conifers, **2**:202
  fire resistance, **1**:64, **2**:26, 202, **4**:39, 57
  formation, **1**:64, **2**:25, **4**:59, 111, 173
  as wood product, **4**:179
  See also Cork cambium
Bark beetles, **2**:61, *62*, 83, *84*

Barley (*Hordeum*), **2**:184, 185, **3**:86, 174, **4**:*55*
  cultivation, **1**:7–9, 21, **2**:*187*
  origins and domestication, **1**:6, **2**:*187*
Barley malt, **1**:20, 21, *23*, 24–25
Barrens, **1**:76
Basal angiosperms, **1**:45–46, **2**:78
Basal cell division, **2**:104–105
Base cations, acid rain and, **1**:2
Basidiomycetes, **3**:58, 89, 113
Basipetal, defined, **3**:20 and Glossary
Basipetal movement, **3**:20
Basta, **2**:170
Bast fibers, **1**:64, **2**:138–139
Bateson, William, **4**:153
Bats
  as pollinators, **1**:114, **2**:115, 145, **3**:*46*, 179, **4**:69
  rain forests, **4**:3, 8
Bauhin, Caspar, **3**:64
Bay leaf, **1**:46
Beach grass, **2**:4
Beach naupaka, **2**:4
Beadle, George, **3**:68
Beans, **1**:6, 8, 68, **2**:132, **4**:129, *155*
  broad (*Vicia faba*), **2**:*178*, **3**:92
  pests and defenses, **3**:112, **4**:129
  Rhizobium and, **3**:94
  seeds, **4**:51, *52*, 53, 113, 143
  See also Soybean
Beech (*Fagus*), **1**:77, **2**:47, **3**:89, 112
Beechdrops (*Epifagus*), **3**:112
Beer, **1**:20, *23*, 24–25, **2**:164, 189
Beer industry, **1**:20–22, **4**:28
Bees, **2**:58, **4**:82
  as pollinators, **1**:114, **2**:50, *145*, **3**:177, *177*–178, **4**:8
  See also Honey
Beet (*Beta vulgaris*), **1**:98, **3**:157, **4**:119, 156
  See also Sugar beet
Beetles, **2**:*58*, **4**:44
  ambrosia beetles, **2**:61
  bark beetles, **2**:61, *62*, 83, *84*
  flea beetles, **2**:60
  leaf beetles, **4**:7, 8
  as pollinators, **1**:48, 114, **2**:*145*, 147, **3**:179, **4**:8, 15
  rain forests, **4**:3, 7, 8
  rove beetles, **4**:3, 8
Beggar's ticks (*Bidens*), **4**:43–44
Beilschmiedia, **4**:44
Belladonna, **1**:32, **3**:70, 171, 173, 174, **4**:*68*
  defined, **1**:32, **3**:171, **4**:68 and Glossary
Bellis, **3**:142
Bennettitales, **1**:45
Benson, Andrew, **1**:117
Bentham, G., **4**:100
Benthic zone, **1**:*51*
Benzoic acid, **1**:35
Berberidaceae, **1**:77
Bering land bridge, **1**:77, 78, **4**:140
Bermuda grass (*Cynodon*), **2**:189, **3**:181, 183

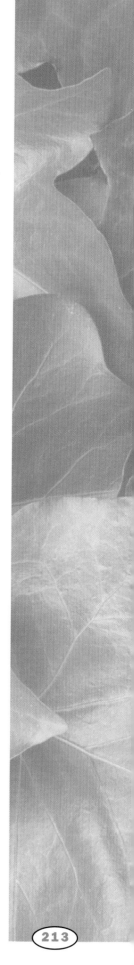

Berries, **2**:*159*, 159
Bessey, Charles, **1:65–66**, **4**:100, 104
Beta-carotene, **1**:129, 130, **3**:157, 165
Beta-glucans, **3**:149
Betalains, **1**:130, **3**:156, 157
Beta vulgaris. See Beet; Sugar beet
Betula. See Birch
Bidens (beggar's ticks), **4**:43–44
Biffen, R. D., **4**:153
Bijugate sequence, **3**:142
Bilateral symmetry, flowers, **2**:130, 146, 147, **3**:177
Bilobalide, **2**:180
Binding proteins, **3**:15
Binomial, defined, **4**:103 and Glossary
Binomial nomenclature. *See* Nomenclature
Biodiesel, **1**:80
Biodirected assays, **3**:70–71
Biodiversity, **1:66–73**
    community fluctuations, **3**:161
    conservation, **1**:72, 162–163, **2**:117, **3**:165
    defined, **2**:98, **3**:5, **4**:1 and Glossary
    extent and hot spots, **1**:68–69, *70*
    levels of, **1**:66
    measures of, **1**:66–67
    organic vs. conventional agriculture, **1**:15
    property rights to, **3**:165
    threats to, **1**:69–72, **2**:63, **3**:49
    See also Endangered species; Extinctions; Genetic diversity; Species diversity
Biodiversity prospecting, **2**:117, **3**:29–30, 124
    See also Plant prospecting
Bioengineering. *See* Genetic engineering
Biogeochemical cycles (nutrient cycles), **1**:3–4, **73–75**, **2**:85, 98, 193–194
    bacteria in, **2**:121
    deforestation and, **4**:11
    fire and, **2**:94–95, **4**:11
    fluctuations in, **3**:161
    tropical rain forests, **4**:10–11
    See also Decomposers; *specific nutrients*
Biogeography, **1:75–79**, 119, **3**:159, **4**:90
    defined, **1**:80, **3**:159, **4**:90 and Glossary
    island biogeography, **1**:78–79
    plant distribution, **1**:75–78
    regional flora, **2**:143
    See also Biomes; Plant distribution
Biological clocks, **4**:25–26, 136
Biological communities
    community defined, **1**:35 and Glossary

community ecology, **2**:85, 98, **3**:157, 159, **4**:157–158
    See also Plant communities; *specific ecosystem types*
Biological diversity. *See* Biodiversity
Biological pest management, **1**:11, 12
Biological species criterion, **4**:71, 72–73, 76
Bioluminescence, **4**:25
Biomass, **1**:3, **2**:85
    accumulation, **2**:94–95
    defined, **1**:3, **2**:75, **3**:161, **4**:3 and Glossary
    production. *See* Net primary productivity
    and trophic level, **2**:87
Biomass crops, **3**:181
Biomass fuels, **1:79–80**
    peat, **1**:80, **3**:122
Biomass waste, **1**:79
Biomes, **1:80–84**, **3**:159
    climate change and, **1**:84, **2**:182–183, **3**:28
    precipitation and temperature, **1**:*82*
    world biomes mapped, **1**:*81*
    See also Plant distribution; *specific biome types*
Bioremediation, **1:84–86**
Biosphere, defined, **3**:25, **4**:1 and Glossary
Biosphere II, **2**:*103*
Biosynthesis, defined, **3**:13 and Glossary
Biosystematics, **2**:143
Biota, defined, **1**:13, **2**:94, **3**:27, **4**:3 and Glossary
Biotechnology. *See* Genetic engineering
Biotic, defined, **1**:73, **2**:98, **3**:157, **4**:1 and Glossary
Birch (*Betula*), **1**:64, **2**:47, *48*, **3**:176, **4**:55, 138, *139*
Birds, **3**:*46*, 112
    coniferous forests, **2**:19–20
    grasslands, **2**:193
    as herbivores, **3**:46, **4**:139
    nutrient transport by, **1**:74
    as pollinators, **1**:114, **2**:50, 115, *145*, **3**:46, 86, 112, 179, **4**:69
    rain forests, **4**:3, 7–9
    as seed dispersers, **2**:19–20, **4**:43
    shaded coffee lands, **2**:13
    tundra, **4**:139
Bird's-foot trefoil, **2**:55
Birth control pill. *See* Contraceptives
Bisexual plants and flowers. *See* Hermaphroditism
Blackberries (*Rubus*), **2**:160, **4**:18, 35
Black gum (*Nyssa*), **1**:77
Black nightshade (*Solanum nigrum*), **3**:171
Black pepper (*Piper nigrum*), **1**:46, **3**:11, 174
Black pepper family. *See* Piperaceae
Bladderworts (*Utricularia*), **1**:*127*, 128, **3**:143

Blastomycosis, **2**:165
Blending inheritance, **3**:74
Bluebell family. *See* Campanulaceae
Blueberries, tundra species, **4**:*138*
Bluegrass, **3**:86
Blue-green algae. *See* Cyanobacteria
Boehmeria nivea (ramie), **2**:138, **4**:113
Bogs, **1**:51, 76, **3**:121–122, **4**:166
    plants, **3**:86, 103, 121–122, **4**:137
    See also Peat bogs; Wetlands
Bois d'arc, **2**:160
Bolivia, Beni Biosphere Reserve, **2**:*108*
Bonpland, Aimé, **3**:31
Bonsai, **1:86–88**, *87*
Boojum tree, **2**:77, **4**:*25, 26*
Bordeaux mixture, **2**:165, **3**:185
Boreal forests, **2**:17, 18–19, 20, 202, **3**:89
    climate change and, **2**:88, **3**:28
    lichens in, **3**:60, 61
    mapped, **1**:*81*
    See also Coniferous forests
Boreal steppes, **2**:188
Borlaug, Norman E., **1:88–89**, *88*, 98
Bormann, E. Herbert, **2**:98
Boron, **3**:97, 98, **4**:63, 64
Borthwick, Harry, **3**:155
Botanical gardens, **1**:72, **91–93**, **3**:6
    curators of, **2:35–36**
    endangered species and, **2**:110, 111
    New York Botanical Garden, **1**:102–103, **4**:117
    Royal Botanic Gardens, Kew, **3**:*6*, 12, 13, **4**:103
Botanical illustrators, **1:89–91**
Botanical insecticides
    nicotine, **1**:32, **2**:59, **4**:116
    pyrethrum, **1**:58
    triterpenoids, **2**:55
Botanical nomenclature. *See* Nomenclature
Botanical Society of America, **2**:34
Botanists, ethnobotanical research by, **2**:116
Botany, **1:93**, **4:103–104**
    economic, **2**:115–116
    ethnobotany. *See* Ethnobotany
    forensic, **2:150–151**
    Humboldt's contributions, **3**:31
    paleobotany, **1**:103, 104, **4**:90
    systematic. *See* Systematics; Taxonomy
Botany education, **1**:65
Bourbon, **2**:189
Boxelder (*Acer negundo*), **3**:50
Boxwood family. *See* Buxaceae
Boysen-Jensen, Peter, **3**:155
Bracken fern (*Pteridium aquilinum*), **2**:133, 135
Bradyrhizobium, **3**:93
Branches
    development, **3**:77, **4**:60
    growth mechanisms and patterns, **3**:78, **4**:59, 60–61, 79–80

root branching, **4**:33, 123
specialized (runners or stolons),
   1:41, **2**:186, **4**:18, 41, 59
tree branching, **4**:123
Brassica
   campestris, **3**:*102*
   juncea (Indian mustard), **1**:*85*
   napus, **1**:98, **3**:*102*
   oleracea, **1**:98, **2**:60, **4**:156
   See also Broccoli; Cabbage;
      Turnips
Brassicaceae (Cruciferae) (cabbage
   or mustard family), **1**:102, **2**:7,
   59, 78, 157
   mycorrhizae lacking, **3**:90
   pest defenses, **2**:56, 60
   pests and diseases, **3**:42, 117–118
   tundra species, **4**:*139*
Brassinosteroids, **3**:66
Braun-Blanquet, Josias, **3**:159
Brazil, **2**:11–12, 31, **4**:27, 157
   See also Amazonia
Brazilian rubber tree (*Hevea*), **4**:34
   See also Rubber
Breeders, **1**:93–95, 96, **2**:167
   Borlaug, **1**:88–89, *88*, 98
   Burbank, **1**:109–111, *109*
Breeding, **1**:94, **95–99**, **3**:196
   breeding program components,
      1:96–97
   classical/traditional, **2**:168, 169,
      3:85
   disease resistance, **2**:57, 165,
      3:91, 186, **4**:153
   drought resistance, **3**:91
   food crops, **1**:8–9, 98–99, **3**:85,
      91, 171, **4**:129–130
   germplasm preservation, **1**:72,
      99, **4**:48–50
   hybridization and, **3**:33
   Mendelian basis for, **3**:75
   molecular tools for, **3**:85
   pest resistance, **2**:61, **4**:129–130
   shuttle breeding, **1**:89
   successes, **1**:98–99
   synthetic polyploids, **3**:183
   systematics and, **4**:94
   See also Genetic engineering;
      Green Revolution; Hybrids and
      hybridization; *specific plants*
Breeding systems, **1**:99–102, **2**:145
   See also Pollination biology; Re-
      production, sexual; *specific plants
      and plant groups*
Brewing industry, **1**:21–22, **4**:28
Brewing science programs, **1**:22
Bristlecone pine (*Pinus aristata, P.
   longaeva*), **2**:17, 21, 198, **4**:15, 56,
   127
Britain, **1**:25, 66, 67, *68*, **4**:7
Brittleworts, **1**:*27*
Britton, Nathaniel, **1**:102–103
Broad bean (*Vicia faba*), **2**:178, **3**:92
Broadleaf conifers, **2**:17, 21, 199
Broadleaf forests. *See* Deciduous
   forests, temperate
Broccoli, **1**:98, 102, **3**:183, **4**:156

Bromeliads (Bromeliaceae), **3**:87
   epiphytic, **1**:68, **2**:114, 115, **3**:43,
      86, 111
   flowering, **3**:19, 20
   record-holding, **4**:*14*
Brongniart, Adolphe, **1**:103–104
Broomrake, **3**:45
Broomrape (*Orobanche*), **3**:112
Brown algae, **1**:29, 31, 156, **2**:80,
   3:141, 165, **4**:17
Brownian Motion, **3**:39–40
Brown, Robert, **4**:100
Brugmansia (angel's trumpet),
   3:193–194
Brunfelsia, **4**:68
Brunfels, Otto, **3**:4
Brussels sprouts, **1**:98, **2**:60, **4**:156
Bryologist, defined, **1**:103 and Glos-
   sary
Bryophyllum, **3**:142
Bryophyta. *See* Mosses
Bryophytes, **1**:42, **104–109**, **2**:121,
   3:145, 166
   distinguishing characteristics,
      1:*106*
   ecological roles, **1**:108
   evolution, **1**:105, **2**:121, 123,
      3:*144*, 146
   flavonoids in, **2**:140
   leaves, **1**:42
   reproduction, **1**:105, **2**:125, 166,
      4:17, 20, 23, 77
   taxonomy, **1**:105, *106*, **4**:102
   vascular tissues, **1**:42, **3**:*144*,
      4:152
   See also Hornworts; Liverworts;
      Mosses
Bt-toxin, **2**:171–172
Buckbrush (*Ceanothus*), **1**:148–149
Buckwheat (*Fagopyrum esculentum*
   Moench), **2**:184
Budding and grafting, **3**:188–190
Buds
   adventitious, **4**:80
   apical, **2**:179, **3**:18, *141*
   axillary/lateral, **2**:179, **3**:18, 19,
      76, 77
   formation, **3**:19
Buffon, Georges-Louis Leclerc de,
   2:128
Bulbils, **4**:41
Bulbs, **1**:41, **3**:87, 127, **4**:26, 80
Bulk flow, **4**:163
Bundle sheath cells, **1**:40, **3**:132
Bünning, Erwin, **4**:25
Burbank, Luther, **1**:109–111, *109*
Burrill, Thomas, **3**:114
Butomus umbellatus, **3**:*38*
Buttercup family. *See* Ranunculaceae
Buttercups (*Ranunculus*), **1**:65, **3**:174
Butterflies
   Bt-toxin and, **2**:172
   as pollinators, **2**:50, *145*,
      3:178–179, **4**:8
   rain forests, **4**:7, 8
Butterworts (*Pinguicula*), **1**:*127*, 128
Buttress roots, **1**:42, **4**:34, 125

Buxaceae (boxwood family), **2**:79

C

C_3 photosynthesis, **1**:40, **2**:77, 188,
   3:129–130, 133, 150
C_4 photosynthesis, **1**:40, **2**:77, 188,
   3:99, 131–133, 150
Cabbage, **1**:8, 98, **2**:60, **3**:*57*, **4**:156
Cabbage aphid, **2**:60
Cabbage butterflies, **2**:7
Cabbage family. *See* Brassicaceae
Cabbage worm, imported, **2**:60
Cable roots, **4**:34
Cacao (*Theobroma cacao*), **1**:32,
   111–113, *112*, **3**:*102*, 189, 194
   See also Chocolate; Cocoa
      butter
Cacti (Cactaceae), **1**:113–116,
   2:114, **4**:*81*
   adaptations, **1**:69, 113–114, **2**:4,
      52, 77, **3**:*57*, *146*
   Christmas cactus, **1**:116
   distribution and diversity,
      1:114–115, **2**:78
   Echinocactus, **3**:*142*
   horticultural interest, **1**:115–116
   peyote cactus, **1**:115, **3**:192
   photosynthetic pathway, **1**:114,
      3:132
   prickly pear cacti, **3**:43
   record-holding, **4**:*15*
   saguaro, **1**:*114*, 115, **2**:77,
      3:43–44, **4**:15
   spines, **2**:60, *61*, **3**:57
   taxonomy, **1**:115
Cactoideae, **1**:115
Cactus moth, **3**:43
Cadmium, **1**:85, *85*
Caffeine, **1**:32, *33*, 113, **2**:59, **3**:172,
   194, **4**:106
Cage, John, **3**:8
Calabash (*Cresentia cujete*), **4**:43
Calamitales, **4**:126
Calcite, **1**:74
Calcium, **1**:74
   acid rain and, **1**:2
   in hormonal signaling, **3**:15, 16
   as nutrient, **3**:97, 98, **4**:63
   in soil, **4**:63
   uptake, **4**:32
Calcium carbonate, **1**:74, **2**:75
Calcium oxalate, **1**:139, **3**:172, **4**:54
Caliche, **2**:75
California, **1**:14, 24, 69
California chaparral, **1**:147–151,
   148
California coastal sage, **1**:149
California poppy (*Eschscholzia califor-
   nica*), **2**:56, 146
Callose, **4**:120–121, 151
Calorie sources, human, **1**:6, 8, 122,
   2:30, **3**:101, **4**:82
Calvin, Genevieve Jemtegaard,
   1:116, 117
Calvin, Melvin, **1**:116–117, *116*,
   3:154

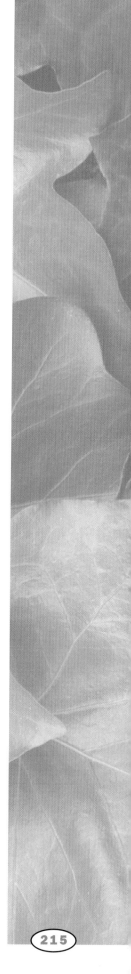

Calvin-Benson cycle, **1**:117, 154, **3**:129–132, 134, 139, 150, 152, 167

Calyx, **2**:144, 147

CAM. *See* Crassulacean acid metabolism

Cambial initials, **4**:171

Cambium/cambia, **1**:37, **3**:18
  See also Cork cambium; Lateral meristems; Procambium; Vascular cambium

Cambrian period, **2**:124

Camellia, **2**:146, 148
  sinensis. *See* Tea

Campanulaceae (bluebell family), **1**:79

Campanulate, defined, **4**:69 and Glossary

Canada, **1**:*68*, 68–69, **2**:19, 28, **3**:122, **4**:38

Cancer-causing agents, **3**:172–173, 194, **4**:107

Cancer protection
  carotenoids, **1**:130–131
  garlic, **1**:36
  See also Anticancer agents

Candolle, Alphonse de, **1**:118–119, **4**:100

Candolle, Augustin de, **1**:117–119, **4**:100

Cane
  giant or switch, **1**:62
  See also Sugarcane

Cannabis, **1**:101, **119–120**, *120*
  hemp, **1**:119, 143, **2**:*138*, **3**:109
  marijuana, **1**:101, 119–120, **3**:194

Canola, **3**:182

Canola oil, **3**:*102*

Canopy science. *See* Rain forest canopy

Capillarity, **4**:67, 151, 162

Capitulum, **3**:141
  defined, **3**:141 and Glossary

Capsella bursa-pastoris, **2**:*105*, 106

Capsules (fruit type), **2**:*159*, 160

Caraway, **3**:152

Carbohydrate polymers, **3**:97

Carbohydrates, **1**:**120–122**, **4**:82
  in cell walls, **1**:136, **3**:97–98
  chemical structures, **1**:*121*, 122, **3**:97
  product of photosynthesis. *See* Photosynthesis, carbon fixation and
  storage. *See* Food storage in plants
  See also Cellulose; Hemicelluloses; Pectins; Polysaccharides; Starches; Sugars

Carbohydrate transport. *See* Translocation

Carbon, **1**:74
  as carbohydrate component, **3**:97
  as nutrient, **3**:96, **4**:63
  in soil, **4**:63
  storage in plants, **3**:65

Carbonation, **1**:24, 25

Carbon cycle, **1**:59, **122–126**, *124*

computer modeling, **2**:89
ecological research, **2**:88
forests' role, **2**:64, 88, **4**:1–2
global warming and, **2**:183

Carbon dioxide
  aquatic plant growth, **1**:52
  atmospheric, ancient decrease in, **2**:38, 121
  concentration in cells, **1**:154
  emissions from fossil fuel combustion, **1**:74–75, *124*, 125, **2**:181, 183, **3**:27
  emissions from soil, **2**:183
  fermentation product, **1**:22
  increases, plant responses to, **1**:124, 125, **2**:88, **3**:133
  produced by yeast, **2**:164, **4**:170
  release by plants. *See* Photorespiration
  uptake by plants, **3**:129, 132, **4**:113, 159–160
  See also Carbon cycle; Carbon fixation; Global warming; Greenhouse effect

Carbon dioxide fertilization, **1**:124, 125, **3**:133

Carbon fixation, **1**:114, **4**:1
  photosynthetic. *See* Photosynthesis, carbon fixation and

Carbonic acid, in rain, **4**:64

Carboniferous period
  atmospheric changes during, **2**:121
  plants, **1**:104, **2**:121, 125, **4**:45, 126

Carcinogens. *See* Cancer-causing agents

Cardenolides, **3**:152

Cardiotonic, defined, **3**:72 and Glossary

Careers
  agroecologist, **1**:3, 5
  agronomist, **1**:**16–18**
  alcoholic beverage industry, **1**:18–22
  arborist, **1**:**54–56**
  botanical illustrator, **1**:**89–91**
  breeder, **1**:**93–95**, 96
  college professor, **2**:**14–15**
  curator of a botanical garden, **2**:**35–36**
  curator of an herbarium, **2**:**36–38**, **3**:8
  ecologist, **1**:5, **2**:85–86
  ethnobotanist, **2**:118, **3**:5
  flavor or fragrance chemist, **2**:**141–142**
  floristic botanist, **2**:143
  food scientist, **2**:141, **149–150**
  forester, **2**:**152–153**, 154–156, **3**:8
  genetic engineer, **2**:**166–168**
  horticulturist, **1**:92–93, **3**:**23–25**
  landscape architect, **3**:**52–53**
  pathologist, **3**:**120–121**
  pharmaceutical scientist, **3**:**123–124**

physiologist, **3**:**146–147**
taxonomist, **4**:**96–97**
turf management, **4**:**140–141**

Caribbean Islands, **1**:13, 69, 74, **4**:115

Carnation, **2**:148

Carnegiea gigantea (saguaro), **1**:*114*, 115, **2**:77, **3**:43–44, **4**:15

Carnivorous plants, **1**:**126–128**, **2**:61, **3**:57, **4**:137
  Darwin's work, **2**:45
  pitcher plants, **1**:77, 126–128, *127*, **4**:129, *130*
  sundews, **1**:126, *127*, 128, **2**:45, 61, **3**:122, **4**:63
  Venus's-flytrap, **1**:126, *127*, 128, **4**:*110*, 136–137
  Warming's work, **4**:157

Carob, **4**:53, 82

Carotenes, **1**:129, *130*, **3**:157, 165

Carotenoids, **1**:56, **129–131**, **3**:152, 156
  in abscisic acid synthesis, **3**:14
  defined, **3**:14, **4**:56 and Glossary
  economic importance, **1**:131, **2**:59
  role in animals, **1**:130–131, **3**:157
  role in plants, **1**:129–130, **3**:130, 135, 153, 156–157, 168
  senescence and, **4**:56
  structure and occurrence, **1**:129, 139, 140, **3**:156–157, 168, **4**:108
  synthetic, **1**:131

Carpellate flowers, **2**:145

Carpels, **1**:38, 43, 101, **2**:144, 173–174, **3**:77
  defined, **1**:38, **2**:144, **3**:77 and Glossary
  early angiosperms, **1**:47
  See also Flower structure

Carrageenan, **1**:29

Carrot family, **3**:11

Carrots, **1**:*130*, **2**:55, **3**:152, 157, **4**:119, *147*, 156

Carthamus tinctorius, **3**:*102*

Carver, George Washington, **1**:**131–132**, *131*, **3**:8

Carya (hickory), **2**:47, **3**:176, **4**:43, 128

Caryophyllales, **1**:46

Caryophyllidae, **1**:45, 46, **2**:78, 79

Caryopses, **2**:*159*, 160, 186

Cashew, **3**:170

Casparian band or thickenings, **1**:38, **4**:32, 164

Cassava (*Manihot*), **1**:6–8, **3**:181, **4**:32

Cassia (senna), **3**:70

Castanea. *See* Chestnut, American (*Castanea dentata*); Chestnut blight

Castilleja (Indian paintbrush), **3**:111, **4**:*139*

Castor bean (*Ricinus communis*), **3**:173, **4**:51, *52*, 53

Castor oil, **3**:101

Catabolism, **3**:148, *151*, 151–152
Catasetum, **3**:178
Catastrophism, defined, **2**:41 and Glossary
Catha edulis, **3**:194
Catharanthus roseus. See Madagascar periwinkle
Cathinone, **3**:194
Cation, defined, **1**:2 and Glossary
Cation exchange capacity, **4**:31, 63
Catkins, **1**:65, **4**:100–101, *101*
    defined, **1**:65, **3**:176, **4**:100 and Glossary
Cattails *(Typha latifolia)*, **4**:24
Cauliflower, **4**:156
Caves, insect populations, **4**:31
Cavitation, **4**:163–164
    See also Air bubbles
cdc2 gene, **1**:134–135
Ceanothus (buckbrush), **1**:148–149
CEC. *See* Cation exchange capacity
Cecropia, **4**:10
Cedar, **2**:24
Ceiba pentandra (kapok), **2**:*138*, 139, **4**:34
Celery, **2**:55
Celery pine *(Phyllocladus)*, **2**:17
Cell cycle, cell division, **1:132–135,** *133, 134*
    anastral division, **1**:133–134
    asymmetric division, **2**:81, 104
    auxins in cell differentiation, **3**:18–19
    basal division, **2**:104–105
    circadian rhythms, **4**:25
    coumarins' effect on, **2**:55
    cytokinesis, **1**:*133*, 134, 140
    phases, **1**:133–134
    plastids, **2**:112–113
    regulation, **1**:34–35
    senescence, **4**:56
    See also Differentiation and development; Growth; Meiosis; Meristems; Mitosis; *specific cell components and types*
Cell elongation, **3**:10, 15, **4**:58, 149
Cell membrane (plasma membrane), **1**:*136*, 136–137, 146, **2**:120
    calcium in, **3**:98
    hormone detection, **3**:15
    See also specific cell types
Cellophane, **1**:144, 147
Cells, **1**:36, **135–140**
    components, **1**:135–140, *136, 137*
    identifiability of plants from, **2**:151
    leaf, **1**:*146*
    plant and animal cells compared, **1**:*139*
    polarity, **2**:80–81, 81–82, 178
    specialized types, **1:140–144,** **2**:80
    See also Cell cycle; *specific cell components and types*
Cellulases, **1**:122, **3**:119
Cellulose, **1**:141, **144–145,** **2**:31, 151
    conversion to fermentable sugars, **1**:80
    economic importance, **1**:144, 147
    structure, **1**:121–122, 144, **3**:149
    synthesis, **1**:137
    See also Cell walls
Cellulose enzymes, **3**:118, 119
Cellulose microfibrils, **1**:121, 135–136, 137, 140, 144–146
    cell elongation, **3**:15
    synthesis, **1**:146–147
Cellulose synthases, **1**:146–147
Cell walls, **1**:36, 135–136, **145–147,** **2**:123, **3**:149, **4**:110
    bacteria, **2**:120
    collenchyma, **4**:112
    composition and architecture, **1**:36, 134, 135–136, 141, 144, 145–146, **3**:97–98, 150, **4**:110
    defensive strengthening of, **2**:57
    durability, **2**:151
    economic importance, **1**:147
    endodermis, **1**:38, **4**:32, 164
    fiber cells, **2**:137, 139, **4**:113
    fragments in defensive responses, **2**:57
    fruit development, **2**:158
    function, **1**:135, *137, 139*
    fungi, **2**:162
    germinating seeds, **2**:175
    lignified, **1**:36, 136, 141, 146, **2**:137, **4**:112–113, 149–150, 173
    proteins in, **1**:136, 146
    roots, **4**:32
    sclerenchyma, **4**:112–113
    secondary wall deposition patterns, **4**:*151*
    sieve elements, **4**:120–121
    synthesis, **1**:140, 146–147
    xylem, **4**:114, 124, 149, 161, 163, 171
    See also Cell elongation; Cellulose; Wood anatomy
Cenchrus (sandbur), **2**:187
Centers of origin theory, **4**:154
Central America, **1**:69, **2**:11–12, 18, **4**:4, 5
    See also Mesoamerica; *specific countries*
Centrifugation, defined, **3**:101 and Glossary
Centriole, **1**:*139*
Centromeres, **1**:158, 159
Cephaelis ipecacuanha. See Ipecac
Cephaleuros virescens, **1**:29
Cereal grains. *See* Grains; *specific cereal grains*
Cereal science programs, **1**:22
Cesium, **1**:*85*
Chalcones, **3**:157
Chamise *(Adenostoma fasciculatum)*, **1**:148
Chamomile tea, **4**:107
Chaparral, **1:147–151,** *148*, **2**:157
Character polarity, **3**:144–145
Characters, **3**:144
    acquired, **1**:110, **2**:128
analogous, **3**:144
    derived, **3**:144, 145, **4**:102
    homologous, **3**:144–145
    primitive vs. advanced, **3**:*144*
    See also Traits
Character states, **3**:144, *145*, **4**:102
Charales, **2**:123
Charcoal, **4**:179
Charophycean algae, **1**:29, 31, **2**:*122*, 122–124, 127
    See also Chlorophyta; Green algae
Chasmogamy, **1**:101
Chat, **3**:194
Cheeses, **2**:164
Chemical defenses, **2:54–60,** 157, **3**:69, 170–171, **4**:118
    against herbivores, **1**:47, 139, 143, **2**:7, 50, 55, 57–58, **3**:153
    against insects, **1**:143, **2**:57–58, 61, **3**:42, 153, **4**:10
    allelopathy, **1**:35, 150, **2**:7–8, **3**:45, 163, **4**:165
    angiosperms, **1**:47
    calcium oxalate, **1**:139, **3**:172, **4**:54
    effectiveness, **2**:57–59
    human uses, **2**:59
    mechanisms of induced defenses, **2**:56–57
    occurrence, **4**:142, 143
    phytoalexins, **3**:119
    rain forest plants, **4**:10
    resins, **2**:61, **4**:10, 173
    seeds and fruits, **4**:9, 43, 54
    types, **2**:55–56
    See also Alkaloids; Flavonoids; Secondary metabolites; Terpenes; Toxins; *specific plants and plant groups*
Chemical fertilizers, **1**:10–13, **2**:136
    See also Fertilizers
Chemical prospecting, **2**:117
    See also Plant prospecting
Chemosystematics, **4**:95
Cherry *(Prunus)*
    fruit, **3**:172, **4**:35
    wood, **4**:*36*, 175
Chestnut
    American *(Castanea dentata)*, **1**:72, 151, **2**:165
    European, record-holding, **4**:15
    in North American TDBF associations, **2**:46, *47*
Chestnut blight, **1**:151, **2**:50, 165
Chestnuts, **2**:160
Chicory *(Cichorium intybus)*, **1**:58
Chile
    agriculture, **2**:28
    forests, **2**:18, *23*, 48
    species diversity, **1**:68, 69
    wine industry, **1**:24
Chili peppers, **1**:6, **3**:91, **4**:68
China
    agriculture, **1**:6, 7, **2**:31, **4**:27, 69, *106*
    desertification, **2**:71, *72*

China (continued)
  forests, **2:**47–48, **4:**5
  fossil fuel usage, **1:**125
  herbals, **3:**4
  orchids in, **3:**104
  species diversity, **1:***68*
Chinese cabbages, **1:**6
Chitin, **2:**162
  defined, **1:**128, **3:**93 and Glossary
Chitinases, **2:**56
Chloranthaceae, **2:**144
Chlorenchyma cells, **1:**141
Chlorine, **3:**97, 98, **4:**63, 64
Chloroarachniophytes, **3:**145
Chlorobionta, **4:**102
Chlorophyceae, **1:**27, 156
Chlorophylls, **1:**139, **151–152,**
  3:156, 168
  in algae, **1:**27, 30–31, 156
  in bark, **1:**64
  carotenoids and, **1:**130
  chlorophyll *a*, **1:***152, 153,* 156,
    3:*135,* 145, 165
  chlorophyll *b*, **1:**152, *153,* 156,
    3:145, 165
  chlorophyll *c*, **1:**152, **3:**165
  chlorophyll *d*, **1:**152, **3:**165
  constituents and chemical struc-
    tures, **1:**152, **3:**98
  in deciduous leaves, **2:**49, 52
  light absorption spectra, **1:***153*
  in photosynthesis, **1:**151–152,
    3:130, 135, 156–157
  senescence and, **4:**56
  synthesis, **1:**152, 155, **2:**179
  types, **1:**152
Chlorophyta, **1:**27, 29–31, **3:**145,
  4:102
  See also Charophycean algae
Chloroplasts, **1:***136,* 139–140,
  153–156, *154,* **3:***129,* 167
  bacteria, **2:**120
  components and structure, **1:**139,
    152–153, *155,* **3:**66, 134–135,
    136, 167
  cortex cells, **4:**78
  defined, **1:**30, **2:**40, **3:**10, **4:**37
    and Glossary
  development, **1:**155–156, **3:**168
  dinoflagellates, **1:**31
  DNA location, **3:**148
  epidermal cells, **4:**113
  evolution, **1:**156, **2:**40, *112,* **4:**86
  function, **1:**139, 153–155, **3:**134,
    167
  herbicides and, **3:**10
  juvenile (proplastids), **1:**155,
    4:*142*
  leaf parenchyma cells, **3:**55
  See also Plastids
Chlorosis, **3:***96,* 99
Chocolate, **1:**111, 112–113, **2:**59,
  3:194
  See also Cacao; Cocoa butter
Cholesterol, **2:**55, **3:**101
Cholodny, N., **3:**18
Chondrodendron tomentosa. See Curare

Chondrus crispus, **1:**29
Christmas cactus, **1:**116
Chromatids, **1:***158*
Chromatin, **1:***136,* 137
Chromium, **1:***85*
Chromoplasts, **1:**140, **3:**167, 168
Chromosomes, **1:**137, **157–160,**
  158, **3:**80, 148, 180, **4:**24
  in bacteria, **2:**120
  cytogenetics, **4:**95
  McClintock and Creighton's re-
    search, **1:**157, **2:**33–34, **3:**66–68
  numbers, nomenclature,
    3:180–181
  pairing, **1:**158, **3:**180, **4:**24
  See also Cell cycle; Diploidy;
    Genes; Genomes; Polyploidy
Chrysanthemum, **3:***125*
  ox-eye daisy, **3:**48
  Shasta daisy, **1:**110
Chrysophyceae, **1:**27, 156
Cichorium intybus (chicory), **1:**58
Cider, **1:**26
Cigarettes, **1:**32–33, **2:**100
Cinchona. See Quinine
Cinnamic acid, **1:**35
Cinnamon, **1:**46, 64, **3:**11, 174
Cinnamon family. *See* Lauraceae
Circadian, defined, **3:**127 and
  Glossary
Circadian rhythms, **4:**25–26
  nyctinasty and photonasty,
    4:135–136
  temperature, **4:**54–55
Circumscription, defined, **1:**46 and
  Glossary
Cisterna, defined, **1:**138 and
  Glossary
CITES (Convention on Interna-
  tional Trade in Endangered
  Species of Wild Fauna and
  Flora), **2:**110–111
Citronellol, **4:***108*
Citrullus lanatus. See Watermelon
Citrus, **1:**9, **2:**158
  mosquito repellent from, **2:**59
  See also specific citrus fruits
Civets, **4:**8
Clades, **3:**145, **4:**93–94
  defined, **1:**45, **2:**79, **4:**93 and
    Glossary
Cladistics, **3:**144–145, **4:**97, 102, 104
Cladodes, **1:**41–42
  defined, **1:**41 and Glossary
Cladograms. *See* Phylogenetic trees
Cladophylls, **4:**80
Classification. *See* Phylogenetics;
  Systematics; Taxonomy
Claviceps. See Ergot
Clay, **4:**65
Clay loams, **4:**65–66
Clay soils, **4:**66, 67
Clean Air Act (U.S.), **1:**1
Clear-cutting, **1:**59
  See also Deforestation
Cleistogamy, **1:**101
Clements, Edith Schwartz, **1:**160

Clements, Frederic, **1:**82, **160–161,**
  2:85, 98, **3:**159
Clifford, George, **3:**62
Climate
  biomes and, **1:**83–84
  past, dendrochronological recon-
    struction of, **2:**65, 67, **4:**127,
    172
  plant distribution and, **1:**75–76,
    83–84
  plants' influences on, **1:**59, **4:**2
  See also Climate change; Global
    warming; Greenhouse effect;
    Mediterranean climate; Precipi-
    tation; Temperature; *specific
    biome and ecosystem types*
Climate change, **1:**126, **3:**29
  biome distribution and, **1:**84
  and desertification, **2:**71–72
  due to global warming, **3:**28
  and extinctions, **2:**107, **3:**29
  Permian, **2:**121
  Pleistocene, **4:**6
  See also Global warming
Climax state, climax communities,
  1:161, **2:**85, 98
  See also Succession
Climbing plants, **4:**59, 60, 129
  aerial roots, **3:**43, **4:**34
  Darwin's work, **2:**44
  rain forests, **4:**6–7 (*see also*
    Lianas)
  thigmotropism, **4:**135
Clines and ecotypes, **1:161–163,**
  3:34, 128
Clock plant, **3:**57
Clonal germplasm repositories, **4:**48,
  49
Cloning
  DNA/genes, **2:**169
  See also Asexual propagation
Clostridium, **3:**91
Clouds, **2:**64, 182
Clover, **3:**93, 181
Club mosses (lycopods), **2:**125, 166,
  3:58, 141, **4:**45, *47,* 126
  See also Lycophytes
Club root, **3:**117–118
Coal, **1:**60, **2:**125, **3:**27, **4:**45
Coalescence, flowers, **2:**146
Coalescing roots, defined, **4:**3 and
  Glossary
Coal mining, **3:**27
Coastal deserts, **2:**73
Coastal ecosystems, **1:**51, **2:1–4,** **3:**2
  mangroves in, **3:**2, **4:**34
  nitrogen fixation, **3:**92
Coastal sage communities (Califor-
  nia), **1:**149
Coast redwood. *See* Sequoia
Cobalt, **3:**97, 98, **4:**63, 64
Cobbles, **4:**65
Coca (*Erythroxylum, Erythroxylon*),
  1:33, **2:4–6,** *5,* **3:**194
Cocaine, **1:**33, **2:**4–6, 59, **3:**194
Coccidiomycosis (*Coccidioides immi-
  tis*), **2:**165

Coccolithophores (coccol-ithophorids), **1:**31, 123

Cocklebur (*Xanthium strumarium*), **3:***126*, 128

Cocoa butter, **3:**101, *102*
See also Cacao; Chocolate

Coconut milk, **4:**23

Coconut oil, **3:***101, 102*

Coconut palm (*Cocos nucifera*), **2:**157, **3:***102, 106,* 107
coconuts, **1:**6–8, **3:**86, **4:**51
coir, **2:***138,* 139–140

Coconut, double (*Lodoicea maldivica*), **4:**15, 51

Codeine, **2:**59, **3:**103, 165

Coevolution, **2:**6–10, 50
angiosperms and animals, **1:**48, **2:**126–127, 144, 147–148, **3:**112, **4:**8
evidence of, **2:**6–7
herbivores and, **2:**6, 7–8
inhibiting factors, **2:**7–8
mutualisms, **2:**6, 8–9, 50
tolerance of chemical defenses, **2:**57–58

Coffee (*Coffea*), **2:**10–13, *11,* 100, **3:**182, 194, **4:**53
See also Caffeine

Coffee leaf rust, **2:**13

Cogon grass (*Imperata cylindrica*), **2:**189

Cohesion, **3:**154, **4:**162, *163*
See also Transpiration-cohesion-tension mechanism

Coir (*Cocos nucifera*), **2:***138,* 139–140

Coix lacryma-jobi (Job's tears), **2:**187

Colchicine, **3:**70, 183

Colchicum autumnale, **3:**70

Coleochaete, **2:***122,* 123

Coleoptile, **2:**105, **4:**132–133
defined, **3:**155, **4:**53 and Glossary

Coleorhiza, **2:**105, 106

Collards, **4:**156

College professors, **2:14–15**

Collenchyma, **1:**37, 142, **3:**55, **4:**112
defined, **3:**55, **4:**111 and Glossary

Colloids, **4:**31

Colombia, **1:**66, *68,* **2:**11–12
See also Amazonia

Colonize, defined, **1:**53, **2:**41, **3:**50, **4:**11 and Glossary

Colony, defined, **4:**3 and Glossary

Color
chlorophyll's role, **1:**152, **3:**135
corn kernels, **1:**48–49, *49*
flowers, **1:**130, 143, **2:**55–56, **3:***145,* 168, 179
fruit, **1:**130, 131, **2:**157, **3:**167, 168, **4:**43
leaves, **1:**129, 140, 152, **2:**49, 52, 60, **3:**179
repellent to insects, **2:**60
wood, **4:**172–173
See also Pigments

Colpus, **3:**88

Columbian Exchange, **1:**9

Columbus, Christopher, **1:**115, **2:**28, **4:**115

Comet impacts, **2:**107

Comfrey tea, **4:**107

Commelinidae, **1:**45

Commensalisms, **2:**50, **3:**43–44, **4:**84, 86
defined, **3:**43 and Glossary

Commodities, defined, **1:**21, **2:**99, **4:**32 and Glossary

Communities. *See* Biological communities; Plant communities

Community, defined, **1:**35, **2:**1, **4:**1 and Glossary

Community ecology, **2:**85, 98, **3:**157, 159, **4:**157–158
See also Plant communities

Compaction
defined, **4:**11 and Glossary
See also Soil compaction

Companion cells, **1:**144, **4:**114, 121, 151
sieve tube-companion cell complex, **1:**47, 144, **4:**114, 121, 151

Competition, **3:**45, 161–163, **4:**6

Competitive exclusion, **3:**162

Complex hybrids, defined, **1:**110 and Glossary

Compos, **2:**191

Compositae. *See* Asteraceae

Compost, **2:15–16**

Compound, defined, **1:**1, **2:**151, **3:**10, **4:**33 and Glossary

Compound leaves, **3:**54, 56, **4:**6

Computer modeling
in ecology, **2:**89, 104
in forestry, **2:**154
of global warming, **2:**182

Computers, in systematics and taxonomy, **4:**90, 101

Cones, **1:**47
conifers, **1:***100,* **2:**21, 198, *199,* 202
gnetophytes, **2:**201
phyllotaxis of pine cones, **3:**141, 142

Congo, **1:***68*

Congo Basin, **4:**4, 12

Conidia, **2:**163, **3:**113

Conidiophores, **2:**163

Coniferales, **2:**17

Coniferous forests, **2:17–21,** *18,* 22, 202, **4:**128
distribution, **2:**18–19
fire frequency, **1:**64, **2:**93
global warming and, **2:**183, **3:**28
management, **2:**20
mapped, **1:***81*
plant-animal interactions, **2:**19–20
redwood forest, **4:**57

Conifers (Coniferophyta), **2:21–24,** 147, 197, 198–199, **4:**100
bark, **2:**202
broadleaf, **2:**17, 21, 199
cones, **1:***100,* **2:**21, 198, *199,* 202, **3:**141, 142
deciduous, **2:**17, 198–199

distinguishing characteristics, **2:***198*
distribution, **2:**22
ecological significance, **2:**202
economic uses, **2:**22, 23–24, 202, **4:**174
fire and, **2:**202
form, **4:**61
needles/leaves, **2:**17, 21, 52, 126, 198–199, **3:**58
pests/pathogens, **3:**112, 116
resin, **2:**61
seeds and dispersal, **2:**19–20, 21, 199, 202, **4:**53
selected genera, **2:**22
taxonomy, **2:**17
as VOC producers, **1:**59–60
wood and wood species, **2:**22, 23–24, 202, **4:**128, 173–175

Coniine, **1:**32, *33,* **3:**153

Conium maculatum (hemlock), **1:**32, *33,* **3:**153

Conservation
of biodiversity, **1:**72, 162–163, **2:**117
endangered species, **1:**72, **2:***108,* 110–111
forests, **2:**65, **4:**12
grasslands, **2:**193–194, **4:**41
New Environmentalism, **2:**117
seed preservation, **4:48–50**

Conservation biology, **4:**94

Conservation tillage, **1:**12

Consumers (heterotrophs), **2:**86–87, 91

Continental drift, **2:**107, **3:**30
defined, **3:**30 and Glossary

Contraceptives, **2:**83, **3:**11

Contractile, defined, **1:**140, **4:**143 and Glossary

Convective uplift, defined, **2:**191 and Glossary

Convention on Biological Diversity (1992), **3:**165

Convention on International Trade in Endangered Species of Wild Fauna and Flora (CITES), **2:**110–111

Convergence, **2:**126, **3:**144, *146,* **4:**102

Cook Islands, **4:**5

Cook, James, **3:**31

Copper, **1:***85,* **3:**15, *97,* 98, **4:**63, 64

Coppice growth, defined, **3:**160 and Glossary

Corals, **1:**29, **2:**87, **4:**85

Corchorus (jute), **2:***138*

Cordaites, **3:**58

Cordus, Valerius, **2:24–25,** 24

Core eudicots, **1:**46

Coriander (*Coriandrum sativum*), **3:**11

Cork, **1:**38, 64, **2:25–28,** **3:**78–79, **4:**113, 171, 179

Cork cambium, **3:**79, **4:**114
cork production, **1:**38, 64, **2:**25, **3:**78, **4:**79, 113

Cork cambium (continued)
    differentiation and development,
        1:37, **3:***78–79*, **4:**113, 171, 173
    function, **4:**58, 59, 111–113
    structure, **3:**77
    See also Cambium/cambia;
        Lateral meristems
Cork oak (*Quercus suber*), **1:**64, **2:***26,*
    26–27
Corms, **1:**41, **3:**87, **4:**80
Corn (maize) (*Zea mays*), **1:***23,*
    2:28–31, *29,* **3:**86, **4:**156
    chromosomal structure, **1:**97,
        2:33–34, **3:**83–84, 183
    color in corn kernels, **1:**48–49,
        49, 159, **2:**33–34
    cultivation areas, **1:**83, **2:**28, 185,
        187, **3:**102
    economic uses and importance,
        2:29–30, 100, 189, **3:**184, **4:**68
    embryogenesis, **2:**106
    flowers and pollination, **2:**29,
        145, 186, **3:**84, 176, **4:**23
    germination, **2:***175*
    gravitropism, **4:**134
    in human diet, **1:**8, **2:**30, 185
    improvement efforts, **1:**9, 98–99,
        2:165, *170,* 170–171
    leaf structure and arrangement,
        4:61
    McClintock and Creighton's re-
        search, **1:**157, **2:**33–34, **3:**66–69
    oil, **3:***102*
    organic vs. conventional agricul-
        ture, **1:**13, 15
    origins and domestication, **1:**6,
        98–99, **2:**28–29, 184, *187,* **3:**91,
        4:23
    pest defenses, **2:**61, **3:**42–43
    pests and diseases, **2:**61, 165,
        170–171, **3:**112
    photosynthetic pathway, **3:**131,
        139
    production and yields, **1:**14,
        2:29–30, 185, **4:**51
    roots, **4:**134
    seeds, **2:**29, 30, **4:**51
    stem structure, **1:***41*
    sugar source, **4:**82
    transpiration rates, **4:**159
    wild progenitor, **1:**98, **2:**28–29,
        4:23
Corn earworm, **2:**61
Corn oil, **3:***102*
Corn smut, **2:**165
Cornstarch, **4:**23
Corn sweeteners, **4:**83
Corolla, **2:**144, 147
Corpse lily. *See Rafflesia*
Corpus, meristems, **3:**77, *78*
Correns, Carl, **3:**75
Cortex, **1:**38, 41, **2:**106, **4:**78, 112,
    113
    root cortex, **4:**32, 34, 112, 164
Cortical, defined, **1:**38, **2:**81, **3:**40
    and Glossary
Cortical parenchyma, **1:**38

Cortisone, **2:**83, **3:***70*
Corymb, **3:**38
Costus, **4:**61
Cotton (*Gossypium*), **2:31–33,** *31, 32,*
    138, **3:***102,* 109
    fiber structure, **1:**144, 147, **2:**31,
        139
    improvement efforts, **2:**32–33,
        3:183
    pests and defenses, **2:**32–33, 60,
        61, **3:**42, **4:**129
    polyploidy, **3:**182
    terpenoids in, **2:**55
Cotton boll weevil, bollworm, **2:**60,
    61
Cottonseed oil, **3:***102*
Cottonwoods (*Populus*), **3:**89, **4:**128
Cotyledons (seed leaves), **2:**78, 105,
    176, **3:**86, **4:***21,* 53
Coumarins, **2:**55
Coutarea hexandra, **3:**179
Covalent, defined, **1:**135, **2:**120 and
    Glossary
Cover crops, **1:**5
    See also Green manure crops
Cowles, Henry Chandler, **1:**161,
    2:98
Cowpeas, **1:**6
Cows, **2:**53
Cranberries, **1:**8
Crane, Peter C., **1:**105
Crassulaceae, **3:**132, **4:***81*
Crassulacean acid, **1:**114
Crassulacean acid metabolism
    (CAM), **1:**114, **2:**77, **3:**132, **4:**81
    defined, **1:**114, **2:**77, **3:**132, **4:**81
        and Glossary
Creeping plants, **4:**59
Creighton, Harriet Baldwin,
    2:33–34, **3:**67
Creosote bush (*Larrea tridentata*),
    4:15
Cresentia cujete (calabash), **4:**43
Cretaceous plants, **2:**122, 147, 180,
    3:58
Cretaceous/Tertiary comet or aster-
    oid impact, **2:**122
Criminal investigations, forensic
    botany in, **2:**150–151
Crocus, **3:**87
Cronquist, Arthur, **4:**104
Crop plants, **3:**85
    genetic engineering, **1:**8–12,
        2:32–33, 168–169
    genetics, **1:**95
    insect herbivores, **3:**41–42
    mycorrhizal associations, **3:**40
    palms, **3:**107
    parasitic pests, **3:**112
    Rosaceae, **4:***36*
    Vavilov's work on origins and
        distribution, **4:**154
    vertebrate herbivores, **3:**46
    wild types, **3:**24, 171, **4:**29, 94
    See also Agriculture; Energy
        crops; Food crops; Oils, plant-
        derived; *specific crop plants*

Crop residues, **1:**79
Crop rotations, **1:**7, 14–15, **3:**93,
    116, 117
    defined, **1:**7, **3:**93 and Glossary
Crop science, **1:**17
Crop yields. *See* Agricultural yields
Cross-incompatibility, **3:**32
Cross-pollination, **2:**44, 145, **3:**128,
    176
    barriers to, **3:**32, 176, **4:**73–74,
        76
Crotalaria juncea (sunnhemp), **2:***138*
Crown gall disease, **2:**169, **3:**117
Cruciferae. *See* Brassicaceae
Crustaceans, **2:**1
Crustose lichens, **3:**59
Cruz, Martín de la, **3:**5
Cryphonectria parasitica (chestnut
    blight fungus), **1:**151, **2:**50, 165
Cryptophyta, **1:***27,* 31
Crystallography, defined, **3:**143 and
    Glossary
Cuba, **1:**13
Cucumber, **2:**158, 159, **4:***114*
Cucurbitacin, **2:**55
Cucurbita pepo, **2:**161
    See also Squash
Culinary herbs, **3:**11
Culm, **2:**186
Cultivars, **2:34–35,** **4:**146
Cultivated plants. *See* Crop plants
Cultivation, defined, **1:**88, **2:**47,
    4:12 and Glossary
Cupressaceae, **2:**17
Cupressus (cypress), **2:***22*
Curare, **1:**64, **3:***70,* 165
Curarea toxicofera. See Curare
Curators
    botanical gardens, **2:35–36**
    herbaria, **2:36–38,** **3:**8
Cuscuta. See Dodders
Cuscutaceae. *See* Dodders
Custard-apple family. *See*
    Annonaceae
Custer, George A., **3:**8
Cuticle, **3:**57, 118, **4:**54, 81, 113,
    159–160
    defined, **1:**52, **2:**4, **3:**57, **4:**33 and
        Glossary
    See also Waxes
Cutin, **1:**142, **3:**118, 119
Cutinase enzymes, **3:**118, 119
Cuttings, propagation via,
    3:187–188
Cuvier, Georges, **1:**118
Cyanide heap leach gold mining,
    2:88
    defined, **2:**88 and Glossary
Cyanobacteria, **1:***27,* **2:38–40,** **3:**165
    Anabaena, **2:***39*
    defined, **1:***27,* **2:**121, **3:**58, **4:**26
        and Glossary
    nitrogen fixation, **2:**39, **3:**91, 92,
        4:84–85
    Nostoc, **1:**108
    photosynthesis by, **2:**38–39,
        120–121, **4:**26

role in plastid evolution, **1:**156, **2:**113, 121
See also Lichens
Cyanogenic, defined, **2:**55, **3:**153, **4:**10 and Glossary
Cyanogenic compounds, in grasses, **2:**189
Cyanogenic glycosides, **2:**55, **3:**153, 172, **4:**10
Cycads (Cycadophyta), **2:**197, 199–200, *200*, 202, **4:**126
distinguishing characteristics, **2:***198*
pollination, **1:**48
record-holding, **4:**16
reproduction, **4:**20
symbioses, **4:**84–85
Cyclanthaceae, **3:**179
Cyclic tetrapyrroles, **1:**152
Cyclin, **1:**135
Cyclooxygenases, **2:**59
Cyme, **3:**38
Cynara scolymus (artichoke), **1:**58
Cynodon (Bermuda grass), **2:**189, **3:**181, 182
Cyperaceae (sedge family), **3:**86, *87*, 90
See also Sedges
Cypress *(Cupressus)*, **2:***22*
Cypress family, **2:***22*, 23–24
Cypress, swamp or bald *(Taxodium)*, **1:**77, **2:**17, *18*, *22*
Cytochrome *bf* complex, **3:**137–138
Cytogenetics, **4:**95
Cytokinesis, **1:***133*, 134, 140
Cytokinins, **3:**118, 153, 155
applications of, **2:**158, 177
functions and effects, **2:**179, **3:***17*, 19, **4:**56, 109
interactions, **3:**19, 20
synthesis, **3:**14, **4:**32
tissue culture media, **4:**109
Cytologist, defined, **2:**33 and Glossary
Cytology, defined, **3:**66, **4:**99 and Glossary
Cytosine, **3:**81, *148*
Cytoskeleton, **1:***139*, 140
Cytosol, **3:**149
defined, **3:**149 and Glossary
Cytostatic, defined, **1:**33 and Glossary
Czech Republic, **1:**25

D

Daffodil, **3:**87
DAG (diacylglycerol), **3:**65
Daisies, **1:**110, **3:**39, 48, 141, 142
Damping off, **3:**116, 119
Dams, **4:**168
Damselfly, **1:***128*
Dandelion *(Taraxacum officinale)*, **1:**58, 67, **3:**48, 178, **4:**78
asexual seed formation, **4:**18
seeds, **2:**157, **4:***19*
Darwin, Charles, **2:40–46**, *40*

background and early life, **2:**40–41
Beagle voyage, **2:**41
botanical work, **2:**44–45, 129, **3:**155, **4:**132–133
Gray and, **1:**77, **2:**129, 194–196, **4:**103
Hooker and, **2:**42, 129, **3:**13
influences on others, **1:**77, 109, **2:**40, 129, 194–196
interest in genealogies, **4:**103
on flowering plants, **1:**44
on Venus's-flytrap, **1:**126
Sachs' opinion of, **2:**45, **4:**37
Wallace and, **2:**43
See also Natural selection, Darwin's theory of; *On the Origin of Species*
Darwin, Francis, **3:**155, **4:**132–133
Darwinism
Lysenko's opposition to, **4:**154
synthesis with Mendelian theory, **2:**43–44, 129, **3:**75, **4:**104
Darwin's "abominable mystery," **1:**45, **2:**147
Dates, date palm, **1:**6, **3:**86, 107, **4:**31, 53, 82, 171
Dating, tree-ring. *See* Dendrochronology
Datura (jimsonweed), **3:**193–194
Daubenmire, Rexford, **3:**159
Daucus carota (Queen Anne's lace), **4:**44
Dawn redwood *(Metasequoia)*, **1:**77, **2:**17, *18*, 22
Day-length sensitivity. *See* Photoperiodism
Daylilies, **3:**157
Day-neutral plants, **3:**125, *126*, 127, **4:**26
See also Photoperiodism
DDT, **1:**85, **2:**88–89
Deadly nightshade. *See* Belladonna
de Bary, Anton, **3:**114, 185
Deciduous forests, temperate, **2:46–51**, **3:**176, **4:**7, 128
U.S. deciduous forest associations, **2:**46, *47*, **4:**128
Deciduous forests, tropical, **1:**71, **2:**46
Deciduous habit, **1:**47, **2:**49, 51–53, 130
Deciduous plants, **2:51–53**
conifers, **2:**17, 198–199
summer-deciduous plants, **1:**149
Decomposers, **1:**122, **2:53–54**, 87
earthworms, **1:**126, **2:**45, 53, *54*, **4:**8, 10
fungi, **2:**53–54, 162
termites, **4:**10, 40
tropical rain forests, **4:**10
See also Bacteria
Decomposition, **2:**121, **4:**63
cellulase in, **1:**122
rain forests, **4:**10–11
rates, global warming and, **2:**183
Deductive, defined, **3:**1 and Glossary

Deer, **2:**50, 53, 109, **4:**8
Defenses. *See* Chemical defenses; Physical defenses; *specific plants and plant groups*
Deforestation, **2:63–65**, *64*, 98
alternative strategies, **2:**64–65
causes, **2:**63, **3:**27
effects on atmosphere and climate, **1:**59, 125, **2:**64, **3:**27
effects on biodiversity, **1:**69, 71, **2:**63, 108, 109, **3:**29
effects on soil and water, **2:**63, **4:**11
nutrient cycling and, **4:**11
rates and statistics, **1:**69, **2:**46, 63, 98, **3:**26, 29
See also specific locations and forest types
Degree of specialization, disease resistance and, **4:**153
Dehiscent fruits, **2:**157, *159*, 159–160
Delta-tetrahydrocannabinol (THC), **1:**119
De Materia Medica (Dioscorides), **3:**4, **4:***92*
Dendrochronologist, defined, **4:**172 and Glossary
Dendrochronology, **2:65–68**, **4:**127, 172
Deoxyribonucleic acid. *See* DNA
Deoxyribose, **3:**148
Deparia acrostichoides, **2:***134–135*
Depressants
kava *(Piper methysticum)*, **3:**195
opium poppy, **1:**32, *33*, **3:102–103**, *103*, 174, 195
Depth accommodation growth, **1:**52
Derivatives, **3:**76, 77, **4:**171
Derived characters, **3:**144, 145, **4:**102
Dermal tissues, **1:**38, 140, 142, **4:***111*, 111–112, 113
Dermatophytes, defined, **2:**164 and Glossary
Descent with modification, **2:**124, 126, 129
See also Natural selection
Deschampsia antarctica (Antarctic hair grass), **2:**187
Desertification, **2:**63, **70–73**, 183, **3:**28
defined, **2:**64 and Glossary
Desert plants, **1:**114, **2:**4, 74, 75–77, **4:**30
adaptations, **2:**75–77, **3:**57, *146*
See also Cacti
Deserts, **1:**75, **2:73–77**, *74*, *76*
distribution, **2:**73, *75*
mapped, **1:***81*
natural, **2:**71
polar, **4:**139
Desiccate, defined, **2:**74 and Glossary
Desiccation, defined, **2:**60, **4:**85 and Glossary
Desmids, **1:**27, **2:**127

Desmodium (tick-trefoil), **4**:44
Desulphovibrio, **1**:85
Determinate inflorescences, **3**:37–38
Detritus, defined, **2**:1 and Glossary
Devonian period, **2**:121, **3**:57–58
DeVries, Hugo, **3**:75
Dextrose, **4**:82
Diacylglycerol (DAG), **3**:65
Diammonium phosphate, **2**:136
Diamondback moth larvae, **3**:42
Diaspore, **4**:41
Diatomaceous earth, **1**:29
Diatoms, **1**:27, 29, 31, 156, **3**:165
    defined, **1**:29, **3**:165 and Glossary
Dicaeum (mistletoe bird), **3**:112
Dichasium, **3**:38
Dichogamy, **1**:101
Dichotomous keys, **3**:36, **4**:96, 97, 103
Dicots, **1**:46, 65, **2**:78–79
    embryogenesis, **2**:105–106
    flowers, **1**:39, 46, 47, **2**:145–146, 146
    leaves, **1**:39, 40, **2**:78, **3**:53–56, 58
    major families, **2**:78
    roots, **2**:78, **4**:30, 32
    seeds, **1**:39, **2**:78, **3**:86, **4**:53
    stems, **3**:86, **4**:77
    See also Eudicots
Dicotyledons. *See* Dicots
Dictyophora indusiata (stinkhorn), **2**:162, 163
Dictyosome, **1**:36, 138
    defined, **1**:36 and Glossary
    See also Golgi apparatus
Dieffenbachia, **3**:170, 172
Diener, Theodor, **3**:115
Diet, human, **3**:22
    calorie sources, **1**:8, 122, **2**:30, **3**:101, **4**:82, 169
    cereals in, **4**:51
    fats and oils in, **3**:101
    fiber, **1**:147
    fungi in, **2**:164, 165
    grasses in, **2**:185, 187, 188–189
    lichens in, **3**:61
    Rosaceae in, **4**:35–36
    seeds in, **4**:51
    See also specific food plants
Differential growth
    and plant form, **4**:58, 60
    See also Tropisms and nastic movements
Differentiation and development, **2**:80–83, **3**:80
    See also Cell cycle; Genetic mechanisms and development; Growth; Meristems; *specific cell components and types*; *specific plant parts*
Diffuse porous wood, **4**:173
Diffusion, **4**:146, 160
Digalactosyldiacylglycerol, **3**:66
Digestive enzymes, **3**:119, **4**:142
Digitalis (drug), **3**:172
Digitalis (foxglove), **3**:11, 70, 71–72, 72, 170, 172

Digitoxin, **3**:11, 70, 72, 172
Digoxin, **3**:70, 72, 172
Dilleniidae, **1**:45, 46–47, **2**:78, 79
Dimensional lumber. *See* Lumber; Wood products
Dinoflagellates, **1**:27, 29–30, 31, 156
Dinophyta (Pyrrhophyta), Dinophyceae. *See* Dinoflagellates
Dinosaurs, **2**:122
Dioecious, defined, **1**:105 and Glossary
Dioecy, **1**:101–102, **2**:145, **4**:23
Dionaea. See Venus's-flytrap
Dioon edule, **4**:16
Dioscorea. See Yams
Dioscorides, **3**:4, **4**:92
Diosgenin, **2**:83, **3**:70
Dioxin contamination, **3**:10
Diploid stage (2N), **1**:158–159
    See also Alternation of generations; Sporophytes
Diploidy, **1**:97, 158, **3**:34, 83–84, 180
    diploid, defined, **1**:97, **2**:145, **3**:33, **4**:16 and Glossary
    diploid-triploid crosses, **3**:66–67
    evolution from polyploidy, **3**:183
Direct marketing of agricultural produce, **2**:102
Disaccharides, **1**:121, **4**:81
Discontinuous transition, **3**:142
Disease resistance
    breeding for, **2**:57, 165, **3**:91, 186, **4**:153
    Vavilov's work, **4**:153
Diseases
    as selection mechanism, **2**:7–8
    systematic studies of, **4**:94
    threats to native plants, **1**:72
    See also Bacterial diseases; Fungal diseases; Pathogens; Viruses and viral diseases; *specific diseases*
Disease vectors, **3**:42, 116–118
Disharmonious species distribution, **1**:79
Disjunctions, **1**:76–78
Disk florets, **1**:58
Dissipate, defined, **1**:126, **2**:91 and Glossary
Distal roots, **4**:123–124
Distichous leaf arrangement, **3**:56
Distilled spirits, **1**:23, 26, **2**:164, 189
Disuse, **2**:128
Diterpenes (diterpenoids), **3**:152, **4**:108
Diurnal, defined, **4**:8 and Glossary
Divergence, **4**:71, 72, 102
    and Darwin's natural selection theory, **2**:42, 128–129
Divergence angle, **3**:142
Diversity. *See* Biodiversity; Genetic diversity; Species diversity
Dixon, Henry, **3**:154, **4**:163
DMT (N,N-dimethyltryptamine), **3**:193
DNA (deoxyribonucleic acid), **1**:56, 137, 139, 157, **3**:80–84

chemical structure, **3**:80, 80–81, 81, 148
in eubacteria, **2**:120
from herbarium specimens, **3**:6
location in cells, **3**:80, 148, 166
mutations, **3**:84, 183
protein synthesis, **3**:81, 83, 148
replication, **3**:82, 82–83, 84
transfer DNA, **4**:117–118
transposable DNA elements (transposons, jumping genes), **1**:157, 159, **2**:33–34, **3**:68
viruses, **3**:114
    See also Chromosomes
DNA analysis, **1**:57, **4**:87–88, 90, 95, 97
    See also Molecular genetics; Molecular systematics
DNA cloning, **2**:169
DNA fingerprinting, **3**:84
DNA insertion techniques, **2**:169–170, **4**:117–118
DNA polymerase, **3**:82
DNA synthesis
    in cell cycle. *See* S-phase
    germinating seeds, **2**:175
Dobzhansky, Theodosius, **4**:91
Dodders (Cuscutaceae), **3**:45, 111, 111–112, 112
Dogwoods, **1**:72
Doi, Yoji, **3**:115
Domesticate, defined, **1**:6, **2**:28, **3**:171, **4**:68 and Glossary
Domestication of crop plants, **1**:6–9, 98, **3**:171, **4**:68
    See also specific crop plants
Dominant traits, **3**:74
Dormancy
    photoperiodism, **3**:127, **4**:26
    seeds, **1**:149, **2**:126, 175–178, **3**:19, 20, **4**:54–55
Dormant, defined, **1**:149, **2**:75, **3**:103, **4**:23 and Glossary
Double coconut (*Lodoicea maldivica*), **4**:15, 51
Double fertilization, **1**:43–44, **2**:145, **4**:51
Douglas-fir (*Pseudotsuga*), **2**:199, **3**:112, 158, **4**:126
    distribution, **2**:19, 22
    uses, **2**:22, 23, **4**:174
Douglass, Andrew Ellicott, **2**:66
Downy mildews, **2**:165, **3**:114, 116–118
Doxorubicin, **4**:106
Dracaena, **3**:86
Dracontium, **3**:178
Dragon fruit, **1**:115
Drinking water, **1**:26
Dropsy, **3**:71, 72
Drosera. See Sundews
Drought
    adaptations. *See* Xerophytic adaptations
    and desertification, **2**:71, 72
    grasslands and, **2**:191

Drought resistance, breeding for, **3:**91

Drude, Oscar, **1:**160

Drugs, plant-derived. *See* Alkaloids; Medicinal plants and fungi; Phyto-pharmaceuticals; *specific drugs*

Drupes, **2:***159,* 159, **4:**35
defined, **2:**11 and Glossary

Dry deposition, **1:**1, **4:**64

Dry fruits (nonfleshy fruits), **2:**157, *159,* 159–160, **4:**35, 51, 53

Drylands, **2:***70,* 72
See also Desertification; Deserts

Dryobalanops, **4:**7

Dry soils, mycorrhizae and, **3:**90

Duboisia myoporoides. See Belladonna

Duckweeds, **4:**31
Lemna, **1:**43, **3:**53
Wolffia angusta, **4:**15

Dumbcane (dieffenbachia), **3:**170, 172

Dunes, **2:**3–4, 76

Dutch elm beetle, **2:**61, 83

Dutch elm disease, **2:**50, **83–84,** *84,* 165

Dwarf mistletoe, **3:**112, 116, **4:**85
See also Mistletoes

Dyes, **2:**59, **3:**61

Dynamical system theory, defined, **3:**143 and Glossary

E

Earlywood, **4:**172, 173, 175

Earthquakes, Humboldt's work, **3:**30–31

Earth's magnetic field, polarity reversals, **3:**30

Earthworms, **1:**126, **2:**45, 53, *54,* **4:**8, 10

ECB (European corn borer), **2:**170–172

Echinacea angustifolia (purple coneflower), **1:**118

Echinocactus, **3:**142

Eck, Paul, **2:**102

Ecological niches, **3:**162, **4:**6, 7

Ecological planning and design, **3:**53

Ecological succession. *See* Succession

Ecology, **1:**160, **2:84–90,** **3:**99–100, **4:**90
computer modeling in, **2:**89, 104
energy flow, **1:**3, **2:**85–87, *86,* **90–92,** *91,* 98
food webs and chains, **2:**86–87, 89, 90–91, 92
history of, **2:**84–85, **96–99,** **4:**156, 157–158
naming of field, **2:**97
in natural resource management, **2:**88–89
See also Agroecology; Community ecology; Fire ecology

Economic botany, **2:**115–116
See also Ethnobotany

Economic Botany (journal), **2:**116

Economic importance of plants, **2:99–102,** **4:**68
ethnobotanical research and, **2:**117, **3:**5
See also Agriculture; Crop plants; Fiber and fiber products; Oils, plant-derived; Phyto-pharmaceuticals; Wood products; *specific plants and plant groups*

Ecophysiological, defined, **4:**1 and Glossary

Ecoregions, **1:**84
See also Biomes; *specific ecosystem types*

Ecosystems, **2:102–104**
boundary definition, **2:**102–103
coining of term, **2:**85
defined, **1:**1, **2:**20, **3:**2, **4:**2 and Glossary
key traits, **1:**3–5
modeling, **2:**89, 104
Odum's promotion of concept, **2:**98, **3:**99–100
size of, **2:**103
stability of, **2:**103–104
succession in, **3:**161

Ecosystems ecology, **2:**85, 88–89, 98

Ecosystem services, **1:**69, 71
mangroves, **3:**2, **4:**34

Ecosystems management, **2:**88–89, *108,* 111

Ecotone, **4:**38

Ecotypes, **1:161–163,** **3:**34, 128

Ectomycorrhizae, **2:**164, **3:**40, *88,* 89
See also Mycorrhizae

Ectosymbiosis, **2:**111–112
See also Symbiosis

Ecuador, **2:**12, **4:**7

Edaphic savannas, **4:**38

Eddy covariance, **2:**88

Edema, **3:**71, 72

Eggplant (*Solanum melongena*), **2:**161, **4:**68

Eggs
formation and fertilization, **4:**20–21, 22, 23
See also Fertilization; Gametes; Zygotes

Egypt, **1:***6,* 20, **3:**4

Ehrlich, Paul, **2:**6

Eichhornia crassipes (water hyacinth), **1:**52, *53,* 102, **4:**31

Elaeis, **3:***102*
See also Palm kernel oil; Palm oil

Elaioplasts, **3:**168

Elaters, defined, **4:**46 and Glossary

Elderberry (*Sambucus*), **4:***114*

Electrical impulses, in defensive responses, **2:**57

Electric potential, photosynthetic energy, **3:**139

Electron transfer system, **1:**140, **3:**130, 135, *136,* 136–139, *138,* **4:**145

Electropism, **4:**135

Elemicin, **3:**193

Elephant ficus, **4:***30*

Elephants, **4:**8, 40, 41, 43

Elm (*Ulmus*), **1:**72, **2:**160, **4:**173
American (*U. americana*), **2:**47, 83–84
Dutch elm disease, **2:**50, **83–84,** *84,* 165

Elm bark beetles, **2:**61, 83

El Niño, **1:**84

Elodea, **1:**53, **4:**32

Embryogenesis, **2:104–106,** *105,* 178–179, **4:**20–21, 23, 51
gymnosperms, **2:**198
mosses, **1:**106, **4:**20
See also Fertilization

Embryophytes (Embryophyta), **2:**124, **4:**102

Embryos, **2:**124, 176, **4:**50, 53
angiosperms, **2:**145
germination process, **2:**174–176
nutrition for. *See* Endosperm; Placenta
structure, **4:**53
See also Embryogenesis; Germination; Seeds; Sporophytes; Zygotes

Embryo sac, **2:**166, **4:**17, 21

Emerson, Robert, **3:**154

Empedocles, **2:**127

Empirical formula, defined, **1:**120 and Glossary

Emulsifiers, defined, **1:**29 and Glossary

Encarsia wasps, **1:***13*

Encroachment, defined, **2:**70 and Glossary

Endangered species, **2:106–111,** **3:**112, **4:**94
biodiversity hot spots, **1:**69, *70*
endangered plant statistics, **2:**109–110
lone survivors, **2:**109
protecting, **1:**72, **2:***108,* 110–111
species maintained in cultivation, **2:**110
threats to, **1:**71–72, **2:**107–109
See also Biodiversity

Endangered Species Act (ESA), **2:**110

Endemic, defined, **1:**45 and Glossary

Endemism, **1:**67, 69

Endlicher, S., **4:**100

Endodermis, **1:**38, **4:**32, 164

Endomembrane system, **1:**138–139

Endomycorrhizae, **3:**40, 89–90
See also Mycorrhizae

Endophyte, defined, **3:**40 and Glossary

Endoplasmic reticulum (ER), **1:***136,* *137,* 138, *139,* **3:**15, 166
defined, **3:**15, **4:**119 and Glossary

Endosperm, **2:**145, 176
cereal grains, **2:**105, **4:**51, 53–54
defined, **1:**25, **2:**29, **3:**16, **4:**21 and Glossary
formation, **4:**21, 22–23, 51

Endosperm (continued)
legumes, **4**:53–54
monocots, **4**:53
persistence, **4**:51
triploid nature, **1**:47, **2**:145, **4**:23
Endosporic, defined, **2**:166 and Glossary
Endosymbiosis, **1**:156, **2**:40, **111–113**, 121, **3**:145, **4**:86
defined, **3**:146 and Glossary
See also Symbiosis
Energy crops, **1**:79–80
Energy efficiency, photosynthesis, **2**:77, 91–92, **3**:132–133, 139, **4**:83
Energy flow, **1**:3, **2**:85–87, *86*, **90–92**, 98
food webs and chains, **2**:*91*, 92, **4**:83, 86
solar vs. chemical energy sources, **2**:90–91
Energy use
impacts of Industrial Revolution, **3**:27
organic vs. conventional agriculture, **1**:*14*
Engler, Adolf, **1**:77, **4**:100
Enhanced greenhouse effect, **2**:181
See also Greenhouse effect
Enlightenment, **2**:128
defined, **2**:128 and Glossary
Enology, **1**:18–19, **3**:22
See also Oenologists; Wine
Entisols, **2**:75
Entomologist, defined, **4**:4 and Glossary
Entomopalynology, **3**:108
Envelope, plastids, **3**:166
Environment, genotype-environment interaction (GxE), **1**:98
Environmental legislation, U.S., **1**:1, **2**:110
Environmental movement, **3**:100
Enzyme inhibitors, **4**:143
Enzymes, **2**:54–56, **3**:98, 146, **4**:37, 87
amylases, **1**:25, **3**:15–16, 19, 119
ATP synthase, **3**:139
in Calvin-Benson cycle, **1**:154–155, **3**:129–130, 131, 134
cellulases, **1**:122, **3**:119
cellulose synthases, **1**:146–147
in cell wall synthesis, **1**:146–147
chitinases, **2**:56
cutinases, **3**:118, 119
cyclooxygenases, **2**:59
defined, **1**:24, **2**:39, **3**:19, **4**:10 and Glossary
digestive, **3**:119, **4**:82, 142
DNA polymerase, **3**:82
in DNA replication, **3**:*82*, 82–83
in endosperm, **4**:54
expansin, **3**:15
glycosyl transferases, **1**:147
hydrolases, **2**:175
insect-produced, **4**:10
isopentenyl transferase, **3**:14

kinase (p34), **1**:135
lipases, **3**:119
location in cells, **3**:167
nitrogenase, **2**:39
oxidases, **2**:56
in pathogenesis, **3**:118, 119
PEP carboxylase, **3**:132, 133
phosphatases, **3**:130
proteases, **3**:119
RNA polymerase, **3**:83
rubisco, **1**:154–155, **3**:129–130, 131
tea fermentation, **4**:106
See also Proteins
Eoplasts, **3**:166–167, 168
Eperua, **4**:6
Ephedra, **1**:44, **2**:*198*, 201, 202
sinica (ephedra, ma huang), **3**:*70*
See also Gnetophytes
Ephedrine, **2**:202, **3**:*70*
Ephemerals, **2**:76
defined, **1**:106, **2**:75 and Glossary
Epiblast, **2**:105
Epicuticle, **2**:60
defined, **2**:60 and Glossary
Epidemiologists, **3**:120
Epidermal cells, **1**:143
Epidermal hairs. *See* Trichomes
Epidermis, **1**:38, 143, **4**:81, 111, 171
defined, **2**:106 and Glossary
lateral meristems, **3**:78
leaves, **1**:39, 53, **3**:55, 118
roots, **4**:32, 34
stems, **4**:78
structure and function, **4**:111–112, 113
Epifagus (beechdrops), **3**:112
Epiphytes, **1**:76, **2**:113–115, **3**:43, **4**:3
bromeliads, **1**:68, **2**:114, 115, **3**:43, 86
cacti, **1**:115–116
defined, **1**:68, **3**:86, **4**:1 and Glossary
fork ferns (psilophytes), **2**:166, **4**:46, *47*, 48
nitrogen fixation, **4**:11
orchids, **1**:68, **2**:*114*, **3**:43, **4**:3, 34
vs. parasites, **3**:111
roots, **3**:43, **4**:34
tropical forests, **1**:68, **3**:43, 86, **4**:3, 4, 6, 7, 11
Epizoochorous fruits, **4**:43–44
Equisetaceae, Equisetophyta, **3**:99, **4**:45, 46, *47*
See also Horsetails
Equisetum. See Horsetails
ER. *See* Endoplasmic reticulum
Eragrostis spectabilis, **2**:187
Erebus (research vessel), **3**:12
Ergot, **2**:165, 185, **3**:174
Ericaceae (heather family), **3**:90, **4**:*138*
Erosion. *See* Soil erosion
Erotactin, **4**:20
Erwin, Terry, **4**:1, 8

Erythroxylum, Erythroxylon (coca), **1**:*33*, **2**:**4–6**, *5*, **3**:194
Escarpment, defined, **2**:28 and Glossary
Eschscholzia californica. See California poppy
Espeletia, **4**:140
Essential nutrients. *See* Nutrients, plant
Essential oils, **3**:11, 152, 153, **4**:108
See also Sesquiterpenes; Terpenes
Estrogen, **2**:83
Estuaries, **1**:51, **2**:3, **4**:44
Ethanol fermentation, **1**:22, 80
Ethanol production in plants, **4**:166–167
Ethereal oils, **1**:46
Ethnobotanists, **2**:118, **3**:5, 124
defined, **3**:5, **4**:94 and Glossary
Ethnobotany, **2**:115–119, **3**:5, 164, **4**:94
defined, **3**:70 and Glossary
indigenous knowledge, **2**:117, 118, **3**:5, 70, **4**:11, 94
Ethological isolation, **3**:32
Ethylene, **3**:*17*, 18–20, 153, 155
abscission, **2**:51
aquatic plants, **1**:52
fruit ripening, **2**:158, **3**:16, 20
receptor protein, **3**:15, 16
root hair development, **2**:82
seedling growth, **2**:179, **3**:16
synthesis, **2**:82, **3**:14
Etioplasts, **3**:168
Etoposide, **3**:*70*, 71
Euasterids, **1**:46
Eubacteria. *See* Bacteria
Eucalyptus, **1**:43, 61, **3**:54–55, **4**:39, 126–127
regnans, **4**:15
Eudicots, **1**:*44*, 45, 46–47, **2**:79
flowers, **1**:47
See also Dicots
Eugenics, **3**:75
Euglenophytes, euglenoids (Euglenophyta), **1**:27, 31, **3**:145
Euglossine bees, defined, **4**:8 and Glossary
Eukaryotes, **1**:56, 152, **2**:120, **3**:165, 166, **4**:86
Eukaryotic, defined, **1**:28, **2**:38, **3**:113, **4**:86 and Glossary
Euphorbia
esula (leafy spurge), **3**:48, 50
as potential fuel crop, **1**:117
Euphrates River, **1**:6
Euphyllophytes, **2**:126
Europe
deforestation, **3**:27
desertification, **2**:*71*
herbals, **3**:4–5
herbaria, **3**:6
Pleistocene extinctions in, **1**:77–78
species diversity, **1**:67
temperate deciduous forest, **2**:46–47

See also specific countries
European corn borer (ECB),
2:170–172
Eurosids, 1:46, 2:79
Eutracheophytes, 2:125
Evaporation. *See* Transpiration
Everglades, 4:168
Evergreens, 2:52
See also Conifers
Evolution
convergent, 2:126, 3:144, *146*
theories of, 2:127–129
See also Natural selection
Evolutionary biology, 2:129, 4:91
Evolutionary synthesis, 2:44, 129,
3:75, 4:104
Evolutionary trees. *See* Phylogenetic
trees
Evolutionary uniqueness, 1:67
Evolution of plants, 2:121–127
alternation of generations,
4:17–18
dioecy, 1:101–102
diversification of plants,
2:124–127
history of, 2:127–129
homology, 4:87
parasitism, 3:111–112
pollination mechanisms,
4:100–101
seed production, 4:51
sexual reproduction, 4:23
study of, 2:123, 143 (*see also* Phylogenetics; Systematics)
See also Natural selection; *specific
plant groups*
Excitation energy, 3:135
Exotic species, impacts of, 1:71–72,
2:109, 3:29
See also Invasive species; Weeds
Expansin, 3:15
Explant, 3:190
Extinction rates, 1:71, 2:109–110,
3:29
Extinctions, 2:109, 110
climate change and, 2:107, 3:29
Cretaceous/Tertiary comet or
asteroid impact, 2:122
natural, 2:107
Pleistocene, 1:77–78
Sixth Extinction, 3:29–30
See also Endangered species
Extinction threat, biodiversity hot
spots, 1:69, *70*
Extrafloral, defined, 2:61 and
Glossary
Extreme-climate plants, global
warming and, 2:182–183
Extreme environments, organisms
in, 1:56–57, 2:38
Exudation, defined, 1:35, 3:11 and
Glossary

F

Fabaceae. *See* Legumes
FACE system, 2:88

Facultative, defined, 2:161, 3:111
and Glossary
Facultative parthenocarpy, 2:161
Fagales, 4:100
Fagopyrum esculentum. See Buckwheat
Fagus (beech), 1:77, 2:*47*, 3:89, 112
Fallowing, 1:7
False hellebore (*Veratrum califor-
nicum*), 3:173
False morel (*Gyromitra esculenta*),
2:164
Families, Jussieu's groupings, 4:103
Family, 2:132–133, 4:99
See also Taxonomy
Farming. *See* Agricultural ecosys-
tems; Agriculture
Fats and oils
conversion of sucrose to, 1:140
in human diet, 3:*101*, 4:82
storage in plants, 3:65, 100, 168,
4:51, 112
See also Lipids; Oils, plant-
derived
Fatty acids, 1:137, 155, 2:57, 3:65,
101, 150
Feedbacks, 2:182
Feeder roots, 4:34
Fens, 1:51, 3:121–122, 4:166
See also Wetlands
Fenugreek, 4:53–54
Fermentation, 1:80, 2:164
alcoholic beverages, 1:22, 23, 25,
2:164
cacao processing, 1:112
ethanol, 1:22, 80
tea, 4:105–106
wheat gluten and, 4:170
Fern allies. *See* Seedless vascular
plants
Ferns, 1:42, 2:133–135, 3:166
aquatic, 1:53
bracken fern, 2:133, 135
distribution, 2:135
diversity, 2:127
epiphytic, 2:114, 4:3
evolution, 2:121, 125–126
floating, 1:*53*
leaves, 1:42, 2:126, 133
mycorrhizal associations, 3:89
reproduction, 1:42, 2:133–135,
134–135, 166, 4:17, 20, 23,
45
seed-producing, 2:126
silvery glade fern, 2:*134–135*
speciation, 4:74
tree ferns, 4:60, 126, 140
vascular tissues, 1:42, 44, 4:148
Ferredoxin, 3:138
Fertigation, defined, 3:22 and Glossary
Fertile Crescent, 1:6
See also Mesopotamia
Fertilization, 1:158, 2:157, 3:32,
176, 4:20–21, 22–23
barriers to, 3:32, 176, 4:73–74,
76
double, 1:43–44, 2:145, 4:51

See also Pollination; Pollination
biology; Reproduction, sexual;
specific plant types
Fertilizer grade, 2:136
Fertilizers, 2:135–137, 4:37
and algal blooms, 1:72, 4:64–65
application, 2:136–137
commercial/inorganic, 1:10–13,
2:136
leaching/pollution, 1:11, 12,
4:168
organic, 2:136–137
See also Compost; Green manure
crops; Nutrients, plant
Fescue, 3:86
Fescue endophytes, 3:40
Fiber and fiber products, 1:147,
2:137–140, 4:113, 178–179
bast fibers, 1:64, 2:138–139
cellulose in, 1:144
flax/linen, 1:144, 147, 2:*138*,
4:113
hard fibers, 2:138, 139
hemp, 1:119, 143, 2:*138*
major fiber plants, 2:*138*
ramie, 2:*138*, 4:113
rayon, 1:144, 147
sclerenchyma fibers, 1:142–143,
4:173
seed or fruit fibers, 2:138, 139
sisal, 1:143, 2:*138*, 139
synthetic, 2:31
tencel, 2:156
See also Cotton
Fiber cells, 2:137–139, 4:113, 114,
148
Fiber, dietary, 1:147
Fibonacci, Leonardo, 3:141
Fibonacci angle, 3:142
Fibonacci sequence, 3:141–142
Fibrous roots, 1:42, 4:30, 31, *32,*
123–124
Ficus (fig), 1:6, 2:160, 4:14, *30,* 34
fig wasps, 2:8, *9,* 4:8
rain forests, 4:6, 9
strangler fig, 3:*44,* 4:3, 7
Fiddleheads, 1:42, 2:133
Fig. *See Ficus*
Fig wasps, 2:*8, 9,* 4:8
Figwort family. *See* Scrophulariaceae
Filament, defined, 1:31, 2:119, 3:89
and Glossary
Filamentous, defined, 1:105, 2:38,
3:113 and Glossary
Fir (*Abies*), 2:19, 22, 4:59, 173, 174
Fir club moss (*Lycopodium selago*),
3:141
Fire
nutrient cycling and, 2:94–95,
4:11
revegetation programs, 1:150
Fire adaptations, 1:64, 149, 2:93
savanna plants, 4:39–40
Fire blight, 3:114
Fire ecology, 2:92–96
Fire management, 1:149, 2:20, 88,
95–96, 4:39, 41

Fire-prone ecosystems, **1:**64, 75, **2:**93
  bark and, **1:**64, **2:**26, **4:**39
  chaparral, **1:147–151,** *148,* **2:**157
  conifers in, **2:**202
  See also Grasslands; Savannas
Fire regimes, **2:**94
Fire-triggered germination, **1:**149
Fire-triggered seed dispersal, **2:**157
Fire use, aboriginal humans, **2:**95
Fish, **2:**1, 3, **3:**46, **4:**8, 44
Fisher, R. A., **3:**75
Fission, in plastids, **2:**113
Fitzroya (alerce), **2:**21–22, *23*
Flagella, **1:**56
  defined, **1:**56, **2:**120, **3:**114, **4:**20
    and Glossary
Flame-weeding, **1:**16
Flavin, **4:**133
Flavones, **2:**140, **3:**157
Flavonoids, **1:**35, **2:**56, **140–141,**
  180, **3:**156, 157
  chemical structure, **2:***140*
  defined, **1:**35, **2:**56, **3:**93 and
    Glossary
  legumes, **3:**93
  See also Anthocyanins; Pigments
Flavonols, **2:**140, **3:**157
Flavor and Extract Manufacturers
  Association, **2:**141
Flavor and fragrance chemists,
  2:141–142
Flavor components, **2:**59, **3:**152,
  4:108
Flax (*Linum usitatissimum*), **2:***138,*
  4:113
  See also Linen
Flea beetles, **2:**60
Fleming, Alexander, **2:**164
Fleshy fruits, **2:**157, 158, *159,* **4:**35,
  51
Flies
  larvae, carnivorous plants and,
    1:128
  as pollinators, **2:**50, 147, **3:**112,
    178, **4:**8, 15
Flooding
  deforestation and, **2:**64
  root growth and, **4:**33
Floodplain forests, **4:**166
Flora, floras, **2:142–144**
Floral meristems, **2:**148, 173–174
Florets, **1:**58
Floriculture, **3:**22, 23
Florida, **1:**69, **3:**49
  Everglades, **4:**168
Florigen, defined, **3:**127 and
  Glossary
Floristic, defined, **1:**44, **2:**194, **3:**5,
  4:140 and Glossary
Floristic botanists, floristic research,
  2:143, **3:**5
Floristry, **3:**23–24
Flowering
  circadian rhythms, **4:**25
  form and, **4:**59
  hormones in, **3:**19, 20, 127, 133,
    4:118

patterns, **1:**62, **4:**42
photoperiodism, **3:**19, *125,*
  125–127, 128, **4:**26
rain forests, **4:**6, 8
Flowering plants. *See* Angiosperms
Flowers, **2:144–149**
  bisexual. *See* Hermaphroditism,
    flowers
  catkins, **1:**65, **4:**100–101, *101*
  coevolution with pollinators,
    1:48, **2:**6, *8,* 8–9, 126–127, 144,
    147–148, **3:**112, **4:**8
  color, **1:**130, 143, **2:**55–56,
    3:*145,* 168, 179
  development, **2:**148, 173, **3:**77,
    84
  diversity, **2:**144, 145–146
  evolution, **1:**65, **2:**147–148, 174
  function, **2:**145
  as modified leaves, **2:**174, **3:**77
  nastic movements, **4:**136
  parts, **2:**144
  pollination adaptations, **2:**8–9, 44
  record-holding, **4:***14,* 15
  senescence, **3:**20, **4:**56
  sex determination, hormones
    and, **3:**19
  shoot removal to encourage,
    4:60–61
  See also Breeding systems; Flow-
    ering; Flower structure; Inflo-
    rescences; Pollination biology;
    specific plants and plant groups
Flower stalks. *See* Inflorescences
Flower structure, **1:**38, *39,* 65,
  2:144–147, 173
  bilateral symmetry (zygomor-
    phy), **2:**130, 146, 147, **3:**177
  Cretaceous period, **2:**147
  early angiosperms, **1:**47, 65, **2:**147
  genetic mechanisms, **2:**173–174
  pollination and, **1:**100–102,
    2:8–9, 44, **3:**176, 178–179
  radial symmetry, **2:**146
  Warming's research, **4:**157
  *See also specific flower parts; specific
    plants and plant groups*
Fluoride, **1:**60
Flux rates, **1:**74
Fly agaric (*Amanita muscaria*), **2:**164,
  3:*175*
Fog, **4:**5
Foliose lichens, **3:***59,* 59–60
Follicles, **2:***159,* 160, **4:**35
  defined, **4:**35 and Glossary
Food chemistry, **2:**59
Food colors, **1:**131
Food crops
  cacti, **1:**115
  genetic engineering, **1:**8–12,
    2:168–169
  loss of diversity, **1:**8, 9
  native, **3:**91, **4:***50*
  origins and domestication, **1:**6–9,
    98, **3:**171, **4:**68, 154
  selection and breeding, **1:**8–9,
    98–99, **3:**85, 91

sugar crops, **4:**82
vanilla, **3:**86, 104
vegetables, **3:**22, **4:**50, **155–156**
See also Grains; *specific crop
  plants*
Food plants
  allergies to, **3:**174
  nutritional composition, **4:**118
Food science careers
  alcoholic beverage industry,
    1:18–22
  flavor chemist, **2:141–142**
  food scientist, **2:149–150**
Food storage in plants
  bulbs, **3:**87, **4:**80
  carbohydrates, **1:**121, 141, 144,
    154, **4:**112, 119, 143
  fats and oils, **3:**65, 100, 168,
    4:51, 112
  fruits, **4:**119
  minerals, **4:**143
  proteins, **4:**112, 143
  rhizomes, **3:**87, **4:**80
  roots, **4:**31–32, 112, 119
  seeds, **4:**53–54, 119, 143 (*see also*
    Endosperm)
  starch, **1:**140, 141, 154, **3:**150,
    168, **4:**31–32
  stems, **4:**112, 143
  sugar, **1:**121, 139, 141, 154, **3:**57,
    4:82, 143
  tubers, **1:**140, 141, **3:**184, **4:**80,
    119
  vacuoles, **4:**143
Food webs and chains, **2:**86–87, 89,
  90–91
  aquatic, **1:**29, 50–51, **4:**85
  coastal, **2:**1
  energy flow through, **2:***91,* 92,
    4:83, 86
Foot (sporophytes), **4:**77
Forbs, **2:**192, 193
  defined, **1:**82, **2:**192 and Glossary
Forensic botany, **2:150–151**
Foresters, **2:152–153,** 154–156,
  3:8
Forest products
  economic value, **2:**100
  See also Paper; Wood products
Forestry, **2:**65, 152, **153–156**
  agroforestry, **2:**65, 153
  plantation forests, **2:**20, 154–155
  U.S. Forest Service management
    policy, **2:**20, 88
Forests, **1:**75
  acid rain in, **1:**1–2
  and atmosphere, **1:**59, **2:**64, 183
  canopy significance, **4:**1–2 (*see
    also* Rain forest canopy)
  composition, **4:**128
  conversion to agriculture, **1:**7,
    125, **2:**50, 63, **3:**26, **4:**11–12
  floodplain forests, **4:**166
  germination in, **4:**55
  plantation forests, **2:**20, 154–155
  plant-plant interactions, **3:**43
  types mapped, **1:***81*

See also Coniferous forests; Deciduous forests; Deforestation; Rain forest canopy; Rain forest plants; Rain forests

Fork ferns (psilophytes), **2:**166, **4:**46, *47*, 48

Form. *See* Shape and form

Forma, **4:**146

Forman, Richard, **3:**159

Forster, Johann, **3:**31

FORTOON, **2:**154

Fossil fuel combustion, **2:**183
  impacts, **1:**74–75, *124*, 125–126, **2:**183, **3:**27, **4:**64

Fossil fuels, **1:**125, **3:**27

Fossil fuel usage, **1:**125

Fossil plants, **2:**125
  angiosperm evolution and, **1:**45
  Arcto-Tertiary geoflora, **1:**77–78
  Brongniart's classification of, **1:**104
  study of, **2:**122, **3:**107, *144*
  See also Paleobotany

Founder events, **4:**72

Foxglove (*Digitalis*), **3:**11, *70*, 71–72, *72*, 170, *172*

Fragaria. See Strawberries

Fragrance chemists, **2:141–142**

Fragrance emissions, **4:**25

France, **1:**24, *68*

Franklinia (Franklin tree), **2:**110

Franklin, Benjamin, **3:**39

Fraxinus (ash), **2:**160, **4:**41, 176

Free-Air CO$_2$ Enrichment system, **2:**88

Free fatty acids, **3:**101

Free radicals, **3:**10
  defined, **3:**10 and Glossary

Freshwater ecosystems, **1:**49–50, 75, 76
  See also Aquatic ecosystems; Estuaries; Wetlands

Frog's-bit family (Hydrocharitaceae), **3:**86, *87*

Fronds, **1:**42, **2:**133

Fructose, **1:**121, 122, **4:**81, 82

Frugivores and frugivory, **3:**46, **4:**8

Fruit and vegetable rots, **3:**116, 117, 119

Fruit drop, **2:**158
  See also Abscission

Fruit fibers, **2:**138, 139

Fruiting patterns, **4:**42
  rain forests, **4:**6

Fruits, **1:**38, **2:**59, 145, **156–161**
  color, **1:**130, 131, **2:**157, **3:**167, 168, **4:**43
  composition, **4:**112
  cyanogenic compounds in, **2:**55
  development, **2:**156–158, **4:**51, 118
  dispersal. *See* Seed dispersal
  function, **2:**157
  ripening, **2:**158, **3:**14, 16, 20, 167, 168, **4:**56
  seedless, **2:**158, **160–161**
  types, **2:**158–160, *159*

See also specific plants and plant groups

Fruit trees, budding and grafting, **3:**189–190

Fruticose lichens, **3:**60

Fuchs, Leonhart, **3:**4

Fucus, **2:**80
  spiralis, **3:**141

Fuels
  biomass, **1:79–80**
  peat, **1:**80, **3:**122
  research in plant-derived fuels, **1:**117
  See also Fossil fuels

Functional genomics, **3:**85

Fundamentals of Ecology (Odum), **3:**99–100

Fungal diseases, **2:**50–51, 164–165, **3:**114, 116–119
  chestnut blight, **1:151, 2:**50, 165
  damping off, **3:**116, 119
  Dutch elm disease, **2:**50, **83–84**, *84*, 165
  ergot, **2:**165, 185, **3:**174
  fruit and vegetable rots, **3:**116, 117, 119
  of humans, **2:**164–165
  leaf diseases, **3:**116, 117
  mildews, **2:**165, **3:**114, 116–118
  potato blight, **2:**165, **3:**114, **185–186**, *185*
  root rots, **3:**116, 119
  rusts and smuts, **2:**13, 165, **3:**113, 116, 117
  vascular wilts, **3:**116–117, 119

Fungi, **2:162–165, 4:**65
  aquatic, **2:**163
  cell structure, **3:**113
  classification, **1:**93, **2:**162, **3:**113–114, 165, **4:**94
  as decomposers, **1:**122, **2:**53–54, 162
  in ethnobotanical research, **2:**115
  genetic engineering uses, **2:**161
  human uses, **2:**164
  nutrition, **2:**162, 163–164
  as pathogens, **3:**21, 113–114, *115*, 118, 119 (*see also* Fungal diseases)
  vs. plants, **3:**165
  rain forests, **4:**3, 9
  sac fungi, **3:**58
  specimen preparation, **3:**7
  spores, **2:**162–163, **3:**60, 113, **4:**16
  sporophytes, **4:**11
  structure and life cycle, **2:**162–163, **3:**113–114, **4:**16
  symbiotic relationships. *See* Lichens; Mycorrhizae
  toxins, **2:**164, **3:**172–173 (*see also* Mushrooms, toxic)
  vacuole function, **4:**143
  See also Fungal diseases; Hyphae; Interactions, plant-fungal; Lichens; Molds; Mushrooms; Mycorrhizae

Fungicides, **2:**165, **3:**185, 186

Fungi Imperfecti, **3:**113

Fusiform initials, **3:**77, 78

Futures markets, **2:**100–101

G

G1 (postmitotic interphase), **1:***133*, 133–135

G2 (postsynthetic interphase), **1:***133*, 134–135

G6P (glucose 6-phosphate), **1:**154, **3:**130

GA (gibberellic acid). *See* Gibberellins

Galapagos Islands, **1:**77, **2:**41

Galls, **2:**61, 169, **3:***117*, 117–118

Gametangia, **4:**16–17, 18
  defined, **2:**166 and Glossary

Gametes, **3:**33, 180
  formation, **1:**158, **2:**81, **3:**33, 181, **4:**20, 24
  zygote formation, **4:**16–17
  See also Eggs; Sperm; Zygotes

Gametophytes, **2:**123, **165–166,** **4:**16–18, 20
  bisexual vs. unisexual, **2:**134–135
  defined, **1:**43, **2:**123, **4:**20 and Glossary
  formation and development, **4:**16, 20–21, 22–24
  See also Alternation of generations; *specific plant groups*

Gametophytic self-incompatibility (GSI), **1:**102

Gamma diversity, **1:**66

GA-myb, **3:**16

Gap 1 (G1), **1:***133*, 133–135

Gap 2 (G2), **1:***133*, 134–135

Garlic, health benefits, **1:**36

Garner, Wightman W., **3:**125

Gas diffusion, in soils, **4:**67

Gaseous fuels, **1:**80

Gases, van Helmont's investigations, **4:**144

Gause, G. F., **3:**162

GCMs (global circulation models), **2:**182

Geitonogamy, **1:**100

Gel electrophoresis, defined, **4:**88 and Glossary

Gene banks, **1:**99

Gene cloning, **2:**169, **4:**95

Gene-for-gene resistance, **2:**57

Genera. *See* Genus/genera

Genes
  coding for proteins, **3:**81
  DNA structure, **3:***80*, 80–81, *81*
  Mendel's work proving existence of, **3:**33
  proof of carriage on chromosomes, **1:**157, 159, **2:**33–34
  quantitative trait loci, **3:**85, **195–196**
  study of. *See* DNA analysis; Molecular genetics; Molecular systematics

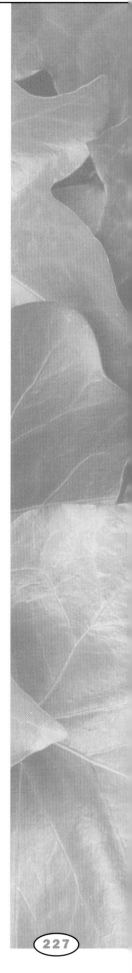

Genes (continued)
  transgenes, **2:**169–170
Genetically modified organisms
  (GMOs). *See* Genetic engineering; Transgenic plants
Genetic diversity, **1:**66
  food crops, **1:**8, 9, 12, **4:**48, 50
  rain forests, **4:**10
  seed/germplasm preservation,
    1:72, 99, **4:48–50**
  See also Biodiversity; Genetic
    variation; Species diversity
Genetic engineering (biotechnology), **1:**35, **2:168–172**, **3:**80, 84,
    4:12
  benefits and concerns, **2:**171–172
  crop plants, **1:**8–12, **2:**32–33,
    168–169, **3:**24, **4:**170
  debate over, **2:**168, 171–172, **3:**85
  forest trees, **2:**155
  goals, **2:**166–167
  herbicide resistance, **2:**155, **3:**10
  pest resistance, **2:**32–33,
    170–172, **3:**24
  plasmids in, **2:**120
  process, **2:**169–170, **4:**117–118
  seedless fruits, **2:**161
  transgenic plants, **2:**169, **3:**84–85
  unintended consequences, **2:**172
Genetic engineers, **2:166–168**
Genetic loci, **1:**157
Genetic mechanisms and development, **2:173–174**, **3:**80
  programmed cell death, **4:**56
  See also Differentiation and development; Genetics; Growth
Genetics, **4:**101
  Mendelian basis for, **3:**73, 75
  molecular plant genetics,
    3:80–85
  in Stalinist Russia, **4:**154–155
  Vavilov's work, **4:**152–155
Genetics Society of America, **3:**68
Genetic variation, **1:**9, 66,
  2:134–135, **3:**84, 176
  agamospermy and, **4:**19
  genotypical vs. phenotypical variation, **2:**129
  homologous series, **4:**153
  rain forests, **4:**10
  sexual reproduction and, **4:**24
  transposons as source of, **1:**159
  See also Clines and ecotypes
Genomes, **1:**97–98, 157, **3:**195
  crop plants, **1:**95, **2:**168–169,
    3:68
  defined, **1:**139, **2:**148, **3:**33, **4:**88
    and Glossary
  duplication, **3:**34
  transposable elements, **1:**157,
    159, **2:**33–34, **3:**68
  See also Chromosomes
Genomics, **3:**84–85
Genotype, defined, **3:**34 and
  Glossary
Genotype and environment interaction (GxE), **1:**98

Genotypes, genotypical variation,
  2:129
Genus/genera, **2:**132, 133, **4:**93, 99
  defined, **1:**36, **3:**63, **4:**6 and
    Glossary
  Jussieu's groupings, **4:**103
  Linnaeus's definition, **3:**63, 64
  See also Taxonomy
Geological nutrient transport mechanisms, **1:**74
Geology, **1:**103, **2:**128, **3:**107
Geophytic plants, **1:**114
Geotropism (gravitropism), **3:**18,
  168, **4:**32, 131, 134–135
Geranium, **4:**61
Gerard, John, **3:**4
Germany, **1:**13, 24, 25
Germination, **2:174–176**, *175*
  aids to, **2:**177, **3:**19, **4:**54
  cues for, **4:**54–55
  fern spores, **2:**135
  fire-triggered, **1:**149
  grains, **3:**15–16
  and growth, **2:176–179**
  gymnosperms, **2:**198
  hormones in, **3:**19, 155
  nurse logs, nurse plants, **3:**43,
    44
  orchids, **3:**90, 103
  radicle emergence, **2:**174, **4:**130
  seed dormancy, **1:**149, **2:**126,
    175–178, **3:**19, 20, **4:**54–55
  strategies, **4:**44
  See also Seedlings; Seeds
Germplasm
  defined, **4:**48 and Glossary
  preservation, **1:**72, 99, **4:**48–50
Gesneriaceae, **3:**179
Giant fan palm (*Lodoicea maldivica*),
  4:15, 51
Giant kelp, **1:**28, *30*, **2:**23, **3:**144
Giant sequoia (*Sequoiadendron giganteum*), **2:**19, 21–22, 198, **4:**57, 127
  record-holding trees, **4:**13, 15
Gibberellic acid (GA). *See* Gibberellins
Gibberellins, **3:**118, 153, 155
  in alpha-amylase production,
    3:15–16, *17*, 19
  biosynthesis, **3:**14
  effects, **3:**19, **4:**56
  fruit treatment with, **2:**161
  GA$_1$, **3:**14
  GA$_3$, **3:**17
  germination and, **2:**176, 177
  interactions, **3:**20
  seed treatment with, **2:**177
  senescence and, **4:**56
  in stem elongation, **3:**16
Gilbertiodendron, **4:**7
Ginger family. *See* Zingiberaceae
Ginkgetin, **2:**180
Ginkgo biloba (maidenhair tree),
  2:179–181, *180*, 200–201, **4:**20
  characteristics, **2:***198*
  extinction in wild, **2:**110, 180,
    200–201

medicinal properties, **2:**180–181,
    202
  taxonomy, **1:**67, **2:**17, 180
Ginkgolides, **2:**180
Ginkgophyta, **2:**17, 197, *198*,
  200–201
Ginseng (*Panax*), **2:**108, **4:**32
Giraffes, **3:**179–180, **4:**40
Gladiolus, **4:**80
Glandular trichomes, **4:**129
Glaucoma, **2:**117
Glaucophyta, **1:**27, 31
Gleason, Henry Allan, **2:**85, 98, **3:**160
Gliricidia sepium, **2:**132
Global circulation models (GCMs),
  2:182
Global warming, **2:181–184**, **3:**28
  biome distribution and, **1:**84,
    2:182–183, **3:**28
  carbon dioxide and, **1:**122–123,
    4:1
  causes, **2:**181
  and desertification, **2:**72, **3:**28
  extent and pace, **2:**181–182
  impacts on plants, **2:**182–183
  TDBF phenological cycles and,
    2:49
  See also Climate change; Greenhouse effect
Globose, defined, **4:**46 and Glossary
Globular proteins, **3:**149
Glucomannans, **3:**150
Glucose, **1:**121–122, 144, **3:**152,
  4:81, 82
  in cellulose microfibrils,
    1:135–136
  production in photosynthesis,
    1:154
Glucose 1-phosphate, **3:**151, 152
Glucose 6-phosphate (G6P), **1:**154,
  3:130
Glucosinolates, **2:**56, 59
Glume, **2:**186
Glutamic acid, **1:**152, **3:**150
Glutamine, **3:**150
Gluten, **4:**169–170
Glyceraldehyde 3-phosphate, **1:**154
Glycerolipids, **3:**65–66
Glycine, **3:**150 *See also* Soybean.
Glycolysis, **3:**151, 152
Glycoproteins, **1:**146
Glycosides, **3:**11, 69, 172
  cyanogenic, **2:**55, **3:**153, 172, **4:**10
  medicinal, **3:**70, 72
  mustard oil, **3:**153
Glycosyl transferases, **1:**147
Glyoxylate cycle, **3:**151
Glyoxysomes, **1:**140
Glyphosate, **3:**10
GMOs (genetically modified organisms). *See* Genetic engineering;
    Transgenic plants
Gnetales. *See* Gnetophytes
Gnetophytes (Gnetophyta, Gnetales), **1:**44–45, 48, **2:**126, 197,
  198, 201
Gnetum, **1:**44, **2:***198*, 201

Goats, **2:**109

Goats-beard (*Tragopogon*), **3:**32

Gold, in genetic engineering process, **2:**169

Golden brown algae, **1:***27*, 156, **3:**165

Golden number, **3:**142

Goldenrod, **2:**55, **3:**178

Golden Triangle, **3:**102

Gold mining, **2:**88

Golgi apparatus, **1:**134, *136, 137,* **3:**166, **4:***142*
    structure and function, **1:**138–139, *139,* 147
    See also Dictyosome

Gossypium. See Cotton

Gossypol, **2:**55

Gradient, defined, **3:**160, **4:**122 and Glossary

Gradient analysis, **2:**98

Grafting and budding, **3:**188–190

Grains (caryopses, fruit type), **2:***159,* 160, 186

Grains, **1:**68, **2:184–185,** *187,* **3:**26, 167
    cereal science programs, **1:**22
    in crop rotations, **1:**7
    genetic engineering, **2:**169
    McClintock's work, **3:**66
    nutrient storage in stems, **4:**119, 143
    origins and domestication, **1:**6, **2:**184
    pests, **3:**42, 45
    seed development and germination, **2:**105, 106, **3:**15–16, 19, **4:**51, 53–54
    Vavilov's work, **4:**153, 154
    See also specific grains

Gramineae. *See* Grasses

Gram stain, **2:**120

Granal thylakoids, **1:**139, 153, **3:**167

Grant, Verne, **3:**33, 34

Grapefruit, **1:**9

Grapes, **1:**6, 8, 18, **2:***157,* 158, **3:**157
    seedless, **2:**158, 160, 161, **3:**19
    wild, **3:**50
    wine grapes, **1:**18, 22, 24, **2:**165
    See also Wine

Grasses (Poaceae), **1:**62, 68, **2:185–189,** **3:**86, *87,* **4:**26
    distribution, **2:**187–188, 191, **4:**6
    economic importance, **2:**188–189, **4:**68
    European grasses in North America, **1:**72, **2:**109
    fire and, **1:**75, **2:**188, 191–192, **4:**39
    flowers, **1:**62, **2:**148, 186
    in human diet, **2:**185, *187,* 188–189
    inflorescences, **2:**186
    leaves, **2:**186, **3:**54
    nutrient storage, **4:**143
    parasites, **3:**40
    photosynthesis in, **2:**188
    pollination and seed dispersal, **2:**148, 186–187

record-holding, **4:**13, 15, 16
    root growth, **4:**30
    savannas, **4:**39, 40
    seed dispersal, **2:**186–187
    seeds, **2:***188*
    speciation, **4:**74
    tundra species, **4:***138*
    turf management, **4:140–141**
    See also Grains; *specific genera*

Grasslands, **2:**188, **189–194**
    conversion/destruction of, **1:**7, 71, **2:**189, 193–194
    extent and distribution, **1:***81,* **2:**189
    fire and, **1:**148, **4:**39
    fire in, **2:**93, 94, 188, 191–192, **4:**38
    global warming and, **2:**183
    See also Prairies; Savannas; Steppes

Gravel, **4:**65

Graves's beach plum, **2:**110

Gravitropism (geotropism), **3:**18, 168, **4:**32, 131, 134–135

Gravity, **4:**136
    sensing of, **4:**134–135

Gray, Asa, **1:**65, 77, **2:194–196,** *194,* **4:**117
    and Darwin, **1:**77, **2:**129, 194–196, **4:**103

Grazers and grazing, **1:**71, **2:**187, 192–193
    food chain, **2:***91*
    overgrazing, **2:**71, 192
    prairies, **1:**74
    savannas, **2:**87, **4:**40, 41
    toxic plants and, **3:**173
    tundra, **4:**139
    See also Herbivores and herbivory

Green algae, **1:***27, 28,* **3:***144,* 145, 165, **4:**102
    charophyceans, **1:**29, 31, **2:***122,* 122–124, 127
    Coleochaete, **2:***122,* 123
    isomorphic alternation of generations, **4:**17
    symbiotic relationships. *See* Lichens

Greenhouse effect, **1:**122–123, 124–126, **2:**181, **3:**133
    modern carbon dioxide buildup, **1:**75, *124,* 124–126, **2:**181, 182, **3:**27, 133
    simulated, **2:***182–183*
    See also Global warming

Greenhouse gases, **2:**181, 182–183, **3:**27
    See also Carbon dioxide

Green manure, defined, **2:**132 and Glossary

Green manure crops, **1:**12, **2:**132, 137
    defined, **1:**12 and Glossary

Green Revolution, **1:**89, **2:**185, **196–197,** **4:**29
    achievements, **1:**9, 98, **2:**197
    criticisms of, **1:**9, **2:**197

Gregarious flowering, bamboos, **1:**62

Ground cherries, **4:**68

Ground meristems, **2:**106, **4:**111, 112

Groundnuts. *See* Peanuts

Ground tissues, **1:**38, 140–143, **2:**106, **4:***111,* 112–113, 171
    See also Collenchyma; Cortex; Parenchyma; Sclerenchyma

Groundwater, bogs, **3:**122

Groundwater pollution, bioremediation, **1:**86

Growing season length
    global warming and, **2:**183
    and plant distribution, **1:**75–76, **2:**183

Growth, **1:**37
    abnormal, pathogen-caused, **3:**118
    accelerated, as defensive mechanism, **2:**61
    allometric, **3:**57
    aquatic plants, **1:**52
    areas of, **2:***177*
    boron in, **3:**98
    cell elongation, **3:**10, 15, **4:**58, 149
    excessive, herbicide-caused, **3:**10
    grazed vs. ungrazed plants, **2:**193
    hormonal control and development, **3:13–17**
    isometric, **3:**57
    lateral/secondary. *See* Lateral meristems; Secondary growth
    monocots, **3:**86–87
    phytochrome regulation of, **3:**156
    roots. *See* Root growth
    seedlings, **2:**178–179, **3:**16, **4:**30
    speed of, record-holding plants, **4:**16
    wood. *See* Wood growth
    See also Germination; Meristems; Shape and form; Tropisms and nastic movements; *specific plant parts*

Growth regulators. *See* Hormones, plant

GSI (gametophytic self-incompatibility), **1:**102

Guadua, **2:**189

Guaiacum officinale (lignum vitae), **4:**177

Guanine, **3:**81, *148*

Guano, **1:**74

Guard cells, **1:**143, **3:**16, 19–20, **4:**113

Guatemala, **1:**6, **2:**28–29

Guianas, **4:**12

Gums, **3:**150

GxE (genotype and environment interaction), **1:**98

Gymnosperms, **1:**67, **2:**17, 127, 147, **197–202**
    defined, **1:**44, **2:**121, **3:**86, **4:**13 and Glossary

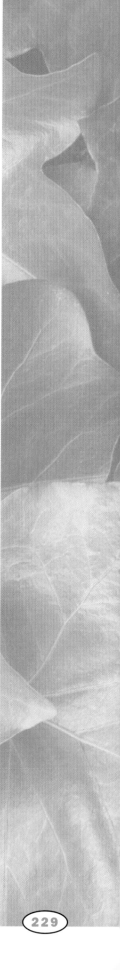

Gymnosperms (continued)
   ecological significance, **2:**202
   economic significance, **2:**202
   extinction threat, **1:**71
   Gnetales, **1:**44–45, 48, **2:**126
   groups, **2:***198*, **3:**166
   mycorrhizal associations, **3:**88–89
   origins and evolution, **2:**121–122,
      126, **3:***144*
   phloem structure, **4:**119, 121,
      150
   pollination and reproduction,
      1:47, 48, **2:**197–198, **4:**17, 21
   seeds, **2:**197, **4:**53
   stems, **3:**86, **4:**77
   xylem structure, **4:**148
   See also Conifers; Cycads;
      Ginkgophyta; Gnetophytes
Gynodioecious plants, **1:**101
Gynoecium, **2:**144, 145
   defined, **2:**144, **4:**69 and Glossary
Gypsipherous, defined, **2:**75 and
   Glossary
Gypsy moth, **2:**50
Gyromitra esculenta (false morel),
   2:164

H

Haberlandt, Gottlieb, **4:**134
Habit. *See* Deciduous habit; Shape
   and form
Habitat degradation, **1:**69, 70–71,
   2:108
HABs. *See* Algal blooms
Hackling, **2:**138–139
Haeckel, Ernst, **2:**84–85, 97, **3:**143
Haldane, J. B. S., **3:**75
Hales, Stephen, **3:**1–2, *1*, 153, 154
Hallucinogenic, defined, **1:**33, **2:**164
   and Glossary
Hallucinogens and hallucinogenic
   plants, **3:**192–194
   angel's trumpet and jimsonweed,
      3:193–194
   ayahuasca, **2:***116*, **3:***193*
   marijuana, **1:**101, 119–120, **3:**194
      (*see also Cannabis*)
   mushrooms, **2:**164
   nutmeg and mace, **1:**46, **3:**174,
      192–193
   ololioqui, **3:**193
   peyote, **1:**115, **3:**192
Halophilic Archaea, **1:**56
Halophytes (salt plants), **1:**56, **2:**1, 3,
   77, **3:**2
   See also Mangroves
Hamamelidaceae, **1:**77
Hamamelidae, **1:**45, 46–47, **2:**78
Haploid, defined, **1:**47, **2:**145, **3:**180,
   4:16 and Glossary
Haploid cells, **1:**158
   See also Gametes
Haploid stage (1N), **1:**158–159
   See also Alternation of genera-
      tions; Gametophytes
Haptonema, **1:**31

Haptophyta, **1:***27*, 31
Hard fibers, **2:**138, 139
Hardwoods, **4:**128, 173–177
Harmaline, **3:**193
Harmful algal blooms (HABs). *See*
   Algal blooms
Harmine, **3:**193
Harshberger, John W., **2:**116
Hartig net, **3:**89
Harvey, William, **3:**2
Hatch-Slack cycle, **3:**150
   See also C_4 photosynthesis
Haustorial, defined, **2:**180 and
   Glossary
Haustorium/haustoria, **2:**180, **3:**45,
   110, 111, 118
Hawaiian Islands, **2:**4, **3:**92, **4:**31
   endangered species hot spot, **1:**69
   invasive species, **3:**49
   plants of, **1:**101
   species diversity, **1:**78–79
   threatened plants, **1:**71
Hawk moths, **1:**114, **3:**178–179, **4:**8
Hay fever, **3:**174
Head (inflorescence type), **3:**38
Heart disease, **3:**11, *70*, 71–72, 172
Heartwood, **4:**172
Heather family. *See* Ericaceae
Heaths, tundra species, **4:***138*
Heat stress, adaptations, **4:**80
   See also Xerophytic adaptations
Heavy metal contamination
   bioremediation, **1:**85
   phytoremediation, **1:***85*
Heavy metal uptake, **4:**32
Helianthus. See Sunflowers
Helical patterns, **3:**56, 141–142
Heliothis, **3:**42
Helmont, Jan Baptista van. *See* van
   Helmont, Jan
Hemicelluloses, **1:**80, 134, 136, 145,
   147, **2:**175
Hemileia vastatrix (coffee leaf rust),
   2:13
Hemiparasites, **3:**111, 112
Hemiterpenes, defined, **4:**108 and
   Glossary
Hemlock (*Conium maculatum*), **1:**32,
   33, **3:**153
Hemlock (*Tsuga*), **2:**19, *22*, **3:**112
Hemoglobin, rhizobial nodules,
   3:93, 94
Hemp, **1:**119, 143, **2:***138*, **3:**109
   Manila. *See* Abacá
   sunnhemp, **2:***138*
   See also Cannabis
Henbane (*Hyoscyamus niger*), **3:***126*,
   171, **4:**68
Hendricks, Sterling, **3:**155
Henequen (*Agave fourcroydes*), **2:***138*,
   139
Hennig, Willi, **3:**144, **4:**102, 104
Henslow, John Stevens, **2:**41
Herbals and herbalists, **3:**3–5
   herbalism/herbal medicine,
      3:4–5, 11–12
   herbals, **2:**25, **3:**3, *4*, **4:***92*

Herbaria, **1:**91, 92, 118, **2:**36–38,
   3:5–8, 4:103
   curators of, **2:36–38, 3:**8
   notable herbaria listed, **3:**6
   specimen collection and han-
      dling, **3:**7–8, 36–37, 164
   Torrey's collections, **4:**117
Herbicide resistance, **3:**10, 49
   genetic engineering for, **2:**155,
      3:10, 85
   genetic engineering process and,
      2:170
   monocots, **3:**10
Herbicides, **3:9–10, 4:**143, 166
   allelochemicals as, **1:**35
   application methods, **3:**9
   mechanisms, **3:**10
   U.S. usage, **3:**9
   See also Weed control
Herbivores and herbivory, **2:**1, 86,
   109, **3:**46, 162
   chemical defenses against, **1:**47,
      139, 143, **2:**7, 50, 55, 57–58,
      3:153
   coevolution and, **2:**6, 7–8
   defined, **1:**32, **2:**1, **3:**41, **4:**8 and
      Glossary
   insects. *See* Insect herbivory
   physical defenses against,
      2:60–62, 188, 200
   rain forests, **4:**2, 9, 10
   savannas, **2:**87, **4:**40
   tundra, **4:**139
   See also Grazers and grazing
Herbs, **3:**3, **11–12**
   culinary, **3:**11
   herbal medicine, **3:**4–5, 11–12
   rain forests, **4:**6
Heredity, **3:**80
   chromosomal theory of inheri-
      tance, **3:**67
   and Darwin's natural selection
      theory, **2:**43
   Mendel's investigations, **1:**9, 95,
      157, **2:**43, 129, **3:**33
   particulate inheritance, Mendel's
      elucidation of, **3:**73–75
   synthesis of Darwinian and
      Mendelian theory, **2:**43–44,
      129, **3:**75, **4:**104
   See also Characters; Genomes;
      Hybrids and hybridization;
      Traits
Hermaphroditism, **1:**100, 101–102
   flowers, **1:**47, 100, 101, **2:**145,
      3:107, **4:**23, 68
   plants, **1:**100, 101, **2:**44,
      3:106–107, **4:**23 (*see also*
      Monoecious plants)
Heroin, **3:**103
Hesperidium, **2:***159*
Hesperoyucca whipplei, **4:**16
Heteroblasty, **3:**54–55
Heterocyclic, defined, **1:**32 and
   Glossary
Heterokontophyta (Ochrophyta),
   1:*27*, 31

Heteromorphic alternation of generations, **4**:17
Heterophylly, **1**:53, **3**:54–55
Heteropogon, **2**:187
Heterosis (hybrid vigor), **2**:44, **3**:33, 34
Heterosporous, defined, **2**:166, **4**:45 and Glossary
Heterostylous, defined, **1**:101 and Glossary
Heterostyly, **1**:101, 102
Heterotrophic algae, **1**:31
Heterotrophic bacteria, **3**:91
Heterotrophs (consumers), **2**:86–87, 91, **3**:157
defined, **1**:31, **2**:39 and Glossary
Heterozygousness, **3**:184
Hevea (Brazilian rubber tree), **4**:34
See also Rubber
Hexane, **3**:100
Hibiscus, fiber species, **2**:*138*
Hickory *(Carya)*, **2**:47, **3**:176, **4**:43, 128
Hierarchical/Linnaean classification systems, **2**:127, **3**:61, 63–64, **4**:93, 95, 117
Hill, Robin, **3**:154
Hingston, R. W. G., **4**:3
Histogenesis, leaves, **3**:56
Histones, **3**:148
Histoplasmosis *(Histoplasma capsulatum)*, **2**:165
Historic preservation and reclamation, **3**:53
Hofmeister, W., **4**:100
Holistic, defined, **1**:96, **2**:98, **3**:31 and Glossary
Holly, **3**:194, **4**:23
Holoparasites, **3**:111, 112
Homeotic, defined, **2**:148 and Glossary
Homeotic mutations, **2**:148
Homologous characters, **3**:144–145
Homologous series, **4**:153
Homologues, **3**:67
Homology, **4**:87, 100
defined, **4**:100 and Glossary
Homoplasy. *See* Convergence
Homoploid hybrid speciation, **3**:33, 34, **4**:71, 74
Honey, **1**:26, **3**:107–108, **4**:82
Honeybees, **3**:177, **4**:82
See also Bees
Honeysuckle *(Lonicera)*, **3**:48
Japanese, **1**:71–72
Hooker, Joseph Dalton, **2**:42, 129, **3**:12–13, *12*, **4**:100
Hooker, Sir William Jackson, **3**:12
Hops and hop industry, **1**:20–21, 25
Hordeum. See Barley
Hormone application
auxins, **3**:18
cuttings, **3**:188
cytokinins, **3**:19
ethylene, **2**:158, **3**:20
gibberellins, **2**:161, 177, **3**:19
and senescence, **4**:56

Hormones, human, synthetic, plant sources of, **2**:83
Hormones, insect, **2**:55
Hormones, plant, **1**:137, **2**:45, 57, **3**:13, **17–21**
biosynthesis, **3**:14
detection and binding proteins, **3**:15
discovery, **3**:17, 154, 155
florigens, **3**:127
flowering, **3**:19, 20, 127, 155
fruit formation and ripening, **2**:158, **3**:14, 16, 20
functions and effects, **3**:*17,* 18–20, 153, **4**:56, 118
in genetic engineering, **2**:170
germination, **3**:155
hormonal control and development, **3**:**13–17**, 18–20, **4**:56
interactions, **3**:20
principal hormones listed, **3**:17
production, **4**:32
rhizobial nodulation, **3**:93–94
senescence and, **4**:56
signal transduction, **3**:15
sterols, **3**:66
terpenes, **4**:108
tissue culture media, **4**:109
transport within plants, **3**:14–15, 20, **4**:118
See also Abscisic acid; Auxins; Cytokinins; Ethylene; Gibberellins
Horneophyton, **2**:125
Hornworts, **1**:42, 105, 107, 108, **2**:123, 127, **3**:146
Anthoceros, **2**:*125*
distinguishing characteristics, **1**:*106*
reproduction, **1**:108, **2**:*125*, 166
See also Bryophytes
Horsechestnut *(Aesculus)*, **4**:61
Horses, **4**:43
Horsetails *(Equisetum)*, **3**:99, 166, **4**:46, *47*, 126
evolution and classification, **2**:125–126
phyllotaxis, **3**:141
reproduction, **2**:166, **4**:46
Horticulture, **3**:**21–23**
See also Ornamental plants
Horticulture therapy, **3**:23
Horticulturists, **1**:92–93, **3**:**23–25**
Host, **4**:**84–86**
See also Parasitism; Symbiosis
Hot springs, **1**:56–57
Houseplants, **3**:22, 23, **4**:61
HR (hypersensitive response), **2**:57, 61
Human ecology, **2**:86
Human impacts, **3**:**25–30**, 100
agriculture, **1**:7–8, **3**:25–27
on biodiversity, **1**:69, 71–72, **3**:29–30
desertification, **2**:**70–73**
endangered species and, **2**:107–108
fire use and suppression, **1**:149,

2:20, 88, 95–96, **4**:39
Industrial Revolution, **3**:27
spread of fungal diseases, **2**:50–51
study of (human ecology), **2**:86
See also Acid rain; Deforestation; Global warming; Greenhouse effect; Invasive species; *specific ecosystem types*
Humans, nutrient transport by, **1**:74–75
Humboldt, Alexander von, **1**:160, **2**:97, **3**:**30–31**, *30*, 159
Hummingbirds, **1**:114, **3**:*46*, 179, **4**:8, 68
Humulus lupulus. See Hops and hops industry
Humus, **2**:15
defined, **2**:15, **4**:3 and Glossary
Hunger, **1**:8
Hunt, Tim, **1**:135
Hunting and gathering, **1**:7, **3**:25, 27
Hura crepitans, **4**:44
Hurricanes, mangroves and, **4**:34
Huxley, Thomas Henry, **2**:43
Hybrid breakdown, **3**:32
Hybrid inviability, **3**:32, **4**:74
Hybrids and hybridization, **3**:**32–35**, 183
barriers, **3**:32, 176, **4**:73–74, 76
Burbank on hybrids, **1**:110
complex hybrids defined, **1**:110 and Glossary
history of scientific study, **3**:32–33
hybrid, defined, **1**:6, **2**:28, **3**:73 and Glossary
hybridization, defined, **1**:9, **3**:22, **4**:71 and Glossary
hybrid speciation, **3**:33–35, **4**:71, 74
Mendel's work, **3**:74–75
natural, **3**:32–34
polyploid formation, **3**:182–183
quadruple hybrids defined, **1**:110 and Glossary
seedless hybrids, **2**:160–161
tendency to reversion, **3**:33
types of hybridization, **3**:33–35
See also Polyploidy; Speciation
Hybrid seed, **1**:11, 12
Hybrid sterility, **2**:160–161, **3**:32–34, 182, 183, **4**:74
Hybrid vigor (heterosis), **2**:44, **3**:33, 34
Hydnora family (Hydnoraceae), **3**:*111*
Hydrarch succession, **3**:161
Hydrocharitaceae, **3**:86, *87*
Hydrocortisone, **2**:83
Hydrogen, **1**:74, **3**:15, 97, **4**:63
as nutrient, **3**:97, **4**:63
Hydrogenation, **3**:101
Hydrogen bonds
transpiration, **4**:162
See also Protons

Hydrogen cyanide, **2**:55
Hydrogen sulfide, in photosynthesis, **2**:39
Hydroids, **4**:152
Hydrolases, **2**:175
Hydrological cycle
    defined, **2**:64 and Glossary
    forests' role, **2**:64
Hydrolytic enzymes, **3**:119
Hydrome, **1**:42
Hydrophobic, defined, **1**:137 and Glossary
Hydrophytes, adaptations, **3**:57
Hydroponic, defined, **3**:22, **4**:37 and Glossary
Hydroponics, **3**:35–36, 90, 96, 154, **4**:37
Hydrostatic pressure, **3**:154, **4**:122
    See also Turgor pressure
Hydrothermal vents, **1**:56–57, **4**:85
Hydrotropism, **4**:135
Hydroxyl, defined, **1**:48, **2**:55 and Glossary
Hydroxyproline, **1**:46, 136
Hylocereus undatus (dragon fruit), **1**:115
Hyophorbe amaricaulis, **2**:109
Hyoscyamus niger (henbane), **3**:*126*, 171, **4**:68
Hypanthium, **4**:35
Hyperaccumulators, **1**:*85*
Hyperarid lands, **2**:72
    See also Deserts
Hypersensitive response (HR), **2**:57, 61
Hyperthermophiles, **1**:57
Hyphae, **2**:56, 162, **3**:*41*, 113, **4**:142
    defined, **2**:56, **3**:40, **4**:142 and Glossary
    mycorrhizae, **3**:40, 89, 90
    See also Haustorium/haustoria
Hypocotyl, **2**:105, 106, **4**:53
Hypodermis, **1**:38
Hypophysis, **2**:106

I

IAA (indoleacetic acid). *See* Auxins
ICBN (International Code of Botanical Nomenclature), **4**:95, *100, 101*
Ice Age extinctions, **2**:107, 109
Iceland, **1**:78
Identification of plants, **3**:36–37, **4**:129, 149
    See also Keys
Ilex. See Holly
Illiciaceae, **1**:77
Illicit, defined, **2**:6 and Glossary
Illicium, **1**:45
Illustrators, botanical and scientific, **1**:89–91
Imbibition, **2**:174, **3**:2
Impatiens, **4**:62
    capensis (jewelweed), **3**:169
    touch-me-not, **4**:*137*
Impede, **2**:25

defined, **2**:11, **3**:116, **4**:31 and Glossary
Imperata cylindrica (cogon grass), **2**:189
Inbreeding, inbreeding depression, **1**:100–101, **4**:23
Incense-cedar, **2**:24
Income, from agriculture, **1**:14–15
Income growth, **2**:99
Indehiscent fruits, **2**:157, 160
Indeterminate inflorescences, **3**:37–38
India, **4**:68
    agriculture, **1**:7, 89, **2**:31, 197, **4**:27, 28, *106*
    species diversity, **1**:*68*
Indian fig (*Opuntia ficus-india*), **1**:115
Indian paintbrush (*Castilleja*), **3**:111, **4**:*139*
Indian pipe (*Monotropa*), **3**:110
Indigenous peoples
    ethnobotanical research and, **2**:117, 118, **3**:5, 70, **4**:11
    tropical rain forests, **4**:11
Indole-3-acetic acid, **3**:17
Indoleacetic acid (IAA). *See* Auxins
Indole-butyric acid, **3**:17
Indoleglycerophosphate, **3**:14
Indonesia, **1**:68, **2**:12, **4**:27, *106*, 140
Indoor plants, **3**:22, 23, **4**:61
Inducible defenses, **2**:57
Indusium, **2**:*134–135*
Industrial crops, **1**:7
Industrial emissions, and acid rain, **1**:1–2
Industrial Revolution, impacts of, **3**:27
Inert, defined, **1**:29, **3**:35 and Glossary
Inferior ovaries, **2**:146
Inflorescences, **3**:37–39
    defined, **1**:25, **2**:11, **3**:176, **4**:14 and Glossary
    grasses, **2**:186
    record-holding, **3**:*14*
Infrared light, **1**:152
Infraspecific variation, **4**:146
    See also Clines and ecotypes; Cultivars
Infrastructure, defined, **2**:101 and Glossary
Inga, **3**:179
Ingenhousz, Jan, **3**:39–40, *39*, 154
Inheritance. *See* Heredity; Hybrids and hybridization; Traits
Initials, meristems, **3**:76, 77–78
Injury, plant responses to, **4**:120–121, 151
Inoculation
    defined, **3**:93 and Glossary
    mycorrhizae, **3**:90, 93, 95
Inositol triphosphate, **3**:16
Insect herbivory, **2**:50, 60, **3**:41–42, 117, 118
    conifers, **2**:19
    crop plants, **3**:41–42 (*see also specific crop plants*)
    tropical forests, **4**:3, 9, 10, 42

Insecticides, **1**:10–13
    allelochemicals as, **1**:35
    botanical, **1**:32, 58, **2**:55, 59, **4**:116
    DDT, **1**:85, **2**:88–89
    triterpenoids, **2**:55
Insectivorous, defined, **4**:131 and Glossary
Insectivorous plants. *See* Carnivorous plants
Insect pollinators, **1**:48, **2**:50, 115, 146, **3**:86
    bees, **1**:114, **2**:50, *145*, **3**:*177*, 177–178, **4**:8
    beetles, **1**:48, 114, **2**:*145*, 147, **3**:*179*, **4**:8, 15
    butterflies, **2**:50, *145*, **3**:178–179, **4**:8
    cacti, **1**:114
    coevolution with flowers, **1**:48, **2**:6–9, 126–127, 144, 147–148, **3**:*177*, **4**:8
    early angiosperms, **2**:147
    flies, **2**:50, 147, **3**:112, 178, **4**:8, 15
    midges, **4**:8
    moths, **1**:114, **2**:8, 50, *145*, **3**:178–179, **4**:8
    orchids and, **2**:8–9, 44, 146, **3**:104
    thrips, **4**:8
    tropical rain forests, **4**:8
    wasps, **2**:8–9, 50, **3**:104, **4**:8
Insect resistance. *See* Pest resistance
Insects
    beneficials, **1**:5
    as biocontrol agents for weeds, **3**:43, 50, **4**:166
    carnivorous plant prey, **1**:126
    caves, **4**:31
    chemical defenses against, **1**:143, **2**:57–58, 61, **3**:42, 153, **4**:10
    coastal ecosystems, **2**:1
    as decomposers, **2**:54
    grasslands, **2**:193
    light detection, **3**:157
    as pathogens and disease vectors, **3**:42, 116–118
    rain forest canopy, **4**:3
    See also Insect herbivory; Insect pollinators; Interactions, plant-insect; Pest control; *specific insects*
Institut de France, **3**:62
Institute of Food Technologists, **2**:141
Integrated pest management (IPM), **1**:12, 15
Intensive tillage, **1**:10
Interactions
    decomposers, **2**:53–54
    ecological significance, **4**:86
    rain forest canopy, **4**:3
    See also Symbiosis
Interactions, plant-animal
    antagonistic relationships, **2**:50
    commensal relationships, **2**:50, **3**:43–44, **4**:84, 86
    coniferous forests, **2**:19–20
    TDBFs, **2**:49–50

vertebrates, **2**:115, **3**:45–47
vertebrates and epiphytes, **2**:115
See also Chemical defenses; Co-evolution; Interactions, plant-insect; Mutualisms; Physical defenses; Pollinators and pollen vectors; Seed dispersal; Symbiosis
Interactions, plant-bacterial
  bacterial pathogens, **2**:120, **3**:113, 114, *115*
  endosymbiosis, **1**:156, **2**:40, **111–113**, 121
  hornworts and cyanobacteria, **1**:108
  See also Nitrogen fixation
Interactions, plant-fungal, **3**:40
  fungal pathogens. *See* Fungal diseases
  See also Lichens; Mycorrhizae
Interactions, plant-insect, **3**:41–43
  commensal relationships, **2**:50, **3**:43–44, **4**:84, 86
  epiphytes, **2**:115
  insectivorous plants, **1**:126–128, **2**:45
  insects as disease vectors, **3**:42, 116–118
  See also Chemical defenses; Insect pollinators; Physical defenses
Interactions, plant-plant, **3**:43–45
  allelopathy, **1**:35, 150, **2**:7–8, **3**:45, 163, **4**:165
  competition, **3**:45, 161–163, **4**:6
  parasitic plants, **2**:199, **3**:44, 45, **110–112**, 113, 116
  See also Plant communities
Interactions, plant-vertebrate. *See* Interactions, plant-animal
Interbreeding, speciation and, **4**:71, 72, 75–76
Intercalary, defined, **3**:56 and Glossary
Interchange chromosomes, **3**:67
Intercontinental disjunctions, **1**:77–78
Intercropping, **1**:7, **3**:102
Interference, **3**:45
  See also Allelopathy
Intergovernmental Panel on Climate Change, **3**:28
Intermediate-day plants, **3**:125–126
  See also Photoperiodism
International Biological Program, **1**:82, **2**:98, **3**:100
International Center for the Improvement of Wheat and Corn, **1**:9
International Code of Botanical Nomenclature (ICBN), **4**:95, *100, 101*
International Congress of Genetics, **4**:153
International Rice Research Institute, **1**:9
Internodes, **1**:40, **2**:186, **4**:60, 78
  defined, **4**:60 and Glossary

Interspecific hybridization
  defined, **3**:34, **4**:74 and Glossary
  See also Hybrids and hybridization
Intertidal, defined, **2**:1 and Glossary
Intracellular bacteria, defined, **4**:86 and Glossary
Intraspecific taxa, **3**:33, 34–35
  defined, **3**:33 and Glossary
Introgression, **3**:34–35
Intuiting, defined, **3**:63 and Glossary
Inulin, **3**:150
Invasive species, **3**:47–50, **4**:94
  exotics, **1**:71–72, **2**:109, **3**:29, 47, **4**:168
  See also Weeds
Ion content, aquatic ecosystems, **1**:49
Ionic, defined, **2**:56 and Glossary
Ions, defined, **3**:2, **4**:118 and Glossary
Iowa Farmers' Institute, **1**:65
Ipecac (*Cephaelis ipecacuanha, Psychotria ipecacuanha*), **2**:10, **3**:172, 173
IPM (integrated pest management), **1**:12, 15
Ipomoea
  batatas. See Sweet potato
  violacea, **3**:193
Iran, **2**:48
Iraq, **2**:63
Ireland, **3**:122
Iris, **2**:146, 160, **3**:87
Irish potato famine, **2**:165, **3**:114, 185
Iron
  high-iron rice, **3**:85
  as nutrient, **3**:96, *97*, 98, **4**:63, 64
  in soil, **4**:63
Ironweeds (*Vernonia*), **1**:58
Irradiation, **3**:67
Irreversible, defined, **2**:91 and Glossary
Irrigation, **1**:4, 10, 11
Isidia, **3**:60
Island biogeography, **1**:78–79
Islands, biodiversity hot spots, **1**:69, *70*
Isoetaceae. *See* Quillworts
Isoetes, **2**:125
  See also Quillworts
Isoflavonoids, **2**:140
Isoginkgetin, **2**:180
Isometric growth, **3**:57
Isomorphic alternation of generations, **4**:17
Isopentenyl transferase, **3**:14
Isoprene, **1**:59, 60, **2**:55, **4**:*108*
Isozyme variability, **4**:87
Italy, **1**:13, 24
Ivory Coast, **2**:12
Ivy, **3**:54–55, **4**:59

J

Jaborandi (*Pilocarpus*), **3**:70
Jack-in-the-pulpit, **3**:87
Japan, **1**:*68*, **2**:18, 48, **4**:5, *106*

Japanese honeysuckle, **1**:71–72
Jasmonates, **4**:56
Jasmonic acid (JA), **2**:57, 59
Jefferson, Thomas, **1**:126
Jemtegaard, Genevieve. *See* Calvin, Genevieve Jemtegaard
Jesuits' bark (*Cinchona*), **3**:*70*
  See also Quinine
Jewelweed (*Impatiens capensis*), **3**:169
Jimsonweed (*Datura*), **3**:193–194
Job's tears (*Coix lacryma-jobi*), **2**:187
Johansen, Wilhelm, **2**:129
Joly, John, **3**:154
Josselyn, John, **3**:5
Juglandaceae, **4**:100
Juglans. See Walnut
Jumping genes (transposable DNA elements), **1**:157, 159, **2**:33–34, **3**:68
Juniper (*Juniperus*), **2**:17, 19, 21, 22, 24
Juniper berries, **2**:24
Jussieu, Antoine-Laurent de, **4**:100, 103
Jute (*Corchorus*), **2**:138
Juxtaposition, defined, **1**:148 and Glossary

K

Kale, **4**:156
Kant, Immanuel, **2**:97, **3**:31
Kapok (*Ceiba pentandra*), **2**:*138*, 139, **4**:34
Kauri (*Agathis*), **2**:21–22
Kava (*Piper methysticum*), **3**:195
Kelp, **1**:31
  giant, **1**:28, *30*, **3**:144
Kenaf (*Hibiscus cannabinus*), **2**:*138*
Kenrick, Paul, **1**:105
Kenya, **4**:*106*
Ketones, **1**:121
Kew Gardens. *See* Royal Botanic Gardens, Kew
Keys, **3**:36, **4**:*96*, 97, 103
Khat, **3**:194
Kimmins, J. P., **2**:154
Kinase (p34), **1**:135
Kingdoms, classification, **4**:94
Klácel, Matthew, **3**:73
Kohlrabi, **4**:156
Kölreuter, Joseph Gottlieb, **3**:32–33
Krameria family (Krameriaceae), **3**:*111*
Kranz anatomy, **1**:40, **3**:132
Krebs cycle, **1**:140, **2**:39, **3**:*151*, 152
Kricher, John, **3**:159
Kudzu (*Pueraria lobata*), **3**:29, 48, **50–52**, *51*

L

Labor use, organic vs. conventional farms, **1**:*14*, 15
Lacerate, defined, **2**:61 and Glossary
Lactuca. See Lettuce
Ladybugs, **1**:33

Lamarckian inheritance, **4**:154
    defined, **4**:154 and Glossary
Lamarck, Jean-Baptiste, **1**:110, 118,
    2:128, 129, **4**:100
    proponents of Lamarckian the-
        ory, **4**:154, 157
Lamella/lamellae, **1**:42, **3**:98, 119
    defined, **1**:42, **4**:149 and Glossary
Laminaria, **1**:31
Laminar stamens, **1**:47
Lanatosides, **3**:70, 72
Land development planning, **3**:53
Land-grant universities, **1**:17, **3**:121
    defined, **3**:121 and Glossary
Land plants
    groups, **3**:165–166
    origins and diversification, **1**:29,
        31, **2**:122–127, **3**:90, 145–146,
        165–166
    reproduction, **4**:23
    See also specific plant groups
Landrace, defined, **1**:9, **4**:48 and
    Glossary
Landscape architects, **3:52–53**
Landscape design, **3**:52, 53
Landscape ecology, **2**:85–86, **4**:4
Landscape mosaic, **3**:159
Landscaping, landscape plants. *See*
    Horticulture; Ornamental plants
La Niña, **1**:84
Lapland, Linnaeus' explorations,
    3:61–62
Larch (*Larix, Pseudolarix*), **2**:17, 19,
    198
Largest plants. *See* Record-holding
    plants
Larix. See Larch
Larrea tridentata (creosote bush), **4**:15
Lateral, defined, **1**:37, **2**:10, **3**:18,
    4:44 and Glossary
Lateral buds, **2**:179, **3**:18, 19, 76, 77
Laterally, defined, **4**:79 and Glossary
Lateral meristems, **1**:37, **2**:179, **3**:76,
    77–79, **4**:58–59, 111
    See also Cambium/cambia; Cork
        cambium; Secondary growth;
        Secondary tissues; Vascular
        cambium
Lateral roots, **4**:123, *124*, 125
Latewood, **4**:172, 173, 175
Latex, **2**:*58*, 59
Lauraceae (laurel or cinnamon fam-
    ily), **1**:45, 46, **2**:*78*, **3**:*111*
Laurel, **1**:46
Lavauden, L., **2**:70
Lavender, **4**:108
Laver, **1**:29
Lawn grasses, **3**:86
    turf management, **4:140–141**
Layering, **4**:18
Leaching
    fertilizers and herbicides, **1**:11,
        12, **4**:166
    nutrients, **1**:4
Lead, **1**:*85*, **4**:32
Leaf bases, **4**:80
    nonwoody trees, **4**:126

Leaf beetles, **4**:7, 8
Leaf blade, **1**:39–40, **3**:53–54, 55,
    4:61
Leaf-bud cuttings, **3**:188
Leaf-cutter ants, **4**:*9*
Leaf cuttings, **3**:188
Leaf design, ecological view,
    2:87–88
Leaf diseases, **3**:116, 117
Leaf expansion, **3**:56–57
Leaf fibers. *See* Hard fibers
Leaf growth, **2**:179
Leafhoppers, **4**:129
Leaflets, **4**:61
Leaf primordia, **3**:76, 77, **4**:78
Leaf shapes, **3**:54, 56–57, **4**:61
    heterophylly, **1**:53, **3**:54–55,
        4:61
Leaf sheath, **2**:186, **3**:53, 56, 87,
    4:61
Leaf suction, **3**:2
Leaf veins, **1**:39, 142, **2**:125–126,
    3:55, 87–88
Leafy mistletoe, **3**:116
Leafy spurge (*Euphorbia esula*), **3**:48,
    50
Leaves, **3:53–58**, *54*
    adaptations, **2**:52, 126, **4**:6
    anatomy, **3**:55, **4**:112, 113
    arrangement, **3**:56, *142*, **4**:61–62
    cells, **1**:*146*
    chlorophylls in, **1**:129, **2**:49, 52
    chlorosis, **3**:*96*, 99
    color, **1**:129, 140, 152, **2**:49, 52,
        60, **3**:179
    dicots, **1**:39, 40, **3**:53–56, 58
    differentiation and development,
        1:39, **3**:56–57, 76–77, **4**:78
    epidermis, **1**:39, 53, **3**:55, 118
    etiolated, **3**:168
    evolution, **2**:126, **3**:57–58
    flowers as modifications of,
        2:174, **3**:77
    fungal penetration, **3**:118
    modifications, **3**:57
    monocots, **1**:39, 40, **3**:54–57
    movement, **3**:127, **4**:25
    nastic movements, **4**:134,
        135–136
    photoperiod sensors, **3**:127
    photosynthetic tissue, **3**:55
    pollution damage, **1**:61
    protein synthesis, **3**:149
    record-holding, **4**:13
    senescence, **3**:19, 20, **4**:56
    structure, **1**:39–40, *40*, 53, 141,
        3:53–54, *54*, **4**:61
    translocation and, **4**:119
    transpiration, **1**:59
    types, **3**:53–55
    vascular tissues, **3**:55, 57
    wilting, **3**:17, 19–20
    See also Deciduous habit; *specific
        plants and plant groups*
Lebanon, **2**:63
Lectins, **3**:173, **4**:10
Leeks, **4**:61

Legumes (Fabaceae), **1**:68, **2**:*78*,
    130–132, 130
    alkaloids in, **2**:55
    in crop rotations, **1**:7
    cyanogenic compounds in, **2**:55
    defined, **1**:6, **2**:13, **3**:44, **4**:44 and
        Glossary
    economic importance, **2**:130,
        131, **4**:51, 68
    flavonoids in, **3**:93
    fruits, **2**:130, *159*, 159–160
    green manuring with, **2**:132, 137
    in human diet, **4**:51, 69
    leaves, **2**:130
    nastic movements, **4**:135–136
    nitrogen fixation, **2**:9–10,
        131–132, **3**:44, *92*, 92–95, **4**:69,
        84
    parasitic weeds, **3**:45
    seeds and dispersal, **2**:130, **4**:44,
        53–54
    See also specific genera
Leguminosae. *See* Legumes
    (Fabaceae)
Lemma, **2**:186
Lemna (duckweeds), **1**:43, **3**:53
Lemon, **4**:143
Lemurs, **3**:180
Lenin (Vladimir Ilyich Ulyanov),
    4:153
Lennoa family (Lennoaceae), **3**:*111*
Lenticels, **4**:34
Lentils, **1**:6, **2**:132, **3**:174
Lepidium, **2**:146
Lepidodendrales, **4**:126
Leptoids, **4**:152
Leptome, **1**:42
Lettuce (*Lactuca sativa, L. serriola*),
    1:58, **2**:55, **3**:36
    seeds, **4**:51, *52*, 53, *55*
Leucaena leucocaphala, **2**:132
Leucoplasts, **3**:168
Lewis, Gilbert Newton, **1**:116
Lianas, **4**:3, 4, 6
Lichens, **3**:7, **58–61**, *59*, **4**:84, *85*
    component organisms, **1**:29,
        2:38, 162, **3**:58–59, **4**:84
    diversity, **3**:58
    ecology, **1**:29, **3**:60
    rain forests, **4**:6
    tundra, **4**:138, 140
    types and reproduction, **3**:59–60
Liebig, Justus von, **4**:62
Light, plant responses to
    circadian rhythms, **4**:25–26
    etiolation, **3**:168
    nyctinasty and photonasty,
        4:135–136
    seed dormancy termination,
        2:177–178, **4**:54–55
    solar tracking, **4**:134
    See also Photoperiodism; Pho-
        totropism; Phytochromes
Light, ultraviolet, **1**:32, 56
Light absorption, **3**:135
    anthocyanins, **4**:143
    chlorophylls, **1**:152, *153*, **3**:135

phototropism, **4**:133
phycobilisomes, **2**:38
Light intensity, and photoperiodism, **3**:126
Light production, bacteria-marine animal symbioses, **4**:85
Light reactions, in photosynthesis. *See* Photosynthesis, light reactions and
Light sensing, **3**:155–156, 155–157, 167
 phototropism and, **4**:132–133
 phytochromes, **2**:178–179, 179, **3**:127, 155–156, **4**:55
 seeds, **2**:177–178, **4**:55
Lignified, defined, **1**:36, **2**:124, **4**:54 and Glossary
Lignins, **1**:36, 141, **3**:150, **4**:149
 decomposition, **2**:162
 effect on insects, **2**:61
 fiber cells, **2**:137, **4**:112–113, 173
 in pulp production, **3**:109
 sclerenchyma tissue, **4**:112–113, 173
 strength of, **1**:146, **2**:124, **3**:149, **4**:173
 structure and function, **1**:136, 146, **3**:149, 152, **4**:112
 synthesis, **3**:150
 See also Wood anatomy
Lignum vitae (*Guaiacum officinale*), **4**:177
Ligules, **2**:186, **4**:45
Likens, Gene, **2**:98
Liliidae, **1**:45
Liliopsida. *See* Monocots
Lily family (Liliaceae), **1**:35, **3**:54, 87, **4**:54
Lime, **4**:64
Limnology, **1**:49
Limonin, **3**:152
Limonoids, **3**:152
Lineage, defined, **1**:29, **2**:38, **3**:143, **4**:74 and Glossary
Linen, **1**:144, 147, **2**:138
Linnaeus, Carolus (Carl), **1**:77, **2**:96–97, 127, **3**:61–65, 61
 classification system, **3**:61, 63–64, **4**:93, 100, 103, 117
 education and works, **3**:61–63, 65
 hybridization studies, **3**:32–33
 nomenclatural system, **3**:61, 64–65, **4**:93, 103
Linum usitatissimum (flax), **2**:138, **4**:113
 See also Linen
Lipases, **3**:119
Lipids, **1**:137, 154, **3**:65–66
 cell membranes, **1**:137, **2**:120, **3**:134
 conversion to sugar, **3**:151
 nectar, **2**:148
 synthesis, **1**:138, 154, **3**:150
Lipo-chito-oligosaccharides, **3**:93
Liquidambar (sweet gum), **1**:77
Liquid fuels, **1**:80
Liquor. *See* Spirits

Liriodendron, **1**:77, 78, **2**:146
Littoral zone, **1**:51, 51
Liverworts, **1**:42, 107–108, **2**:114, 127, **3**:144, 146
 common liverwort, **1**:107
 distinguishing characteristics, **1**:106
 evolution, **1**:105, **2**:123
 reproduction, **1**:107–108, **2**:166, **4**:20, 77
 See also Bryophytes
Livestock
 plants poisonous to, **3**:173
 savannas, **4**:41
Lizards, **2**:115
Llanos, **2**:191
Loams, **4**:65–66
Lobed leaves, **3**:54, 56, 57
Lobelia, **4**:140
Loci, defined, **4**:23 and Glossary
Lockeretz, W., **1**:13
Lodgepole pine, **4**:126
Lodging, defined, **4**:29 and Glossary
Lodicule, **2**:186
Lodoicea maldivica (double coconut, giant fan palm), **4**:15, 51
Lolium multiflorum (annual ryegrass), **1**:150
Long-day plants, **3**:125, 126, 127, 128, **4**:26
 See also Photoperiodism
Lonicera. See Honeysuckle (*Lonicera*), Japanese
Lophophora williamsii (peyote cactus), **1**:115, **3**:192
Loranthaceae. See Mistletoes
Lumber, **4**:174–175
 See also Wood products
Lund, P. W., **4**:157
Lupine alkaloids, **2**:55
Lupulin, **1**:25
Lutein, **1**:129, 130–131
Lycopene, **1**:130–131
Lycophytes (Lycophyta), **2**:125–127, **3**:166, **4**:45–46
Lycopodiaceae, *Lycopodium. See* Club mosses
Lycopods. *See* Club mosses
Lycopsids, **2**:125
Lyell, Sir Charles, **2**:41, 42
Lysenko, Trofim, **4**:152, 153–154
D-lysergic acid amide, **3**:193
Lysichitum. See Skunk cabbage
Lysine, **2**:30, **4**:169
Lythrum salicaria (purple loosestrife), **3**:29, 49, 50, **4**:168
Lytic, defined, **4**:142 and Glossary

M

Macaranga, **4**:10
Mace (*Myristica fragrans*), **3**:192–193
 See also Nutmeg
Macroalgae. *See* Seaweeds
Macrocystis. See Giant kelp
Macromolecules, **3**:114, 148–150, **4**:87

Macronutrients, **3**:96–97, 97, **4**:63
Macrophytes, aquatic, **1**:50
Macropores, **4**:67
Macroscopic, defined, **3**:41 and Glossary
Madagascar, **1**:68, 69, **3**:180
Madagascar periwinkle (*Catharanthus roseus*), **3**:70, 175
Magnesium
 acid rain and, **1**:2
 fertilizers, **2**:136
 as nutrient, **3**:97, 98, **4**:63
 in soil, **4**:63, 64
Magnesium carbonate, **4**:64
Magnolia, **1**:44, 77, 78
Magnoliaceae (Magnolia family), **1**:45, 46, 77, **2**:78
Magnoliidae, **1**:45–47, **2**:78, 79
Magnoliophyta. *See* Angiosperms
Magnoliopsida. *See* Dicots
Mahogany, **4**:173
Ma huang, **3**:70
Maidenhair tree. *See* Ginkgo biloba
Mairan, Jean de, **4**:25
Maize. *See* Corn (maize) (*Zea mays*)
Malaria, **4**:108
Malate, **3**:132
Malay Peninsula, **4**:7
Malic acid, **3**:132
Malpighi, Marcello, **3**:154
Malt and malt industry, **1**:20–21, 23, 24–25
Malthus, Thomas, **2**:42, 99
Mammals
 coniferous forests, **2**:20
 grasslands, **2**:193, **4**:40, 139
 nutrient transport by, **1**:74
 as pollinators, **3**:179–180 (*see also* Bats)
 rain forests, **4**:3, 7
 seed predation and dispersal, **2**:20, **3**:46, **4**:8, 43
 TDBFs, **2**:50
 See also specific mammals
Mandrake, **4**:68
Manganese, **3**:97, 98, **4**:63, 64
Mango (*Mangifera*), **1**:6, 8, **3**:170, **4**:19
Mangroves, **2**:3, **3**:2, 3, **4**:5, 34, 44
Manihot. See Cassava
Manila hemp. *See* Abacá
Manure
 as fertilizer, **2**:136–137
 See also Green manure crops
Manzanita (*Arctostaphylos*), **1**:149
 Presidio, **2**:107, 109
Maple (*Acer*), **1**:77, 78, **2**:47, **3**:176, **4**:56, 59
 Japanese, **4**:58
 red (*A. rubrum*), **1**:76
 seeds and dispersal, **2**:160, **4**:41, 42, 55
 sugar (*A. saccharum*), **2**:48, **4**:82
 wood, **4**:173, 175
Marchantia, **4**:77
 polymorpha (common liverwort), **1**:107

Marchantiophyta. *See* Liverworts
Marijuana, **1:**101, 119–120, **3:**194
    See also Cannabis
Marine ecosystems, **1:**50, 57, **4:**85
    corals, **1:**29, **2:**87, **4:***85*
Mariposa lily, **2:**110
Marketing of agricultural products,
    2:100–102, **4:**83
Markov, Georgi, **3:**173
Marshes, **1:**51, **3:**86, **4:**166, 168
    See also Wetlands
Martin, Gary J., **2:**118
Mascarene Islands, **2:**109
Mass flowering/fruiting, **4:**42
Mathematical patterns, **3:**141–142
    See also Phyllotaxis
Mattheck, Claus, **4:**125
Mattioli, Pier Andrea, **3:**4
May-apple (*Podophyllum peltatum*),
    3:*70, 71*
Mayr, Ernst, **4:**104
McClintock, Barbara, **1:**157, 159,
    2:33–34, **3:66–69,** *66*
McKenna, Malcolm, **1:**78
Mead, **1:**26
Mean residence time (MRT), **1:**74
Medicago sativa. See Alfalfa
Medicinal plants and fungi, **1:**32,
    107, **2:**59, **3:69–72**
    Cannabis, **1:**119
    coca, **2:**4
    common plants and uses, **3:***70*
    conifers, **2:**202
    defensive chemicals in plants,
      2:59 (*see also* Chemical de-
      fenses)
    determining value of, **3:**70–71,
      4:94
    Echinacea angustifolia, **1:**118
    ergot, **2:**165, 185, **3:**174
    ethnobotany and, **2:**117, **3:**70
    foxglove, **3:**11, *70, 71–72, 72,*
      170, 172
    Ginkgo biloba, **2:**180–181
    herbal medicine, **3:**4–5, 11–12
    herbal teas, **4:**107
    Madagascar periwinkle, **3:***70*, 175
    may-apple, **3:***70, 71*
    opium poppy, **1:**32, *33,*
      3:102–103, *103,* 174, 195
    overharvesting, **2:**108
    Pacific yew, **1:***34,* **2:**202, **3:***70,*
      173–174, **4:**109
    physic gardens, **1:**91
    prospecting for, **2:**117, **3:**29–30,
      70, 124, 164–165, **4:**94
    Solanaceae, **4:**68
    synthetic drugs based on, **2:**83,
      3:11
    tea, **4:**106
    toxic plants, **3:**172, 173–174
    See also Alkaloids
Medicinal preparations, rosa-risa,
    2:*116*
Mediterranean basin, **1:**69
Mediterranean climate, **1:**69, 148,
    149

Medulla, defined, **3:**60 and Glossary
Megaphylls, **2:**126
    defined, **2:**126 and Glossary
Megaspores, **4:**22, 46
Meiosis, **1:**158, 159, **3:**182, **4:***17*
    cytogenetics, **4:**95
    defined, **3:**181, **4:**22 and Glossary
    gametogenesis, **4:**16, 45
    sporogenesis, **4:**16, 20, 22, 77
    sporophyte evolution and,
      4:17–18
    See also Alternation of genera-
      tions; Differentiation and de-
      velopment
Melaleuca, **3:**29
Melissopalynology, **3:**107–108
Meloidogyne, **3:**118
Melons, **1:**6
Membrane G protein, **3:**15
Mendelian theory
    Lysenko's opposition to, **4:**154
    synthesis with Darwinian theory,
      2:43–44, 129, **3:**75, **4:**104
Mendel, Gregor, **2:**129, **3:73–76,** *73*
    hybridization experiments and
      inheritance theory, **1:**157, **3:**33,
      74–75
    rediscovery and influence of, **1:**9,
      95, **2:**43, **3:**75
    tallness gene, **3:**14
Mentha x *piperita. See* Peppermint
Meristematic, defined, **1:**133, **2:**148,
    3:166, **4:**111 and Glossary
Meristematic cells (meristemoids),
    1:36, **2:**81, **3:**166
Meristems, **1:**37, **2:**106, *177,*
    3:76–80, *79,* **4:**111
    apical. *See* Apical meristems
    cell division, **3:**75
    cell walls, **1:**145
    defined, **1:**64, **2:**10, **3:**56, **4:**78
      and Glossary
    floral, **2:**148, 173–174
    ground, **2:**106, **4:**111, 112
    intercalary, **3:**56
    lateral. *See* Lateral meristems
    primary, **4:**111, 112, 114, 147
    procambium, **2:**106, **4:**111, 112,
      114, 147
    protoderm, **4:**111
    roots, **4:**32–33
    secondary. *See* Lateral meristems
    seedling growth, **2:**178–179
    tropisms and, **4:**131
Mescaline, **2:**59, **3:**192
Mesic, defined, **2:**68 and Glossary
Mesoamerica, **1:**6, **2:**28–29
    See also Central America
Mesophyll, **1:**39, 40, **3:**55, 132,
    4:112, 113, 121
Mesopotamia, **1:**24
    See also Fertile Crescent
Mesorhizobium, **3:**93
Mesozoic era, **2:**121–122, 180
Messenger ribonucleic acid
    (mRNA), **1:**155–156, **3:***83,* 149
Metabolism. *See* Physiology, defined

Metabolites
    primary, **3:**11, 152, 153
    secondary, **3:**11, 69, 152–153,
      171 (*see also* Alkaloids;
      Flavonoids; Glycosides;
      Steroids; Terpenes)
Metals
    bioremediation, **1:**85
    phytoremediation, **1:***85*
Metaphase, **1:**133–134
Metaphyta, **2:**124
Metasequoia (dawn redwood), **1:**77,
    2:17, 18, 22
Meteorological nutrient transport
    mechanisms, **1:**74
Methane, **1:**56, **3:**27
Methane fuels, **1:**80
Methanogens, **1:**56
Methanol, **1:***153*
Methanospirillum hungatii, **1:***57*
Methione, **3:**81
Methionine, **3:**14
Methyl salicylate, **2:**56
Mexico, **1:**6, *68,* 88–89, **2:**11–12, 18,
    28
    See also Mesoamerica
Mice, **2:**20, **3:**46
Microbes
    defensive responses to, **2:**57
    See also Pathogens
Microbodies, **3:**166
Microfibrils
    defined, **3:**15 and Glossary
    See also Cellulose microfibrils
Microfilaments, **1:***136, 137,* 140
Micromolecules, **4:**87
Micron, defined, **3:**166 and Glossary
Micronutrients, **3:**96–97, *97,* **4:**63
Microorganisms, **1:**15, 84–85, 122
    See also Archaea; Bacteria; Myc-
      orrhizae; Soil bacteria
Microphylls, **2:**125
    defined, **2:**125 and Glossary
Micropores, **4:**67
Micropropagation. *See* Tissue
    culture
Microspores, **2:**81, **4:**22, 46
Microsporium canis (athlete's foot),
    2:164–165
Microtubules, **1:***136, 137,* 140
Middle East, **1:**6, 24, 25
    See also specific countries
Midges, **4:**8
Migrations, **1:**77–78, **4:**140
Mile-a-minute weed (*Polygonum per-*
    foliatum), **3:**48
Milkweeds, **3:***146,* 170–171
Millets, **2:**184, 185, *187,* **3:**86
Mimosa (sensitive plant), **4:***136, 137*
Mineralization, **2:**137
Minerals. *See* Nutrients, plant;
    specific minerals
Mineral transport. *See* Nutrient
    transport
Mint, **3:**174
Mint family, **3:**11, **4:**62
Misodendraceae. *See* Mistletoes

Mistletoe bird, **3**:112
Mistletoes, **3**:45, *111*, 112, 116
Mites, **1**:126, 127–128, **4**:3
Mitigation, defined, **2**:70 and Glossary
Mitochondria, **1**:*136*, **2**:55, 120, **3**:148, 166, **4**:*142*
   composition and function, **1**:*137*, *139*, 140, **2**:113
   defined, **3**:130, **4**:86 and Glossary
   origins, **2**:113, 121, **4**:86
Mitochondrion (mt) genome, **1**:97
Mitosis, **1**:105, *133*, 133–135, 140, 157, 159, **2**:80
   defined, **1**:105, **2**:120, **4**:17 and Glossary
   seed development, **4**:51, 53
   sporophyte evolution and, **4**:17
   See also Differentiation and development
Modeling
   of ecosystems, **2**:89, 104, 154
   of phyllotaxis, **3**:142–143
   See also Computer modeling
Moisture availability, biome type factor, **1**:83–84
Molasses, **1**:*23*
Molds, **2**:162–164, **3**:172–173
   Aspergillus, **1**:26, **2**:164, **3**:172–173
   Neurospora, **3**:68
   Penicillium, **2**:*163*, 163, 164
   Rhizopus, **2**:83, 163
   See also Fungi; Slime molds
Molecular biology, **1**:95
Molecular genetics, **1**:95, **3**:80–85, 155
   breeding and, **3**:85
   DNA structure and replication, **3**:80–83
   mutations and polymorphisms, **3**:84
   protein synthesis, **3**:83
   See also Chromosomes; Genes; Genomes; Molecular systematics; Polyploidy
Molecular systematics, **2**:122, 143, **3**:*145*, **4**:87–90, 104
   defined, **2**:122, **4**:90 and Glossary
Molles, Manuel, **3**:159
Mollusks, **1**:126, **2**:1
Molybdenum, **3**:97, 98, **4**:63, 64
Monarch butterfly, **2**:172
Monardes, Nicholas, **3**:5
Monera, **2**:162, **4**:94
Mongolia, **2**:76
Monkeyface, **3**:173
Monkeys, **3**:179, **4**:43
Monoammonium phosphate, **2**:136
Monocots, **1**:*44*, 46, **2**:78, 145–146, **3**:86–88, *87*
   anatomy, **2**:145–146, **3**:54–58, 86–88
   embryogenesis, **2**:105–106
   flowers, **1**:39, **2**:145–146, **3**:88
   herbicide resistance, **3**:10
   leaves, **1**:39, 40, **2**:78, **3**:54–58

origins, **1**:45, 65, **2**:79
   parasitism lacking in, **3**:111
   rain forests, **4**:6
   roots, **2**:78, **3**:86, **4**:30, 32
   seeds, **1**:39, **2**:78, **3**:86, **4**:53
   stems, **3**:86, 87, **4**:77, 78, 171
   See also Noneudicots; *specific monocot families*
Monocotyledons. *See* Monocots
Monocultures, **1**:10, 12–13
   defined, **1**:6, **3**:50 and Glossary
Monoecious plants, **1**:101, **2**:145, **4**:23
   See also Hermaphroditism, plants
Monographic (revisionary) studies, **2**:143, **3**:5
Monomethyhydrozine (MMH), **2**:164
Monophyletic, defined, **2**:123, **3**:144, **4**:102 and Glossary
Monophyletic groups, **3**:144, 145, **4**:102
Monosaccharides, **1**:121, **4**:81
Monostichy, **3**:143
Monoterpenes (monoterpenoids), **1**:59–60, **2**:55, **3**:152, **4**:108
Monotropa (Indian pipe), **3**:110
Monstera (Swiss cheese plant), **3**:96
Montane, defined, **1**:68, **4**:4 and Glossary
Montane tropical rain forests, **4**:5
Mora, **4**:7
Morgan, Thomas Hunt, **3**:67
Morning glories, hallucinogenic, **3**:193
Morphine, **1**:32, *33*, **3**:103, 153, 174, 195, **4**:143
Morphological, defined, **1**:28, **2**:38, **3**:45, **4**:42 and Glossary
Morphologically, defined, **4**:24 and Glossary
Morphological systematics, **4**:87, 93, 95, 100, 104–105
Morphology
   defined, **1**:43, **2**:76, **3**:110, **4**:87 and Glossary
   Warming's studies, **4**:157
Morphology of Organisms (Haeckel), **2**:97
Mosquito repellent, citrus, **2**:59
Mosses, **1**:42, 105–107, **2**:123, **3**:7, *144*
   distinguishing characteristics, **1**:*106*
   distribution and diversity, **1**:105, **2**:114, 127, **4**:6, 138, 140
   economic importance, **1**:108
   epiphytic, **4**:6
   mycorrhizal associations, **3**:89
   peat moss, **1**:80, 108, **2**:127, **3**:121, *122*
   reproduction, **1**:105–107, **2**:166, **4**:20, 23, 77
   See also Bryophytes; Club mosses; Spike mosses
Moss forests, **4**:5
Mother-of-thousands plant, **3**:*187*

Moths, **4**:8
   Bt-toxin and, **2**:172
   Heliothis, **3**:42
   as pollinators, **1**:114, **2**:8, 50, *145*, **3**:178–179, **4**:8
Motile, defined, **1**:31, **2**:163, **3**:114, **4**:23 and Glossary
Mountain geography, **1**:77–78, **2**:48
Movement in plants. *See* Tropisms and nastic movements
MRT (mean residence time), **1**:74
mt genome, **1**:97
Mucigel, **4**:31
Mucilages, **3**:150, **4**:32, 54
Mucilaginous, defined, **3**:118 and Glossary
Multiple fruits, **2**:158, *159*, 160
Münch, E., **3**:154
Müntzing, Arne, **3**:33
Murein, **2**:120
   defined, **1**:56 and Glossary
Musa. See Abacá; Bananas
Musaceae (banana family), **3**:87–88
Musanga, **4**:10
Muscarine, **2**:164
Muscimol, **2**:164
Mushrooms, **2**:53, 163, 164, **3**:40, 58, 175
   edible, **2**:165, **4**:156
   stinkhorn, **2**:*162*, 163
   toxic/hallucinogenic, **2**:*163*, 164, **3**:170, *175*
   See also Fungi
Mustard, Indian (*Brassica juncea*), **1**:*85*
Mustard family. *See* Brassicaceae
Mustard oil glycosides, **3**:153
Mutant analysis, **3**:84–85
Mutationism, **3**:75
Mutations, **2**:148, **3**:67, 84–85, 183, **4**:23
Mutualisms, **2**:6, 50, **3**:44, 46, 162, **4**:84
   defined, **1**:4, **3**:162, **4**:3 and Glossary
   examples, **2**:8–10, **3**:44, 46
Myanmar, **4**:27, *106*
Mycelium, **2**:162, 164
   defined, **3**:112 and Glossary
Mycology, **2**:162
   See also Fungi; Mushrooms
Mycoplasma-like organisms, **3**:115
Mycorrhizae, **2**:162, 164, 166, **3**:44, **88–90**, *88, 89, 90*
   ecological importance, **3**:90, **4**:85, 86
   epiphytes, **2**:114
   ferns and mosses, **3**:89
   inoculation, **3**:90, 93, 95
   legumes, **2**:131
   mycotrophs, **3**:110–111
   nutrient uptake and, **2**:164, **3**:44, 89–90, 113, **4**:31
   orchids, **3**:90, 103
   threats to, **1**:72
   tropical rain forests, **4**:11
   types, **2**:164, **3**:40, 89–90

Mycotrophs, **3:**110–111
Myristicaceae, **1:**46
Myristica fragrans. See Mace; Nutmeg
Myristicin, **3:**193
Myxomycota, **2:**162

N

NADP+, **3:**130, *136,* 137, 138
    defined, **3:**136 and Glossary
NADPH, **1:**153, 154, **3:**130, 132,
    134
    defined, **1:**153, **3:**134 and
        Glossary
    production, **3:**130, 137–138
Naka, John Yoshio, **1:**87
Naming of plants. *See* Nomenclature
Nanometer, defined, **1:**144, **2:**38,
    3:135 and Glossary
Napp, F. C., **3:**73
Narcotic alkaloids. *See* Depressants,
    opium poppy
Narcotine, **3:**103
Nastic movements, **4:**131, 135–137
    solar tracking, **4:**134
Nasturtium, **3:**57
National Plant Germplasm System,
    4:48–50
National Research Council, **1:**13
National Seed Storage Laboratory,
    4:49, 50
Native food crops, **3:91,** **4:***50*
Native plants, threats to, **1:**71–72,
    2:108
Native Seeds/Search, **3:***91,* **4:***50*
Natural resource management
    ecology in, **2:**88–89
    ecosystems management,
        2:88–89, *108,* 111
    fire management, **1:**149, **2:**20,
        88, 95–96, **4:**39, 41
    See also Forestry
Natural selection
    coevolution, **1:**48, **2:6–10**
    convergence, **2:**126, **3:**144, *146*
    hybrids and, **3:**33
    selection mechanisms, **2:**7–8
Natural selection, Darwin's theory
    of, **2:**84–85, **3:**75, **4:**91
    clines and ecotypes as confirma-
        tion of, **1:**162
    formulation of, **1:**161, **2:**42,
        128–129
    Gray's advocacy of, **2:**194, 196
    Hooker and, **2:**129, **3:**13
    influence of, **2:**40, 97, **3:**143,
        4:93, 100, 103
    reactions to, **2:**43–44, **3:**13
    synthesis of Darwinian and
        Mendelian theory, **2:**43–44,
        129, **3:**75, **4:**104
Near East, **2:**48, 71, 72
    See also specific countries
Necrosis diseases, **3:**115, 116, 117
Nectar, **2:**58, 61, 148, **4:**82
Nectaries, **1:**142, **2:**148
    defined, **1:**142 and Glossary

Needles, conifers, **2:**17, 21, 52, 126,
    198–199, **3:**58
Negative feedback, defined, **2:**102,
    182 and Glossary
Nematodes, **2:**193, **3:***114,* **4:**65
    as pathogens, **3:**113, *115,*
        115–116, 118, 119
Nematologists, **3:**120
Neoxanthin, **1:**129
Net primary productivity (NPP),
    1:73, **2:**92, **3:**27
    tropical rain forests, **4:**10–11
Neuromuscular junction, defined,
    2:59 and Glossary
Neurospora, **3:**68
Neurotransmitter, defined, **2:**55 and
    Glossary
Neutral lipids, **3:**65
Neutral soils, **4:**64
New Caledonia, **1:**69, **2:**126
New Environmentalism, **2:**117
New Guinea, **4:**11
    agriculture, **2:**12
    deforestation, **2:***64*
    rain forest, **4:**4, 7, 12
    species diversity, **1:***68*
New York Botanical Garden,
    1:102–103, **4:**117
New Zealand, **1:***68,* 69, 101, **4:**5
Niacin deficiency, **2:**30
Niche, defined, **2:**41 and Glossary
Niches, ecological, **3:**162, **4:**6, 7
Nickel, **1:***85,* **3:**97, 98, **4:**63, 64
Nicotiana. See Tobacco
Nicotinamide adenine dinucleotide
    phosphate. *See* NADPH
Nicotine, **1:**32–33, *34,* **2:**59, **3:**192,
    194
    as insecticide, **1:**32, **2:**59,
        4:116
Night-length sensitivity, **3:**127
    See also Photoperiodism
Nightshade family. *See* Solanaceae
Nile Valley, **1:**6
Nitrates, in protein synthesis,
    3:150
Nitrogen, **1:**74
    alkaloids and, **1:**32
    conversion to organic forms,
        3:168
    desert environments, **2:**75, **3:**60
    excess, and algal blooms, **4:**64–65
    function in plants, **3:**98
    lichens as source of, **3:**60
    as nutrient, **3:**97, 98, **4:**63
    role in acidification, **1:**2
    seeds' provision of, **3:**149
    soil nitrogen, **1:**15, **2:**190, **3:**60,
        168, **4:**31
Nitrogenase, **2:**39
Nitrogen compounds
    in acid rain, **1:**1–2
    legume seeds, **2:**130
    in runoff, impacts, **1:**72
Nitrogen cycle, fire in, **2:**95
Nitrogen deficiency, **3:***96, 99*
Nitrogen deposition, **1:**72, 74

Nitrogen emissions, fossil fuel com-
    bustion, **1:**75
Nitrogen fertilizers, **2:**135–136
Nitrogen fixation, **1:**7, 48, **3:91–95,**
    4:31
    bacteria, **3:**91–92, **4:**31, 32 (*see
        also* Rhizobia)
    cyanobacteria, **2:**39, **3:**91,
        4:84–85
    ecological importance, **4:**86
    epiphytes, **4:**11
    essential nutrients, **3:**97, 98
    isoflavonoids and flavones in,
        2:140
    legumes, **2:**9–10, 132, **3:**44,
        93–95, **4:**69
    levels and rates, **3:**92–93, 95,
        4:84
    nitrogen-fixing organisms,
        3:91–93
    rhythms, **4:**25
Nitrogen oxides, in ozone forma-
    tion, **1:**60–61
Nitrous oxides, **1:**74
Nobel Prize awards, **1:**89, 116, 117,
    159, **3:**66–69
Nodes, **1:**40, **2:**186
    defined, **3:**51 and Glossary
Nod factors, **3:**93
Nodulation, rhizobia, **3:**93–95
Nodulins, **3:**94
Nomenclatural, defined, **3:**64, **4:**11
    and Glossary
Nomenclature, **1:**103, **2:**55, **4:**95, 98
    binomial/Linnaean, **3:**61, 64–65,
        4:93
    cultivar names, **2:**34
    ICBN, **4:**95, *100, 101*
    taxonomic ranks, **4:**93, *99*
Nondehiscent fruits, **2:**157, *159,* 160
Noneudicots, **1:**45, 46
    See also Basal angiosperms;
        Monocots
Nonmotile, defined, **4:**20 and
    Glossary
Nonpolar, defined, **1:**137, **3:**19 and
    Glossary
Nonsecretory, defined, **4:**129 and
    Glossary
Nonvascular plants. *See* Algae;
    Bryophytes
Nopales/nopalitos, **1:**115
Norephedrine, **3:**194
Norfolk Island pine (*Araucaria het-
    erophylla*), **2:**24
Nori, **1:**29
Norpseudoephedrine, **3:**194
North America
    coniferous forests, **2:**19, **4:**57
    deserts, **2:***71,* 74, *75*
    grasslands, **4:**38–39
    temperate deciduous forest, **2:**46,
        47, 48
    tree diversity, **4:**128
    See also specific countries
North Carolina, Green Swamp Na-
    ture Preserve, **1:**128

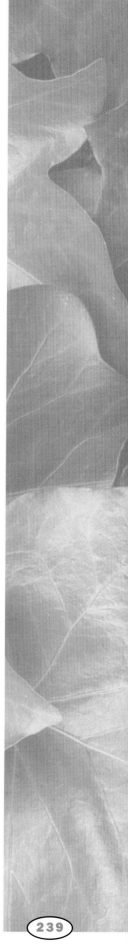

Northern blot, defined, **4:**118 and Glossary
Nostoc, **1:**108
Nothofagus, **2:**48, **4:**7
NPGS. *See* National Plant Germplasm System
NSSL. *See* National Seed Storage Laboratory
Nucellar tissue, **4:**53
Nuclear envelope, **1:***136,* 137, 138
Nucleic acids, **3:**98, 150, 152
Nucleolar, defined, **3:**67 and Glossary
Nucleolus, **1:***136,* 137, **4:***142*
Nucleoplasm, **1:**137, **4:***142*
Nucleotide sequences, **4:**88
Nucleus/nuclei, **1:***136,* **3:**80, 148, 166, **4:***142*
 sieve elements, **1:**144, **4:**119, 121
 structure and function, **1:***136,* 137–138, *139*
Numerical taxonomy. *See* Phenetics
Nuphar, **1:**52
Nurse, Paul, **1:**134
Nurse logs, **3:**43
Nurse plants, **2:**75, **3:**43, 44
Nurseryman, defined, **1:**109 and Glossary
Nursery production, **3:**22, 24
Nutmeg *(Myristica fragrans),* **1:**46, **3:**174, 192–193
Nutmeg family. *See* Myristicaceae
Nutrient availability, **4:**63
 deciduousness and, **2:**52–53
 decomposition and, **2:**53, 192–193
 deserts, **2:**74–75
 grasslands, **2:**190, 192–193
 mycorrhizae and, **3:**89–90
 organic fertilizers, **2:**137
 and soil pH, **4:**64
 See also Nutrient uptake; Soil fertility
Nutrient cycles. *See* Biogeochemical cycles (nutrient cycles); *specific nutrients*
Nutrient leaching, **1:**4
Nutrients, human/animal, carotenoids, **1:**130–131
Nutrients, plant, **1:**73, **3:95–99,** **4:**31, 62
 deficiency/toxicity, **3:**98, 99
 essential nutrients, **3:**95–96, *97,* **4:**63–64
 excess, effects of, **4:**64–65
 functions, **3:**98–99
 Sachs' investigations, **4:**37
 See also Food storage in plants; Nutrient availability; Nutrient transport; Nutrient uptake; *specific nutrients*
Nutrient transport, **4:**33, 78, 114
 bryophytes, **4:**152
 fungi, **2:**163
 halophytes, **3:**2
 mechanisms, **1:**74–75
 trees, **1:**64

See also Nutrient uptake; Phloem; Translocation; Vascular tissues; Xylem
Nutrient uptake, **2:**69, **3:**154
 acid rain and, **1:**2, **4:**31
 mycorrhizae and, **2:**164, **3:**44, 89–90, 113, **4:**31
 roots in, **4:**31–34, 118, 158–159, 162, 164
 soil pH and, **4:**64
 See also Nutrient transport
Nutritional composition of plant foods, **4:**118
Nutrition, human, **3:**22
 calorie sources, **1:**6, 8, 122, **2:**30, **3:**101, **4:**82
 fats and oils, **3:***101*
 sugars/carbohydrates, **4:**82
 See also Diet, human
Nutrition, plant
 Saussure's work, **2:**69
 van Helmont's work, **4:**144
Nuts, **2:**157, 158, *159,* 160
Nyctinasty, **4:**135–136
Nymphaeaceae (water lily family), **1:**45, **2:***78*
Nyssa (black gum), **1:**77

O

OAA (oxaloacetic acid), **3:**132
Oak *(Quercus),* **2:***48, 52,* 56, **3:**89, **4:**59, 61
 acorns, **2:**160, **4:**53
 bark and wood, **4:**53, 128, 173, 175
 cork *(Q. suber),* **1:**64, **2:**26, *26–27*
 European TDBF, **2:**47
 flowers and pollination, **2:**145, **3:**176
 root growth, **4:**30
 seed dispersal, **4:**43, 53
 U.S. TDBF, **2:**47
Oak savannas, **4:**38–39
Oak woodlands, **1:**148
Oats *(Avena sativa),* **1:**8, **2:**184, *187,* **3:**182, **4:***55*
Obligate, defined, **3:**45 and Glossary
Obligate parasites, **3:**117–119, **4:**85–86
 defined, **3:**117 and Glossary
Obligate symbioses, **3:**162, **4:**85–86
Oceanography, **1:**49
Oceans
 carbon cycle and, **1:**123–124, *124,* 125, 126
 role in coastal ecosystems, **2:**2, 3
 temperature alterations, **1:**84
 See also Marine ecosystems
Ochroma (balsa tree), **3:**179, **4:**177
Ochrophyta (Heterokontophyta), **1:**27, 31
Ocotillo, **2:**77
Odorants, **3:**42–43
 defined, **3:**42 and Glossary
Odor sources. *See* Aroma components

Odum, Eugene, **2:**98, **3:99–100,** 161
Oeconomy of Nature, The (Linnaeus), **2:**96–97
Oelhaf, R.C., **1:**13
Oenologists, **1:**24
 See also Enology
Oil palm, **1:**6, **3:**86, 107
Oils. *See* Fats and oils; Lipids; Oils, plant-derived; Volatile oils
Oils, plant-derived, **3:100–102,** *102,* **4:**51
 formation, **3:**168
 fuels from, **1:**80
 potential oil crops, **3:**2
 seeds as source, **3:**65, 100
 soybean oil, **3:***102,* **4:**70–71
 See also Essential oils
Olax family (Olacaceae), **3:***111*
Oldest plants. *See* Record-holding plants
Olea europea, **3:**102
Oleander, **3:**57, **4:**62
Oleoresin, **2:**61
Olericulture, **3:**22
Oligosaccharides, **1:**121
Olive oil, **3:**100, 101, *102*
Ololiuqui, **3:**193
Olyreae, **1:**62
1N (haploid stage), **1:**158–159
 See also Alternation of generations; Gametophytes
Onion family (Alliaceae), **1:35–36**
Onions, **1:**8, 36, **3:**87, **4:**80, 156
On the Origin of Species (Darwin), **2:**44, 85, 129, 196, **3:**13, 143
 publication of, **2:**43
 significance of, **2:**40, 97, **4:**93
Oomycetes, **3:**113–114
Oospores, **3:**114
Oosting, Henry J., **3:**159
Ophiostoma ulmi (Dutch elm disease), **2:**50, *83–84, 84,* 165
Opilia family (Opiliaceae), **3:***111*
Opium, **2:**59
Opium poppy *(Papaver somniferum),* **1:***32, 33,* **3:102–103,** *103,* 174, 195
Opuntia, **1:**115
Oranges, **1:**6–9, **2:**158, **3:**157
Orchids (Orchidaceae), **3:103–105**
 Catasetum, **3:**178
 Darwin's studies, **2:**44, 129
 diversity and range, **3:**86, *87,* 103
 economic importance, **3:**104
 endangered status, **2:**109
 epiphytic, **1:**68, **2:***114,* 114–115, **3:**43, 103, 111, **4:**3, 6, 16, 34
 flower structure, **2:**146, **3:**104
 Hawaii, **1:**79
 leaves, **3:**54
 mycorrhizal associations, **3:**90, 103, **4:**85
 Paphiopedilum, **3:***104*
 pollination syndromes, **2:**8–9, 44, 115, 146, **3:**104, 178, **4:**73
 rain forests, **1:**68, **4:**3, 6
 roots, **4:**34

Orchids (Orchidaceae) (continued)
 seeds and dispersal, **3:**90, 103,
  4:16, 44, 51, 53
 vanilla orchid, **3:**86, 104, **4:**34
Order, **2:**132
Ordovician period, **2:**121, 124
Organelles, **2:**113, 120, **3:**166
 defined, **1:**40, **2:**38, **3:**113, **4:**119
  and Glossary
 See also Chloroplasts; Endoplas-
  mic reticulum; Golgi apparatus;
  Mitochondria; Nucleus/nuclei;
  Peroxisomes; Plastids; Vacuoles
Organic acids, **3:**152
Organic agriculture, **1:**5, **12–16**, *14*,
 2:16, 33
Organic fertilizers, **2:**136–137
 See also Compost; Green manure
  crops
Organic foods sales, **1:**13
Organic matter, **1:**74, **4:**63
 and soil fertility, **4:**63
 and soil structure/tilth, **1:**12,
  4:66–68
 See also Compost; Decomposi-
  tion; Humus
Organic pest control, **1:**5, 11, 16
*Origin of Species. See On the Origin of
 Species*
Ornamental plants, **3:105–106,** 181,
 186
 conifers, **2:**24
 Rosaceae, **4:***36*
 Solanaceae, **4:**68
 See also Horticulture; *specific
  genera*
Orobanche (broomrape), **3:**112
Orthids, **2:**75
Orthophosphate, **1:**73
Oryza. See Rice; Wild rice
Osage orange, **2:**160
Osmosis, **4:**164
 defined, **4:**122 and Glossary
Osmotic, defined, **3:**154 and
 Glossary
Outcrossing, outbreeding,
 1:100–101, **2:**145, **4:**23, 26
Outgroup method, cladistics, **3:**145
Ovaries, **1:**38, **2:**144, **3:**176
 fruit formation, **2:**156–158
 seed formation, **2:**176
 superior vs. inferior, **2:**146
Overcompensation, **2:**193
Overcultivation, **2:**71
Overgrazing, **2:**71, 192
Overharvesting of native plants,
 1:72, **2:**108
Oviposition, defined, **2:**10 and
 Glossary
Ovules, **1:**47, **2:**144, 176, **3:**176,
 4:22
 differentiation and development,
  1:38, **4:**51, 53
 gymnosperms, **2:**197–198, 199,
  200
Oxalates, **1:**139, **3:**172, **4:**54
Oxalis (shamrock), **1:**102

Oxalis (wood sorrel), **4:**136
Oxaloacetic acid (OAA), **3:**132
Ox-eye daisy (*Chrysanthemum leucan-
 themum*), **3:**48
Oxidases, **2:**56
Oxidation, defined, **2:**55, **3:**137 and
 Glossary
Oxidation reactions, **3:**137–138
Oxycarotenoids. *See* Xanthophylls
Oxygen, **1:**74
 ancient atmospheric increase,
  2:38, 121, **3:**25, 134
 aquatic plants and, **1:**52, **4:**166
 as carbohydrate component, **3:**97
 consumption by fossil fuel combustion, **1:**125
 consumption by plants, **1:**59, 123
 as nutrient, **3:**97, **4:**63
 and photosynthetic rates, **3:**131,
  132
 plants' influences on atmospheric
  oxygen, **1:**59, **2:**64, 121,
  3:133–134
 in soils, **4:**33, 34, 63, 67
Oxygen depletion, aquatic ecosystems, **4:**64–65
Oxygen production
 by photosynthetic bacteria,
  2:120, **3:**25, 133
 Photosystem II, **3:**98
 by plants and algae, **1:**29, 59,
  2:64, 185, **3:**22, 133–134 (*see
  also* Photosynthesis, oxygen
  production in)
Oxygen transport, rhizobial nodulation, **3:**93, 94
Oxyria digyna (alpine sorrel), **3:**128
Ozone depletion, **3:**29
Ozone formation, **1:**60–61
Ozone-resistant plants, **1:**61

P

Paál, Arpad, **3:**155
Pachycereus weberi, **4:***15*
Pacific Islands, **4:***5*
Pakistan, **4:**27, 28
Palea, **2:**186
Paleobotany, **1:**103, 104, **4:**90
 defined, **4:**90 and Glossary
 See also Fossil plants
Paleoherbs, **1:**46
Palisade parenchyma, **3:**55, **4:**112
Palmae. *See* Palms (Arecaceae)
Palmate leaves, **3:**54, 106, **4:**61
Palm kernel oil, **3:***101, 102*
Palm oil, **3:***101, 102*
Palms (Arecaceae), **3:**86, *87*,
 106–107, **4:**126
 endangered species, **2:**109
 extinction threat, **1:**71
 flowers, **3:**106–107
 form, **4:**60
 leaves, **3:**53, 54, 56, 106, **4:**13
 pollination, **3:**179
 rain forests, **4:**6
 record-holding, **4:**13, 15

root growth, **4:**30
 See also specific genera
Palynology, **2:**150, 151, **3:107–109,**
 4:95
 See also Pollen; Spores
Palynomorphs, **3:**107
Pammel, L. H., **2:**97
Pampas, **2:**190
 See also Grasslands; Steppes
Panax. See Ginseng
Pandanus, **4:***161*
Pangenesis, defined, **3:**75 and Glos-
 sary
Pangenesis theory, Darwin's reliance
 on, **3:**75
Panicle, **3:**38
 defined, **3:**38, **4:**14 and Glossary
Panicum maximum, **2:**187
Papaveraceae (poppy family), **1:**46,
 2:*78, 79*, 160
Papaverine, **3:**103
Papaver somniferum (opium poppy),
 1:32, *33*, **3:102–103,** *103*, 174,
 195
Papayas, **1:**6
Paper, **1:**144, 147, **3:109–110,**
 4:128, 178
 nonwood sources, **1:**63, **2:**138,
  3:109
 See also Wood products
Paphiopedilum, **3:***104*
Papilionoideae, **3:**177
Papua New Guinea. *See* New
 Guinea
Papyrus, **4:**60
Parallel leaf venation, **1:**39, **3:**87–88
Parallel variation, **4:**153
Paraphyletic groups, **4:**102
 defined, **4:**102 and Glossary
Paraquat, **3:**10
Parasitic wasps, **1:***13*, **3:**42–43, **4:**8
Parasitism, **3:**113, **4:**84
 algal parasites, **1:**29
 fungal parasites, **2:**164–165, **3:**40
 obligate parasites, **3:**117–119,
  4:85–86
 plant parasites, **2:**199, **3:***44,* 45,
  110–112, 113, 116, **4:**53, 85–86
 threats to native plants, **1:**72
 See also Pathogens; Symbiosis
Parastichies, **3:**141
Parenchyma, **1:**37, 139, *141*,
 141–144, **3:**78
 cortical, **1:**38
 defined, **1:**105, **3:**55, **4:**78 and
  Glossary
 leaves, **3:**55
 in phloem, **4:**114 (*see also* Companion cells)
 stems, **4:**78
 structure and function, **4:**112,
  114
 succulents, **4:**81
 in xylem, **4:**114, 172, 173
Park planning, **3:**52
Parmelia caperata, **3:***59*
Parrots, **4:**9

Parsimony, **3:**145

Parthenocarpy, **2:**161

Particle bombardment, **2:**169, 171

Particle research, **3:**39–40

Particle sizes, USDA system, **4:**65

Particulate inheritance, **3:**73–75

Particulates, **1:**1

Passion flower (*Passiflora vitifolia*), **3:***46*

Pastoralists, defined, **2:**95 and Glossary

PAT gene, **2:**170

Pathogens, **3:113–120**
  bacteria as, **2:**120, **3:**113, 114, *115*
  coevolutionary interactions with plants, **2:**7–8, 9–10
  defensive responses to, **2:**57
  defined, **1:**9, **2:**9, **3:**11, **4:**118 and Glossary
  disease-causing mechanisms, **3:**116–118
  host recognition and penetration, **3:**118–119
  role of enzymes, toxins, and phytoalexins, **3:**119
  types and characteristics, **3:**113–116, *115*
  See also Bacterial diseases; Diseases; Fungal diseases; Viruses and viral diseases; *specific diseases*

Pathologists, **3:**8, **120–121**

Patterns on plants. *See* Phyllotaxis

PCR (polymerase chain reaction), **2:**170

PCR studies, **1:**57, **4:**88

Peaches, **1:**6, **2:**159, **3:**189, **4:**35

Peanut oil, **3:***102*

Peanuts (*Arachis*), **1:**6–8, 132, **3:**84, *102*, 174, **4:**51
  breeding efforts, **3:**183
  carcinogenic molds on, **3:**172–173
  polyploidy, **3:**182

Pears, **3:**189, **4:**35, 113

Peas (*Pisum sativum*), **1:**8, 9, 68, **2:**132, **3:**177, **4:**156
  Mendel's experiments, **1:**157, **3:**33, 73, 74
  pods, **4:**119
  seeds, **4:**51, 53, 143
  tendrils, **4:**135

Peat, **1:**80, **3:**122

Peat bogs, **1:**127, **2:**127, **3:121–123**

Peat moss (*Sphagnum*), **1:**80, 108, **2:**127, **3:**121, *122*

Pectins, **1:**134, 136, 145–146, 147, **3:**150, **4:**110
  in bast fibers, **2:**138
  collenchyma, **4:**112
  pathogenesis and, **3:**119

Pectolytic enzymes, **3:**119

Pedicel, defined, **3:**38 and Glossary

Pelagic zone, **1:***51*

Pellagra, **2:**30

Penetration peg, **3:**118

Penicillin, **2:**164

Penicillium, **2:***163*, 164
  notatum, **2:**164

Pennisetum. *See* Millets

Pentoxylon, **1:**45

PEP carboxylase, **3:**132, 133

Peperomia, **4:**62

Pepinos, **4:**68

Pepos, **2:***159*

Pepper, black (*Piper nigrum*), **1:**46, **3:**11, 174

Peppermint (*Mentha* x *piperita*), **3:**11, **4:**108

Peppers, **1:**6, **3:**184, **4:**68

Peptides, **2:**57

Peptidoglycan layer, **2:**120

Percolate, defined, **2:**4 and Glossary

Perennials, desert, **2:**76–77

Perfect flowers. *See* Hermaphroditism, flowers

Perforation plates, **4:***149*

Perfumes, **2:**59, **3:**61, **4:**108
  flavor and fragrance chemists, **2:141–142**
  prospecting for fragrance plants, **2:**142
  See also Aroma components

Perianth, **2:**144, 147

Peribacteroid, defined, **3:**93 and Glossary

Peribacteroid membrane, **3:**93

Pericarp, **4:**51–52

Pericycle, **1:**38, **4:**33

Periderm, **3:**78, *79*, **4:**111–113

Periodic flowering, bamboos, **1:**62

Perisperm, **4:**53

Permaculture, **2:**65

Permafrost, **4:**138

Permeability, defined, **3:**119 and Glossary

Permian period, **2:**121, 126

Peroxisomes, **1:***136*, *137*, *139*, 140

Peroxyacetyl nitrate, **1:**61

Perry, Donald, **4:**4

Peru, **1:**68, **2:**12, **3:***28*, **4:**7, *14*
  See also Amazonia

Pest control, **3:**42–43
  biological pest management, **1:**11, 12
  chemical, **1:**10, 11–12
  integrated pest management (IPM), **1:**12, 15
  organic/biological, **1:**5, 11, 16
  See also Insecticides

Pesticide resistance, **2:**57–58, 171–172

Pesticides. *See* Chemical defenses; Fungicides; Herbicides; Insecticides

Pest resistance
  breeding for, **2:**61
  genetically-engineered, **2:**32–33, 170–172, **3:**24
  mycorrhizal, **3:**40

Petals, **1:**38, **2:**144, 173–174, **3:**77
  See also Flower structure

Petioles, **1:**39, **3:**53–54, 57, **4:**61
  defined, **3:**19, **4:**13 and Glossary

Petunia, **3:**184, **4:**68

Peyote cactus (*Lophophora williamsii*), **1:**115, **3:**192

Pfiesteria, **1:**30

PGA (3-phosphoglyceric acid), **3:**129–130, 131

pH, **4:***64*
  acid rain, **1:**1–2
  auxin transport and, **3:**14–15
  defined, **1:**1, **3:**122, **4:**64 and Glossary
  expansin activation and, **3:**15
  freshwater ecosystems, **1:**49
  peat bogs, **3:**122
  of soil, **4:**64
  vacuoles, **4:**143
  of water, and carbon dioxide availability, **1:**53

pH gradient, photosynthetic energy, **3:**139

Phallotoxins, **2:**164

Pharmaceuticals
  semisynthetic, **3:**71
  See also Medicinal plants and fungi; Phyto-pharmaceuticals

Pharmaceutical scientists, **3:123–124**

Pharmacognosy, defined, **3:**124 and Glossary

Pharmacopeia, defined, **3:**3 and Glossary

Phaseolus. *See* Beans

Phellem. *See* Cork

Phellogen. *See* Cork cambium

Phenetics, **3:**144, **4:**101–102, 104

Phenolics, **2:**55–56, 58, 59, **3:**152, **4:**54
  See also Anthocyanins; Flavonoids; Lignins; Tannins

Phenological cycles, TDBFs, **2:**49

Phenology, **2:**49, **3:**32
  defined, **4:**3 and Glossary

Phenotypical variation, phenotypic plasticity, **2:**129

Phenyl-acetic acid, **3:**17

Pheromones
  to attract pollinators, **2:**146, **3:**104
  defined, **2:**146, **3:**104 and Glossary

Philippines, **1:**68, 69, **4:**27

Philodendron, **3:**87, 172, 179, **4:**61

Philosophie zoologique (Lamarck), **2:**128

Phloem, **1:**38, **3:***79*, 144, **4:***114*, *120*
  bark, **1:**64, **3:**154, **4:**173
  development and differentiation, **1:**37, **3:**18–19, 77–78, **4:**171
  ferns, **1:**42
  fiber cells, **2:**137, 138
  function, **1:**144, **3:**18, 154, **4:**78, 114, 146, 147 (*see also* Translocation)
  hormones and, **3:**14, 18, 20
  internal, in Solanaceae, **4:**69
  lacking in bryophytes, **1:**42, **3:***144*

Phloem (continued)
  leaves, **3:**55
  primary, **4:**147
  roots, **4:**32–33
  secondary, **1:**41, **4:**79, 171, 173
  structure, **1:**41, 144, **4:**114, 119–121, 150
  See also Sieve elements; Sieve-tube members; Vascular tissues
Phloem loading and unloading, **4:**121–122
Phloem necrosis, **3:**116, 117
Phloem sap, **1:**144, **4:**118, 121–123
Phosphatases, **3:**130
Phosphates
  in DNA, **3:***80*, 81
  mycorrhizal associations and, **3:**89–90
  orthophosphate, **1:**73
Phosphinothricin acetyl-transferase (PAT) gene, **2:**170
Phosphoenolpyruvate (PEP) carboxylase, **3:**132, 133
3-phosphoglycerate, **1:**154
3-phosphoglyceric acid. *See* PGA
Phospholipids, **1:**137, **3:**65–66, 101
Phosphorus, **1:**74, **4:**11, 31
  desert environments, **2:**75
  as nutrient, **3:**97, 98, **4:**63, 64
  rock phosphorus, **3:**90
  in runoff, impacts, **1:**72, **4:**64–65
Phosphorus cycle, **1:**73–74, 75
Phosphorus fertilizers, **2:**135–136
Phosphorus mining, **1:**75
Phosphorus pollution, **1:**75
Photonasty, **4:**135–136
Photons, **3:**135, 137
Photooxidate, defined, **1:**129 and Glossary
Photoperiod, defined, **1:**9 and Glossary
Photoperiodism, **3:125–128**, **4:**26
  deciduousness and, **2:**51
  flowering and, **3:**19, *125*, 125–127, 128, **4:**26
  wheat breeding to eliminate, **1:**89
Photoprotectants, **4:**143
  defined, **4:**143 and Glossary
Photoreceptors. *See* Phytochromes
Photorespiration, **1:**59, 75, 123, 140, **2:**88, **3:**130–133
  absent in CU4u plants, **3:**132
  Priestley's experiments, **3:**39
  Saussure's experiments, **2:**69
Photosynthesis, **1:**59, 120, **3:128–140**, 150, *151*
  air pollution and, **1:**61
  anoxygenic (hydrogen sulfide), **2:**39
  aquatic plants, **1:**29, 50, 53
  bacterial. *See* Cyanobacteria; Photosynthetic bacteria
  C₃, **1:**40, **2:**77, 188, **3:**129–130, 133, 150
  C₄, **1:**40, **2:**77, 188, **3:**99, 131–133, 150
  Calvin's work, **1:**117

CAM photosynthesis, **1:**114, **2:**77, **3:**132, **4:**81
carbon dioxide fertilization, **1:**124, 125, **3:**133
circadian rhythms, **4:**25, 26
conifers, **2:**17
efficiency, **2:**77, 91–92, **3:**132–133, 139, **4:**83
equations, **3:**128, 134, 154
forest canopies, **4:**1
global warming and, **2:**183
glucose production in, **1:**154, **2:**91
grasses, **2:**188
herbicide disruption of, **3:**10
high-temperature, **1:**60
history of investigation of, **3:**153–154
oxygen concentrations and, **3:**130
oxygen production in, **1:**59, **2:**120, **3:**39, 98, 153–154, **4:**145
photosynthetic bark, stems, and roots, **1:**64, 114, **3:**57, **4:**34, 78
pigments in, **1:**129–130, 151–152, **3:**130, 135, 156–157
proteins in, **1:**155
Saussure's experiments, **2:**69, **3:**154
varying rates of, **3:**131–133
Photosynthesis, carbon fixation and, **1:**120, 123, 154, **3:128–133**
  Calvin's research, **1:**117
  carbon dioxide uptake, **3:**129, 132, **4:**113, 159–160
  chloroplasts' role, **1:**139, 153–154, **3:**167
  Ingenhousz' investigations, **3:**39, 154
  pathways, **3:**129–132
  Sachs' investigations, **4:**37
  significance of carbon fixation reactions, **3:**132–133
Photosynthesis, light reactions and, **3:133–140**
  ATP production, **3:**130, 137, 138–140
  carotenoids' role, **1:**129–130, **3:**130, 135
  chlorophyll's role, **1:**151–152, **3:**130, 135
  chloroplasts' role, **1:**139, 153–154, 155, **3:**134–135, 167
  electron transport, **1:**140, **3:**130, 135, *136*, 136–137, *138*, **4:**145
  light absorption, **3:**135
  NADPH production, **3:**137–138
  van Niel's work, **4:**145
  water in, **3:**133, 134, 137, 138, **4:**159
Photosynthetic bacteria, **1:**93, 152, **2:**120, **3:**25, 133
  nitrogen fixation, **3:**91, 92
  as plastid ancestor, **2:***112*, 112–113, 121
  prochlorophytes, **2:**40
  van Niel's investigations, **4:**145
  See also Cyanobacteria

Photosynthetic capability, loss of, **3:**112, **4:**85
Photosynthetic membrane. *See* Thylakoids, thylakoid membrane
Photosystem I, **3:**10, 137–138
Photosystem II, **3:**10, 98, 137–138
Phototaxis, **4:**131
Phototoxins, **3:**172
Phototropism, **3:**18, 155, **4:131–134**, 135
  auxins in, **3:**17, 18
  Darwin's work, **2:**44–45, **3:**155, **4:**132–133
Phragmoplast, **1:**134, **2:**123
  defined, **2:**123 and Glossary
Phycobilins, **3:**165
Phycobilisomes, **1:**156, **2:**38
Phycologists, **1:**28
Phyllocladus, **2:**17
Phyllotaxis, **3:**56, **140–143**, **4:**61–62
Phylogenetic, defined, **1:**45, **2:**38, **4:**91 and Glossary
Phylogenetics, **1:**45, 65, **3:143–146**, **4:**95, 101
  cladistics, **3:**144–145, **4:**97, 102, 104
  green plants, **3:**145–146
  systematics/classification, **3:**144, **4:**91, 93–94, 97, 102
  See also Evolution of plants; *specific plant types*
Phylogenetic species criterion, **4:**71, 75–76
Phylogenetic Taxonomy of Flowering Plants (Bessey), **1:**65
Phylogenetic trees (cladograms), **2:**122, **3:**145, **4:***90*, 91, 95, 101, 102
Physical defenses, **1:**145, **2:**54, **60–62**, *62*
  against herbivores, **2:**60–62, 188, 200
  grasses, **2:**188
  inflorescences, **3:**38
  seeds, **4:**54
  spines, **2:**60, *61*, **3:**57, **4:**80
  See also Trichomes; *specific plants and plant groups*
Physic gardens, **1:**91
Physiological ecology, **2:**85
Physiologists, **3:146–147**
Physiology, **3:**146, **148–153**, **4:**90
  defined, **1:**32, **2:**34, **3:**1, **4:**37 and Glossary
  history of, **3:153–155**
  Sachs' contributions, **3:**154, 155, **4:**36–37
Phytoalexins, **3:**119
Phytochromes, **2:**177–178, 179, **3:**127, **155–156**, **4:**55
Phytogeographer, defined, **4:**152 and Glossary
Phytography, **4:**99
Phyto-pharmaceuticals, **1:**33, 107, **3:**24, 69–71, *70*
  artemisinin, **4:**108
  digitalis, **3:**172

pilocarpine, **2:**117, **3:***70*, 165
taxol, **1:**33, *34*, **2:**24, 202, **3:***70*,
174, **4:**108, *109*
from tropical rain forest sources,
3:164–165
vinblastine and vincristine, **3:***70*,
165, 174
See also Medicinal plants and fungi
Phytophthora, **3:**114
infestans (potato blight fungus),
2:165, **3:**114, **185–186**, *185*
infestans (wheat rust), **2:**165
Phytoplankton, **1:***50*, **2:**2
Phytoplasmas, **3:**113, *115*, 117,
118–119
Phytoremediation, **1:***85*, **3:**22
Phytosterols, **3:**152
Picea (spruce), **2:**19, *22*, 23, **4:**59,
173, 174
Pigments, **3:156–157**, **4:**108
bacteriorhodopsin, **1:**56
betalains, **1:**130
defined, **3:**101, **4:**56 and Glossary
in eukaryote lineages, **3:**165
flavin, **4:**133
insects and, **3:**157
occurrence and function,
3:156–157, 168
in oils, **3:**101
in photosynthesis, **1:**129–130,
151–152, **3:**130, 135, 156–157
phototropism and, **4:**133
phycobilins, **3:**165
phycobilisomes, **1:**156, **2:**38
phytochromes, **2:**177–178, *179*,
3:127, **155–156**, **4:**55
senescence and, **4:**56
xanthophylls, **1:**129, **3:**156
See also Anthocyanins;
Carotenoids; Chlorophylls;
Color
Pignoli, **2:**202
Pigs, **4:**8
Pilocarpine, **2:**117, **3:***70*, 165
Pilocarpus (jaborandi), **3:***70*
Pimentel, D., **1:**13
Pine *(Pinus)*, **1:***100*, **2:**21, *22*, 46, 61,
4:77
bristlecone, **2:**17, 21, 198, **4:**15,
56, *127*
cones, phyllotaxis, **3:***141*, 142
economic importance, **2:**22–23
growth rings, **2:***66*
lodgepole, **4:**126
Monterey, **2:**17
mycorrhizal associations, **3:**89, 90
North American distribution,
2:19
parasitic pests, **3:**112
seeds, **4:***52*, 55
singleleaf pinyon, **1:***148*
stone pine, **3:***141*, 142, **4:***52*
in U.S. TDBF associations, **2:***47*
wood, **4:**173, 174
Pine, celery *(Phyllocladus)*, **2:**17
Pine, Japanese umbrella *(Sciadopitys)*,
2:17

Pine, Princess *(Lycopodium)*, **4:**45
Pineapple, **1:**6, **2:**160, **3:**19, *20*, 132,
141–142
Pineapple family. *See* Bromeliads
Pinedrops, **3:**45
Pine nuts, **2:**202
Pin flowers, **1:**101
Pinguicula. See Butterworts
Pinnae, **2:**133, *134–135*
Pinnate leaves, **3:**54, 106, **4:**61
Pinus. See Pine
Piper, **4:**6
methysticum (kava), **3:**195
nigrum. See Black pepper
Piperaceae (black pepper family),
1:46, **2:***78*
Pistils, **1:**38, **2:**166
defined, **1:**38, **2:**156, **3:**63, **4:**22
and Glossary
in Linnaean classification system,
3:63–64
See also Stigma
Pisum. See Peas
Pitcher plants, **1:**77, 126–128, *127*,
4:*130*
Sarracenia, **1:**128, **4:**129
Pith, **1:**38, 41, **2:**106, **3:***79*, **4:**112
Pit membrane, **4:**149
Pits, **4:**114, 149
Placenta, **2:**123
Plantae (Plant kingdom), **2:**124,
4:94
Plant associations. *See* Plant communities
Plant breeding. *See* Breeders; Breeding
Plant collecting, **3:**7, 11–12, 164
See also Plant prospecting
Plant communities, **3:157–163**
community concept, **3:**158–160
community defined, **1:**35 and
Glossary
community ecology, **2:**85, 98,
3:157, 159, **4:**157–158
competition in, **3:**45, 161–163,
4:6
organization, **3:**159–160
species diversity, **3:**162
succession and climax in, **1:**161,
2:85, 98, 151, **3:**160–161
as superorganisms, **1:**160,
3:159–160
See also Biogeography; Biological
communities; Biomes; Interactions, plant-plant; *specific community types*
Plant defenses. *See* Chemical defenses; Physical defenses; *specific
plants and plant groups*
Plant distribution, **2:**85, **4:**71, 72
circumpolar, **1:**77, **4:**140
factors in, **1:**75–77, **2:**182–183,
3:28, 127–128, **4:**39
Gray's work, **2:**195–196
intercontinental disjunctions,
1:77–78
See also Biogeography

Plant domestication, **1:**6–9, 98,
3:171, **4:**68
See also specific crop plants
Plant growth. *See* Germination;
Growth
Plant identification. *See* Identifica-
tion of plants; Keys
Plant kingdom, **2:**124, **4:**94
Plant migrations, **1:**77–78, **4:**140
Plant patent laws, **1:**111
Plant pathologists, **3:**8, **120–121**
Plant pathology, **2:**165
See also Diseases; Pathogens
Plant production, **3:**22, 106
See also Horticulture; Ornamental
plants
Plant propagation. *See* Propagation
Plant prospecting, **2:**117, 142,
3:29–30, 70, 124, **164–165**, **4:**10
See also Plant collecting
Plants, **3:165–166**
vs. algae and fungi, **3:**165
Plant systematics. *See* Systematics
Plasma membrane. *See* Cell mem-
brane
Plasmids, **2:**120
Plasmodesmata, **1:**134, **2:**123
defined, **2:**123, **4:**151 and Glossary
Plasmodiophora brassicae, **3:**117–118
Plasmopara viticola. See Downy
mildews
Plastid (pt) genome, **1:**97, **3:**166
Plastids, **1:***137*, *139*, **2:**40, 112–113,
3:166–169
amyloplasts, **1:**140, **3:**168, **4:**134
chromoplasts, **1:**140, **3:**167, 168
elaioplasts, **3:**168
eoplasts, **3:**166–167, 168
etioplasts, **3:**168
general features, **3:**166
gravity sensing, **4:**134–135
leucoplasts, **3:**168
origins, **2:***112*, 112–113, 121
rhodoplasts, **2:**112, 113
See also Chloroplasts
Plastocyanin, **3:**136, 138
Plastoquinone, **3:**137–138, 139
Platanaceae (sycamore family), **1:**46,
2:*79*
Plateau phase, germination, **2:**175
Pleistocene climate changes, **4:**6
Pleistocene glaciations, and plant
distribution, **1:**77–78, **4:**140
Plesiomorphy, **3:**144, *145*, **4:**102
Plums, **1:**110, **2:**110, 159, **3:***172*,
4:*35*, *55*
Plumule, **4:**53
Plywood, **4:**178
Pneumatophores, **4:**34
Poaceae. *See* Grasses
Podocarpaceae, **2:**17, 18, 21
Podocarpus, **2:**22
Podophyllotoxin, **3:***70*, 71
Podophyllum peltatum. See May-apple
Poison ivy *(Toxicodendron radicans)*,
3:169–170, *169*, 174

Poison oak, **3:**170, 174
Poisonous plants, **3:170–175**
 benefits to humans, **3:**173–174
 fungal toxins, **2:**164, **3:**172–173
 irritants and allergens, **3:**169, 174
 livestock and, **3:**173
 poison ivy, **3:169–170**, *169*
 poison oak, **3:**170
 poison sumac, **3:**170
 Solanaceae, **4:**68
 spices, **3:**174
 types of toxic compounds,
  3:171–173
 See also Mushrooms, toxic; Tobacco
Poisons. *See* Toxins
Poison sumac, **3:**170, 174
Poland, Bialowieza National Park,
 1:*67*, **3:***164*
Polanyi, Michael, **1:**116
Polar deserts, **4:**139
Polar glycerolipids, **3:**65–66
Polarity
 of cells, **2:**80–81, 81–82, 178
 Earth's magnetic field, **3:**30
 hormone transport, **3:**14, 18–19,
  20
Pollen, **2:**148, 151, 166, **3:***108*, **4:**17,
 20
 formation and development,
  1:158, **2:**81, 144, 173, **4:**22
 germination of, **3:**176, **4:**22
 prepollen, **2:**179–180
 sperm cell concentrations, **4:**20
 structure, **1:**45, **2:**79, **3:**88
 tubes, **3:**32, 88, 176, **4:**20, 21,
  22
 *See also specific plants and plant
  groups*
Pollen analysis. *See* Palynology
Pollination, **1:**38, **4:**20–21, 22–23
 angiosperms, **1:**47, 48, **2:**145
 cacti, **1:**114
 conifers, **2:**17
 grasses, **2:**186
 gymnosperms, **1:**47, 48
 seed formation without, **4:**18, 19
 TDBF trees, **2:**50
 tropical rain forests, **4:**8
 wind. *See* Wind pollination
Pollination biology, **3:175–180**
 barriers to natural hybridization,
  3:32, 176, **4:**73–74, 76
 breeding systems, **1:99–102,**
  2:145
 cross-pollination, **2:**44, 145,
  3:128, 176
 flower structure and, **1:**100–102,
  2:8–9, 44, **3:**176, 178–179
 inflorescences, **3:**38
 pollination mechanisms,
  3:176–180 (*see also* Pollinators
  and pollen vectors; Wind pollination)
 self-fertilization, **1:**100–101,
  3:175–176, **4:**19, *23*
 tropical plants, **3:**176, 179

 See also Fertilization; Flower
  structure; Hybrids and
  hybridization
Pollination syndromes, **3:**177
 orchids, **2:**8–9, 44, 115, 146,
  3:104, 178, **4:**73
Pollinators and pollen vectors, **3:**32,
 46
 bats, **1:**114, **2:**115, *145*, **3:**46,
  179, **4:**8, 69
 birds, **1:**114, **2:**50, 115, *145*,
  3:46, 86, 112, 179, **4:**8, 69
 insects. *See* Insect pollinators
 various mammals, **3:**179–180
Pollinia, **3:**178
Pollution, **3:**29
 bioremediation, **1:84–86**
 and HABs, **1:**30
 phytoremediation, **1:***85*, **3:**22
 threats to native plant species,
  1:72
 wetlands as filters, **4:**167–168
 See also Air pollution; Waste;
  Water pollution
Pollution-resistant plants, **1:**61
Polycultures, **1:**6
Polygalaceae, **4:**6
Polygalacturonic acid, **1:**146
Polygons (tundra feature), **4:**138
Polygonum perfoliatum (mile-a-minute
 weed), **3:**48
Polyhedral, defined, **4:**112 and
 Glossary
Polymerase chain reaction. *See* PCR
 studies
Polymers, **3:**149, **4:**112
 defined, **1:**135, **2:**38, **3:**83, **4:**112
  and Glossary
Polymorphisms, **3:**84
Polynomial, defined, **3:**64 and
 Glossary
Polypeptides, **3:**149
Polyphenols, **2:**59, **4:**106
Polyploidy, **1:**97–98, **3:**33, 34,
 83–84, **180–184**, **4:**71
 allopolyploidy, **1:**97–98, **3:**33–34,
  181–182
 ancient polyploidy in diploids,
  3:183
 autoallopolyploidy, **3:**182
 autopolyploidy, **1:**97–98, **3:**181,
  182, 184
 defined, **1:**98, **4:**91 and Glossary
 evolutionary importance, **3:**183
 natural polyploid speciation,
  4:74
 polyploid formation, **3:**182–183
 seed fertility and, **3:**181, 182
 seedlessness and, **2:**160–161
 See also Diploids; Hybrids and
  hybridization; Tetraploidy
Polysaccharides, **1:**121, 139, 145,
 147, **3:**149–150, 152
 algal, **1:**29
 callose, **4:**120–121, 151
 defined, **1:**29, **4:**109 and Glossary
 tissue culture media, **4:**109

 See also Cellulose; Hemicellu-
  loses; Pectins; Starches
Polysporangiates, **2:**125
Polyunsaturated fatty acids, **3:**101
Pomes, **2:***159*, 159, **4:**35
Pomology, **3:**22, 23
Pondweeds, **4:**166
Poplars (*Populus*), **1:**79–80, **3:**89,
 4:18, 41, 42
Poppy, California (*Eschscholzia cali-
 fornica*), **2:***56*, 146
Poppy family. *See* Papaveraceae
Population, defined, **1:**66, **4:**8 and
 Glossary
Population ecology, **2:**85
Populations, plant, **1:**76, **4:**71, 72
 genetic variation among. *See*
  Clines and ecotypes
 genetic variation within, **1:**66
 loss of, and loss of genetic diver-
  sity, **1:**69, 162–163
 See also Plant communities
Population, human, **2:**42, 63, 99,
 3:27, 29
 agriculture and population
  growth, **1:**7–8, **3:**26
Populus. See Cottonwoods; Poplars
Pores. *See* Stomata
Porosity, defined, **2:**53, **4:**66 and
 Glossary
Porosity of soils, **2:**53, **4:**66–67
Porphobilinogen, **1:**152
Porphyra, **1:**29
Positional information, in cell devel-
 opment, **2:**81–82
Positive feedback, defined, **2:**182
 and Glossary
Postmitotic interphase (G1), **1:***133*,
 133–135
Postsynthetic interphase (G2),
 1:*133*, 134–135
Potamogeton, **1:**53
Potassium, **4:**31
 acid rain and, **1:**2
 desert environments, **2:**75
 in hormonal signaling, **3:**16
 as nutrient, **3:**97, 98, **4:**63
 in soil, **4:**63, 64
Potassium chloride, **2:**136
Potassium fertilizers, **2:**135–136
Potassium-magnesium sulfate, **2:**136
Potassium sulfate, **2:**136
Potato (*Solanum tuberosum*),
 3:184–185, **4:**68, 156
 alkaloids in, **1:**32, *34*, **3:**171
 breeding efforts, **1:**109, **3:**186,
  4:129
 diseases, **2:**164, **3:**114, 115,
  185–186, *185*
 importance, **1:**8, **3:**184, **4:**68, 156
 introduction to Europe, **1:**9,
  3:171, 185, **4:**68
 origins and domestication, **1:**6–7,
  3:91, 184
 pigments in, **3:**157
 polyploidy, **3:**180, 181
 toxicity, **3:**170, 171

tuber formation and starch storage, **1**:140, 141, **3**:184, **4**:80, 119
wild species, **3**:184, 186
Potato blight, **2**:165, **3**:114, **185–186,** *185*
Potato famine, **2**:165, **3**:114, 185
Powdery mildews, **3**:116–118
p34 (kinase), **1**:135
P-protein, **4**:151
PQ. *See* Plastoquinone
Prairies, **1**:75, 83, **2**:188, 190, **3**:86
human impacts, **2**:193–194, **3**:*26,* 26–27
tallgrass, **1**:*76,* **2**:109, 190, 192, 193, **4**:39
See also Grasslands; Steppes
Praying mantis, **4**:*130*
Precipitation
defined, **2**:5 and Glossary
mean annual precipitation and temperature of biomes, **1**:*82*
and nutrient transport, **1**:74
See also Rainfall
Pre-Columbian, defined, **2**:4 and Glossary
Precursor, defined, **3**:14 and Glossary
Predation, **3**:162, **4**:6
defined, **1**:8, **4**:6 and Glossary
See also Herbivores and herbivory; Seed predation
Predators, **2**:86–87
Prepollen, **2**:179–180
Prescribed burning, **2**:95–96
Pressure chambers, **4**:*163*
Pressure mechanisms, **4**:143
cell elongation, **3**:15
nastic movements, **4**:137
translocation, **1**:144, **3**:154, **4**:122, 150–151
transpiration, **4**:160–164
Pretracheophytes, **2**:125
Prickly pear cacti, **3**:43
Priestley, Joseph, **3**:39, 153–154, *154*
Primary consumers, **2**:86
Primary meristems, **4**:111, 112, 114, 147
Primary metabolites, **3**:11
Primary producers. *See* Autotrophs (primary producers), defined
Primary root, **3**:86
Primary succession, **3**:161
Primates, **3**:179, **4**:8, 43
Primordial, defined, **2**:106 and Glossary
Primordium/primordia
arrangement. *See* Phyllotaxis
defined, **2**:148, **3**:56, **4**:78 and Glossary
leaf primordia, **3**:76, 77, **4**:78
Primrose *(Primula)*, **2**:133, **3**:141
Primrose family (Primulaceae), **2**:133
Princess pine *(Lycopodium)*, **4**:45
Proanthocyanidins, **2**:140

Procambium, **2**:106, **4**:111, 112, 114, 147
Prochlorophytes, **2**:40
Producers. *See* Autotrophs (primary producers), defined
Progenitor, defined, **1**:8, **2**:28, **3**:34, **4**:23 and Glossary
Progesterone, **2**:83
Programmed cell death, **2**:57, **4**:56
Progymnosperms, **2**:126
Prokaryotes, **1**:30–31, 152, **2**:120, **3**:91
defined, **1**:27, **2**:38, **3**:165, **4**:145 and Glossary
See also Archaea; Bacteria; Cyanobacteria
Prolamellar bodies, etioplasts, **3**:168
Propagate, defined, **1**:6, **2**:35, **3**:118, **4**:18 and Glossary
Propagation, **3**:186–192
cuttings, **3**:187–188
grafting and budding, **3**:188–190
nursery production, **3**:22, 24
pest and pathogen susceptibility, **3**:118–119, 187
runners, **4**:18, 59, 80
seed/sexual, **3**:186
tissue culture, **2**:*170,* **3**:190–191, **4:109–110**
Prophase, **1**:133–134
Proplastids, **1**:154, **4**:*142*
Prop roots, **1**:42
See also Buttress roots
Prostrate growth, **4**:59
Protandry, **1**:101
Proteaceae (protea family), **1**:46
Protease inhibitors, **4**:10
Proteases, **3**:119
Protein engineering, **3**:84
Proteins, **3**:152
in cell membrane, **1**:137, **3**:15
in cell walls, **1**:136, 146
in chromosomes, **1**:157
components, **3**:98
in defensive responses, **2**:57
function in cell reactions, **3**:80
histones, **3**:148
in hormonal signal transduction, **3**:15
hormone receptors, **3**:15
human digestion, **4**:82
in lipid layer, **1**:137
molecular investigations of, **4**:87
mutations and, **3**:84
in nectar, **2**:148
nodulins, **3**:94
in photosynthesis, **1**:155, **3**:135, 136–139 *(see also* Rubisco)
phytochromes, **2**:177–178, 179, **3**:127, **155–156, 4**:55
P-protein, **4**:151
structure and function, **3**:149
in tonoplast, **1**:139
as toxins, **3**:172, 173
in wheat, **4**:169–170

See also Amino acids; Enzymes; Protein sequencing; Protein synthesis
Protein sequencing, **4**:87
Protein synthesis, **1**:138, 140, **3**:150
in chloroplasts, **1**:156
DNA and, **3**:81, 83, 148
RNA and, **3**:149
Protist, defined, **1**:29, **2**:113, **4**:84 and Glossary
Protista, **4**:95
Protists, **1**:29
Protoderm, **2**:106, **4**:111
Protogyny, **1**:101
Protonema, **1**:105
Proton motive force, **3**:139
Proton pumping, **3**:15, **4**:143
Protons
cation exchange, **4**:31
transport, photosynthesis, **3**:137–138, 139
Protoplasmic, defined, **4**:150 and Glossary
Protoplast, **1**:36, 136–137
defined, **1**:36, **4**:149 and Glossary
Prunus
wood species, **4**:*36*
See also Cherry
Pseudolarix. See Larch
Pseudomonas syringae, **2**:161
Pseudotsuga. See Douglas-fir
Pseudo-whorled leaf arrangements, **4**:61–62
Psilocin, **2**:164
Psilocybe cubensis, **2**:164
Psilocybin, **2**:164
Psilophytes (Psilophyta) (fork ferns), **2**:166, **4**:46, *47,* 48
Psychoactive, defined, **1**:119 and Glossary
Psychoactive plants, **3**:192–195
angel's trumpet, **3**:193–194
chat or khat, **3**:194
coca, **1**:*33,* **2**:4–6, *5,* **3**:194
coffee, **2**:10–13, *11,* 100, **3**:182, 194
depressants, **3**:195
hallucinogens, **3**:192–194
holly, **3**:194
jimsonweed, **3**:193–194
kava, **3**:195
marijuana, **1**:101, 119–120, **3**:194 *(see also Cannabis)*
mushrooms, **2**:164
nutmeg and mace, **1**:46, **3**:174, 192–193
ololioqui, **3**:193
opium poppy, **1**:32, *33,* **3:102–103,** *103,* 174, 195
peyote, **1**:115, **3**:192
stimulants, **3**:194
tea, **1**:32, **2**:56, **3**:152, 194
traditional usage, **3**:192
See also Cacao; Tobacco
Psychotria, **3**:193 *(see also* Ayahuasca)
ipecacuanha. See Ipecac
Pteridium aquilinum. See Bracken fern

Pteridophytes (Pteridophyta),
2:114
See also Ferns; Seedless vascular
plants
Pterophyta. See Ferns
pt (plastid) genome, 1:97, 3:166
Pubescence, 2:60–61
defined, 2:60 and Glossary
See also Trichomes
Pueraria lobata (kudzu), 3:29, 48,
50–52, 51
Pulp, 2:100, 4:128, 178
Pulse-reserve resource availability,
2:74–75, 76
Pulses, 2:130, 132
See also Beans; Lentils; Peas
Pulvinus, 3:57
Pumpkins, 2:158, 159
Punnett, R. C., 4:153
Purines, 3:150
Purple coneflower (Echinacea angus-
tifolia), 1:118
Purple loosestrife (Lythrum salicaria),
3:29, 49, 50, 4:168
Pussy willow (Salix discolor), 4:101
Puya raimondii, 4:14
Pyrethrum (Tanacetum cinerari-
ifolium), 1:58
Pyridine alkaloids, 4:116
Pyrimidines, 3:150
Pyrolysis oils, 1:80
Pyrones, 3:195
Pyrophosphate, 4:143
Pyrrophyta. See Dinoflagellates
Pyruvate, 3:151
Pyruvic acid, 3:132, 4:82
defined, 4:82 and Glossary
Pythium, 3:114

Q

QTLs (quantitative trait loci), 3:85,
195–196
Quadruple hybrids, defined, 1:110
and Glossary
Qualitative traits, 3:85
Quantitative, defined, 3:1, 4:116 and
Glossary
Quantitative trait loci (QTLs), 3:85,
195–196
Quantitative traits, 3:85, 195, 196
Queen Anne's lace (Daucus carota),
4:44
Quercus. See Oak
Quid, defined, 2:5 and Glossary
Quiescence (seeds), 4:54
Quiescent center, meristems, 3:76,
4:32–33
Quillworts (Isoetaceae), 4:45, 46, 47,
126
See also Lycophytes
Quinine, 1:32,, 34, 64, 2:10, 3:70,
165
Quinoa, 3:91
Quinones
plastoquinone, 3:137–138, 139
sorgoleone, 1:35

R

Rabbits, 3:173
Raceme, 3:38
Radial patterning, embryogenesis,
2:106
Radial symmetry, flowers, 2:146
Radiation budget, 1:59
Radicle (embryonic root), 2:126,
174–175, 4:30, 53
Radii, defined, 2:67, 4:32 and
Glossary
Radiocarbon dating, 2:66
Radioisotopes, defined, 3:154 and
Glossary
Radishes, 3:125
Raffia
farinifera. See Raffia palm
taedigera. See Bamboo palm
Raffia palm (Raffia farinifera), 3:53,
4:13
Rafflesia, 1:43, 2:144, 3:112, 4:85, 86
arnoldii (corpse lily), 4:15
Rafflesia family (Rafflesiaceae),
3:111
Rainfall
forests as producers, 2:64
impact on plant distribution,
1:75–76
nutrient leaching, 1:4
and transpiration, 1:59
See also Acid rain; Precipitation;
specific biome types
Rain forest canopy, 2:115, 4:1–4, 6,
128
Rain forest plants, 4:6–8
chemical defenses, 4:10
epiphytes, 1:76, 2:115, 3:43, 4:1,
3, 7
leafing, flowering, and fruiting
patterns, 4:6
pollination and seed dispersal,
4:8–9
record-holding, 4:13, 15
roots, 4:3, 11
See also specific plants and plant
groups
Rain forests, temperate, 2:18, 19,
4:5
Rain forests, tropical, 1:60, 83–84,
4:4–13
animals, 4:3, 6, 7–8
conservation, 4:12
destruction of, 1:69, 71, 2:98,
3:29, 4:11–12
herbivory and decomposition,
4:10
indigenous peoples, 4:11
mapped, 1:81
montane, 4:5
nutrient cycling, 4:10–11
plant components, 3:107
regeneration and succession,
4:8–10, 11
secondary, 4:9–10
species diversity, 1:66, 68–69,
3:164–165, 4:1, 6–8

structure, 4:6
threats to, 4:11–12
See also Rain forest canopy; Rain
forest plants
Rainshadow deserts, 2:73–74
Rambling habit, defined, 2:83 and
Glossary
Ramie (Boehmeria nivea), 2:138,
4:113
Ranunculaceae (buttercup family),
1:46, 2:78, 79, 4:138, 139
Ranunculales, 1:46, 2:79
Ranunculus (buttercups), 1:65, 3:174,
4:139
Raspberries, 2:60, 160, 4:35
Rats, 3:46
Rauwolfia serpentina, 3:70
Raven, Peter, 2:6
Ray florets, 1:58
Ray initials, 3:77, 78
Raymer, William, 3:115
Rayon, 1:144, 147
Rays, 4:173
Ray, John, 4:93
Reaction centers
defined, 1:151, 3:10 and Glossary
photosynthesis, 3:135–138
See also Photosystem I; Photosys-
tem II
Reactive oxygen species (ROS), 2:56
Receptacle, 2:144
Receptor proteins, 3:15
Recessive traits, 3:74
Record-holding plants, 4:13–16,
126–127
Recreational planning, 3:52
Red algae, 1:29, 31, 156, 2:112,
3:165, 4:17, 102
Redox, defined, 3:138 and Glossary
Red tide, 1:29–30
Reduction, defined, 3:137 and
Glossary
Reduction reactions, 3:130, 137–138
Redwood, coast. See Sequoia
Redwood, dawn (Metasequoia), 1:77,
2:17, 18, 22
Redwood, giant or Big Tree. See
Giant sequoia
Reeds, 3:109, 122
Regulation of populations, 1:4
Regulatory proteins, signal transduc-
tion, 3:15
Reiter, Hans, 2:97
Relative humidity, transpiration and,
4:160
Relay planting, 1:7
Renaissance, defined, 4:92 and
Glossary
Reproduction
interbreeding and speciation,
4:71, 72, 75–76
lichens, 3:60
and plant form, 4:59
reproductive isolation, 3:32–34,
4:71, 72–74, 76
See also specific plants and plant
groups

Reproduction, asexual, **1:**38, 53, **4:18–19**, 24, 41
Reproduction, sexual, **1:**158, **4:21–24**
 advantages, **4:**24, 41
 alternation of generations, **1:**158–159, **2:**123, **4:16–18**, 20, 45 (*see also* Diploid stage; Gametophytes; Haploid stage; Sporophytes)
 vs. asexual, **1:**38, **4:**24, 41
 breeding systems, **1:99–102**
 chromosome replication and division, **1:**158–159
 evolution of, **4:**23
 fertilization and, **4:20–21**, 22–23 (*see also* Fertilization)
 Linnaeus' investigations, **3:**32
 See also Embryogenesis; Fertilization; Hybrids and hybridization; Pollination; Pollination biology; Seed dispersal; Seed release; Seeds; *specific plants and plant groups*
Reproduction, vegetative, **1:**53, **4:**18, 24, 41, 80
Reproductive isolating barriers, **3:**32, 176, **4:**73–74, 76
Reproductive isolation, speciation and, **3:**32–34, **4:**71, 72–74, 76
Reptiles, **4:**3, 7, 8
Research Institute for Fragrance Materials, **2:**141
Reserpine, **3:**70
Resin acids, **3:**152
Resins, **4:**10, 108
 conifers, **2:**61, **4:**173
 medicinal, **3:**70, 71
 as toxins, **3:**71, 172
Resource partitioning, **3:**162
Respiration
 cellular, **1:**140, **2:**174, **3:**130
 by plants. *See* Photorespiration
Restriction site analysis, **4:**88, 89
Reticulate leaf venation, **1:**39, **2:**125–126, **3:**87
Retting, **2:**138–139
Revegetation programs, **1:**150
Revisionary (monographic) studies, **2:**143
Rheum raponticum (rhubarb), **3:**172
Rhizobia, **2:**9–10, 132, **3:**92–95, 98, **4:**69
Rhizobium, **2:**9–10, **3:**92, 93, 94, **4:**69
Rhizobium Research Laboratory, **3:**95
Rhizomes, **1:**41, **2:**126, **4:**18, 80
 ferns, **1:**42, **2:**133
 grasses, **2:**186, **3:**87
Rhizopus, **2:**83, 163
Rhododendron, **3:**13, 105
Rhodophyta, Rhodophyceae, **1:**27, 31, 156
Rhodoplasts, **2:**112, 113
Rhodospirillum, **3:**91
Rhozophora (red mangrove), **3:**3, **4:**34, 44

See also Mangroves
Rhubarb (*Rheum raponticum*), **3:**172
Rhyniophytes, **1:**105
Rhythms in plant life, **4:24–26**
 nyctinasty and photonasty, **4:**135–136
Ribonucleic acid. *See* RNA
Ribose, **3:**83, 148
Ribosomal RNA, **3:**149
Ribosomes, **1:**136, 138–139, 155, 156, **2:**120, **3:**83
RIBs. *See* Reproductive isolating barriers
Ribulose 1,5-bisphosphate. *See* RuBP
Ribulose 1,5-bisphosphate carboxylase. *See* Rubisco
Riccia, **4:**77
Rice (*Oryza sativa*), **1:**52, **2:**189, **3:**86, **4:26–29**
 alcoholic beverages from, **1:**23, 26, **2:**189
 chromosomal structure, **1:**97, **3:**183
 cultivation, **1:**7, **4:**27, 28
 cyanobacteria and, **2:**39
 cyclins in, **1:**135
 economic importance, **2:**100, **3:**184, **4:**68
 Green Revolution and, **1:**9, 89, **2:**185, 196–197, **4:**29
 growth mechanisms, **1:**52
 harvest and milling, **4:**38–39
 in human diet, **1:**8, **2:**185, **4:**26
 improvement efforts, **1:**9, 130, **2:**62, 185, **3:**85, **4:**29
 origins and domestication, **1:**6, **2:**184, **3:**91, **4:**26
 production and yields, **2:**184–185, 187, 197, **4:**26–27, 51
 See also Wild rice
Rice paddies, **4:**27
 nitrogen fixation, **3:**92
Ricin, **3:**173
Ricinus communis. See Castor bean
Ring porous wood, **4:**173
Riparian zone, **1:**51, 51
Rivea corymbosa, **3:**193
RNA (ribonucleic acid), **1:**56, 137–138, **3:**80, 166
 mRNA, **1:**155–156, **3:**83, 149
 ribosomal RNA, **3:**149
 structure, synthesis, and function, **3:**83, 148–149
 tRNA, **3:**149, 150
 viroids, **3:**115
 viruses, **3:**114
RNA analysis, **3:**85, **4:**89, 90
 See also Molecular genetics; Molecular systematics
RNA polymerase, **3:**83
Rock, carbon fixation in/release from, **1:**74, 123–124, 125, 126
Rockefeller Foundation, **1:**88
Rock outcrops, **1:**76
Rock phosphorus, **3:**90

Rodents, **2:**20, 53, **3:**46, **4:**8, 43, 139
Root amyloplasts, **3:**168
Root apical meristems, **2:**105–106, 178–179, **3:**76, **4:**33–34, 171
Root cap, **2:**179, **3:**76, **4:**32, 33, 56
Root cortex, **4:**32, 34, 112, 164
Root cuttings, **3:**188
Root growth, **3:**78, **4:**31, 33–34, 56
 desert plants, **2:**76
 dicots vs. monocots, **4:**30
 hormones and, **3:**18–19
 layering, **4:**18
 radicle emergence, **2:**174–175, 178, **4:**30
 seedlings, **2:**178–179, **4:**30
 tropisms, **3:**168, **4:**131, 134, 135
 See also Root apical meristems
Root hairs, **4:**32, 56, 65, 113
 function, **1:**38, **4:**31, 32
 mycorrhizae and, **3:**89
 origination and development, **1:**38, **2:**81–82, **4:**31
 rhizobia infection, **3:**93
Root knot nematode diseases, **3:**115–116, 118
Root parasites, **3:**111, **4:**6
Root pericycle, **1:**38
Root pressure, **3:**2
Root rots, **3:**116, 119
Roots, **1:**37, 38, 42, **3:**89, 90, **4:29–35**
 adventitious, **2:**78
 aerial/aboveground, **3:**43, **4:**34
 anatomy, **1:**38–40, **3:**19, **4:**32–33, 112, 161, 164
 aquatic plants, **1:**52, **4:**31, 32, 166
 buttress roots, **1:**42, **4:**34, 125
 cable roots, **4:**34
 dicots vs. monocots, **2:**78, **3:**86, **4:**31, 32
 embryonic (radicle), **2:**105, 106, 126, 174–175, **4:**30, 53
 epidermis, **4:**34
 fibrous, **1:**42, **4:**30, 31, 32, 123–124
 food storage in, **4:**31–32
 formation, **3:**76
 functions, **4:**30–32, 158
 haustoria, **2:**180, **3:**45, 110, 111
 lateral, **4:**123, 124, 125
 modified, **4:**34
 mycorrhizal associations. *See* Mycorrhizae, threats to
 nutrient uptake, **4:**31, 32–33, 34, 118, 158–159
 photosynthetic, **4:**34
 as plant stabilizers, **4:**60
 rain forest plants, **4:**3, 11
 record-holding, **4:**13–14
 sinker, **4:**124, 124, 125
 as soil stabilizers, **4:**30, 34
 taproots, **1:**41, **3:**86, **4:**30, 32, 119, 123–125
 translocation sinks, **4:**119
 trees, **4:**123–124, 124, 125, 126
 water transport and, **4:**162

Roots (continued)
    water uptake and, **3**:2, **4**:31,
        32–33, 158–159, 162, 164
Rootstocks, **3**:189, 190
Root vein (vascular cylinder, stele),
    1:38–40, **3**:19, **4**:32–33
ROS (reactive oxygen species), **2**:56
Rosaceae, **1**:68, **2**:55, 78, **4:35–36**,
    35, 138, *139*
Rosa-risa, **2**:*116*
Rose (*Rosa*), **2**:60, 148, **3**:157, **4**:108,
    172
Roselle (*Hibiscus sabdariffa*), **2**:*138*
Rosette plants, **4**:60, 78, 140
Rosewoods, **2**:132
Rosidae, **1**:45, 46, 47, **2**:78, 79
Rosids, true, **1**:46
Ross, James Clark, **3**:12
Rotenone, **2**:59
Rots. *See* Fruit and vegetable rots;
    Root rots
Roughage, **1**:147
Roundup®, **3**:10
Roundup-Ready soybeans, **3**:85
Roundworms. *See* Nematodes
Rove beetles, **4**:3, 8
Royal Botanic Gardens, Kew, **3**:*6*,
    12, 13, **4**:103
Rubber, **1**:7, **2**:*58*, 59, **4**:34, 108
Rubiaceae, **1**:77, **2**:10
Rubisco (ribulose 1,5-bisphosphate
    carboxylase), **1**:154–155,
    3:129–130, 131, 149, **4**:88
RuBP (ribulose 1,5-bisphosphate),
    1:155, **3**:129–130, 131
Rubus, **4**:*139*
    See also Blackberries; Raspberries
Rum, **1**:*23*, **2**:189
Ruminants, toxic plants and, **3**:173
Runners, **4**:18, 59, 80
Runoff, **1**:30, 72, **4**:11, 67
Russia, **2**:18–19, **4**:154–155
Rusts, **2**:13, 165, **3**:113, 116–118
Ruta, **3**:141
Rwanda, **1**:69
Rye (*Secale cereale*), **2**:184, 185, *187*,
    3:*32*, 183
    ergot fungus, **2**:165, 185, **3**:174
    root system, **4**:13
    spirits from, **1**:*23*
Ryegrass, **3**:181

S

Saccharides, **1**:120–122
Saccharomyces
    cerevisiae, **1**:23, 25
    uvarum, **1**:25
Saccharum. *See* Sugarcane
Sac fungi, **3**:58
Sachs, Julius von, **1**:65, **2**:45, **3**:36,
    154, 155, **4:36–37**
    opinion of Darwin's work, **2**:45,
        4:37
    tissue systems concept, **4**:111
Safflower oil, **3**:*102*
Sage (*Salvia*), **1**:149, 150

Sagebrush (*Artemisia*), **1**:58, 149,
    150
Sagittaria, **1**:53
Saguaro cactus (*Carnegiea gigantea*),
    1:*114*, 115, **2**:77, **3**:43–44, **4**:15
Sake, **1**:26, **2**:189
Salicaceae, **4**:100, *101*
Salicornia, **3**:2
Salicylic acid, **2**:57
    defined, **2**:57 and Glossary
Saline soils, **1**:12, **2**:71, **3**:90, 98–99,
    4:31
Salinity profiles, estuaries, **2**:3
Salinization, defined, **2**:71 and
    Glossary
Salix. *See* Willow
Salpiglossis, **4**:68
Salt
    buildup in soil. *See* Saline soils
    high-salt environments, **1**:56
Salt marshes, **1**:51, **4**:168
Salt marsh grasses, **4**:168
    Spartina, **2**:3, **4**:166
Salt-tolerant plants, **1**:56, **2**:1, 3, 77,
    132, **3**:2
    See also Mangroves
Saltwater, in estuaries, **2**:3
Saltwater contamination, **1**:12
Salvia (sage), **1**:149, 150
Samaras, **2**:*159*, 160
    defined, **4**:42 and Glossary
Sambucus, **4**:*114*
Sandalwood family (Santalaceae),
    3:*111*
Sandbur (*Cenchrus*), **2**:187
Sand dunes, **2**:3–4, 76
Sand particles, **4**:65
Sandy soils, **4**:66, 67
Sap. *See* Phloem sap; Xylem sap
Sap circulation. *See* Nutrient trans-
    port; Translocation; Transpira-
    tion
Saponins, **2**:83, **3**:70
Saprophytes, **4**:6
    defined, **4**:6 and Glossary
Sapwood, **4**:173
SAR (systemic acquired resistance),
    2:57
Sargasso Sea, **1**:31, 50
Sargassum, **1**:31
Sarracenia. *See* Pitcher plants
Sarria, Daniel, **1**:*96*
Sassafras, **1**:46, 78
Sassafras tea, **4**:107
Saturate, defined, **1**:2, **2**:103 and
    Glossary
Saturated fats and oils, **3**:*101*, 102
Saururaceae, **1**:77
Saussure, Nicolas-Théodore de,
    2:68–69, **3**:154
Savanna grasses, **2**:187
Savannas, **1**:64, 75, **2**:188, **4:38–41**
    food web, **2**:87
    See also Grasslands
Saxifraga, **4**:138, *139*
Scala naturae, **2**:127

Schisandra, **1**:45
Schisandraceae, **1**:77
Schlumbergera (Christmas cactus),
    1:116
Scholander, Per, **4**:*163*
Schwartz, Edith, **1**:160
Sciadopitys, **2**:17
Science (journal), **1**:65
Scientific illustrators, **1:89–91**
Scions, **3**:189, 190
Sclereids, **1**:143, **4**:*113*
Sclerenchyma, **1**:37, 136, 142–143,
    3:55, 57
    defined, **3**:55, **4**:111 and Glossary
    fibers, **1**:142–143, **4**:173
    structure and function,
        4:112–113
    in wood, **4**:172–173
Scopolamine, **3**:*70*, 194, **4**:68
Scotch thistle, **3**:50
Scouring rushes, **3**:99, **4**:46
    See also Equisetaceae, Equiseto-
        phyta
Scrophulariaceae (figwort family),
    3:*111*, 111–112
Scutching, **2**:138–139
Scutellum, **2**:106, **4**:53
Sea grasses, **1**:50, 52, **2**:1, 3, **4**:166
Seashells, **1**:74
Seaweeds, **1**:29, 31, 50, **2**:2, 123,
    4:102
Secale cereale. *See* Rye
Secondary cell walls, **1**:36, 136, 141,
    146, **2**:137, **4**:161
    deposition patterns, **4**:149–150,
        151
Secondary consumers, **2**:86–87
Secondary growth, **2**:197, **3**:77–79,
    4:60
    monocots, **3**:86, 87, 106
    wood as result of, **2**:197, **3**:86,
        4:172
    See also Lateral meristems;
        Secondary tissues
Secondary meristems. *See* Lateral
    meristems
Secondary metabolites, **3**:11, 69,
    152–153, 171, 192, **4**:10
    See also Alkaloids; Flavonoids;
        Glycosides; Steroids; Terpenes
Secondary succession, **3**:160–161,
    4:9–10, 12
Secondary tissues, **3**:77, **4**:171, 172
    See also Lateral meristems
Second messengers, **3**:13
Sedge family (Cyperaceae), **3**:86, *87*,
    90
Sedges, **3**:54, 122, **4**:138, *139*
Sedgwick, Adam, **2**:41
Sedimentary rock, carbon cycle and,
    1:74, 123–124, 125, 126
Sedimentation, **3**:161
    defined, **1**:74, **3**:161 and Glossary
Sedoheptulose, **3**:150
Seed agriculture, **1**:6, 7
Seed banks, **1**:*72*, **4**:48–50
    See also Germplasm, preservation

Seed coat, **2:**176–178, **4:**51, 54, 113
oils from, **3:**100
Seed dispersal, **1:**47, **2:**157, **4:41–44,**
54
animals, **2:**19–20, **3:**46, **4:**8,
43–44
coniferous forests, **2:**19–20
fire-triggered, **2:**157, 202
mechanical, **2:**130, 157, 176,
4:43, 44, 54, 137
speciation and, **4:**71, 72
tropical forests, **4:**8–9, 42
water, **2:**157, **4:**44
wind, **2:**21, 157, 160, 187, **4:**16,
41–43
*See also specific plants and plant
types*
Seed fibers, **2:**138, 139
Seed leaves (cotyledons), **2:**78, 105,
176, **3:**86, **4:**21, 53
Seedless fruits, **2:**158, **160–161,**
3:19
Seedless vascular plants, **2:**197,
4:45–48, 148
club mosses (lycopods), **2:**125,
166, **3:**58, 141, **4:**45, 47, 126
fork ferns (psilophytes), **4:**46,
46–47, 47, 48
horsetails and scouring rushes,
2:125–126, 166, **3:**99, 141, 166,
4:46, 47
life cycle, **4:**45
quillworts, **4:**45, 46, 47, 126
spike mosses, **2:**125, **4:**45, 46, 47,
126
See also Ferns
Seedlings
damping off, **3:**116, 119
growth, **2:**178–179, **3:**16
nitrogen provision to, **3:**149
predation in rain forests, **4:**9
See also Germination
Seed plants
evolution, **4:**51
fertilization, **4:**20–21, 51
groups, **3:**165
origins/rise of, **2:**121, 125–126,
197
See also Angiosperms; Gymnosperms
Seed predation, **2:**20, **3:**46, 162,
4:44, 54
See also Seed dispersal
Seed preservation, **1:**72, **4:48–50**
Seed-producing ferns, **2:**126
Seed release, **2:**159–160
Seeds, **1:**38, **2:**160, **4:50–55**
advantages of, **2:**126
angiosperm innovations, **1:**47,
2:144
asexually formed, **4:**18, 19
chemical defenses, **4:**9
dicots, **4:**53
dispersal. *See* Seed dispersal
dormancy, **1:**149, **2:**126,
175–178, **3:**19, 20, **4:**54–55
dry fruits, **2:**157, **4:**35

evolution, **4:**51
fats and oils in, **3:**65, 100, **4:**51
fertility, **3:**181, 182
fleshy fruits, **2:**158, **4:**35
formation and development,
2:176, **4:**118
germination. *See* Germination
gymnosperms vs. angiosperms,
2:197
legumes, **2:**130
light sensitivity, **2:**177–178
monocots, **4:**53
proteins in, **3:**149
quiescence, **4:**54
record-holding, **4:**15–16
seedless fruits, **2:**158, **160–161,**
3:19
storage, **4:**49
structure and development,
2:105, 176, **3:**176, **4:**19, 51, *52,*
53–54
See also Embryogenesis; Embryos; Endosperm; Fruits; Seed
coat; Seed dispersal; Seed predation; *specific plants and plant
types*
Seed Savers Exchange, **4:**50
Seismic waves, Humboldt's work,
3:30–31
Seismonasty, **4:**136–137
Selaginella, **2:**125
Selaginellaceae. *See* Spike mosses
Selection. *See* Breeding; Natural
selection
Selenium, **1:***85,* **2:**189
Self-compatibility, **1:**102
Self-incompatibility (SI), **1:**102,
2:145
Selfing, self-fertilization, **1:**100–101,
3:175–176, **4:**19, 23
Semidwarfing, defined, **1:**89 and
Glossary
Semisynthetic pharmaceuticals, **3:**71
Senescence, **3:**19, 20, **4:56–57**
Senescent, defined, **1:**150 and
Glossary
Senna, **3:***70*
Sennoside, **3:***70*
Sensing in plants, **4:**132
gravity, **4:**134–135
light. *See* Light sensing
Sensitive plant (mimosa), **4:***136, 137*
Sepals, **1:**38, **2:**144, 173–174, **3:**77
defined, **1:**38, **2:**130, **3:**77, **4:**35
and Glossary
See also Flower structure
Sequoia, **2:***22,* **4:57–58**
sempervirens (coast redwood),
2:17, 19, 68, 198, **4:**15, *57,*
57–58, 126
Sequoiadendron giganteum. See Giant
sequoia
Serology, defined, **4:**87 and Glossary
Sesame oil, **3:***102*
Sesamum indicum, **3:***102*
Sesquiterpenes (sesquiterpenoids),
2:55, **3:**152, **4:**108

See also Essential oils
Seta (sporophytes), **4:**77
Setaria. See Millets
Sewage, **1:**79
Sexual reproduction. *See* Reproduc-
tion, sexual
Shaking, plant responses to,
4:136–137
Shamrock *(Oxalis),* **1:**102
Shape and form, **4:58–62**
Shasta daisy *(Chrysanthemum leucan-
themum hybridum),* **1:**110
Sheep, **3:**173
Shelford, Victor, **1:**82
Shellfish contamination, algal toxins,
1:30
Shen Nung, **3:**4
Shoot apical meristems, **3:**76, *79,*
4:58, 78, 171
branching, **4:**58, 60–61
differentiation and development,
2:105–106, 178
leaf differentiation, **1:**39, **3:**56,
76–77, **4:**78
Shoot growth, **3:**18
See also Shoot apical meristems
Shoot system, **4:**78, 158
Shorea, **4:**6
Short-day plants, **3:***125, 126,* 127,
128, **4:**26
See also Photoperiodism
Shortgrass prairies, **2:**190, 193–194
See also Steppes
Shuttle breeding, **1:**89
SI. *See* Self-incompatibility
Sieve areas, **4:**150–151
Sieve cells, **4:**119–121, 150
Sieve elements, **1:**144, **4:**119–122,
150–151, 173
Sieve plates, **1:**144, **4:**120, 150
Sieve-tube members, **3:**20, **4:**114,
120, 150
function, **1:**41, **4:**120, 150
origination, **3:**78
sieve tube-companion cell com-
plex, **1:**47, 144, **4:**114, 121, 151
structure, **1:**144, **4:**114, 120, 150,
151
Sieve tubes, **4:**114, *120,* 150
Signal transduction, **3:**13, 15
Silage, defined, **2:**30 and Glossary
Silica, **1:**31, **2:**61, 188
Siliceous, defined, **1:**31 and Glossary
Silicified, defined, **1:**104 and
Glossary
Silicon, **3:**99, **4:**63
Silt, **4:**65
Siltation, **2:**63
Silurian period, **2:**121
Simard, Suzanne, **4:**85
Simple fruits, **2:***159,* 159–160
Simple leaves, **3:**54
Simpson, Gaylord, **4:**104
Sinker roots, **4:***124,* 124, 125
Sink regions, **4:**119, 122, 147
Sinorhizobium, **3:**93
Sinus, **3:**57

Sisal (*Agave sisalana*), **1**:143, **2**:*138*, 139

Sister clades, **3**:145

Sister taxa, **3**:145

Site planning, **3**:52

Sixth Extinction, **3**:29–30

Skin irritants, **3**:169, 174

Skunk cabbage, **3**:87, 172, 178, 179

Slash-and-burn agriculture. *See* Swidden/slash-and-burn agriculture

Sleep movements (nyctinasty), **4**:135–136

Slime molds, **2**:162

Slugs, carnivorous plant prey, **1**:126

Smallest plant, **3**:15

Smith, Erwin F., **3**:114

Smith, Robert Angus, **1**:1

Smith, Robert Leo, **3**:159

Smith, Thomas M., **3**:159

Smog, **1**:60, 61, 72

Smuts, **2**:165, **3**:113

Snails, **1**:126

Snapdragon (*Antirrhinum*), **2**:146, 148, 161, 173

Society of Flavor Chemists, **2**:142

Socrates, **1**:32

Sodic soils, **4**:64

Sodium
   halophytes and, **3**:2
   as nutrient, **3**:*97*, 98–99
   in soil, **4**:63
   See also Salt

Sodium carbonate, **4**:64

Softwoods, **4**:128, 173, 174

Soil, earthworms and, **2**:45

Soil additives, peat, **3**:122

Soil bacteria, **1**:74, **4**:31
   Agrobacterium, **2**:169, **3**:117, **4**:117–118
   See also Rhizobia

Soil bulk density, **4**:67

Soil characteristics, physical, **4**:65–68
   particles, **4**:65
   porosity, **2**:53, **4**:66–67
   structure and texture, **4**:31, 33, 34, 65–67
   tilth, **1**:12, **4**:67–68
   See also specific ecosystem types

Soil chemistry, **4**:62–65
   chemical components, **4**:63
   pH, **1**:61, **4**:64
   See also Nutrients, plant

Soil compaction, **1**:11, **4**:11, 67
   defined, **1**:11, **4**:11 and Glossary
   root growth and, **4**:31, 33

Soil degradation
   deforestation, **2**:63
   desertification, **2**:71
   modern agriculture, **1**:11
   salt buildup, **1**:12
   See also Soil erosion

Soil detoxification. *See* Bioremediation

Soil development, **3**:161

Soil erosion, **4**:30, 34, 166

agriculture and, **1**:11, 12, 15, **2**:71
deforestation and, **2**:63, 64, **4**:11

Soil fertility
   acid rain and, **1**:2, 72, **4**:31
   cation exchange capacity, **4**:31, 63
   decomposition and, **2**:53
   mycorrhizal associations and, **3**:89–90
   organic matter and, **4**:63
   See also Nutrient availability; Soil degradation; *specific ecosystem types*

Soil fungi. **1**:74
   See also Mycorrhizae

Soil health, in organic farming, **1**:12

Soil horizon, defined, **2**:75 and Glossary

Soil nitrogen, **1**:15, **2**:190, **3**:60
   See also Nitrogen fixation

Soil science, **1**:17

Solanaceae, **3**:184, 185, **4**:68–69, 129
   hallucinogens, **3**:193–194
   See also specific genera

Solanine, **1**:32, *34*

Solanum
   melongena. *See* Eggplant
   nigrum (black nightshade), **3**:171
   tuberosum. *See* Potato

Solar radiation, **1**:59

Solar tracking, **4**:134

Solute, defined, **1**:142, **2**:174, **3**:16, **4**:109 and Glossary

Soredia, **3**:60

Sorghum, **1**:35, 80, **2**:184, **3**:183, **4**:82
   origins and cultivation, **1**:6, 8, **2**:185, *187*
   pests, **3**:112
   photosynthetic pathway, **3**:131

Sorgoleone, **1**:35

Sori, **1**:42, **2**:*134–135*

Source regions, **4**:119, 122, 147

South Africa, **1**:24, *68*, 69

South America
   deserts, **2**:71, 73, 74, *75*
   forests, **2**:48, **4**:5
   grasslands, **4**:38
   Humboldt's explorations, **3**:31
   origins of agriculture, **1**:6, **4**:68
   See also Amazonia; Andes mountains; *specific countries*

Southern blot, defined, **4**:118 and Glossary

Southwestern Endangered Aridlands Resource Clearinghouse, **3**:91

Soybean (*Glycine max*), **4**:51, **69–71**, *70*
   breeding, **1**:9
   cultivation, **1**:8, **4**:69
   economic importance and uses, **2**:100, 130, **4**:69, 70–71
   growth, **4**:59
   nitrogen fixation, **3**:93
   organic vs. conventional agriculture, **1**:13, 15

origins and domestication, **1**:6, **4**:69
   pest defenses, **4**:129
   photoperiodism, **3**:125
   photosynthesis, **3**:139
   polyploidy, **3**:182
   Roundup-Ready, **3**:85
   seeds, **4**:51
   wild progenitor, **4**:69

Soybean oil, **3**:*102*, **4**:70–71

Spain, **1**:24, **2**:*190*

Spanish Inquisition, **4**:144

Spanish moss (*Tillandsia*), **3**:111

Spartina, **4**:166
   alterniflora (Atlantic cord grass), **3**:47

Spasticity, defined, **1**:120 and Glossary

Speciation, **2**:129, **4**:6, **71–75**, 93, 102
   defined, **1**:78, **2**:7, **3**:33 and Glossary
   hybrid speciation, **3**:33–35, **4**:71, 74
   reproductive isolation and, **3**:32–34, **4**:71, 72–74
   See also Hybrids and hybridization

Species, **4**:75–76
   recognition criteria, **4**:71, 75, 76

Species diversity, **1**:66, 69
   climatic influences on, **1**:75–76
   coevolution's role in, **2**:6
   ecological niches and, **3**:162, **4**:6, 7
   grasslands, **2**:192, 193
   mapped, selected countries, **1**:*68*
   Polish forest, **1**:*67*
   savannas, **4**:39–40
   temperate deciduous forest, **2**:48, 50, **4**:128
   and temperature, **2**:19
   threats to, **1**:69, 70–72 (*see also* Endangered species)
   tropical forests, **1**:66, 68–69, **3**:164–165, **4**:1, 3, 6–8, 128
   See also Biodiversity

Species richness, **1**:66

Specimens
   collection and handling, **3**:7–8, 36–37
   defined, **1**:89, **2**:14, **3**:1, **4**:117 and Glossary
   type specimens, **2**:127

Speciose, defined, **1**:79 and Glossary

Speckling, sources of, **1**:159

Sperm, **3**:176
   bryophytes, **1**:105–106, **4**:20, 23
   ferns, **2**:*134–135*, 135, **4**:20, 23
   Ginkgo, **2**:180, **4**:20
   seed plants, **4**:20–21
   See also Fertilization; Gametes; Zygotes

Sphagnum. *See* Peat moss

S-phase, **1**:*133*, 133

Spices, **3.11–12**, *87*, 174
   aroma components, **1**:46, **3**:152

Spiders, **1:**126, **2:**115, **4:**3, 8
Spike, **3:**38
Spikelet, **2:**186
Spike mosses (Selaginellaceae), **2:**125, **4:**45, 46, *47*, 126
  See also Lycophytes
Spinach, **3:**125
Spindle tuber, **3:**115
Spines, **4:**80
  cacti, **2:**60, *61*, **3:**57
  See also Trichomes
Spiral patterns, **3:**141–142
Spirits, **1:**23, *26*, **2:**164, 189
Spongy parenchyma, **3:**55, **4:**112
Sporangia, **2:**124, 133, *134–135*, **4:**16, 18, 77
  fern allies, **4:**45, 46
Spores, **2:**151, 166, **4:**16, 18
  algae, **4:**16
  bryophytes, **1:**106–107, 108, **4:**20, 23
  fern allies, **4:**45, 46
  ferns, **1:**42, **2:**133–134, *134–135*, 135, **4:**23, 45
  formation, **2:**166, **4:**16, 20, 22, 45, 77
  fungi, **2:**162–163, **3:**60, 113–114, **4:**16
  lichens, **3:**60
  See also Palynology
Sporogenesis. *See* Spores, formation
Sporophytes, **2:**165, **4:**16, **76–77**, *77*
  defined, **1:**105, **2:**123, **4:**20 and Glossary
  genetic variation in sporophyte generation, **2:**134–135
  origins and evolution, **2:**123–124, **4:**17–18
  See also Alternation of generations; *specific plant groups*
Sporophytic self-incompatibility (SSI), **1:**102
Sporopollenin, **2:**123
Sporotrichosis, **2:**165
Sporulate, defined, **3:**185 and Glossary
Sprengel, Carl, **4:**62
Spruce (*Picea*), **2:**19, *22*, 23, **4:**59, 173, 174
Spurges, **3:***146*
Squamulose lichens, **3:**60
Squash, **1:**6, **2:**158, 159, 161, **4:**156
  pest defenses, **2:**55, 61
  See also specific types
Squash vine borer, **2:**62
Squirrels, **2:**20, **3:**46, **4:**9, 43, 139
Sri Lanka, **1:**69, **4:***106*
SSI. *See* Sporophytic self-incompatibility
Stabilized introgression, **3:**33–34
Stadler, Lewis, **3:**67, 68
Stalinist Russia, genetics in, **4:**153–154
Stalin, Josef, **4:**152
Stamens, **1:**38, 47, **2:**144, 147, 173–174, **3:**77

in Linnaean classification system, **3:**63–64
  See also Flower structure
Staminate flowers, **2:**145
Stands, **3:**158
St. Anthony's fire, **2:**185
Star anise, **1:**46
Starches, **1:**154, **3:**149, 150, **4:**82
  in beetle pollination syndromes, **3:**179
  and gravitropism, **4:**134–135
  storage, **1:**140, 141, 154, **3:**150, 168, **4:**31–32
  structure, **1:**121, 122, 144, **3:**149
  in vegetables, **4:**156
Statical method, **3:**1
Stebbins, George Ledyard, Jr., **2:**129, **3:**33, 34, **4:**104
Stele (vascular cylinder, root vein), **1:**38–40, **3:**19, **4:**32–33
Stem cuttings, **3:**187–188
Stem fibers. *See* Bast fibers
Stem parasites, **3:**111
Stems, **4:78–80**
  branching, **4:**59, 79–80
  function, **1:**38, **3:**57
  grasses, **1:**62, **2:**186
  growth, **2:**179, **3:**16, 19, 78, 155, **4:**59–61, 78–79 (*see also* Phototropism)
  leaf arrangement on, **3:**56, *142*
  light sensing, **4:**133
  modified, **1:**41–42, 113, **3:**87, **4:**80 (*see also* Corms; Rhizomes; Runners; Stolons; Tubers)
  monocots, **3:**86, 87
  photoperiodism, **3:**127
  photosynthetic, **1:**114, **3:**57, **4:**78
  as storage organs, **4:**112
  structure, **1:**38, 40–41, *41*, **3:**86, **4:**78, 112
  succulent, **1:**69, 113, **4:**80
  toughness as defense mechanism, **2:**61–62
Stem suckering, **4:**41
Steppes, **1:**75, *81*, **2:**188, 190
  See also Grasslands
Sterile, defined, **1:**108, **2:**70, **3:**32 and Glossary
Sterility
  hybrid, **3:**32–34, 182, 183
  triploidy and, **2:**160–161, **3:**183
Steroids, **2:**55, **3:**11, 69
  in *Dioscorea*, **2:**83, **3:**70
Sterols, **3:**66, 101
  defined, **3:**102 and Glossary
Stigma, **1:**38, **2:**144, 147, **3:**176, **4:**22
Stilt roots, **4:**34
Stimulants, **3:**194
  chat or khat, **3:**194
  chocolate, **1:**111, 112–113, **2:**59, **3:**194
  coca, **1:***33*, **2:**4–6, *5*, **3:**194
  coffee, **2:**10–13, *11*, 100, **3:**182, 194
  holly, **3:**194

tea, **1:**32, **2:**56, **3:**152, 194
  See also Nicotine; Tobacco
Stimulus, defined, **2:**158 and Glossary
Stinging nettle (*Urtica*), **2:**60–61, **3:**174
Stinkhorn (*Dictyophora indusiata*), **2:***162*, 163
STMs. *See* Sieve-tube members
Stolons, **1:**41, **2:**186, **4:**18, 41, 80
  defined, **1:**41 and Glossary
Stomata, **1:**61, *142*, 143, **3:**16, 55, 118, **4:***159*
  abscisic acid in stomatal closure, **3:**16, 17, 19–20
  aquatic plants, **4:**166
  defined, **2:**4, 77, **3:**55, **4:**78 and Glossary
  desert plants, **2:**77, **3:**57
  formation, **2:**81, *82*
  function, **4:**113, 159–160
  stomatal crypts, **3:**57
  stomatal movements, **4:**25
Stone fruits, **2:**159
  See also Drupes
Stone pine (*Pinus pinea*), **3:***141*, 142, **4:***52*
Stones, **4:**65
Stoneworts (Charophyceae), **1:**27, **2:**123
Storage tissues. *See* Food storage in plants; Water storage tissues
Stramenopila, **2:**162, 163
Strangler fig (*Ficus*), **3:**44, **4:**3, 7
Strasburger, Eduard, **4:**161–162
Stratification, defined, **4:**3 and Glossary
Stratigraphic geology, **1:**103, **3:**107
  defined, **1:**103 and Glossary
Stratigraphy, defined, **3:**107 and Glossary
Straw, **3:**109
Strawberries (*Fragaria*), **3:**84, **4:**18, 59, 130
  fruits, **2:**158, 160, **4:**35
Strelitzia, **3:**180
Streptophyta, **3:**145
Striga (witchweed), **3:**45, 112
Striping, sources of, **1:**159
Strobili, **1:**44
  defined, **1:**44 and Glossary
Stroma, **1:**139, 153–154, **3:**166
Stromatolites, **2:**38
Strontium, **1:***85*
Strychnine (alkaloid), **1:**33, *34*, **3:**103
Strychnine (*Strychnos nux-vomica*), **1:***34*, **3:**174
Style, **1:**38, **2:**144, 147, **3:**176
Subalpine, defined, **2:**19 and Glossary
Suberin, **1:**38, **3:**78
Subfamily, **2:**132
Subsidiary cells, **4:**113
Subspecies, **3:**33, **4:**146
Substrate, defined, **1:**105, **2:**80, **4:**3 and Glossary

Subtropical rain forests, **4**:5
Succession, **1**:161, **2**:85, 98, 151,
   3:160–161, **4**:9–10
   defined, **2**:151 and Glossary
Succulent, defined, **1**:69, **2**:4, **3**:188,
   4:80 and Glossary
Succulents, **1**:69, **2**:4, 77, **3**:2,
   4:80–81, *81*, 112
   See also Cacti
Suckers, **4**:41
   defined, **3**:188 and Glossary
Sucrose, **1**:121, 122, 154, **3**:150,
   4:81, 82, 121
   conversion from stored fats,
     1:140
   storage, **1**:121, 139, **4**:143
   structure, **1**:121, **4**:81
Suffrutescent, defined, **1**:149 and
   Glossary
Sugar, **2**:100, **4**:81–84
   See also Fructose; Glucose;
     Sucrose; Sugars
Sugar beet, **1**:8, **3**:127, *181*, **4**:*83*
   seeds, **4**:*52*, 53
   sugar storage, **1**:121, **4**:82, 143
Sugarcane (*Saccharum*), **1**:6–8, *23*,
   2:62, *187*, **3**:109, 131
   energy efficiency, **4**:83
   nitrogen fixation, **3**:92
   polyploidy, **3**:180, 181
   sugar storage, **1**:121, **4**:82, 143
Sugarcane borer, **2**:62
Sugar maple (*Acer saccharum*), **2**:48,
   4:82
Sugars, **1**:120–122, **3**:152, **4**:81–84
   in DNA, **3**:80, 80–81, *81*, 148
   in phloem sap, **4**:118
   in RNA, **3**:83, 148
   secreted by roots, **4**:31, 32
   storage in plants, **1**:141, 154,
     3:57, **4**:82
   transport. *See* Phloem; Translo-
     cation
   See also Carbohydrates; Fructose;
     Glucose; Polysaccharides;
     Sucrose; Sugar
Sulcus, **3**:88
Sulfate
   defined, **1**:1 and Glossary
   in rain and surface waters, **1**:1–2
Sulfur, **1**:74, 75
   fertilizers, **2**:136
   as nutrient, **3**:*97*, 98, 99, **4**:63
Sulfur bacteria, **1**:*85*, **4**:85, 145
Sulfur compounds, in acid rain,
   1:1–2
Sulfur dioxide, **3**:60
   emissions, **1**:1–2, 60, **2**:182
Sulfur dioxide-resistant plants, **1**:61
Sulfur-metabolizing Archaea, **1**:56,
   57
Summer-deciduous plants, **1**:149
Sundews (*Drosera*), **1**:126, *127*, *128*,
   2:45, 61, **3**:122, **4**:*63*
Sunflower family. *See* Asteraceae
   (Compositae)
Sunflower oil, **3**:*102*

Sunflowers (*Helianthus*), **1**:*58*, **3**:38,
   102, 112, 125, **4**:172
   breeding efforts, **4**:130
   hybrid speciation, **4**:74
   phyllotaxis, **3**:141, 142, **4**:62
   pollination, **3**:178
   seeds, **2**:160, **4**:53
Sunnhemp (*Crotalaria juncea*), **2**:*138*
Sun spot activity, **2**:181
Superior ovaries, **2**:146
Surface waxes, **2**:60, **3**:2, 57, 66
Susceptibility, defined, **2**:7 and
   Glossary
Suspensor, **2**:104–105, *105*, 106,
   4:*21*
Sustainability, agricultural ecosys-
   tems, **1**:3, 13, 14
Suture, defined, **2**:160 and Glossary
Swamp cypress (*Taxodium*), **1**:77,
   2:17, 18, *22*
Swamps, **1**:51, **4**:166
   See also Wetlands
Sweden, **3**:122
Sweet gum (*Liquidambar*), **1**:77
Sweet potato (*Ipomoea batatas*),
   1:*6–8*, 130, 132, **3**:184, **4**:32
Sweetsop family. *See* Annonaceae
Sweet sorghum. *See* Sorghum
Sweet woodruff, **4**:60, *62*
Swezey, Sean, **1**:5
Swidden/slash-and-burn agriculture,
   2:63, **3**:*28*, 102, **4**:12
   swidden agriculture defined, **2**:63
     and Glossary
Swiss cheese plant (*Monstera*), **3**:96
Switchgrass, **1**:80
Sycamore family (Platanaceae), **1**:46,
   2:79
Symbiodinium, **1**:29
Symbiont, **4**:84–86
   defined, **3**:40 and Glossary
Symbiosis, **2**:111, **4**:84–87, *85*
   bacteria, **2**:120, **3**:91
   cyanobacteria, **1**:108, **2**:38,
     39–40, **3**:91
   defined, **1**:29, **3**:91 and Glossary
   hornworts, **1**:108
   nitrogen fixation relationships,
     3:92
   See also Commensalism; Lichens;
     Mutualisms; Mycorrhizae; Par-
     asitism
Symmetry, in flowers, **2**:130, 146,
   147, **3**:177
Sympatric speciation, **4**:72
Symplastic movement, **4**:121
Symplocarpus. *See* Skunk cabbage
Synapomorphy, **3**:144
Synecology. *See* Community ecology
Synthetic fertilizers, **1**:10–13
Synthetic pesticides, **1**:12–13
   See also Herbicides; Insecticides
Syria, **2**:63
Systema Naturae (Linnaeus), **3**:62–63
Systematics, **3**:63, **4**:90–96, *96*, 98,
   101
   benefits of, **4**:94

biosystematics, **2**:143
and classification, **4**:93–94, 95
history of, **4**:91–93
molecular, **2**:122, 143, **3**:*145*,
   4:87–90, 104
morphological, **4**:87, 93, 95, 100,
   104–105
phylogenetic. *See* Phylogenetics
subdisciplines, **4**:95
vs. taxonomy, **4**:95, 99
See also Phylogenetics; Taxonomy
Systematists, **1**:28
   defined, **1**:161, **3**:72, **4**:90 and
   Glossary
Systemic, defined, **2**:57, **3**:117 and
   Glossary
Systemic acquired resistance (SAR),
   2:57
Systemin, **2**:57
System stability and change, **1**:4–5
Systems theory, ecosystems applications, **2**:104

T

Taiga. *See* Boreal forests
Tall cordgrass, **4**:168
Tallest plants. *See* Record-holding
   plants
Tallgrass prairies, **1**:76, **2**:109, 190,
   192, 193, **4**:39
Tamarillo, **4**:68
Tambourissa, **2**:144
Tanacetum cinerariifolium
   (pyrethrum), **1**:58
Tank epiphytes, **2**:115
Tannins, **1**:64, 139, **2**:56, **3**:152,
   153, 157
   defined, **1**:24, **2**:56, **3**:152, **4**:172
   and Glossary
   in heartwood, **4**:172–173
   as toxins, **3**:172
   uses, **1**:64, **2**:59
Tansley, Arthur, **2**:85, 98, 102
Tanzania, **1**:*68*
Taproots, **1**:41, **3**:86, **4**:30, *32*, 119,
   123–125
Tarantulas, **2**:115
Taraxacum officinale. *See* Dandelion
Taro, **1**:7
Tasmania, **4**:5
Taxa
   defined, **1**:46, **2**:60, **3**:32, **4**:95
   and Glossary
   intraspecific, formation, **3**:33,
   34–35
   See also Taxonomy
Taxales, **2**:17
Taxodiaceae, **2**:17
Taxodium (bald cypress, swamp
   cypress), **1**:77, **2**:17, 18, *22*
Taxol, **1**:33, *34*, **2**:24, 202, **3**:70,
   174, **4**:108, *109*
Taxonomic keys, **3**:36, **4**:96, *97*,
   103
Taxonomists, **3**:5–8, **4**:96–97, 100
Taxonomy, **4**:96, **98–103**

artificial vs. natural classifications, 4:99–100
Bessey's work, 1:65
Candolle's system, 1:118
cladistics, 3:144–145, 4:97, 102, 104
evolutionary bases for, 2:133
flowering plants, 1:65, 118, 2:25
fossil plants, 1:104
herbaria and taxonomic research, 3:5–8
history of, 4:91–93, 100–102, **103–105**
Linnaean system, 2:127, 3:61, 63–64, 4:93, 95, 117
monographic (revisionary) studies, 2:143
Natural System of, 4:117
phenetic systems, 3:144, 4:101–102, 104
Ray's system, 4:93
sexual system, 3:64
significance of plant descriptions, 2:25
vs. systematics, 4:95, 99
taxonomic ranks, 4:93, 99
See also Phylogenetics; Systematics; specific plant groups; specific taxonomic ranks
Taxus. See Yew, Pacific or Western (Taxus brevifolia)
TDBFs. See Deciduous forests, temperate
Tea (Camellia sinensis), 1:34, 2:56, 3:152, 194, **4:105–108**, 105
parasites, 1:29
Teasel, 2:109
Teas, herbal, 4:107
Teff, 3:86
Teliospores, 3:113
Telophase, 1:133–134
Temperate forests
coniferous. See Coniferous forests
deciduous. See Deciduous forests, temperate
rain forests, 2:18, 19, 4:5
species diversity, 1:66
Temperate grasslands, 1:71, 2:190
See also Grasslands; Prairies; Steppes
Temperature
in aquatic ecosystems, 1:49
biome type factor, 1:82, 83–84
and deciduousness, 2:51
effects on plants, Sachs' investigations, 4:37
extreme-temperature environments, 1:56–57
influence on plant distribution, 1:75–76
ocean temperature alterations, 1:84
photoperiodism and, 3:126–127
photosynthesis at high temperatures, 1:60
rain forests, 4:4–5
seed dormancy and, 4:54–55

and species diversity, 2:19
vegetation's influences on, 1:59
of water, and carbon dioxide availability, 1:53
See also Climate; Global warming; specific ecosystem types
Tendrils, 1:41–42, 4:135
Tensile forces, defined, 4:124 and Glossary
Tension, 4:162
Tent caterpillars, 3:42
Teosinte, 1:98, 2:28–29, 4:23
Tepals, 1:47, 2:144
defined, 1:47, 2:144 and Glossary
Tequila, 1:23
Termites, 4:10, 40
Terpenes (terpenoids), 1:35, 2:55, 59, 3:69, 152, **4:108–109**
Terrestrial ecosystems, vs. coastal, 2:2
Tertiary period
defined, 1:77, 2:180 and Glossary
extinctions, 1:77–78
plants, 1:77–78, 2:180
Testa. See Seed coat
Testosterone, 2:83
Tetrahydrocannabinols, 1:119, 3:194
Tetraploidy, 1:97–98, 3:34, 84, 180, 181
defined, 2:139, 3:34 and Glossary
diploid-tetraploid crosses, 3:183
See also Polyploidy
Tetrastigma, 3:112
Tetraterpenes (tetraterpenoids), 3:152
Texas, 1:69
Textiles. See Fiber and fiber products
Thailand, 4:27, 28
Thallus, defined, 1:107, 2:80 and Glossary
THC. See Tetrahydrocannabinols
Theanine, 4:106
Thebaine, 3:103
Theobroma cacao. See Cacao
Theobromine, 1:113, 3:194
Theophrastus, 2:127, 4:92
Theophylline, 1:113, 3:194
Thermal gasification, 1:80
Thermoacidophiles, 1:56–57
Thermodynamics, laws of, 2:90, 91–92
Thermogenesis, pollination syndromes, 3:179
Thigmomorphogenesis, 4:125
Thigmonasty, 4:136–137
Thigmotropism, 4:135
Thiobacillus, 3:91
Thorns, 1:42
See also Trichomes
Threatened species, 2:106, 110
See also Endangered species
Thrips, 4:8
Thrum flowers, 1:101
Thuja plicata (western red-cedar), 2:24

Thylakoids, thylakoid membrane, 1:139, 152–153, 155, 3:134–136, 167, 168
cyanobacterial, 2:38
Thymine, 3:81, 83, 148
Tick-trefoil (Desmodium), 4:44
Tidal flats, 3:92
Tigris River, 1:6
Tillandsia (Spanish moss), 3:111
Tillers, 1:41–42
Tilth, 1:12, 4:67–68
defined, 1:12 and Glossary
Timber. See Wood plants; Wood products
Timothy, 3:86
Tissue culture, 2:170, 3:190–191, **4:109–110**
Tissues, 1:37–38, 42, **4:110–114**
See also specific tissue types
TNT, 1:85
Toads, 1:32
Tobacco (Nicotiana), 1:102, 2:116, 3:194, 4:68, **115–116**, 115
alkaloids in, 1:32, 34, 3:171
breeding efforts, 4:130
economic importance, 2:100
flower structure, 2:146
photoperiodism, 3:125
polyploidy, 3:182
seeds, 4:51, 55
Tobacco hornworm, 1:32
Tomatillos, 4:68
Tomatine, 2:55
Tomato (Lycopersicon), 2:158, 3:36, 184, 4:51, 68, 156
breeding efforts, 4:129
origins and cultivation, 1:6, 8, 9, 4:156
pest defenses, 2:55, 57
pests and diseases, 3:112, 185
photoperiodism, 3:125
pigments in, 1:131
Tonoplast, 1:136, 139, 4:142
defined, 4:142 and Glossary
Topographic, defined, 1:148, 2:74, 4:128 and Glossary
Torrey Botanical Society, 4:117
Torrey, John, 2:194, 195, **4:116–117**, 116
Totipotent, defined, 4:109 and Glossary
Touch-me-not plant (impatiens), 4:137
Touch, plant responses to, 4:136–137
Tournefort, Joseph Pitton de, 3:63
Toxic algal blooms, 1:29–30, 72
Toxic cyanobacterial blooms, 2:38
Toxicodendron. See Poison ivy; Poison oak; Poison sumac
Toxic plants. See Poisonous plants
Toxic waste, bioremediation, **1:84–86**
Toxins
benefits to plants, 3:170–171
defined, 1:30, 2:7, 3:116, 4:143 and Glossary

Toxins (continued)
fungal, **2**:164, **3**:172–173
in grasses, **2**:189
pathogen-produced, **3**:119
types, **3**:171–173
See also Alkaloids; Chemical
defenses; *specific toxins*
Trace elements. *See* Micronutrients
Tracheary elements, **4**:148–150, *151*
tracheary cells, **3**:20
See also Vessel elements
Tracheids, **1**:41, 143, **4**:114, 148,
149, 161
defined, **1**:41, **4**:56 and Glossary
softwoods, **4**:173
Tracheophytes, **1**:104, 105
See also Vascular plants
Tragopogon (goats-beard), **3**:32
Traits
dominant vs. recessive, **3**:74
qualitative, **3**:85
quantitative, **3**:85, 195, 196
See also Characters
Transcription (RNA synthesis), **3**:83
Transcription factors, defined,
2:174, **3**:15 and Glossary
Transfer cells, **1**:142, 143
Transfer DNA (tDNA), **4**:117–118
Transfer RNA (tRNA), **3**:83, 149,
150
Transgenes, **2**:169–170
Transgenic plants, **2**:169, **3**:84–85,
4:117–118
See also Genetic engineering
(biotechnology)
Translation (protein synthesis), **3**:83
Translocate, defined, **1**:73, **2**:163,
3:98, **4**:173 and Glossary
Translocation, **1**:73, 144, **3**:98, 154,
4:78, **118–123**
pathway, **1**:121, **4**:119–121, 147,
173
phloem loading and unloading,
4:121–122
pressure-flow mechanism, **1**:144,
4:122, 150–151
rates, **4**:123
See also Nutrient transport;
Phloem
Translocation chromosomes, **3**:67
Translucent, defined, **2**:113 and
Glossary
Transmembrane proton electro-
chemical potential, **3**:139
Transmutation, defined, **2**:40 and
Glossary
Transmutationism, **2**:128
Transpiration, **1**:59, **3**:97, 154,
4:150, 159–164
adaptations to reduce, **1**:143,
2:51, 77, **4**:81
CAM plants, **2**:77, **4**:81
causes, **4**:159–160
defined, **1**:143, **2**:64, **3**:97, **4**:56
and Glossary
forests, **2**:64
functions, **4**:160

Hales' experiments, **3**:2, 154
mechanisms, **3**:154, **4**:162
quantified, **4**:159
See also Water transport; Water
uptake
Transpiration-cohesion-tension
mechanism, **4**:160–164
Transposon mutagenesis, **1**:159
Transposons (jumping genes), **1**:157,
159, **2**:33–34, **3**:68
Transverse, defined, **2**:80 and
Glossary
Trapa (water chestnut), **4**:32
Tree ferns, **4**:60, 126, 140
Tree-of-heaven *(Ailanthus altissima)*,
3:48, 50
Tree-ring dating. *See* Dendrochronology
Trees, **1**:38, 41, **4**:**126–129**
age determination, **3**:160–161,
4:127
architecture, **4**:6, **123–126**
bonsai, **1**:**86–88**, *87*
branching, **4**:123
Carboniferous, **4**:126
cold hardiness, **4**:26
diversity, **4**:128
fire and, **2**:192
form, **4**:59
growth rings, **2**:65, *66*, **4**:*172*,
173
identification, **4**:129
mycorrhizal associations, **3**:40
nonwoody, **4**:126, 171
nutrient transport in, **1**:64
propagation, **3**:189–190
record-holding, **4**:13, 15, 16,
126–127, *127*
root systems, **4**:34, 123–124, *124*,
125
savannas, **4**:39–40
vs. shrubs and vines, **4**:126
and smog, **1**:60
species diversity, **1**:68–69
uses and value, **1**:54, **3**:22, **4**:128
water transport in, **4**:160, 162,
163
wetlands, **4**:*168*
wind and, **4**:123–125, *124*
See also Arboriculture; Dendrochronology; Forestry;
Forests; Wood; *specific forest
types; specific genera*
Triacylglycerol, **3**:65
Tribe, defined, **1**:62 and Glossary
Trichomes, **1**:143, **2**:60–61, **3**:2, 57,
4:113, **129–130**
tobacco, **4**:116
Triglycerides, **3**:101
Trimenia, **1**:45
Triploidy, **3**:34, 181
corn, McClintock's work, **1**:157,
2:33–34, **3**:66–67
diploid-triploid crosses, **3**:66–67
endosperm, **1**:47, **2**:145, **4**:23
sterility and, **2**:160–161, **3**:183
See also Polyploidy

Tripsacum, **2**:28–29
Trisaccharides, **1**:121
Trisomics, **3**:67
Triterpenes (triterpenoids), **3**:152,
4:108
Triticale *(Triticosecale Wittmack)*,
2:184, **3**:*32*, 183
Triticum aestivum (bread wheat),
1:97
See also Wheat
Trochodendron, **4**:*113*
Tropane alkaloids, **3**:194, **4**:68
Trophic, defined, **2**:86 and Glossary
Trophic levels, **2**:86–87, 90–91
and energy flow, **2**:*91*, 92
Tropical forests
deciduous, **1**:71, **2**:46, **4**:4–5
epiphytes in, **3**:86
food webs, **2**:87
medicinal plants, **3**:5
plants, **3**:107
seasonally dry, **4**:4–5, 42
See also Rain forest canopy; Rain
forests, tropical
Tropical grasslands, **2**:188, 191
See also Grasslands; Savannas
Tropical plants
photoperiodism, **3**:127–128
See also Rain forest plants
Tropical rain forests. *See* Rain forest
canopy; Rain forests, tropical
Tropisms and nastic movements,
3:18, **4**:25, **130–137**
Cholodny-Went theory, **3**:18
Darwin's work, **2**:44–45
electrotropism, **4**:135
gravitropism (geotropism), **3**:18,
168, **4**:32, 131, 134–135
hydrotropism, **4**:135
nastic movements, **4**:131, 134,
135–137
phototropism, **2**:44–45, **3**:17, 18,
155, **4**:131–134, 135
thigmotropism, **4**:135
Truffles, **2**:163
Tryptophan (tryptophane), **2**:30,
3:14
Tschermak, Erich von, **3**:75
Tsuga (hemlock), **2**:19, *22*, **3**:112
Tubers, **1**:41, **3**:87, 127, 184, **4**:26,
80, 119
Tulip, **2**:144, **3**:88, **4**:136
Tulip tree *(Liriodendron)*, **1**:77, 78,
2:146
Tundra, **1**:*81*, **2**:87, **4**:**138–140**, *139*
Tung oil, **3**:101
Tunica-corpus arrangement, meris-
tems, **3**:77, *78*
Turesson, Gote, **1**:161, 162
Turf grasses, **3**:86
Turf management, **4**:**140–141**
Turgor, **1**:144, 145, **2**:175
defined, **1**:144 and Glossary
Turgor pressure, **3**:15, **4**:137, 143
defined, **3**:15, **4**:137 and Glossary
See also Hydrostatic pressure
Turkey, **4**:*106*

Turnips, **1**:9, **3**:183, **4**:*21*
Turpentine, **4**:108, 179
Tuskegee Institute, **1**:132
Twining, defined, **1**:62, **2**:44 and Glossary
2N (diploid stage), **1**:158–159
2,4-D, **3**:9, 10
2,4,5-T, **3**:10
    See also Alternation of generations; Sporophytes
Type genus, **2**:133
Type specimens, **2**:127
Typha latifolia (cattails), **4**:24

U

Uganda, **2**:12
Ulloco, **3**:91
Ulmus. See Elm
Ultrastructural, defined, **1**:31 and Glossary
Ultraviolet light, **1**:32, 56
Umbel, **3**:38
Uniformitarian, defined, **2**:41 and Glossary
United Kingdom, **1**:25, 66, 67, *68*, **4**:7
United States
    agricultural production. *See specific crop plants*
    biodiversity hot spots, **1**:69
    biomes, **1**:82–83
    coniferous forests, **2**:17, *18*, 19, **4**:57
    deciduous forests, **2**:46, *47*, **3**:26, **4**:72, 128
    deserts, **2**:72, 73, *74*, 74–75
    endangered species hot spots, **1**:69
    grasslands, **1**:82–83, **2**:190, **4**:38–39
    herbaria, **3**:6
    horticulture production areas, **3**:25
    invasive species in, **3**:49, 51
    loss of biodiversity, **1**:71
    organic farming in, **1**:13–15
    species diversity, **1**:*68*, **4**:128
    subtropical forests, **4**:5
    sugar consumption, **4**:83–84
    tea consumption, **4**:107
    weed costs, **4**:165
    See also specific states
U.S. Department of Agriculture (USDA), **1**:14–15, **3**:22, 121, 125
    National Plant Germplasm System, **4**:48–49
    Plant Introduction Stations, **1**:99, **4**:49
    soil classifications, **4**:65
U.S. Forest Service, **2**:20, 88
Unsaturated fats and oils, **3**:*101*, **4**:70
Uplift, defined, **1**:74 and Glossary
Uracil, **3**:83, 148
Uranium, **1**:85
Urbanization, **2**:99
    defined, **1**:52, **2**:71 and Glossary

Urban planning, **3**:52
Urea, **2**:136
Urea-ammonium nitrate, **2**:136
Uredospores, **3**:113
Urena, **2**:*138*
Urtica (stinging nettle), **3**:174
Urticaceae, **3**:176, **4**:6
Urushiol, **3**:169
Use and disuse, **2**:128
Usnic acid, **3**:61
Ustilago maydis (corn smut), **2**:165
Utricularia (bladderworts), **1**:*127*, 128, **3**:143

V

Vacuoles, **1**:*136*, *137*, **3**:76, 166, **4**:**142–143**, *142*
    defined, **1**:36, **2**:80, **3**:2 and Glossary
    flavonoids in, **2**:140
    function, **1**:*139*, **4**:142–143
VAM (vesicular-arbuscular mycorrhizae), **2**:164, **3**:40, 89–90, *90*
Vanilla, **3**:86
Vanilla orchid (*Vanilla planifolia*), **3**:86, 104, **4**:34
Van't Hof, Jack, **1**:134
van Helmont, Jan (Jean-Baptiste), **3**:153, **4**:**143–144**, *143*
van Neil, C. B., **3**:154, **4**:**145–146**
Variation. *See* Genetic variation
Variation and Evolution in Plants (Stebbins), **2**:129
Variegation, corn kernels, **1**:48–49, *49*
Varieties, **2**:34, **3**:33, **4**:146
Vascular, defined, **1**:37, **2**:78, **3**:14 and Glossary
Vascular bundles, **1**:39, 40, **3**:86, **4**:78, 113
    dicots vs. monocots, **4**:*79*
Vascular cambium, **3**:*79*, **4**:*114*, 171
    differentiation and development, **4**:171, *172*
    hormone transport, **3**:14
    structure and function, **1**:37, 40, **3**:77–78, **4**:58–59, 111, 112
    wood formation, **4**:79, 126, 147
    See also Cambium/cambia; Lateral meristems; Wood anatomy; Wood growth
Vascular cylinder (root vein, stele), **1**:38–40, **3**:19, **4**:32–33
Vascular disease, **3**:71–72
Vascular plants (tracheophytes), **1**:104, 105, **4**:102, 147
    defined, **4**:126 and Glossary
    flavonoids, **2**:140
    gametophytes, **2**:125, 166
    origins and rise of, **2**:121, 123, 124–125, **4**:147
    seedless. *See* Seedless vascular plants
Vascular rays, **3**:78

Vascular system. *See* Nutrient transport; Translocation; Vascular tissues; Water transport
Vascular tissues, **1**:38, 140, **3**:*79*, **4**:*111*, **146–152**, 158
    bryophytes, **1**:42, **3**:*144*, **4**:151–152
    composition and function, **1**:143–144, **4**:112, 113–114, 146–147
    differentiation and development, **4**:112, 147, 171
    evolution, **3**:*144*
    fiber cells, **2**:137, 138
    leaves, **3**:55, 57
    lignification, **2**:124
    roots, **1**:38–40, **3**:19, **4**:32–33, 164
    See also Cambium/cambia; Nutrient transport; Phloem; Translocation; Water transport; Xylem
Vascular wilts, **3**:116–117, 119
Vavilov Plant Industry Institute, **4**:49
Vavilov, N. I., **1**:119, **4**:*49*, **152–155**, *152*
Vector, defined, **2**:9, **3**:116, **4**:118 and Glossary
Vegeculture, **1**:6–7
Vegetable oils. *See* Oils, plant-derived
Vegetables, **3**:22, **4**:50, **155–156**
    See also specific vegetables
Vegetation types and patterns, **1**:84
    See also Biomes; Plant communities; *specific ecosystem types*
Vegetative propagation. *See* Asexual propagation
Vegetative reproduction, **1**:38, 53, **4**:18, 24, 41, 80
Velamen, **4**:34
Veld, **2**:190, 191
    See also Grasslands; Steppes
Venezuela, **2**:64
Venus's-flytrap (*Dionaea*), **1**:126, *127*, 128, **4**:*110*, 136–137
Veratrum californicum (false hellebore), **3**:173
Verbenaceae, **4**:6
Vernal, defined, **1**:71 and Glossary
Vernal pools, **1**:76
Vernonia (ironweeds), **1**:58
Vertebrates. *See* Animals; *specific vertebrates and vertebrate groups*
Vesicles, **3**:40, 89, 134–135
    defined, **1**:36, **2**:80, **3**:89 and Glossary
Vesicular-arbuscular mycorrhizae (VAM), **2**:164, **3**:40, 89–90, *90*
Vessel elements (vessel members)
    evolution, **2**:201, **3**:*144*, **4**:148
    function, **1**:41, 143, **2**:201, **4**:114, 149
    occurrence, **1**:44, 47, **2**:201, **3**:*144*
    origination, **3**:78

Vessel elements (continued)
    structure, **1:**41, 143, **2:**201,
        4:114, 150, 161, 163
    wood, **4:**173
Vessels, **4:**114, *149*
Viable, defined, **1:**12, **2:**144, **3:**186,
    4:74 and Glossary
Vicia faba (broad bean), **2:***178*, **3:***92*
Victoria amazonica, **3:***179*
Vietnam, **1:**69, **2:**12, **4:**28, *106*
Vinblastine, **3:**70, 165, 174
Vincristine, **3:**70, 165, 174
Vines, **4:**60, 135
    See also Climbing plants
Vineyard managers, **1:**18, 20
Violaxanthin, **1:**129
Viroids, **3:**113, *115*
Virologists, **3:**120
Viruses and viral diseases, **3:**113,
    114–115, *115*, 117, **4:**65, 94
    propagation and, **3:**118–119, 190
Viscaceae. *See* Mistletoes
Vitamin A, **1:**130, 131, **3:**157, **4:**155
Vitamin C, **4:**155
Vitamins, in plant-derived oils,
    3:101
Viticulture, **1:**18–19, **3:**22, 23
    See also Wine
Vitis. See Grapes
Vitis vinifera. See Wine grapes
VOCs. *See* Volatile organic com-
    pounds
Vogel, Orville, **1:**89
Volatile defenses, **2:**57
Volatile oils, **3:**172, 174
    ethereal oils, **1:**46
    hallucinogenic, **3:**193
    in liverworts, **1:**107
Volatile organic compounds
    (VOCs), **1:**35, 59–60, 61
    chaparral plants, **1:**150
    terpenes, **1:**35, 59–60, **2:**55, 59
Volatilization, defined, **1:**35 and
    Glossary
Volcanic activity
    carbon cycle and, **1:**74, 124
    extinction cause, **2:**107
Volicitin, **2:**57

W

Wallace, Alfred Russel, **2:**43, **4:**100
Walnut *(Juglans)*, **1:**78, 109–110,
    2:160, **3:**190, **4:**175
Warburg Effect, **3:**131, 132
Warburg, Otto, **3:**131
Warming, Johannes, **1:**161, **2:**97,
    3:159, **4:156–158**
Washington, Booker T., **1:**131
Wasps
    fig wasps, **2:***8, 9*, **4:**8
    parasitic, **1:***13*, **3:**42–43, **4:**8
    as pollinators, **2:***8–9*, 50, **3:**104,
        4:8
Waste, **1:**79, **2:**15
    See also Toxic waste
Water
    distribution on Earth, **1:**49

drinking water, **1:**26
    roles in plants, **3:**97, **4:**159
Water chestnut *(Trapa)*, **4:**32
Water collection, epiphytes, **2:**114,
    115
Water cycle, forests' role, **2:**64
Water dispersal of seeds, **2:**157, **4:**44
Water hyacinth *(Eichhornia crassipes)*,
    1:52, *53*, 102, **4:**31
Water lilies, **1:**52, **3:**179, **4:**166
Water lily family. *See*
    Nymphaeaceae
Watermelon *(Citrullus lanatus)*,
    1:131, **2:**158, 161
Water movement, **4:158–165**
    in soils, **4:**67, 138
    within plants. *See* Transpiration;
        Water transport; Water uptake
Water oxidation, in photosynthesis,
    3:137–139
Water pollution, **1:**72
    bioremediation, **1:**86
    chemical fertilizers, **1:**11
    siltation, **2:**63
Water pressure, in cells. *See* Hydro-
    static pressure; Turgor pressure
Water relations, nutrients in, **3:**98
Water storage tissues, **1:**114, **2:**52,
    3:*146*, **4:**34, 40, 112, 114
    See also Succulents
Water stress
    adaptations. *See* Xerophytic adap-
        tations
    deciduousness and, **2:**51
    grasslands, **2:**191, 192
    stomatal response to, **4:**160
    See also Drought
Water table
    defined, **1:**51, **2:**63, **4:**166 and
        Glossary
    drops in, **2:**63
Water transport, **4:**78, 114, 142,
    146–147
    Hales' work, **3:**1–2, 154
    mechanisms, **4:**114, 149–150,
        160–164
    trees, **4:**160, 162, 163
    See also Transpiration; Vascular
        tissues; Xylem
Water uptake, **3:**2, **4:**159, 162
    epiphytes, **2:**114, 115
    imbibition, **2:**174, **3:**2
    roots in, **4:**31, 32–33, 158–159,
        162, 164
Water use, agricultural, **1:**12
Water vapor, as greenhouse gas,
    3:27
Waxes
    roots (Casparian band), **1:**38,
        4:32, 164
    surface, **2:**60, **3:**2, 57, 66
    See also Cuticle
Weaver, John, **3:**159
Weed control, **1:**5, 10, **3:**49, **4:**166
    aquatic plants, **1:**53–54
    biocontrols, **3:**43, 49–50, **4:**165
    cost of, **3:**49, 50
    flame-weeding, **1:**16

invasive species, **3:**47–50
    See also Herbicides
Weeds, **1:**58, **4:165–166**
    aquatic plants, **1:**53–54, **2:**109,
        3:9
    exotic, **1:**71–72, **2:**109, **3:**29
    grasses, **2:**189
    invasive species, **3:47–50**
    Opuntia, **1:**115
    parasitic, **3:**45
Weevils, **4:**3, 8, 44
Welwitschia, **1:**44, **2:***198*, 201, **4:**30
    See also Gnetophytes
Went, Fritz W., **3:**17, 18, 155, **4:**133
Western red-cedar *(Thuja plicata)*,
    2:24
Wet deposition, **1:**1
Wetlands, **1:**51, **3:**49, 86, **4:166–168**
    carnivorous plant habitat, **1:**127
    loss of, statistics, **3:**122, **4:**167
    peat bogs, **1:**127, **2:**127,
        3:121–123
    plant growth habits, **4:***168*
    threats, **4:**167–168
    See also Freshwater ecosystems
Wet soils
    adaptations, **4:**166
    mycorrhizae and, **3:**90
Wettstein, R. V., **4:**100
Wheat *(Triticum)*, **2:**184, **3:***32*, 86,
    167, **4:169–170**, *169*
    allergies to, **3:**174
    breeding efforts, **1:**9, 88–89,
        2:61–62, 165, 185, **3:**183, **4:**153
    cultivation, **1:**7, 8, 83, **2:**185,
        187, **4:**169, 170
    economic importance and uses,
        2:100, 185, **3:**109, 184, **4:**68,
        169
    genetic engineering, **4:**170
    in human diet, **1:**8, **2:**185, **4:**169
    leaf senescence, **4:**56
    McClintock's work, **3:**66
    origins and domestication, **1:**6,
        2:185, *187*, **3:**91
    pests and diseases, **2:**61–62, 165,
        3:174
    polyploidy, **1:**97–98, **3:**181–182
    production and yields,
        2:184–185, 197, **4:**51, 169
    seeds, **4:***52*, *55*, 169
    types, **4:**170
    Vavilov's work with, **4:**153, 154
Wheat beers, **1:***23*
Wheat rust, **2:**165
Wheat stem sawfly, **2:**61–62
Whiskeys, **1:***23*, **2:**189
Whisk ferns. *See* Fork ferns
Whitefly, **1:***13*
Whittaker, Robert, **1:**82, **2:**98, **3:**160
Whorl, defined, **1:**38, **2:**21, **3:**141,
    4:46 and Glossary
Whorled patterns, **3:**141, **4:**61–62
Wildebeest, **4:**40
Wild-ginger family. *See* Aristolochi-
    aceae
Wild rice *(Zizania palustris, Oryza)*,
    4:29

Wilkes Exploring Expedition, **2**:194
Willdenow, Karl, **3**:31
Willow *(Salix)*, **1**:79–80, **2**:145, **3**:89, **4**:41, 42, 54
  pussy willow *(S. discolor)*, **4**:*101*
  tundra species, **4**:*138*
  wood, **4**:173
Wilson, Edward O., **2**:117
Wilt diseases, **3**:116–117
Wilting, **3**:17, 19–20, 98
Wind
  plant types and, **4**:140
  tree architecture and, **4**:123–125, *124*
  water stress and, **2**:191
Wind pollination, **1**:58, **2**:44, 147, **3**:176
  catkin evolution, **1**:65, **4**:100–101, *101*
  deciduous trees, **2**:50, **3**:176, **4**:41
  grasses, **2**:148, 186, **3**:176
  gymnosperms, **1**:48, **2**:17
  tropics, **3**:176, **4**:8
Wind seed dispersal, **2**:21, 157, 160, 187, **4**:16, 41–43
Wine, **1**:18–20, 22–24, *23*, **2**:59, 164, **3**:152
  wine corks, **2**:27
Wine grapes, **1**:18, 22, 24, **2**:165
Wine industry, **1**:18–20, 24
Wine makers, **1**:18, 19–20
Winged fruits, **2**:157, 160
Winge, Øjwind, **3**:33
Wintergreen, **2**:56
Witchweed *(Striga)*, **3**:45, 112
Withering, William, **3**:71–72
Wolffia, **2**:144, **4**:15
Wollemia, **2**:22
Wolpert, Lewis, **2**:81
Wood
  carbon dioxide stored in, **2**:183
  decomposers, **4**:10
  dendrochronology, **2**:65–68
  forensic botany and, **2**:151
  strength, **4**:124, 173, 174
  types, **4**:128
  woody monocots, **3**:87
Wood anatomy, **4**:171–174
  composition and structure, **1**:37, 41, 145, **2**:124, 197, **4**:124, *148*, 171–173
  grain or figure, **4**:175
  growth rings, **2**:65, *66*, **4**:*172*, 173 (*see also* Dendrochronology)
  heartwood, **4**:172–173
  rays, **4**:173
  sapwood, **4**:173
  secondary tissue differentiation and development, **4**:171–172
  softwood vs. hardwood, **4**:128, 173
  water content, **4**:177
Wood growth, **2**:197, **3**:77–78, 86, **4**:79, 126, 147, 171–172
  environmental factors, **2**:68
  See also Lateral meristems; Vascular cambium; Xylem
Woodlands. *See* Forests

Wood plants, **4**:175–177
  conifers, **2**:22, 23–24, 202, **4**:57–58, 174
  legumes, **2**:*131*, 132
  redwood, **4**:57–58
  Rosaceae, **4**:*36*
Wood products, **1**:144, 147, **2**:155, **4**:174–179
  certified, **2**:65
  conifer sources, **2**:23–24, 202, **4**:128, 174
  economic value, **2**:100
  See also Paper
Wood sorrel *(Oxalis)*, **4**:136
Woody plants, **4**:172–173
  See also Trees; Wood
Worms
  Darwin's work, **2**:45
  earthworms, **1**:126, **2**:45, 53, *54*, **4**:8, 10
Wort, defined, **1**:20 and Glossary
Wright, Sewall, **3**:75

X

Xanthine alkaloids, **3**:194
Xanthium strumarium (cocklebur), **3**:*126*, 128
Xanthophylls, **1**:129, **3**:156
Xenobiotics, defined, **4**:143 and Glossary
Xerarch succession, **3**:161
Xeromorphic, defined, **3**:43 and Glossary
Xerophytes, **1**:114, **3**:57
  defined, **1**:114 and Glossary
  See also Cacti; Desert plants; Succulents
Xerophytic adaptations, **1**:114, **2**:4, 75–77, **3**:*146*
  annual life cycle, **1**:69, **2**:75–76
  CAM photosynthesis, **1**:114, **2**:77, **3**:132, **4**:81
  leaf modifications, **2**:4, 52, 77, **3**:57, **4**:81
  succulence, **1**:69, **2**:4, 52, 77, **4**:81
  summer-deciduous habit, **1**:149
Xylans, **3**:150
Xylem, **1**:37, 38, **3**:79, **4**:*148*, 148–150
  development, **3**:18–19, 77, 78, **4**:56, 111, 114, 149
  differentiation, **3**:76, **4**:171
  evolution, **3**:*144*
  fiber cells, **2**:137, **4**:114
  function, **1**:143, **3**:18, **4**:78, 114, 146
  hormones and, **3**:1, 14, 18–20
  lacking in bryophytes, **1**:42, 105
  leaves, **3**:55, 57
  primary, **4**:147
  roots, **1**:38, **4**:32–33, 164
  secondary, **1**:41, **2**:197, **4**:147, 171 (*see also* Wood anatomy)
  structure, **1**:136, **4**:148, 161
  wood, **1**:37, 41, 145, **2**:197, **4**:79

See also Nutrient transport; Vascular tissues; Water transport
Xylem parasites, **3**:111
Xylem sap, **1**:143

Y

Yams *(Dioscorea)*, **1**:6–8, **2**:*83*, **3**:11, 70, **4**:32, 119
  See also Sweet potato
Yeasts, **2**:162, 163, 164, **4**:170
  alcoholic beverage production, **1**:23, 25, 26, **2**:164
  See also Fungi
Yellow-green algae (golden algae), **1**:27, 156, **3**:165
Yellow River, **1**:6
Yew *(Taxus)*, **2**:17, 22, 24, 200, 202
  Pacific or Western *(T. brevifolia)*, **1**:*34*, **2**:202, **3**:70, 173–174, **4**:*109*
Yew family, **2**:21

Z

Zavala, Javier, **2**:*116*
Zea mays. See Corn (maize)
Zea mexicana, Zea mays ssp. *parviglumis* (teosinte), **1**:98, **2**:28–29, **4**:23
Zeatin, **3**:17, 19, 20
Zebras, **4**:*40*
Zein, **2**:30
Zinc, **1**:*85*, **3**:*97*, 98, **4**:63, 64
Zingiberaceae (ginger family), **3**:*87*, 87–88
Zingiberales, **4**:6
Zingiberidae, **1**:45
Zizania palustris (wild rice), **4**:29
Zonation, defined, **1**:51, **3**:31 and Glossary
Zoospores, **2**:163, **3**:114
  defined, **2**:163 and Glossary
Zooxanthellae, **4**:85
Z-scheme, **3**:136
Zucchini squash, **2**:62, **4**:156
Zurich-Montpellier School of Phytosociology, **3**:159
Zygocactus truncata (Christmas cactus), **1**:116
Zygomorphic (bilaterally symmetrical) flowers, **2**:130, 146, 147, **3**:177
Zygomycetes, **3**:89
Zygotes, **1**:37
  algae, **2**:123–124, **4**:16
  angiosperms, **2**:145
  defined, **1**:37, **2**:80, **4**:16 and Glossary
  development, **4**:16, 17, 22, 51
  division, **2**:104, *105*
  ferns, **2**:*134–135*, 135, **4**:20
  fungi, **4**:16
  mosses and liverworts, **4**:20
  polarization, **2**:80
  sporophyte evolution, **4**:17–18
  See also Embryogenesis; Embryos

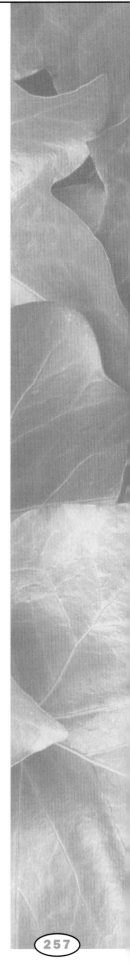